Canadian Women Shaping Diasporic Religious Identities

To Catherine with thanks
& appreciation of
the women of C-NWE.

Studies in Women and Religion
Études sur les femmes et la religion

Studies in Women and Religion is a series designed to serve the needs of established scholars in this new area, whose scholarship may not conform to the parameters of more traditional series with respect to content, perspective, and/or methodology. The series will also endeavour to promote scholarship on women and religion by assisting new scholars in developing publishable manuscripts. Studies published in this series will reflect the wide range of disciplines in which the subject of women and religion is currently being studied, as well as the diversity of theoretical and methodological approaches that characterize contemporary women's studies. Books in English are published by Wilfrid Laurier University Press.

Inquiries should be directed to the series coordinator.

COORDINATOR
Heidi Epstein
St. Thomas More College
University of Saskatchewan

COORDINATRICE
Monique Dumais
Université du Québec, Rimouski

Canadian Women Shaping Diasporic Religious Identities

Becky R. Lee and Terry Tak-ling Woo, editors

WILFRID LAURIER
UNIVERSITY PRESS

This book has been published with the help of a grant from the Canadian Federation for the Humanities and Social Sciences, through the Awards to Scholarly Publications Program, using funds provided by the Social Sciences and Humanities Research Council of Canada. Wilfrid Laurier University Press acknowledges the financial support of the Government of Canada through the Canada Book Fund for its publishing activities. This work was supported by the Research Support Fund.

Library and Archives Canada Cataloguing in Publication

Canadian women shaping diasporic religious identities / Becky R. Lee and Terry Tak-ling Woo, editors.

(Studies in women and religion ; v. 13)
Includes bibliographical references and index.
Issued in print and electronic formats.
ISBN 978-1-77112-153-8 (bound).—ISBN 978-1-77112-154-5 (paperback).—
ISBN 978-1-77112-156-9 (epub).—ISBN 978-1-77112-155-2 (pdf)

1. Women—Religious life—Canada. 2. Feminism—Religious aspects—Canada.
3. Canada—Religion—21st century. I. Lee, Becky R., [date], editor II. Woo, Terry Tak-ling, 1952–, editor III. Series: Studies in women and religion (Waterloo, Ont.) ; v. 13

BL625.7.C35 2016   200.820971   C2015-902615-6
                                                C2015-902616-4

Cover design by Blakeley Words+Pictures. Front-cover illustration copyright © Pittsburgh Post-Gazette, 2014. All rights reserved. Reprinted with permission. Text design by Lime Design, Inc.

© 2016 Wilfrid Laurier University Press
Waterloo, Ontario, Canada
www.wlupress.wlu.ca

RECYCLED
Paper made from recycled material
FSC
www.fsc.org
FSC® C103567

Contents

Part B

New Religions in Canada

Part C

South Asian Religions in Southwest Ontario

Acknowledgements

We would like to thank all of the contributors to this volume for their patience and generosity. Special thanks are owed to those who worked behind the scenes to make this volume possible: the editors at *Studies in Religion/Sciences Religieuses* Francis Landy and Patricia Dold; Heidi Epstein at St. Thomas More University of Saskatchewan and series editor of Studies in Women and Religion; Kerry Fast, our copy editor; and the editorial team at Wilfrid Laurier University Press.

Introduction

Pierre Elliott Trudeau, prime minister of Canada from 1968 to 1984 but for nine months, likened living next to the United States to sleeping with an elephant. Although he was commenting on the political implications, it is equally true in the academic sphere. Today there is a considerable body of scholarly analyses of North American women's participation in their religious traditions.[1] Because of the disparity in size between Canada and the United States, and their geographic proximity, much of that scholarship focuses on American women's experiences. For those same reasons, there is a tendency to assume that Canadian women's experiences approximate American women's. However, the settlement and religious histories of Canada differ significantly from its neighbour to the south. This collection of chapters explores the ways in which women in different religious-cultural communities have contributed to the richly textured, pluralistic society of Canada shaped by those histories.

"Religiosities"
Diasporic Religious Beliefs and Practices in Ordinary Circumstances

THE CHAPTERS IN THIS COLLECTION put women at the centre of their religious traditions and examine the ways in which they have carried and conserved, brought forward and transformed their cultures through religion in modern and contemporary Canada. All of the religious groups represented in these chapters are diasporic settler communities. Some, like the Bahá'í and Hindu communities, arrived relatively recently in Canada. Others, especially Roman Catholics and Anglicans, have such long histories in Canada that we tend to forget that they, too, have been transplanted here from other lands. That tendency is the reason we have chosen to call this collection *Canadian Women Shaping Diasporic Religious Identities.* Paul Bramadat raises "the problematic understanding of Canadian identity" that underlies the common use of the term "diaspora."[2] According to Bramadat, "on some basic level, the concept of diaspora frames members of so-called diasporic communities ... as those who really belong somewhere else,"[3] unlike Christians of European heritage for whom, it is assumed, Canada is their homeland. We agree with Bramadat. The interactions between place, difference, and identity within the Canadian context are far more complex. Bramadat suggests that rather than rejecting the term, we should "broaden the meaning of 'diaspora' to include all communities of people who harbor deep emotional ties to some other place."[4] This collection attempts to do so, examining the intersection of place, difference, and identity in the religiosities of women from the oldest settler communities in Canada to relatively recent immigrant communities.

In addition to different migration histories, the groups represented here embody disparate cosmological beliefs and practices, and occupy a spectrum of socio-economic statuses. Most importantly, there is no unified vision here because women do not, by virtue of gender, form a common constituency. It is the intersection of many factors, including but not limited to ethnicity, culture, socio-economic status, ability, geographic (dis)location, sexuality, and gender that shape one's identity, perspective, experiences, and interactions. There are, however, functional similarities among the communities examined here. The religiosities of the women represented serve as locations for both the assertion of self-identity in diaspora and resistance to institutions old and new, within and without their faith traditions.

We have chosen to focus on women's religiosity rather than on their religions because religiosity encompasses and illuminates the dynamics at the intersection of religion, gender, and diaspora. Cultural anthropologist Mayfair Yang defines religiosity as "the religious feeling or experience of individual believers."[5] Shifting the focus from religions to the religious feelings and experiences of individual believers illuminates and validates the variety of ways women express themselves religiously. Although the religious traditions represented here vary doctrinally in their teachings about women, across those traditions women have been subject to contradictory messages about, and experiences of, their places within their religious communities. As Mary Farrell Bednarowski describes this situation, women are "simultaneously outsiders and insiders."[6] She goes on to suggest that rather than being a disadvantage, women's ambivalent position within their religious traditions can be used creatively to reform and transform those traditions for it allows the distance necessary to view their traditions critically, and to imagine and construct "new visions by combining a tradition's insights with revelations that come from many places in the culture."[7] This is particularly applicable to women in diasporic communities. Separated from their culture of origin, their communities are actively engaged in negotiating the tension between conserving their cultural traditions and embracing the new opportunities available to them.

The chapters in this collection demonstrate that women's ambivalent positions within their religious traditions also motivate and enable them to reform and transform the surrounding culture. Within Canadian society and culture, women also experience being simultaneously outsiders and insiders. As a social institution, religion plays an important role in inculcating and perpetuating societal norms and values via its symbols, rituals, practices, and beliefs. Because they are participatory, those symbols, rituals, practices, and beliefs also provide a forum within which to contest, resist, and manoeuvre within societal norms and values.

Much of women's activity within their religious traditions takes place at the informal, unofficial, and popular levels. Consequently, that is where the chapters in this collection focus their attention. The concept of religiosity, with its attention on the religious feeling or experience of individual believers, renders the distinctions between formal and informal, official and unofficial, elite and popular religion irrelevant. Similarly, it subverts the historical hierarchicalization of beliefs and practices into cult, superstition, religion, and/or philosophy. Resisting those evaluative frameworks, the intention of this collection of chapters is to capture the pluralism that

Canada enjoys, and the different ways in which women express themselves religiously.

Given the informal, unofficial, and personal nature of women's religiosity, it is important that the women whose experiences are being explored speak for themselves. Consequently, the authors rely on first-hand accounts by their subjects, and wherever possible conducted interviews to gather those accounts. The authors themselves bring a variety of experiences to their analyses. Some are insiders of the traditions to which their subjects belong, others are outsiders who have engaged with their subjects as participant observers, and still others are outsiders working with the documents produced by their subjects. The authors also employ a variety of analytical frameworks, illuminating women's religiosity from a number of different angles.

Brief Descriptions of the Contents

THE CHAPTERS IN THIS COLLECTION are organized into three sections: (1) religious communities of European origin, (2) new religions developed in the nineteenth century, and (3) sizable new immigrant populations that arrived after World War II. The first section includes doctrinally diverse, relatively well-established European ethno-religious groups—Anglicans and Roman Catholics from Newfoundland and Toronto, and Jews also from Toronto.

In the first chapter, Marion Bowman traces the growth, spread, and practice of devotion to St. Gerard Majella by Catholic women of Irish descent in Newfoundland to the heights of his popularity in the middle of the twentieth century. A sickly male virgin who died young, St. Gerard was not an obvious candidate for the role of "The Mothers' Saint"; nevertheless, he was called upon for help by women wishing to conceive, pregnant women, women in childbirth, and mothers. Though this devotion to The Mothers' Saint was centred on women and specifically female conditions, it was promoted, controlled, and manipulated at the official level by men—for the saint's popularity owed much to the missions, activities, and devotional literature of the Congregation of the Most Holy Redeemer (CSsR), commonly known as the Redemptorists. Newfoundland's physical, social, and devotional context provided conditions favourable to the positive reception of St. Gerard, and Bowman outlines the religious, cultural, and socio-economic circumstances that impacted this highly gendered devotion in the latter part of the twentieth and early twenty-first centuries.

Also set in Newfoundland, Bonnie Morgan's chapter focuses on the voices of ordinary Anglican women and their participation in the churching of women through a rite of passage officially called "Thanksgiving after Childbirth." This rite of passage remained common among Newfoundland Anglicans well into the twentieth century. In a series of 2011 interviews, the Conception Bay women recall religious beliefs and practices surrounding childbirth from the 1930s through to the 1960s, a period that overlaps with the height of popularity of St. Gerard Majella. The rite as practised in Newfoundland is compared with the experience of English women, and the history of churching in the Church of England demonstrates tension between ideas of "purification" and "thanksgiving." This same gap in Conception Bay reflects different views of churching among women between official and lived religion revealing the influence of class and gender on Christian ritual. The female-centred events of childbirth, lying-in, and churching include embodied practices and beliefs informed by Christian scripture and doctrine, recognition of women's labour within rural households and communities, as well as prescribed notions of female sexuality and reproductive capacity. Given this, women's work, including the work of child-bearing, shaped religious belief and practice into a lived Christianity reflecting the material circumstances of female lives, and which was located in female bodies as they laboured.

In contrast to the first two chapters, which focus on traditional beliefs and practices, Becky Lee examines three Roman Catholic feminist movements that collectively span the history of English-speaking Canada: women's religious communities, the Catholic Women's League, and Canadian Catholics for Women's Ordination/Catholic Network for Women's Equality. She situates these movements in their respective social, historical, and religious contexts, and argues that the women in these movements, who were marginalized on account of their gender and their religion—as Catholic women in a patriarchal church and a predominantly Protestant culture—nevertheless played an active role in shaping their church and society. This was not despite their marginalization in both spheres, but because of it. Lee draws on the work of bell hooks, who considers marginality a site of radical possibility, and concludes that the marginality of those groups enabled them to see beyond the assumptions and prejudices of their church hierarchy and society, and to challenge both to broader visions of what they could be.

Following the three chapters on two major Christian denominations, Aviva Goldberg focuses on women who choose to create and contribute their unique voices in what is non-affiliated Judaism, that is, synagogue worship that is not formally part of denominational institutions. She examines women's voices in two such unaffiliated synagogues in Toronto, Congregation Shir Libeynu, a liberal egalitarian synagogue, and the Toronto Partnership Minyan, an unaffiliated Modern Orthodox community. Her examination is threefold. First, it delineates Orthodox women's advances toward equality in the synagogue in the United States. Second, it assesses the Toronto Jewish Conservative and Orthodox movements and their respective positions on women's participation in worship services. Finally, it examines women's voices in the liturgy, ritual, and leadership of Sabbath worship within these two unaffiliated assemblies. Though quite different in their respective understanding and implementation of *halacha* (rabbinic law), both of these Toronto groups provide women with a venue to be active participants in synagogue worship, leadership, and decision making. Both are in the forefront of what she argues is a radically original and innovative form of non-denominational feminist Jewish worship that, she predicts, will revolutionize North American Judaism.

All three chapters in the second section, new religions, argue that the communities on the cultural periphery greatly influenced the way we practise and understand religion and religiosity today. Included here are the Church of Jesus Christ of the Latter-Day Saints in southern Alberta, the now vanished Theosophy, and the youngest world religion to come out of West Asia, Bahá'í. Katherine Power begins this section, examining how the religious self-identity of female members of the Church of Jesus Christ of Latter-Day Saints Relief Society invokes and recontextualizes other public sphere discourses, particularly multicultural discourse. Power laments the public fetishization of religiously inspired violence, chauvinism, and imperialism that has unfortunately obscured the immense efforts of millions of religious individuals and communities who have devoted themselves to justice, non-violence, and benevolence. It is with a view to countering such obscurantism that she privileges the voices of religious Canadian women over those who might talk or write about them. Her case study, based in the rural town of Claresholm in Alberta, shows that rural Canadian Mormon women produced a sense of their own religious identities by, firstly, categorizing themselves as "belonging to" and/or "separate from" specific religious groups; secondly, by engaging with (including resisting) religious categorization by non-Mormons; and, finally, by projecting attitudinal stances on multi-culturalism. In doing so, she finds that Mormon women do not behave in a consistent manner, despite the official representation of the religion by its spokespeople.

Gillian McCann offers an alternative lens through which to observe social and religious change in Canada. She focuses on women who, through political and religious experimentation, sought to build a spiritually based society anchored in social justice and equity. She does this by placing women who were members of the Toronto Theosophical Society in a larger international context, and tries to understand what attracted them to the movement. She investigates also whether these women participated in the rise of a Theosophical feminism that developed in England and Australia, as documented by scholars Joy Dixon and Jill Roe. McCann examines two oral histories that build on recent works such as the biographies of Rose Henderson and Helen Gutteridge, both Canadian women who were active in public life and interested in alternative religions, including Theosophy. Through her investigation McCann is able to offer an important perspective on why Theosophy appealed to Canadian women, and to assess the impact that their conversion and devotion to such a hybrid religious movement had on later Canadian styles of religiosity.

In the second chapter on new religions, Lynn Echevarria locates the beginnings of the Bahá'í Faith, the youngest of the world religions, in North America in 1893, at the Chicago World Parliament of Religions when the public first heard of Bahá'u'lláh, the prophet-founder of the Bahá'í Faith. Echevarria introduces the Canadian connection through the young woman, Edith Magee, and her mother, sister, and two aunts, who joined the religion in 1898 and formed the first Canadian Bahá'í group in London, Ontario. She argues that during their time, when Bahá'í was in its formative period, women were in the vanguard of community building. Examining the life histories of these Bahá'í women through a sociological lens, Echevarria argues—like McCann—that the attempts Magee, her mother, and her sisters made to construct their religious identities had a measurable impact on society at large; they introduced unfamiliar religious ideas by translating the spiritual principles of a consciousness of oneness, unity in diversity, consultation, and work as worship into their ordinary action.

In the third and final section, we move from the historical influences, populations, and religions of Europe and West Asia to religious communities with ties to South Asia. The recent immigrant communities with ancestral origins in South Asia covered here include two Hindu groups in southwestern Ontario. The authors discuss challenges to patriarchal symbols and mindsets expressed in physical, institutional, liturgical, and ideological changes in the religious groups they study.

In the first chapter, Anne Pearson and Preeti Nayak investigate through interviews the religious lives of first- and second-generation Hindu women immigrants to southwestern Ontario. They discuss the tradition from the point of view of "lived religion"—that is, religion as practised in the women's everyday lives within the challenges of reconstructing and adapting the religion in a diasporic setting. While gendered norms and practices from the homeland like modesty, menstrual taboos, food production, and domestic responsibilities continue to exert strong influences, it is evident that they are subtly contested and have been reconfigured in the Canadian environment. Pearson and Nayak note that while there is a plethora of Hindu texts that prescribe or offer models for female behaviour and responsibilities, there is no definitive single source of authority. This has resulted in an "individualized Hinduism" where many young Hindu women growing up in Canada become resistant to particular practices of Hinduism transmitted by their parents that conflict with their developing hybrid values; most of the younger women interviewed felt quite at ease either rejecting certain practices or transforming their usual meanings to suit their own views, in contrast to their mothers' unquestioning assimilative understandings of Hinduism.

In the second chapter, Nanette Spina studies the roles that women occupy as ritual leaders in the transnational Hindu Adhi Parasakthi Temple Society of Canada in Toronto. She examines how women's ritual authority and leadership have influenced and shaped this tradition in diaspora, and explores the connection and reciprocal relationship this community maintains with its "mother" temple in Melmaruvathur, India. Her study illustrates how women's ritual authority and their collective style of worship have offered a revised definition in worship patterns from traditional priest-mediated ritual performance to a communal style of ritual participation. This movement in worship style has been instrumental in fostering a community identity in the Canadian setting by emphasizing "inclusivity" regarding caste and gender in communal worship patterns.

A bibliography is appended to each chapter in order to facilitate classroom use. We also include at the end of the volume a general bibliography for women and religion in North America. To this we add our volume and we hope that the chapters offered here will spark interest in the topic of women's religiosities, and encourage many more studies, dissertations, journal articles, and books on women's own experiences of religion in Canada. ●

Notes

1. Rosemary S. Keller, Rosemary R. Ruether, and Marie Cantlon, eds., *The Encyclopedia of Women in Religion in North America* (Bloomington: Indiana University Press, 2006).
2. Paul Bramadat and David Seljak, eds., *Religion and Ethnicity in Canada* (Toronto: Pearson/Longman, 2005), 14.
3. Ibid., 15.
4. Ibid., 16.
5. Mayfair Mei-hui Yang, *Chinese Religiosities: Afflictions of Modernity and State Formation* (Berkeley: University of California Press, 2008), 19.
6. Mary Farrell Bednarowski, *The Religious Imagination of American Women* (Bloomington: Indiana University Press, 1999), 17.
7. Ibid., 20.

References

Bednarowski, Mary Farrell. *The Religious Imagination of American Women*. Bloomington: Indiana University Press, 1999.

Bramadat, Paul, and David Seljak, eds. *Religion and Ethnicity in Canada*. Toronto: Pearson/ Longman, 2005.

Keller, Rosemary Skinner, Rosemary Radford Ruether, and Marie Cantlon, eds. *Encyclopedia of Women and Religion in North America*. Bloomington: Indiana University Press, 2006.

Yang, Mayfair Mei-hui. *Chinese Religiosities: Afflictions of Modernity and State Formation*. Berkeley: University of California Press, 2008.

Part **A**

Christianity and Judaism in Newfoundland, Ontario, and Alberta

1 "He's My Best Friend"

Relationality, Materiality, and the
Manipulation of Motherhood in Devotion
to St. Gerard Majella in Newfoundland

MARION BOWMAN THE OPEN UNIVERSITY

Introduction

Devotion to St. Gerard Majella played a significant role in the
lived religious belief and practice of many Catholic women of Irish descent
in Newfoundland in the twentieth century. In this chapter, I explore how
St. Gerard gained particular popularity as The Mothers' Saint in Newfoundland, and how a male religious order, the Congregation of the Most Holy
Redeemer (commonly and hereafter known as the Redemptorists) promoted
devotion to this saint, who concerned himself with two specifically female
conditions, pregnancy and motherhood. By outlining the development,
spread, and conduct of devotion to St. Gerard in Newfoundland, and highlighting the changes in both physical and socio-religious conditions that had
an impact on later generations of Newfoundland Catholic women in relation
to this devotion, we gain valuable insights into "religion as it is lived: as
humans encounter, understand, interpret and practice it."[1]

Devotion to St. Gerard flourished among Catholic Newfoundland
women primarily in response to specific cultural, geographical, and
physical conditions, and in accordance with traditional gendered practices of vernacular Catholicism. Although devotion to saints is central to
Catholicism, ratified and promoted by the church, the actual relationship
between the holy figure and the devotee tends to be conducted largely
outside a controlled environment. As authors such as Christian and Orsi[2]
have demonstrated, the relationships between devotees and holy figures

3

have frequently been outside the approval or beyond the understanding of those notionally "in charge" of the devotions. The Canadian Redemptorists attempted to use St. Gerard's special relationship with women to make him the figurehead of a vigorous campaign to preserve and promote Catholic motherhood in Canada.

This study of devotion to St. Gerard Majella is situated within the methodological context of vernacular religion, which involves "an interdisciplinary approach to the study of the religious lives of individuals with special attention [being paid] to the process of religious belief, the verbal, behavioral, and material expressions of religious belief, and the ultimate object of religious belief."[3] Verbal, behavioural, and material expressions of devotion emerge as particularly significant in the spread and conduct of devotion, as well as the "bidirectional influences of environments upon individuals and of individuals upon environments in the process of believing."[4] While devotion to St. Gerard Majella was and is by no means unique to Newfoundland, local conditions there played a considerable part in the form, role, and significance of the devotion on the island.

St. Gerard and the Redemptorists

I INITIALLY BECAME INTERESTED in St. Gerard Majella while studying folklore at Memorial University of Newfoundland (1977–78) because I kept encountering men called Gerard. Although many men were unaware of why their mothers had chosen the name, it became clear from conversations with women that naming children in honour of St. Gerard was an indication of the widespread devotion to him that had swept the island earlier in the twentieth century.

As a result of my piqued interest, in 1977 and 1978 I conducted fieldwork in St. John's, St. Mary's Bay, Placentia Bay, Bay d'Espoir, Port au Port Peninsula, and Stephenville. The majority of my interviewees were mothers with varying degrees of devotion to St. Gerard, but I also interviewed husbands, single men and women, midwives, nurses, priests, and Redemptorists. In addition, I made considerable use of Redemptorist popular devotional literature as an important source of information on how devotion to St. Gerard was presented to the saint's female devotees. Further visits to

Newfoundland in 1995, 1996, and 2012 enabled additional fieldwork both on the state of devotion to St. Gerard and subsequent social and religious developments there.[5]

To understand St. Gerard's appeal to women and how devotion to him was promoted and manipulated, a brief outline of his life as officially presented follows.[6] Gerard Majella was born in Muro, Italy, on April 6, 1726. Although reputedly a remarkably pious child and an exemplary adolescent, Gerard was twice refused admission to the Capuchin Order due to his poor health, but the Redemptorists finally accepted him in 1749. Gerard made his profession as a lay brother in 1752 and during his six years with the Redemptorists, his piety, humility, and obedience were considered exceptional. Gerard died of tuberculosis in 1755, was beatified in 1893, and was finally canonized on December 11, 1904.

Gerard reputedly persuaded many to make an honest confession and he assisted those wishing to enter holy orders. As a result he was promoted as patron of good confession, and patron of religious vocations. However, he was also believed to have prayed successfully for the well-being of a woman in childbirth. A significant legend further associated him with pregnancy. Gerard is said to have left behind a handkerchief after visiting a family. The daughter of the house ran after him to return it, but Gerard told the girl to keep it as it would one day be useful. Many years later the girl was experiencing great difficulties in childbirth when she remembered the handkerchief. It was found and placed upon her, and she safely and successfully delivered the baby.[7] Although a seemingly unlikely candidate for such a role, it is as The Mothers' Saint that Gerard Majella has been best known and most vigorously promoted, and it is in this capacity that he has gained a large and enthusiastic following in Canada, Ireland, Britain, and throughout the world.

The key to St. Gerard's posthumous success lies with the Redemptorist Order. Redemptorists are members of the Roman Catholic Congregation of the Most Holy Redeemer (CSsR), founded in Italy by St. Alphonsus Ligouri in 1732. Its main activity has traditionally been preaching missions for the faithful, in order to reinvigorate the spiritual lives of those who are already members of the church; Congregation members literally preach to the converted. A Redemptorist mission should complement the work of the parish priest by inspiring the faithful to a fuller practice of the Christian life. Some of my Newfoundland informants in the 1970s recalled the Redemptorists primarily for their "hell fire and damnation" style of preaching. As Laverdure puts it, "missions were to be popular, simple, and, above all, persuasive."[8] They encouraged people to confess and receive the sacraments frequently, but they also promoted private devotions in which they had some vested interest. Pope Pius IX made the Redemptorist Order responsible for the promotion of devotion to the miraculous icon of Our Mother of Perpetual Help, for example, and they also keenly promoted "their" man Gerard. Both through mission activity and publications, the Redemptorists were to find in Newfoundland fertile soil for the dissemination of devotion to St. Gerard in his role as The Mothers' Saint.

The Newfoundland Context

BEYOND THE CAPITAL CITY OF ST. JOHN'S, much Newfoundland settlement traditionally has been in outports, small, often isolated coastal communities. Many lacked electricity and roads until the 1960s or later. They were frequently remote, and bad weather could cut off a community completely. People were vulnerable in the face of illness, the elements, and a physically harsh environment. As one woman in St. Mary's Bay told me, "'twas the roughest kind of life.'"[9]

In some outports, denominational and ethnic identity remained remarkably constant over long periods of time. When conducting fieldwork in Newfoundland in the late 1970s, for example, it was possible to designate certain villages as almost 100 percent Roman Catholic, with inhabitants whose ancestors came from either County Waterford or County Wexford in Ireland. This is still the case in some locations. The connection between Irish and Newfoundland Catholicism had been maintained, not least through a tradition of Irish priests serving in Newfoundland and some Newfoundlanders training for the priesthood in Ireland. Non-liturgical piety and associated vernacular practices were well developed in both Ireland and Newfoundland. Lysaght, for example, points to "the interaction of beliefs of official Catholicism and popular Catholicism" in "the variety of functions which sacramentals fulfilled in nineteenth, and twentieth-century

Ireland."[10] She highlights three areas that were also of considerable significance in Newfoundland: "*prayer*, e.g. the Our Father and liturgical prayers;
dipping, e.g., the use of holy water, and the largest category, *blessings*, which
includes the blessing and use of candles, medals, images and scapulars."[11]

Large families were the norm in Newfoundland. Murray claims that
"a dozen children or more per family was not uncommon in the early part
of the [twentieth] century."[12] As late as 1949, it was claimed in the *Province
of Newfoundland: Statistical Background* that "Newfoundland's birth rate is
among the highest among the white peoples of the world."[13] Because of
their occupation with pregnancy, childbirth, and child care, many married Newfoundland women lacked mobility, being largely tied to the home
while their husbands might participate in seasonal hunting, fishing, seal-
ing, or lumbering activities that could take men away from home for varying periods of time. However, women in Newfoundland tended to be the
religious head of the family, taking responsibility for the spiritual well-
being and religious formation of the family in the home context, and both
initiating and participating in non-liturgical religious activity. The highly
devotional nature of traditional Newfoundland Catholicism was typified
by close relationships with saints (often reflected in the presence of statues, pictures, and prayer cards of saints in the home) and families saying
the rosary together each day. School education remained denomination-
ally based in Newfoundland into the 1990s, which further reinforced the
Catholic liturgical year with its festivals and saints' days, and meant that
religion was taught and experienced both at home and in school.

Saints were traditionally considered able to deal with any eventuality,
and a saint whose efficacy was well attested would be readily added to the
individual's arsenal. Redfield's comments on the cult of the santos in Yucatan
could be applied to innumerable Newfoundlanders' devotion to saints:

> It flourishes in a situation where a need is felt for supernatural aid in the
> course of daily existence and where the common experiences of all mem-
> bers of the community reaffirm the efficacy of such aid and the rightness
> of seeking it.[14]

As I found both in the 1970s and 1990s, personal experience narratives of saintly intervention were candidly recounted and spread, highlighting the important role of the "belief story," characterized by folklorist Gillian Bennett as an informal story that enunciates and validates the current beliefs and experiences of a given community.

Talking of her community before the road was opened and electricity was laid on, one woman said:

> 'Twas only religion then, and your day's work. There was no television and there was no cars coming. You done your day's work and then there was your religion, and the rosary, and your religious books. . . . It was a different type of life then altogether.[15]

While there may well have been some nostalgia in this 1978 comment, it gives the flavour of a lifestyle in which religion was lived in and beyond institutional settings.

Redemptorist Missions

WHEN DEVOTION TO ST. GERARD MAJELLA was introduced into Newfoundland around the turn of the twentieth century, 34.4 percent of the population was Roman Catholic. The first Redemptorists were thought to have visited Newfoundland from Boston in approximately 1881, so when the earliest missions were held on the island, Gerard Majella had not even been beatified. It is reasonable to assume that after his beatification in 1893, his cult would have been promoted, as miracles to secure his canonisation were being sought.

Of St. Gerard's three areas of patronage (good confession, religious vocation, and expectant mothers), undoubtedly the greatest need in Newfoundland was related to pregnancy and childbirth. While there were no instances of the name Gerard in the nineteenth century in the Placentia parish baptismal records, in 1900 (four years before his canonization) one Gerard Majella appears and two boys with Gerard as their middle name. Between 1900 and 1915, 25 percent of Gerard Majella–related names have in the margin the annotation "sub con," indicating that the child had been baptised on the day of its birth due to fears for its survival.

A Redemptorist mission would normally last about one week, and it could be considered a great social as well as a spiritual event in Newfoundland, especially in isolated communities. The missions provided the opportunity not only for preaching about St. Gerard, but for the sale of brief biographies and devotional objects such as medals and statues.

A Redemptorist priest who had preached missions in Newfoundland between the mid-1950s and the mid-1970s recalled:

> When we used to travel round the missions, we would *always*, we'd always mention St. Gerard. Like on Tuesday nights we always had the special instruction for the married people, eh? And in the course of the sermon you'd *always* build up devotion to St. Gerard.[16]

This Redemptorist missionary used to travel with a St. Gerard relic, and commented that if women were pregnant, "they'd come for a blessing, they wanted to be crossed as they say here."[17] One woman remembered hearing about St. Gerard when, as part of the mission, there were separate services for women: "Now they'd do a lot of talking about St. Gerard then, when they had the women's service, see. Like about women, now, expecting, or like women that couldn't have children, he'd tell them to pray to St. Gerard."[18] Another woman mentioned that whenever there was a Redemptorist mission in her area, she would get a supply of St. Gerard medals: "You know, you'd get so many, probably half a dozen or something, then if you knew that some of your friends were expecting, well, I mean . . . you'd offer them then, you know, you help spread devotion."[19] The Redemptorist missions were thus a considerable force in the promotion of devotion to St. Gerard Majella in Newfoundland.

Devotional Magazines and the League of St. Gerard

WHILE MISSIONS WERE IMPORTANT in introducing people to St. Gerard, they were not the only means employed by the Redemptorists to encourage devotion. Devotional magazines were extremely important in this respect. One Newfoundland woman was of the opinion that devotion to St. Gerard had come "through the mail, through the magazines."[20] For the laity, devotional magazines were often the only theological literature encountered, and what appeared in them was taken very seriously. Furthermore, these magazines were aimed primarily at women. Orsi points out the importance of such literature for women devoted to St. Jude, and the role models projected through them.[21] As he comments,

> inert documents stored away in archives were once the living media of real people's engagement with the unfolding events of their times. The challenge is to figure out the relation between these archived pieces of a once-living world and the world from which they came.[22]

Popular devotional literature can be rather overlooked as a source, but its role in the promotion and consolidation of devotion to St. Gerard Majella in Canada (and elsewhere) has been considerable. Detailed study of the devotional magazines produced by the Redemptorists revealed their influence on and significance to Catholic women in Newfoundland, many of whom were having large families into their forties, in frequently harsh physical environments.

The Canadian Redemptorists produced three magazines that were particularly influential in the promotion of devotion to St. Gerard in Canada: *Eikon* (1928–42), *Mother of Perpetual Help* (1942–46), and *Madonna* (1947–67). *Eikon* first appeared in October 1928; the "eikon" which appeared on the cover of the magazine being that of Our Mother of Perpetual Help. St. Gerard was first mentioned in October 1929 in an article entitled "The Mothers' Saint—Saint Gerard." This article condemned the growing unpopularity of motherhood, cited miracles attributed to St. Gerard, and concluded that: "It is our earnest hope that the Catholic mothers of our country will turn to this humble but great Saint in all their needs."[23] In October 1930 *Eikon* contained a picture of St. Gerard and a novena in his honour. From 1931 onward requests from readers for St. Gerard medals were printed, as were letters thanking the saint for favours received.

Another significant development for the dissemination and practice of devotion in Newfoundland was the establishment in 1936 of the League of St. Gerard. St. Gerard was chosen as patron of the League "because he has long been known and invoked as 'The Mothers' Saint,' as well as the protector of the unborn child in every part of the Catholic world."[24] Founder Daniel Ehman, CSsR, had been greatly influenced by Pius IX's 1930 Encyclical on Marriage, *Casti Conubii,* in which artificial contraceptives were vehemently condemned. Ehman was particularly concerned about the "forces of anti-life," which to him were

> all forces, propaganda, movements, agencies or crimes that directly or indirectly attack the Christian family, or debase lawful motherhood. Hence we include in this category: Birth-control propaganda—practises [*sic*] or devices; human sterilisation methods and propaganda; divorce legislation and propaganda.[25]

There was obviously a strong element of propaganda in the League's inception. Devotion to St. Gerard was to be both an expression of values and a means of shaping them, a rallying point against encroachments on the Roman Catholic doctrine on marriage and birth control. There were various categories of League membership, including the Crusader:

> The Crusaders promise to recite daily the prayer to St. Gerard against the forces of anti-life, thereby gaining the indulgences granted—and try to do all in their power to spread a knowledge of The League, and to do battle in their district in every lawful way against the forces of anti-life.[26]

Ehman wrote that one of the aims of the League was "to make St. Gerard known, loved and invoked as 'The Mothers' Saint'"[27] and the League, along with the devotional magazines published by the Redemptorists, became powerful and popular instruments in the fulfillment of this aim.

From 1945 onward, the League's perspective was increasingly strongly expressed, and the magazine became more overtly propagandist. Anti-life was repeatedly condemned, and motherhood extolled as a divine vocation. The following is a typical example of the rhetoric employed:

> Something must be done, and must be done QUICKLY to stop and smash the ghoulish army of anti-life if the white races are to continue to exist. It is our hope that St. Gerard by his tender yet powerful assistance to

mothers in the hour of need will prove to be the bulwark of the Church in her battle to preserve Christian mothers in a pagan world.[28]

From 1950 a League of St. Gerard section became a regular feature of *Madonna* (*Mother of Perpetual Help's* successor) until the magazine's demise in 1967. This section contained exhortative articles and letters from readers thanking St. Gerard, asking for some favour, or requesting devotional objects. The League and *Madonna* magazine together formed a powerful partnership; *Madonna* ceaselessly encouraged membership of the League, while the League promoted *Madonna*. Moreover, the League and *Madonna* became part of the devotional process itself as women instrumentalized League membership and public acknowledgement of St. Gerard's aid. Publication of St. Gerard's success in letters to *Madonna* and joining the League or enrolling others were common forms of thanksgiving or elements of promissory prayer.

Both the devotional magazines (especially *Madonna*) and the League were greeted with enthusiasm by many Newfoundland women. Such was the association between them that some mothers devoted to St. Gerard called their daughters Madonna in his honour. One of my interviewees had the framed cover of the last issue of *Madonna* hanging on her bedroom wall. Another woman commented, "I miss the *Madonna* magazine quite a lot, because that was a lovely magazine."[29]

The magazines were considered a good read and the articles in them were taken very seriously; frequently the magazines were passed round among family and friends. *Madonna* printed two articles on medals, "Catholic Hallmarks"[30] and "Medals in Your Life."[31] In the latter, medals were described as "sacramentals, objects adopted by the Church as a means to obtain for the faithful spiritual and temporal favours from God."[32] Readers were told that medals could help Catholics "by obtaining for them actual grace, forgiveness of venial sin, remission of temporal punishment, health of body, material blessings, and protection from the wiles of the devil."[33] They were reminded that "the effects don't depend upon the medal itself, but upon the mercy of God who regards the prayers of the Church and the dispositions of the wearers of the medal."[34] Nevertheless, the contention that "medals in your life, if worn with faith and devotion, can obtain God's protection for you and endless blessings"[35] implies that medals could be potent sources of divine power. Such articles reinforced the popular practice of wearing medals, and the notion that people could benefit from them. As has been noted in relation to Catholicism in Ireland,[36] the wearing of religious medals was common practice, and to some extent a measure of piety. One Newfoundlander said of someone described as especially pious, "she had every saint you could mention round her neck."[37]

A feature entitled "My Name Is Gerard" appeared regularly in the League pages from the summer of 1958 onward. Children named after the saint were simply listed with their community, and in this section Newfoundlanders were very well represented.[38] In the summer of 1959 a letter from Bellevue was captioned "Community Devotion to St. Gerard" with the writer claiming that "nearly every mother in my community is a subscriber to the Madonna magazine and has special devotion to St. Gerard."[39] Naming in honour of St. Gerard was neither automatic nor standardized, however; one mother of twelve I interviewed demonstrated her devotion in naming one daughter Gerarda, while another woman included Gerard in the names of all three sons.[40] Evidently Gerard Majella–related naming was emblematic of the devotional vogue that swept Newfoundland in the 1950s and 1960s.

Something that had a strong presence in the magazines and that also emerged during my 1977–78 fieldwork was the way in which women could empathize with others, and both rejoice over and contribute to accounts of St. Gerard's successes through the letters pages. Roughly two Newfoundland letters per year were printed in the League of St. Gerard section of *Madonna* between 1950 and 1954, but from early 1955 onward, these numbers increased significantly. In October 1955 it was remarked that "of late Newfoundland is fast being 'covered' for subscriptions by some active promoters."[41] Mothers were repeatedly encouraged to write to *Madonna* as "these authentic letters appear in these pages each month and help, probably more than anything else, to sell St. Gerard to families in need of his help."[42]

Through the League and devotional magazines (particularly *Madonna*), Newfoundland women could participate in and be helped by a widespread devotional, and to some extent therapeutic, community. They could give personal testimony and receive inspiration from that of others; they could relate to women with similar concerns, hardships, and aspirations in the vocation of motherhood. A leitmotif in League literature was protection and this undoubtedly struck a chord with many Newfoundlanders. One woman wrote: "living as we do in a remote community cut off in winter, we feel all the safer, knowing that we are under St. Gerard's special protection."[43] A Fischot Islands woman wrote to *Madonna* with an offering for St. Gerard, and asked for prayers for herself and her family as she was expecting another child in winter. She concluded, "I place all my trust in your prayers and the League Members."[44] There was an extent to which women could enjoy the advantages and fellowship of a pilgrimage centre without actually leaving home. The participatory aspect was undoubtedly very important to many devotees in Newfoundland as their social constraints and isolation did not hinder their involvement and participation in this virtual community.

The Redemptorists used their considerable influence to promote and manipulate devotion to St. Gerard Majella in a situation where the anxieties and responsibilities of pregnancy and motherhood were keenly felt. St. Gerard received widespread publicity through missions, which were important social and spiritual events. The Redemptorists' magazines helped to encourage and consolidate devotion, while the League of St. Gerard, a pragmatic combination of piety and propaganda, provided an important focus for the devotion.

Praxis and Paraphernalia of Devotion

ALTHOUGH THE MALE REDEMPTORISTS were attempting to direct a devotion dealing with a specifically female condition (pregnancy) and vocation (motherhood), and use the devotion to mobilize a certain response to societal trends, we would be misreading the situation if we regarded the female Newfoundland devotees of St. Gerard simply as victims of Redemptorist propaganda. Despite the considerable efforts Redemptorists were making to spread devotion through a variety of means, many women simply learned about St. Gerard from other women as a result of personal experience narratives and assurances that he was effective, and they developed close personal relationships with the saint on that basis. When I asked one Placentia woman how she had become interested in St. Gerard, she replied, "I wasn't very well before the third was born, this friend of mine sent over a book, *The Mothers' Saint*, and so I prayed to him then."[45] Furthermore, Redemptorists I interviewed in the late 1970s and mid-1990s genuinely believed that St. Gerard had the power to help women in childbirth and pregnancy, and offered personal experience narratives of what they felt had been examples of his intercession.

Although many of my informants devoted to St. Gerard either possessed *The Mothers' Saint* or had seen it or similar booklets, in fact the majority could remember little or nothing about St. Gerard's life and miracles. It became clear that what had made the greatest impact were personal recommendations and experience narratives. To quote one mother of nine who had helped spread devotion to St. Gerard: "I've never really known his story.... It has been more or less passed down, I suppose, you know, from mother to daughter, and you know that you can turn to him."[46] One informant mentioned that she had recommended St. Gerard to her daughter, who had in turn told some of her friends about him. She commented, "you know, they spreads it from one to the other, see. I mean, that's the way devotion goes."[47]

The extent to which women prayed to St. Gerard, and the forms such prayers took, varied considerably. There was the novena (a special devotional exercise lasting nine days, usually undertaken to obtain a particular request such as becoming pregnant or having a safe delivery), or a brief exclamation, and also set prayers to St. Gerard, which were readily obtainable. Ehman's widely distributed booklet, "The Mothers' Saint," contained a number of prayers, including "Prayer for Motherhood," "For an Expectant Mother," and "For a Sick Child." The first two prayers frequently appeared on prayer cards featuring a picture of St. Gerard. The prayer, "For an Expectant Mother," was said by women on their own behalf, and frequently also for pregnant friends and relations. Underlining the solidarity women felt with other women, some mentioned that they continued to say the prayer with no one particular in mind on the assumption that there's always someone, somewhere, expecting a baby. Many women were pragmatic in relation to their prayer life. One mother of thirteen told me:

I always said a prayer to St. Gerard. But now, you know, I don't make the novenas like I used to in the early days, because they are long.... The time really comes when you don't hardly have time to pray, I found . . . but I didn't worry because I knew God understood and I know St. Gerard understood. But . . . there's days I've just said "St. Gerard, pray for me," or "St. Gerard, help me," that's all.[48]

One St. John's woman simply said, "I'm talking to him all the time."[49]

Many women greatly valued having St. Gerard medals, prayer cards, pictures, and statues during their pregnancy as tangible symbols and potential conduits of the saint's protection and presence. As Morgan counsels, we need "to study the response to objects as they are displayed, exchanged, destroyed, and circulated in order to determine what they mean to people—that is, how they build and maintain life-worlds. Meaning is not only abstract and discursive, but embodied, felt, interactive, and cumulative."[50] I was told on more than one occasion of a dangerously ill pregnant woman who was cured after drinking holy water in which a St. Gerard medal had been dipped. Many women mentioned that they had a St. Gerard medal with them up to and during the actual delivery. A midwife told me:

> Oh yes, they'd have their medals on, on their nightdress, and if I changed them then they'd have to go back, pinned on again. And some would have them on their neck, have a chain or something, you know. There wasn't too many I went to didn't have a medal or something on them like that.[51]

A woman who had all her children at home said she always kept her St. Gerard medal nearby, "on me person, or on the bed, or somewhere around handy."[52] A number of women encountered St. Gerard in the hospital. In the case room at the Placentia hospital there was a picture of St. Gerard, donated in thanksgiving by a woman in the 1960s. A nurse who worked at the hospital told me, "the lady left that picture, and after she left it there, you know, lots of mothers used to ask me to pass it over to them and put it under them . . . under their pillow."[53]

Similarly, in St. Clare's Mercy Hospital in St. John's, not only did the nursing nuns actively promote St. Gerard and distribute St. Gerard medals in the maternity ward, there was a statue of St. Gerard just outside the delivery room that a number of women mentioned they had seen and been comforted by on their way in. Women who owned a statue of St. Gerard might lend it to others when they needed it.

Of course, women in Newfoundland could and did pray to St. Gerard without having need of a medal or any material object connected with him. However, that people were prepared to go to considerable lengths to get something tangible in some circumstances is demonstrated by the following incident:

> Well, her first baby, you know, she had a lot of trouble, and they come to my place to get the medal, I had a medal then at the time ... her mother come to my place in the middle of the night, twelve o'clock in the night, to get the medal. Yeh, and you know 'twas a rough night, see, in the winter, and she come and asked for the medal.... And she said, "don't think she [the midwife] is going to save her," so she come after the medal twelve o'clock in the night. And eh, she went in and put the medal on her, and the next morning they come out and she said she was all right, she had a baby boy.[54]

Many women in Newfoundland developed relationships with St. Gerard on the basis of the recommendations of friends and family, trust, and positive experiences. The St. Gerard medals, prayer cards, and other devotional items sold and promoted by the Redemptorists through missions, the League, and devotional magazines were considered powerful symbols of the saint's presence and were put to practical use at times of stress and need. In this they had been encouraged by popular practice, and by articles such as "Medals in Your Life," mentioned earlier. Pragmatism and affection were at the heart of many women's interactions with the saint. As Orsi commented in relation to devotees of St. Jude, the saint

> came in a moment of crisis and stayed; the movement here was from a contingent, even contractual association predicated on extreme need to a more lasting, less desperate bond, and many women have remained faithful to this relationship for decades.[55]

I interviewed a number of women in 1977 and 1978 who considered their relationship with St. Gerard the mainstay of their religious lives. As one said,

"He's my best friend."[56] With St. Gerard there could be an intimacy and understanding concerning the details and anxieties of pregnancy and motherhood that might not be shared appropriately with either a priest or a spouse.

Making Gerard Manly

Figure 1.1 › Pre-beatification picture of Gerard, in the possession of a Newfoundland family.
(Source: Marion Bowman, 1978)

JUST AS FEW WOMEN had felt it necessary to know details of St. Gerard's biography, comparatively few women paid particular attention to how Gerard was depicted on the medals and prayer cards. The importance of having a picture, statue, medal, or whatever, tended to lie not in the appearance of the saint, but in the significance and relationality of the object. This makes particularly interesting—and to some extent ironic—the attempts of the Canadian Redemptorists to make "their" saint more attractive to "their" women. Nineteenth-century pictures of Gerard before his canonization, and contemporary pictures of the saint mass-produced in Italy, tend to reflect aspects of his life and legend, depicting him as a delicate young man gazing at a crucifix, frequently with a book (representing the scriptures, learning, and evangelism), a scourge (symbolizing passion and self-discipline), and a stem of white lilies (representing purity and virginity, as well as being a symbol of the Virgin, to whom St. Gerard was especially devoted). (See Figure 1.1.)

Figure 1.2 › Pictures of St. Gerard often hung on bedroom walls of Newfoundland devotees. Many Newfoundland women in the 1970s owned this image as it also appeared on prayer cards and League of St. Gerard membership cards.
(Source: Marion Bowman, 1978)

In the 1970s, the picture of St. Gerard that I was most frequently shown during my fieldwork appeared on prayer cards and League of St. Gerard membership cards in the 1950s and 1960s (Figure 1.2). In this picture the saint is simply depicted holding a large crucifix in his arms, without any other detail. On all the medals I was shown, St. Gerard holds a Latin cross, with lilies, scourge, and skull in the background. Statues (such as the one that used to be outside the delivery room at St. Clare's Mercy Hospital, St. John's) tended to have a skull at their base.

In October 1955 a picture of St. Gerard taken from a statue in the English Redemptorist church in London appeared on the cover of *Madonna*. This illustration also appeared on the League of St. Gerard membership application form that year. The statue had been designed at the request of Cardinal Griffin, then archbishop of Westminster, who wrote: "I am afraid that St. Gerard suffers from his statues . . . so we designed a special statue for him. . . . We ought to make the saints lovable."[57]

Inspired by the English example, in 1956 the Canadian Redemptorists introduced a novel picture of the saint on the cover of Ronald G. Delaney's new pamphlet, "Saint Gerard." He was still holding a large crucifix in his arms, but the traditional halo had disappeared, and there was no sign of the lily or the skull. This picture prompted enquiries about "St. Gerard's 'New Look,'" which were dealt with in *Madonna*. In answer to queries about its authenticity, it was pointed out that "no real picture of St. Gerard has ever been found."[58] Clearly, though, a conscious effort was being made to popularize St. Gerard through this medium: "our new picture is a blending of the English and the Italian concept of St. Gerard. Of course it also has a slight trace of Canadian features which ought to make The Mothers' Saint still more acceptable to our people."[59]

The attempt to make Gerard manly and more attractive to the women the Redemptorists thought of as "our people" was probably not the resounding success they might have hoped for. The new picture survived only on the cover of Delaney's pamphlet, and was not adopted by the League of St. Gerard. I did not encounter it in any of the Newfoundland homes I visited in the 1970s. The picture of St. Gerard that was to appear on subsequent League prayer cards and on the cover of later editions of Ehman's pamphlet, "The Mothers' Saint," showed St. Gerard with one hand

Figure 1.3 › St. Gerard's "new look"
on the cover of Delaney's pamphlet.

(Source: "Saint Gerard," 1956)

resting on the shoulder of a woman who was kneeling at his feet and gazing lovingly at the child in her arms. While the earlier pictures give clues to the saint's life through common Christian symbols, and his appearance is that of a rather otherworldly young man of delicate constitution, in later pictures the only aspect of his life depicted was his association with mothers; emphasis had been shifted away from the saint himself to his role.

St. Gerard was attractive to Newfoundland (and other) women because he was presented as interested in and concerned about the everyday lives and struggles of pregnant women and mothers, and could be called upon as a friend and protector to them. The later pictures, which focused on St. Gerard's role, probably more accurately recognized and reflected the reality of popular devotion that what is important is not how a saint looks, but what he (or she) does.

Women's Business

ALTHOUGH THE REDEMPTORISTS tried to promote St. Gerard as "The Working-man's Friend," and some men would have heard of St. Gerard in the meetings for married couples at missions, devotion to St. Gerard in Newfoundland was in practice the domain of women. Although the high incidence of the name Gerard was what had alerted me to the importance of the devotion in the first place, when asked about their name, many Gerards simply thought that it was traditional, or their mother had just liked it.

Some men whose wives were devotees of St. Gerard either had not heard of him or were unaware of his sphere of influence. The following exchange occurred, for example, while I was interviewing a woman with a son named in honour of the saint:

MR. M: What's Gerard the patron saint of anyways? . . .
MRS. M: Mothers, expectant mothers.
MR. M: Oh geez, I don't know. No wonder I know nothing about the man, I had nothing to do with him.[60]

One man who told me of his mother's great devotion to St. Gerard suddenly turned to his wife and said, "Say, why did you put Gerard on Edmund's name? He's called Gerard," to which his wife replied, "Sure, honey, I was praying my heart out to St. Gerard for Edmund!"[61] Like pregnancy and childbirth, devotion to St. Gerard was very much regarded as "women's business."

Generational Changes and Socio-religious Developments

BY THE LATE 1970S devotion to St. Gerard Majella was in decline. Women who had received help and were devoted to St. Gerard continued to regard him as a friend and helper and attempted to pass on the devotion to daughters and other women, but the St. Gerard fever that had gripped Newfoundland earlier in the twentieth century had abated. Devotion to St. Gerard had given Newfoundland women in a previous era not simply individual spiritual support, but a sense of purpose and solidarity in relation to other women and unborn children, in a context where women's social and religious roles were limited. However, new roles and aspirations were to emerge for a variety of reasons.

Some of the people I interviewed in 1977–78 felt that improved medical facilities and the trend of smaller families contributed to the declining interest in and need for St. Gerard. Devotion to saints generally suffered in the aftermath of Vatican II, and there were some flashpoints of disagreement between parishioners and priests concerning the shift in focus from saints to sacraments. Newer church buildings had neither the space physically nor the place theologically for the statues of saints that had proliferated in some churches; often such statues (including those of St. Gerard) had been donated in thanksgiving and the stories surrounding the donation were part of the church's vernacular tradition. Older church interiors were reconfigured to focus attention on the altar and away from "peripherals." One Placentia woman said with reference to the removal of the statues, "it's not a church anymore, it's like an auditorium."[62]

Whereas at various points there had been Redemptorists at Corner Brook, St. George's, and Whitbourne, by the late 1970s St. Teresa's in St. John's was the only remaining Redemptorist parish in Newfoundland. I observed tensions there between different generations of Redemptorist priests at that time. While one older Redemptorist was happy to recount his experiences of promoting St. Gerard during missions, and his use of a St. Gerard relic to aid women experiencing problems with their pregnancies, a younger priest was dismissive to the point of rudeness of a woman devotee and her stories about St. Gerard's interventions in her life.

By the 1990s, many were blaming changed socio-economic conditions, the advent of roads and television, and the growth of religious and social pluralism for the demise of more traditional ways of life. Seemingly small changes had collectively had a negative impact on devotion to St. Gerard. The St. Gerard picture that had been in Placentia Hospital from the 1960s to the 1980s seems not to have been replaced after the facilities were renovated, and when maternity services in St. John's moved from St. Clare's Mercy Hospital to a Salvation Army hospital, there were no nuns to promote Gerard to a receptive audience.

Undoubtedly one of the most significant turning points for many Newfoundland Catholics came in the last decade of the twentieth century, with revelations of sexual abuse of children in a St. John's boys' home run by a lay order, the Christian Brothers, and of sexual abuse of children by parish priests. One Newfoundlander I met in 1996 referred to herself not as a lapsed but a "collapsed" Catholic, capturing the sense that so many had of the certainties of faith and identity being pulled from under them. Many Catholics, feeling betrayed and disillusioned, simply left the church. Some who had become largely cultural Catholics, belonging without believing, felt justified in distancing themselves from the church. The rate of practice, that is people regularly attending mass on Sunday, fell from an estimated 80 percent of Catholics in the 1970s to around 20 percent in 2012. A non-denominational education system was inaugurated in 1998–89, which has affected religious education and the formation of Catholic children.

However, of those who stayed in the church because they actively wished to be there, a significant number were women. The scandals occasioned considerable soul-searching and self-reflection among the laity, and some openly challenged the Catholic establishment. Condemnations were voiced of the church's traditional attitudes to women and children, and the extent to which the church had colluded in marital inequality and abuse through inaction. Public and vigorous calls were made for an end to priestly celibacy and an increase in the authoritative roles women could hold. The Vatican II vision of the church being the people took on new meaning for many, as some lay people reflected that they had been too inclined to put priests on a pedestal, and that greater co-operation and shared responsibility between clergy and laity were needed. All this, along with the decline in vocations for the priesthood, led to some changes in liturgical practices, with women increasingly serving at the altar and being lay readers. Women in Newfoundland have thus become more visible in church life, their activities having moved increasingly from the domestic to the public sphere. One woman commented that it gave her a great thrill to see women "right up there" reading and serving in church. In her day, she observed, "the only time a woman got near the altar was on her wedding day."[63]

Anxiety about the "vile forces of anti-life" continues, but is expressed in a different form. The all-male Catholic fraternity, the Knights of St. Columba, has a pro-life agenda expressed in the erection of memorial stones ("In memory of all babies killed by abortion," erected at Mount Cashel, 1995; "For all babies lost to abortion. May they rest in peace," St. Patrick's, 1997). Some Newfoundland parishes and individuals participate in the International Perpetual Rosary for Life campaign. As the Priests for Life Canada website explains:

> Prayer is our most powerful weapon against contraception, abortion, euthanasia, and other attacks against the sanctity of human life. Join us, and others throughout the world, through the power of the Holy Rosary, to storm Heaven with prayers in defence of life from conception to natural death.
>
> Our method is simple . . . just pray the Holy Rosary on a regular basis, either daily, a few times each week, or once a week, and offer your intentions to the pro-life cause. With enough involvement, we will ensure that the Rosary for Life is being prayed around the clock on a perpetual basis.[64]

Newfoundland women and men increasingly became engaged in direct action, whether through picketing abortion facilities or running support services for women who would otherwise consider abortion. From the late 1970s the Newfoundland and Labrador Right to Life Association provided a more broadly based and active focus for concerns relating to pregnancy and the rights of the unborn child, relying heavily on female volunteers. The Right to Life Association in St. John's has now been rebranded as The Centre for Life. Its website states:

> The Centre acknowledges that an unplanned pregnancy may present many concerns and issues and provides free, confidential, compassionate, and non-judgemental support with our trained professional counsellors who are only a phone call away. The Centre for Life believes that every human life has intrinsic value and regardless of the circumstances of the pregnancy every woman should be fully informed to ensure their optimum physical and emotional well being.[65]

The Centre is also concerned with other "life issues," such as euthanasia and stem cell research. As one volunteer put it, they are "concerned with life at both ends, from conception to natural death," attempting to counter the "abortive mind-set of the secularised world."[66] They feel that the pro-life movement needs to present itself in non-condemnatory, non-confrontational, ecumenical, compassionate outreach. Much pro-life activity remains faith-based, and prayer campaigns continue, but St. Gerard is no longer the figurehead.

However, the impression should not be given that the Redemptorists are inactive, and that St. Gerard is forgotten in Newfoundland. The Canadian Redemptorists have embraced new technology with enthusiasm. Through their website, information about, pictures of, and prayers to St. Gerard can be accessed (see "Redemptorists"). The League of St. Gerard continues, although I was told in 2012 that there were only five Newfoundland members. Redemptorist TV reaches a wide range of people, for example, through weekly televised devotions to Our Lady of Perpetual Help (widely publicized in Newfoundland Catholic churches), and a variety of devotional resources concerning the saint are available on You-Tube, including broadcasts by Father Ray Corriveau, CSsR, director of the League of St. Gerard. In one broadcast, Father Ray discusses St. Gerard's special role as The Mothers' Saint, and "defender of life from the moment of conception." He recalls his own mother's devotion to St. Gerard and the fact that his elder brother was named Gerard in the saint's honour. He also mentions the letters the League receives either asking for St. Gerard's intercession or expressing thanksgiving for a healthy pregnancy and safe childbirth. A variety of images of St. Gerard feature in the film, including ones alluding to his frailty, as well as a newer image (laughingly described to me by one woman as "sultry St. Gerard"). In addition to St. Gerard's role in relation to mothers, however, much stress is laid on his solidarity with and sensitivity to the poor, and his care and concern for the problems of families; the tuberculosis from which Gerard died is characterized as a disease of the poor.[67] The degree of Newfoundland women's engagement with these resources and the part they might play in their devotional life in future is beyond the scope of this chapter.

Redemptorists are still invited by Newfoundland parishes to organize missions, often on the theme of reconciliation and in situations of community fracture. The stress these days is not on hellfire and damnation preaching, but on "bringing people to an encounter of God's love."[68] One female Redemptorist lay missionary I interviewed in 2012 considered the Redemptorists more open to giving women opportunities that were not always forthcoming in the wider church. She has taken an active and valued role in preparing and conducting missions in Newfoundland, and felt that having a woman on the mission team made a positive difference.

In St. Teresa's Church, it is possible to purchase a variety of St. Gerard paraphernalia, his picture is in the entrance area together with other Redemptorist saints, and a small statue of St. Gerard is tucked away discreetly toward the back of the seating area. There is talk of bringing a larger statue of St. Gerard into the church, and promoting him more vigorously as the "life-affirming" saint (rather than simply presenting him as the "pro-life saint" as he is characterized by some North American congregations). At St. Teresa's in 2012 I encountered a woman who was anxious about her Toronto-based daughter during her labour, and had asked one of the priests to pray for her. He had given the woman a St. Gerard prayer card and she "did a lot of praying that night"; the baby was safely delivered. Another older woman I met there mentioned that she was making a novena to St. Gerard for someone in the parish. The impression I gained both in the late 1970s and mid-1990 was that pockets of devotion to St. Gerard would continue, largely due to the localized influence of family and friends and personal experience narratives of the saint's efficacy. This devotion appears to be operative at the start of the twenty-first century as well.

Conclusion

THE STORY OF THE RISE AND FALL of devotion to St. Gerard Majella in Newfoundland provides a vignette of vernacular religion, in which the verbal and printed testimony of Newfoundland women affords insights into the behavioural, relational, and material expressions of their religious belief in a context that highlights the "bidirectional influences of environments upon individuals and of individuals upon environments in the process of believing."[69] Folklorist Don Yoder succinctly describes folk religion as "the totality of all those views and practices of religion that exist among the people apart from and alongside the strictly theological and liturgical forms of the official religion,"[70] recognizing the huge and frequently understudied area of religious life in which women have so frequently operated. It was this territory that I originally set out to explore in relation to St. Gerard in the late 1970s, and have been privileged to pursue in later decades through the lens of vernacular religious theory. Primiano argues that vernacular religion is "conceptually valuable" because

> the study of vernacular religion, like the study of folklore, appreciates religion as an historic[al], as well as contemporary, process and marks religion in everyday life as a construction of mental, verbal, and material expressions. Vernacular religious theory understands religion as the continuous art of individual interpretation and negotiation of any number of influential sources.[71]

St. Gerard Majella's popularity in Newfoundland was, to a considerably extent, the result of specific social, environmental, and religious conditions Catholic women encountered in twentieth-century Newfoundland. The speed with which devotion spread and the enthusiasm with which it was embraced indicate not simply that it was vigorously promoted, but that it met a perceived—and highly gendered—need. Devotion to The Mothers' Saint, though centred on women and specifically female conditions, was promoted, controlled, and manipulated at the official level by men. Moreover, St. Gerard's "expertise" in relation to pregnancy and childbirth was exploited to make him the figurehead of an anti-modernist campaign to protect traditional Catholic family life and values. However, like so much non-liturgical piety, the devotion could not be tightly controlled. The Canadian Redemptorists' attempts to manipulate the saint's appearance in order to make him more attractive, for example, indicate that the nature and basis of women's relationship with St. Gerard were not fully grasped by his most vigorous promoters. Women creatively embraced and re-narrated this male-mediated devotion, utilizing vernacular forms of relationality and materiality, responding to the saint in gendered and pragmatic ways.

Matthew Engelke claims that "the nature of lived experiences, including lived religion, depends on the particularities of time and place and the exigencies of tradition; it also depends, inevitably, on arguments within traditions."[72] Undoubtedly, from 1900 until well into the 1970s, St. Gerard played a significant role in the spiritual and practical lives of myriad Newfoundland women. However, even by the late 1970s generational differences and tensions between pre- and post–Vatican II belief and practice were obvious, and devotional patterns were changing. Ironically, some would argue that the trauma experienced because of the revelation of clerical sexual scandal in the 1990s had unexpectedly positive gender consequences for the liturgical practices of the Catholic Church in Newfoundland. These, alongside socio-economic change and secularization, have had significant impact on women's lifestyles, expectations, and religious roles. They highlight, in McGuire's words, "the considerable complexity of all the ways people's religion and spirituality are linked with their gender expectations of self and others, their relationships with human and divine others, and their root sense of identity and community."[73] While many remain faithful to St. Gerard, for Newfoundland Catholic women at the start of the twenty-first century, the emphasis has moved significantly from the domestic to the public, from devotional responses to direct action, from motherhood to personhood. ●

Notes

1. Leonard Primiano, "Vernacular Religion and the Search for Method in Religious Folklife," *Western Folklore* 54, no. 1 (1995): 44.

2. William A. Christian Jr., *Person and God in a Spanish Valley* (New York: Seminar Press, 1972); Robert A. Orsi, *The Madonna of 115th Street: Faith and Community in Italian Harlem, 1880–1950* (New Haven: Yale University Press, 1985); Robert A. Orsi, *Thank You, St. Jude: Women's Devotion the Patron Saint of Hopeless Causes* (New Haven and London: Yale University Press, 1996); Robert A. Orsi, *Between Heaven and Earth: The Religious Worlds People Make and the People Who Study Them* (New Haven and London: Yale University Press, 2005).

3. Primiano, "Vernacular Religion," 44.

4. Ibid.

5. Marion Bowman, "Devotion to St. Gerard Majella in Newfoundland: The Saint System in Operation and Transition" (master's thesis, Memorial University of Newfoundland, 1985); Marion Bowman, "Vernacular Religion and Nature: The 'Bible of the Folk' Tradition in Newfoundland," *Folklore* 114, no. 3 (2003); Marion Bowman, "Religion, Sexual Abuse and Controversy: A Case Study," in *Controversial Practices*, ed. Hugh Beattie (Milton Keynes: Open University, 2013), 151–208. For quotations from my 1977–78 fieldwork, references will be cited according to their Memorial University of Newfoundland Folklore and Language Archive (MUNFLA) designation; later material will be referenced by dated field journals. I preserve the anonymity of my informants in accordance with their wishes.

6. Daniel Ehman, CSsR, "The Mothers' Saint" (Toronto: League of St. Gerard, 1951), and Ronald G. Delaney, CSsR, "Saint Gerard" (Montreal: League of St. Gerard, 1956) are typical Redemptorist-produced short biographies of the saint. See Rev. Bernard Kelly, ed., *Butler's Lives of the Fathers*, vol. 5, *Martyrs and Other Principal Saints* (London and Dublin: Virtue & Company, 1954), 408–11, for a more general account.

7. This is reminiscent of cures connected with handkerchiefs recorded in Acts 19:12.

8. Paul Laverdure, "Remarks on the History of Redemptorists in Canada, 1834–1898," *Spicilegium Historicum* 40, no. 1 (1992): 56.

9. MUNFLA, tape, 78-196/C3501.

10. Patricia Lysaght, "The Uses of Sacramentals in Nineteenth- and Twentieth-Century Ireland. With Special Reference to the Brown Scapular," in *Religion in Everyday Life*, ed. Nils-Arvid Bringeus (Stockholm: Konferenser- Kungliga Vitterhets Historie och Antikvitets Akademien, 1994), 193.

11. Ibid., 194.

12. Hilda Chaulk Murray, *More than 50%: Woman's Life in a Newfoundland Outport, 1900–1950* (St. John's: Breakwater Books, 1979), 93.

13. *Province of Newfoundland: Statistical Background* (Ottawa: Bureau of Statistics, Department of Trade and Commerce, 1949), 16.

14. Robert Redfield, *The Folk Culture of Yucatan* (Chicago: University of Chicago Press, 1959), 267.

15. MUNFLA, tape, 78-196/C5851.

16. MUNFLA, tape, 78-196/C3492.

17. Ibid.

18. MUNFLA, tape, 78-196/C5851.

19. Ibid.

20. Fieldnotes, 1978.

21. Orsi, *Thank You, St. Jude,* 70–91.

22. Ibid., xxvii.

23. *Eikon* 2, no. 1 (October 1929): 180.

24. Ehman, "The Mothers' Saint," 58–59.

25. Ibid., 58.

26. Ibid., 59–60.

27. Ibid., 58.

28. *Mother of Perpetual Help,* 3, no. 10 (October 1945): 319.

29. MUNFLA, tape, 78-196/C5851.

30. *Madonna,* 23, no. 12 (December 1950): 329–32.

31. *Madonna,* 33, no. 2 (February 1960): 25–27.

32. Ibid., 27.

33. Ibid.

34. Ibid.

35. Ibid.

36. Lysaght, *Religion in Everyday Life,* 195.

37. MUNFLA, tape, 78-196/C3502.

38. Female Gerard-related names include Gerarda, Gerardine, and Gerardella. Majella usually appeared as a male first or middle name.

39. *Madonna,* 32, no. 7 (Summer 1959): 31.

40. In St. Alban's, Newfoundland, the parish priest Father Hayes had considerable enthusiasm for St. Gerard. Speaking to one woman in that area, I ascertained that

one son born in 1960 had Gerard as part of his name. Confidently expecting an affirmative answer, I enquired whether she had named her son on account of her devotion. She replied, "No, my dear, that was Father Hayes stuck that on him. . . . Father Hayes called everyone Gerard that year." Fieldnotes, 1978.

41. *Madonna*, 28, no. 9 (October 1955): 257.

42. *Madonna*, 31, no. 1 (January 1958): 30.

43. *Madonna*, 32, no. 1 (January 1959): 31.

44. *Madonna*, 35, no. 3 (March 1962): 32.

45. MUNFLA, tape, 78-196/C3499.

46. Ibid.

47. MUNFLA, tape, 78-196/C3501.

48. Ibid.

49. Fieldnotes, 1978.

50. David Morgan, "The Materiality of Cultural Construction," *Material Religion* 4, no. 2 (2008): 228.

51. MUNFLA, tape, 78-196/C3502.

52. MUNFLA, tape, 78-196/C5851.

53. MUNFLA, tape, 78-196/C3500.

54. MUNFLA, tape, 78-196/C3502.

55. Orsi, *Thank You, St. Jude*, 110.

56. Fieldnotes, 1978.

57. Quoted in *Madonna*, 29, no. 5 (May 1956): 158.

58. Ibid.

59. Ibid.

60. MUNFLA, tape, 78-196/C3497.

61. MUNFLA, tape, 78-196/C3500.

62. Fieldnotes, 1978.

63. Fieldnotes, 1995.

64. See "Priests," *Priests for Life*, http://www.priestsforlifecanada.com/English/Resources/perpetual_rosary_for_life.php.

65. See "About Us," *Centre for Life*, http://www.centreforlife.ca/about-us/.

66. Fieldnotes, 2012.

67. See "St. Gerard Majella, C.Ss.R. #2," *Perpetual Help TV Devotions*, http://www.youtube.com/watch?v=tPwzcUytgUo&list=PL7661350C44850DA8.

68. Fieldnotes, 2012.

69. Primiano, "Vernacular Religion," 44.

70. Don Yoder, "Toward a Definition of Folk Religion," *Western Folklore* 33, no. 1 (1974): 14.

71. Leonard Primiano, "Afterword—Manifestations of the Religious Vernacular: Ambiguity, Power and Creativity," in *Vernacular Religion in Everyday Life: Expressions of Belief*, ed. Marion Bowman and Ülo Valk (Abingdon and New York: Routledge, 2012), 383.

72. Matthew Engelke, "Material Religion," in *The Cambridge Companion to Religious Studies*, ed. Robert A. Orsi (Cambridge: Cambridge University Press, 2011), 212.

73. Meredith McGuire, *Lived Religion: Faith and Practice in Everyday Life* (New York: Oxford University Press, 2008), 160.

Bibliography

"About Us." *Centre for Life.* http://www.centreforlife.ca/about-us/.

Bennett, Gillian. "'Belief Stories': The Forgotten Genre." *Western Folklore* 48 (1989): 289–311.

Bowman, Marion. "Devotion to St. Gerard Majella in Newfoundland: The Saint System in Operation and Transition." Master's thesis, Memorial University of Newfoundland, 1985.

———. "Religion, Sexual Abuse and Controversy: A Case Study." In *Controversial Practices*, edited by Hugh Beattie, 151–208. Milton Keynes: Open University, 2013.

———. "Vernacular Religion and Nature: The 'Bible of the Folk' Tradition in Newfoundland." *Folklore* 114, no. 3 (2003): 285–95.

Christian, William A., Jr. *Person and God in a Spanish Valley.* New York: Seminar Press, 1972.

Delaney, Ronald G., CSsR. "Saint Gerard." Montreal: League of St. Gerard, 1956.

Ehman, Daniel, CSsR. "The Mothers' Saint." Toronto: League of St. Gerard, 1951.

Engelke, Matthew. "Material Religion." In *The Cambridge Companion to Religious Studies*, edited by Robert A. Orsi, 209–29. Cambridge: Cambridge University Press, 2011.

"International Perpetual Rosary for Life." *Priests for Life Canada.* http://www.priests forlifecanada.com/English/Resources/perpetual_rosary_for_life.php.

Kelly, Rev. Bernard, ed. *Butler's Lives of the Fathers.* Vol. 5, *Martyrs and Other Principal Saints*, 408–11. London and Dublin: Virtue & Company, 1954.

Laverdure, Paul. "Remarks on the History of Redemptorists in Canada, 1834–1898." *Spicilegium Historicum* 40, no. 1 (1992): 55–69.

Lysaght, Patricia. "The Uses of Sacramentals in Nineteenth- and Twentieth-Century Ireland. With Special Reference to the Brown Scapular." In *Religion in Everyday*

Life, edited by Nils-Arvid Bringeus, 187–224. Stockholm: Konferenser- Kungliga Vitterhets Historie och Antikvitets Akademien, 1994.

McGuire, Meredith. *Lived Religion: Faith and Practice in Everyday Life.* New York: Oxford University Press, 2008.

Morgan, David. "The Materiality of Cultural Construction." *Material Religion* 4, no. 2 (2008): 228–29.

Murray, Hilda Chaulk. *More Than Fifty Percent: Woman's Life in a Newfoundland Outport, 1900–1950.* St. John's: Breakwater Books, 1979.

Orsi, Robert A. *Between Heaven and Earth: The Religious Worlds People Make and the People Who Study Them.* New Haven, CT, and London: Yale University Press, 2005.

———. *The Madonna of 115th Street: Faith and Community in Italian Harlem, 1880–1950.* New Haven: Yale University Press, 1985.

———. *Thank You, St. Jude: Women's Devotion the Patron Saint of Hopeless Causes.* New Haven, CT, and London: Yale University Press, 1996.

Primiano, Leonard. "Afterword—Manifestations of the Religious Vernacular: Ambiguity, Power, and Creativity." In *Vernacular Religion in Everyday Life: Expressions of Belief,* edited by Marion Bowman and Ülo Valk, 382–94. Abingdon and New York: Routledge, 2012.

———. "Vernacular Religion and the Search for Method in Religious Folklife." *Western Folklore* 54 (1995): 37–56.

Province of Newfoundland: Statistical Background. Ottawa: Bureau of Statistics, Department of Trade and Commerce, 1949.

"Redemptorists." *Redemptorists.* http://www.redemptorists.ca.

Redfield, Robert. *The Folk Culture of Yucatan.* Chicago: University of Chicago Press, 1959.

"St. Gerard Majella, C.Ss.R. #2." *Perpetual Help TV Devotions.* http://www.youtube.com/watch?v=tPwzcUytgUo&list=PL7661350C44850DA8.

Yoder, Don. "Toward a Definition of Folk Religion." *Western Folklore* 33, no. 1 (1974): 2–15.

2 "She Couldn't Come to the Table 'til She Was Churched"

Anglican Women, Childbirth, and Embodied Christian Practice in Conception Bay, Newfoundland

BONNIE MORGAN INDEPENDENT SCHOLAR

Introduction

The popularity of churching among Newfoundland Anglicans continued well into the late twentieth century, demonstrated in the April 1968 edition of the diocesan newspaper, *Newfoundland Churchman*. This issue featured a photo of four couples kneeling at the chancel rails of an unnamed church building, "taking part in the Thanksgiving after Child-Birth, following the baptism of their respective children."[1] The inclusion of this photo and caption may have been, in part, an effort by diocesan officials to transform the popularly understood "churching of women," with its connotation of female impurity following childbirth, its multiple customs as well as its history as a female-centred celebration, into its official version as a rite of family thanksgiving. In Conception Bay different views of churching reflect a gap between official and lived religion stretching back to the medieval English church, yet they also reveal the influence of class and gender on Christian ritual. The female-centred events of childbirth, lying-in, and churching included embodied practices and beliefs informed by Christian scripture and doctrine, recognition of women's labour within rural households and communities, as well as prescribed notions of female sexuality and reproductive capacity. In this way, women's work, including the work of child-bearing, shaped religious belief and practice into a lived Christianity reflecting the material circumstances of female lives. It was also a lived Christianity experienced through, and located in, female bodies as they laboured (in varied ways) within the coastal communities of Conception Bay.[2]

This chapter considers Newfoundlanders' continued attachment to the service of churching, exploring the beliefs and practices surrounding this rite as lived by Anglican women of mid-twentieth-century Conception Bay, a large inlet of the Atlantic Ocean located on the southeast corner of the island and forming part of the Avalon Peninsula. In what was then a rural setting of coastal communities, where family labour sustained a household economy (although the household economy was increasingly transitioning to a wage economy after the 1940s), women were actively engaged in agricultural work, including animal husbandry and dairying (mostly small scale), berry picking, laundry, housework, textile production, fish-making, the preparing and serving of food, as well as child-bearing and child care.[3] This chapter focuses on the voices of these ordinary Anglican women, who in a series of 2011 interviews with the author recalled religious beliefs and practices of childbirth from the 1930s through to the 1960s.[4] This inquiry reveals the extent to which religious rituals of childbirth were informed by class and gender. These rituals demonstrated recognition of women's work in the household and community, including that of midwives. With minimal access to medical care, childbirth remained a female-centred event in mid-twentieth-century Conception Bay, with religiously informed practices of lying-in and churching enforced by female kin rather than male clergy. The study demonstrates the importance of embodied religious practices for the women of Conception Bay, revealing lived religiosity informed by gendered notions of cleanliness and female sexuality in ways that official Anglican discourse and doctrine did not.

Churching and Embodied Religious Practice

DURING THE PAST DECADE, scholars of religion have become interested in questions of embodied religious practice, and the ways in which spiritual belief can inform perceptions of, and relationships with, the physical self. R. Marie Griffith, for example, has considered how religious belief contributes to ideological constructions of the body, including popular understanding of "adored and despised" physiognomies, and how this understanding informs the weight loss and fitness industries.[5] Robert Orsi has explored how "sacred presence becomes real in particular times and places," including the role of human bodies in the making of religious cultures:

> The materialization of religious worlds includes a process that might be called the corporalization of the sacred. I mean by this the practice of rendering the invisible visible by constituting it as an experience in a body— in one's own body or in someone else's body—so that the experiencing body itself becomes the bearer of presence for oneself and for others.[6]

In this way, as one Roman Catholic nun writing in the 1930s, quoted by Orsi, said, the "spiritual" is "made concrete."[7]

James Opp has considered the relationship between embodied religious practices and gender in faith healing, arguing that "women were not simply a part of the divine healing movement, their bodies were the movement. It was primarily women's bodies that were healed, and it was primarily women who testified to their experience."[8] "Encountering the divine within the body," Opp asserted, provided late-nineteenth and early-twentieth-century women with a sense of personal holiness and physical "perfection," in contrast to male medical discourses, which characterized the female body as "other" and "prone to sickness."[9]

Concepts of women's bodies as the "despised other" likewise informed male theological discourses, which in turn shaped official beliefs and practices. As argued by Rosemary Radford Ruether, accepting these constructions of female physiognomy meant that

> women could share in the redemptive experience but only through negation of their identities as sexual beings and mothers, only through them becoming the male spirit. . . . In Christian theology this led often to presenting the soul as separate from and superior to the trappings of the body.[10]

For Ruether, women's traditional role in "the processes of life and death," and particularly in childbirth, was perceived by many male theologians as a threat to patriarchal social and cultural power. For this reason, mainstream (male) theologies tended to present female sexuality and maternity as an "inferior aspect" of human experience.[11] In contrast, women's theology "takes seriously the idea that women *as* women—whether as a result of biology or gendered experience—have distinctive insights into the divine to contribute to thinking about God and God's relation to the world."[12] Religious experience and belief, therefore, can be rooted in the experience of pregnancy and childbirth.

As a Christian ritual centred on newly delivered mothers, churching has increasingly interested feminist theologians and liturgists. While some, such as Susan K. Roll, have condemned the rite as "devaluing of women," others see feminist liturgical potential in a Christian ceremony focused exclusively on lay women.[13] Anglican Natalie Knödel, drawing on the pre-Christian origins of the rite as well as the Church of England's official emphasis on churching as a service of thanksgiving rather than purification, has suggested that contemporary Christian women need to revive and reclaim this ancient liturgy as a female-centred celebration of women's bodies and reproductive capacity, rather than "dismiss[ing it] as yet another expression of the church's misogyny."[14]

This dual meaning of churching—purification and thanksgiving—affected how the rite was understood by the women who participated in it. Historians have largely investigated churching in terms of the medieval or early modern European experience, relying almost exclusively on sources about upper- and middle-class women.[15] Scholars such as Susan Karant-Nunn, Paula M. Rieder, and Elizabeth L'Estrange have considered churching as part of a female-centred culture of child-bearing, and argued for churching's role in the construction and expression of gender roles.[16] Rieder, in her work on late medieval France, has linked churching to social and cultural ideas of female sexuality, purification, social standing (legitimacy), and healing.[17] David Cressy has presented churching in Tudor and Stuart England as "an occasion of female social activity, in which the notion of 'purification' was un-contentious, minimal or missing."[18] Arguing for churching as an empowering, female-centred community celebration, historically valued by Anglican women as a "rare opportunity to be the focus of attention within the liturgy of the church and to have their bodily labors recognized, taken seriously, and celebrated," Cressy is sensitive nonetheless to the influence of time and place on interpretation.[19]

"Churching was about many things," he observes, "but not necessarily always the same things. Like many other rituals, its outward form could mask a variety of meanings."[20]

Scholars such as Cressy and Rieder have sought to understand how women themselves felt about participation in this rite, and the nature of its meaning for participants.[21] Despite the belief, presented by some historians, that churching had become obsolete after the eighteenth century, increased attention to the working-class experience has demonstrated otherwise. Sarah Williams has noted how, especially in northern English parishes and working-class districts of London, churching was practised into the twentieth century.[22] Margaret Houlbrooke's 2012 study, *Rite out of Time*, further demonstrates the survival of churching among English working-class families (artisan and labouring), although in decline since the 1960s.[23] Houlbrooke explores the meaning of churching for mid-twentieth-century English women by seeking out the living voices of those who experienced the rite. This is the method I used for this study of Conception Bay women.[24]

History of Churching
Purification or Thanksgiving?

DONNA RAY AND DAVID CRESSY, among others, have considered the history of churching within the Church of England.[25] Much of this work has considered the tension between "custom," including the popular understanding of churching as a purification ritual, and "liturgy," the church's argument that the service was primarily about thanksgiving. This tension is rooted in the historical development of the rite. Part of English custom as early as the seventh century, and described by the Venerable Bede, churching became official church rite only in the medieval era. It was titled "Blessing of a Woman after Childbirth before the Church Porch" in the twelfth-century *Missal of Sarum*, and preserved in the Church of England's first Book of Common Prayer (BCP; 1549) under a new title, "The Order of the Purification of Women." Under pressure from English Protestant leaders, who associated churching with Jewish and Roman Catholic "superstition," by 1552 the Church of England had removed reference to purification and renamed the service "The Thanksgiving of Women after Child Birth, commonly called the Churching of Women," a name retained into the twenty-first century.[26]

In the seventeenth century, Church of England leadership tried to counteract the persistent popular understanding of churching as a purification rite by making liturgical changes to the service for the 1662 version of the BCP. These included emphasizing the language of thanksgiving and replacing Psalm 121, with its call for help and protection from evil, with Psalm 116, a song of thanksgiving after delivery from distress.[27] These changes were not without controversy. Despite the tendency of Anglican clergy to insist that churching as purification was a popular misunderstanding of the church's intentions, English theologians were engaged in the purification/thanksgiving debate. Ray notes how High Church Anglican clerics such as John Donne primarily viewed churching as an act of purification rather than thanksgiving, believing that "only the churching rite, performed by a priest, could bring a clean thing out of filthiness." While Puritans rejected churching, she argues this should be considered more of a political gesture against clerical authority than against ideas of women being "polluted" by conception and childbirth.[28]

Following the Restoration, ecclesiastical and political debates about the rite subsided, yet churching remained a controversial ceremony within the Church of England. Houlbrooke has described the extent to which notions of female impurity after childbirth and the need to be "churched" or else "remain unclean" continued in England after World War II, especially among older women. She likewise describes clerical efforts to "stamp out" churching in the 1950s and 1960s. This including publishing articles in church magazines "condemn[ing] superstition about the ritual": that un-churched women would be unlucky, that their shadows could cause houses to collapse, and that they were impure and could not be seen in public.[29] Similar efforts were made in the Canadian Anglican church, with Rev. Dr. William Armitage noting in 1922 that while the service is "based upon the Old Testament rite of Purification. It is not, however, intended to be a ceremonial suggesting the removal of any defilement through childbirth. . . . Its sole note is that of thanksgiving."[30] In Newfoundland Anglican church leaders were aware of the vernacular interpretation of this service in other jurisdictions, yet believed the island and Labrador were pockets of orthodoxy within a vast landscape of misinterpretation. In March 1926, William White, then bishop of Newfoundland, described the churching of women as an important gesture of public thanks to God for the blessing of a new family member, and stated that "contrary to some other dioceses," the women of Newfoundland understood the "true" meaning of this service.[31] In expressing this opinion, the Anglican bishop may have been wilfully blind, hopeful, or simply out of touch with popular practices among his flock. For the women of mid-twentieth-century Conception Bay, beliefs about churching were laden with notions of female cleanliness, sin, and morality.

Many of the popular beliefs about and practices of churching described by twentieth-century Conception Bay women, such as staying indoors or not preparing food, were part of popular Christian practice from the medieval era onward. Ray describes how before the eleventh century European Christian women were expected to wait for a specified period after childbirth before attending public services of worship and receiving communion. But she notes that the church did not formalize a ritual for this period of waiting and the mother's "return" to the church community. She argues that the churching rite was initially intended by the English clergy to be a thanksgiving ceremony, and that many popular beliefs about purification, such as that an un-churched woman should stay indoors (for fear she would be "attacked by evil spirits" or "defile those around her") were never accepted or promoted by Anglican theologians.[32] In the classic *Religion and the Decline of Magic*, Keith Thomas describes a variety of popular beliefs about un-churched women, including that such women would be burned if exposed to the sun or moon (Psalm 121:6), that meat they touched would spoil, and that grass would not grow in the places they walked. Thomas attributes some of these beliefs to the interpretation, by both clergy and laity, that sexual activity was polluting, and that the physical process of childbirth, with its pain and bloodshed, was evidence that "some stain or other doth creep into this action which had need to be repented."[33] Among early modern clerics, there were theological debates about whether un-churched women were damned and whether or not they could be buried in consecrated ground, a debate tied to the popular belief that women of child-bearing age should avoid the grave of an un-churched woman, for fear their own reproductive capacity would be compromised.[34]

Churching and Newfoundland Anglicans

IN 1922 REV. DR. WILLIAM ARMITAGE, then rector of St. Paul's Anglican Church in Halifax and a leading cleric within the Diocese of Nova Scotia, noted the extent to which the service of "The Thanksgiving of Women after Child-Birth Commonly Called the Churching of Women," had "fallen into . . . general disuse in the Canadian Church." Armitage continued:

> There are parishes in which it is never used, and it would not be far from the truth to say that it never has been used; and no attempt is made, even by way of suggestion, much less by definite instruction, to make the service a part of our normal Church life.[35]

There were some exceptions to this pattern of "general disuse" identified by Armitage, usually led by parishioners who requested the ceremony. While he did not state whether these parishioners were male or female, Armitage did identify their place of origin. "It will be found," he observed, "that as a rule those who ask for it are either from the mother land [England], or from the neighboring dominion of Newfoundland. The Church people of Newfoundland prize this service very highly."[36]

The service "prized highly" by Anglicans of Newfoundland was, by the mid-twentieth century, a brief ceremony for newly delivered mothers conducted on the same Sunday as the infants to whom they had given birth were baptized. Mildred (Butler) Porter (1919–2013) described her experience of churching in the 1940s:

> Well now you went to the service, 11 o'clock service in the morning. Now there was churching of women. Perhaps there would be one, two or three. You would go up to the rail and he had a service to read to you. Then, of course, he passed this book to you to put your bit of money on.[37]

Mildred's daughter Myra (Porter) Rideout similarly recalled women being churched as a group in the 1960s, and the paying of what was once termed "shame money" to the priest:

> I remember when mine were [baptized] it was a bit different. They had their service, morning service. So you went with your baby and you sat with your sponsors [godparents] and you sat in the back of the church.... They baptized your babies and then they had the churching of the women. By this time the church was empty unless it was some of your family, you know. It was a little service after.... You would stay in the back of the church and he would say we are going to have the churching of women ... and all the mothers went up. He'd say a few prayers and then he passed along his book and you put your dollar.[38]

As printed in the Book of Common Prayer, "Thanksgiving After Child-Birth" was exactly that, a service in which women were "called upon to give hearty thanks to God" who "out of his goodness" had "bestowed upon them the gift of a child" and "preserved" them in child-birth.[39] Yet the history of this service, and the popular practices surrounding it, told a different story, one of women's bodies being "polluted" by conception, pregnancy, and childbirth, and of women's need to be cleansed of this "impurity" by participating in the churching rite.[40] As noted by Armitage, as well as by historians of the ritual, by the late nineteenth and early twentieth centuries, many Anglican women had rejected the practice of being churched after childbirth. For some, however, participating in this service remained a regular part of religious life during their child-bearing years.

Conception Bay
Lying-in and Postpartum Care

CLOSELY TIED TO THE RITE OF CHURCHING was the lying-in following childbirth. While originating "in Levitical blood taboos, which required the separation of the newly-delivered woman from the community" during the time of her lochial flow, historians have recognized how the lying-in period "offered mothers valuable care, recognition and a chance for celebration during and after what was a physically demanding time."[41] As argued by Natalie Zemon Davis, lying-in (and churching) led to "the upsetting of traditional gender hierarchies"; through childbirth, women could negotiate their place within patriarchal social structures and, even if temporarily, come out "on top" within households and communities.[42] For aristocratic women of medieval and early modern western and northern Europe, lying-in could last from four to six weeks. L'Estrange recognizes that while "all Christian women adhered" to this practice, the duration depended on the status of the household, especially the amount of help available from "female assistants, relatives, friends or hired midwives."[43]

In mid-twentieth-century Conception Bay, women were aware of risks associated with childbirth, both in terms of the mother's health and the child's chances of survival. Mildred (Butler) Porter noted of her experience in the 1940s: "It was serious having a baby and you had to be so careful."[44] Within the Church of England Women's Association (CEWA), the primary female voluntary organization within the Diocese of Newfoundland, news that members had delivered babies was included in the weekly "sick report." This message could be communicated by midwives who were active in the association, such as on November 22, 1938, at Seal Cove, when "Sister Eve Morgan suggested that we should all go and visit Sister Phoebe Morgan as she has been sick and unable to attend." (Phoebe had delivered a baby boy on November 16.)[45] At Long Pond, the sick report of December 16, 1959, stated that "Sister Doris Bishop and Sister Violet Taylor has a baby girl each," while on September 23, 1964, the secretary noted "Sister Joan Jefford reported sick with a new baby girl." On November 25, 1964, "Sister Edwina Porter reported having her baby and better."[46] Using language of sickness to describe childbirth and the postpartum period reflected women's understanding of the risks of childbirth and the need for a period of rest and recovery after delivery, rather than a notion of childbirth as disease or disability. As well, it afforded the opportunity for women in the community to care for each other during such a time.

In mid-twentieth-century Conception Bay, the services of midwives were highly valued, and went beyond physical delivery of the child. In a 1988 interview, Gladys Butler of Long Pond described how local midwives, "who just took it up as far I know" rather than having formal training, came to the house of a labouring woman, boiled water, got towels ready, and "kept you occupied and talking."[47] Butler compared positively the care given by midwives to that provided later by doctors and hospitals. With a midwife such as "Aunt Nicie" Perrin, she said, after three or four hours of labour "it was all over," and she "never heard of anyone dying in child-birth with the midwives." Butler described how midwives would stay all day with a woman, and for nine days after the birth they would come every day to tend to the mother and child, as well as to wash baby clothes.

This time frame for lying-in was mentioned by several informants from Foxtrap and Long Pond, such as Beulah (Porter) Morgan, who noted, "sure the mother used to stay in bed about nine days after the birth in them days, oh yes."[48] For English women, ten days lying-in before churching appeared to be the twentieth-century standard.[49] Other women recalled seven days of care. In a 1977 interview, Eliza Jane Dawe proudly recalled of her twenty years as midwife in Upper Gullies that she "never lost a mother," going on to describe how she would stay with a woman seven days after a baby was born.[50]

Along with midwives, female relatives could help new mothers during the lying-in period. Myra (Porter) Rideout recalled:

> I was thirteen when my sister was born. She was born home, that was by a midwife. She came for six or seven days after. Mom didn't get out of bed. Before I [went] to school I would bring up [the] face and hand [pan] for her to wash. Then you would bring her breakfast. Then the nurse would come and see to the baby. . . . It was complete bed rest. Even when my first was born, that was in '64, I was in hospital a week and I had no problems whatsoever.[51]

Significantly shorter than the four to six weeks noted by L'Estrange for upper-class women, the seven or nine days described by the rural work-ing women of Conception Bay reflected the socio-economic status of their households and the nature of rural Newfoundland society. Women were actively involved in the family economy, and households depended on adult female labour for both indoor and outdoor work.

The length of time for lying-in was also informed by religious belief. Seven days reflected the period of "uncleanness" following the birth of a male child described in Leviticus 12, the scriptural chapter most associated with the churching custom. Interestingly, the distinction between giving birth to a male child (seven days "unclean") and delivering a female child (twelve days "unclean"), as described in Leviticus, did not survive in local popular practice.[52]

The number seven was also associated with local traditional healing practices. The healing powers of a seventh daughter or a seventh son, a well-documented European folk belief, was also common in Newfoundland and Labrador (although it was more often the seventh son than the seventh daughter who was believed to have healing powers).[53] Asked by the author about religious cures, Pat (Morgan) Woolgar of Kelligrews related her personal experience of being healed by a seventh daughter:

> I actually had it done with me. I had a string of warts down my leg, bunch of little warts. This old aunt of my mom's, old Rachael Hennessey, used to come up now and then. She was a real old woman and [Mom] would say Aunt Rachael was a seventh daughter. You heard tell of seventh sons . . . but she was the seventh daughter. Mom said to me one day when Aunt Rachael comes up now she will take those away for you. So she rubbed her hand over my warts and I don't know what she said or did. I didn't even think of it but it was four or five days later and when I looked they were gone away, whether she took it away or not. That actually did happen to me and it never came back.[54]

Sandra (Taylor) Tilley, who also grew up in Kelligrews, recognized the Christian significance of the number seven, although she was ambivalent about whether or not ordinary people would consider cures by seventh-born children as religious per se:

> I don't know if they perceived it that way or not, but the seven is a biblical number. It is completeness. The seven days of the week and seven tribes and you know and all that. . . . So you would hear talks, people would go to somebody about their tooth. So did they see it as religious? I don't

know what their interpretation was. They didn't talk about why they did it. They just believed in it. They availed of it.[55]

The connection between the number seven and traditional healing practices was also noted by Rachel Fagan and Minnie Bussey of Foxtrap, who reported in a 1972 interview that women caring for sick family members believed that the seventh day of a serious illness was the point at which the person would either start to improve or start to die.[56]

Whether nine days or seven days, women connected the time frame of lying-in with preparation for the religious ceremonies of baptism and churching that ended their confinement. Mildred (Butler) Porter explained how for nine days after delivering a baby "you had to make sure you didn't go out of doors or wet your hands or anything till [the christening]." This was echoed by other women interviewed for this project. Enid (Porter) Haines, discussing religious practices related to childbirth, noted that "you don't take the child out until the child goes and gets baptized. There was no such thing as taking a child outside then before it was baptized." Her mother, Mary (Petten) Porter, added, "they was only baptized on Sunday, you couldn't take them in the store until a couple of days after. I don't know why, but that is it."[57] The practice of not taking your baby out until it was baptized was likewise described by Marge (Saunders) Dawe and Joyce (Andrews) Morgan.[58]

Conception Bay
Honouring the Midwife

IN MID-TWENTIETH-CENTURY CONCEPTION BAY, midwives were often present at churching services by virtue of being asked to stand as godmothers to the children they delivered. Cressy describes churching in early modern England as a female-led celebration, with the newly delivered mother proceeding from her home to the church accompanied by her midwife and other women from the community.[59] While this public processional approach to churching was not practised in Conception Bay, women arranging to have their midwives present for the ceremony suggested a cultural remnant from traditional English churching rituals.[60] During baptism, usually held during the same service in which the mother was churched, godmothers promised to pray for the child and, on his or her behalf, "acknowledge the duty to keep God's holy will and commandments" as well as to "walk steadfastly in the Way of Christ." Eliza Jane Dawe reported that she was often asked to stand as godmother to children she helped deliver.[61] Families may have considered midwives especially appropriate women to serve as godmothers because of their ability to perform emergency baptisms, a religious function normally reserved for male priests and licensed lay readers.[62] At the same time, their very participation in childbirth, a moment of potential death for mother and child, gave midwives a special spiritual status within the local community.

Sandra (Taylor) Tilley recognized the religious aspects of midwifery in relation to her aunt, Dorcas Taylor. Taylor's work with labouring mothers and infants gave her a revered status within the local community. Tilley associated this special spiritual status with midwives' work with mothers and children at a time of high infant mortality. She recalled of her aunt:

> She born all of Mom's children, she would have been there to born the children and she was up and down the shore. She was the person who borned the children. That was always kind of revered. I guess it was revered because back then it was common that every family, I know it was for us, that one child in every family seemed to die ... things that today they would never die. I don't know if it was because [midwives] were so tuned into this, you still go through our cemeteries on Foxtrap Church Road, you see all these one month, two months, three months. ... So I always seemed to recall that Aunt Dorcas and the babies was a revered thing.[63]

Tilley recognized how Dorcas Taylor, as a midwife, was intimately tied to women at moments of potential joy or sorrow, with the outcome of any delivery having profound religious and emotional effects on families and communities. Scholars such as Susanna Morrill have recognized how the death of a child could shape women's theological perspective, with even the most committed Christians doubting and questioning the meaning of God's will when faced with such a loss.[64] Midwives felt first-hand the sorrow of mothers and/or families when a birth went wrong or a child was lost in infancy, as well as suffering her own sense of loss. Eliza Jane Dawe described her lingering sadness at being present at births of dead or deformed and dying children, remembering especially one woman who faced the sorrow of three stillborn deliveries.[65]

Like other Conception Bay Anglican women, midwives participated in the religious life of the community and expressed their need for female-centred Christian practice and service through active participation in the CEWA. Eve Morgan of Seal Cove and Rachel Dawe of Long Pond, for example, received special attention and honour from the women of this association as a result of their work as midwives. At Seal Cove women demonstrated their respect and affection for Morgan in the financial and spiritual support they provided to her in the late 1920s and early 1930s, as she experienced a period of sickness in an otherwise long and healthy life.[66] At Long Pond, women honoured Rachel Dawe at the time of her death in 1953, with a tribute captured by CEWA secretary Elsie Baird:

> The Worthy President [Annie Jefford] now spoke of our late sister Rachel
> Dawe who passed away during the summer. She was a lifelong member
> of the CEWA and did much for this community being a Maternity nurse.
> The sisters were asked to stand for two minutes of silence in her honor.
> This was done. May she rest in peace and light perpetual shine upon her.[67]

While Eve Morgan and Rachel Dawe were identified as midwives in CEWA records, additional names of midwives active on the south side of Conception Bay were found in church baptismal records, as clergy often noted the name of the person who administered an emergency baptism if the child lived to be received into the church at a later date.[68]

Some midwives' medical knowledge went beyond assisting with childbirth and giving postpartum care to mother and child, and this earned them reputations as healers within the community. In a 1988 interview, Gladys Butler of Long Pond referred to midwife Eunice Perrin as a "doctor woman" who would "bind up" broken bones, make ointment for boils, treat infections and cure pneumonia, flu, and bad colds.[69] Likewise, Dorcas Taylor was remembered by fellow midwife Eliza Jane Dawe as the "next thing to a doctor" on the shore.[70] There has been little effort by scholars to understand the interaction between religious belief and vernacular healing in Newfoundland, or how vernacular healing can be understood as embodied religious practice, representing people's understanding of a direct, physical and personal connection between humanity and the Divine.[71] Within the Newfoundland literature, John Crellin and Barbara Rieti have offered secular perspectives on traditional healing, with Crellin noting how "charmers" in rural settings offered "magical treatment ... what was perceived by some people as a form of faith healing."[72] Yet the examples of Eve Morgan, Rachel Dawe, Eliza Jane Dawe, Dorcas Taylor, and Eunice Perrin suggest the potential to understand some aspects of traditional healing as embodied religious practice. Women of Conception Bay, and perhaps elsewhere, used religious language and ritual, along with church-based collective action, to honour and respect the female healers and midwives of their community.

Churching Practices in Conception Bay

MARGE (SAUNDERS) DAWE (1926–2014) of Upper Gullies recalled how Anglican women had to be churched after childbirth, and went on to describe the prohibitions new mothers faced in the home and church prior to participating in the ceremony: "you couldn't take communion 'til you were churched. You couldn't make bread 'til you were churched."[73] Emma (Petten) Warford had similar memories:

> I tell you one thing, you weren't allowed to make bread or do a thing after your baby until your baby was christened ... you weren't allowed to do anything till you went and got the baby christened.... You weren't allowed to touch anything along the food line.[74]

Emma remembered likewise how new mothers could not partake of Holy Eucharist prior to being churched:

> You had to wait before you could go to the service. After you would go and take your communion then, right.... You were churched, that's what they used to call it. You weren't allowed to do anything until you were

churched and the baby christened. I tell you, you had to listen to what they said.

When asked about her feelings about being churched, Emma was positive. "I was so delighted with my baby," she recalled and, reflecting the female-centred nature of the ceremony, went on to remember the names of other women who were churched at the same time. Prudence (Morgan) Rideout (1914–2014) was positive also: "That was part of the service; I don't know how to put it now. But ... if a woman had a baby it seemed like that was the blessing on her like." Daughter Judy (Rideout) Dawe added, "when the baby was brought to the church to be christened, the women were churched. They had to go up to the rail and their prayers and whatever. I remember that."[75]

Other Conception Bay women were more critical of the rules and rituals regarding churching. Marge (Saunders) Dawe considered the prohibitions on touching food or taking communion as evidence that the community (and the church) believed that a new mother "wasn't clean or something," going on to point out "the Lord ordained how babies are born, so how could you be unclean?"[76] Sandra (Taylor) Tilley likewise described how her mother, who grew up outside Conception Bay close to the city of St. John's, resisted her mother-in-law's attempt to impose local customs:

One [religious practice] my mother doesn't speak very highly of. . . . When a child was born the mother was not allowed to sit at the table for the meal until after they had gone to church and been churched. . . . Mom was living on Topsail Road and she married Dad and moved to Kelligrews. And Dad's mother was still alive and living [with them], because Dad looked after her, Nana Taylor. So they were there and when [my brother] was born [in 1937] she would have come to go to the table, [but] she was told by Nana Taylor that she was not to come to the table till she was churched. My mother was a strong woman, I guess too, and she defied that practice. She said having a child was not a dirty thing and she was going to be eating at the table with the family.

An ordained priest, Tilley went on to describe how popular customs around churching had little to with the intention behind "Thanksgiving after Childbirth":

> I think we see it today that it was, over the years, a misconstruing of what [it] was meant to be. The churching of women was really wanting [to give] God thanks for safe delivery, safe baby, healthy baby, safe mother. God's hand at work. Somehow it got turned into you put some money on the Bible and you were forgiven your sins for the dirt you were involved in.[77]

Conclusion

ATTITUDES TOWARD CHURCHING were tied to social standing. By the eighteenth century, members of the English middle and upper classes tended to reject popular ideas about churching, female purity, and restrictions on women's movements and activities following childbirth. However, as demonstrated by Sarah Williams, these ideas remained important to the English working class well into the twentieth century. The practice of and beliefs about churching recalled by Anglican women of rural Conception Bay (settled largely in the period between 1774 and 1845), including restrictions on a new mother's mobility and the belief that these limitations could be lifted only with participation in church ritual, echoed those described by women in 1920s working-class London:

> When I had my Billy I got out of bed to change his napkins [and] they came and caught me and said I was flying in the face of the Lord. You couldn't come out of the door into the open air unless you went straight to the church after you had children and the child wasn't allowed out until it was christened. If you did not you was treated like dirt.[78]

Williams focuses on the social control aspects of churching, with obedience to prescribed behaviours as a test of a woman's piety and respectability, yet other factors may have been at play. In twentieth-century Conception Bay, placing limitations on un-churched women was a popular religious practice preserved (and enforced) by working women. While limitations placed on the newly delivered woman suggest female impurity that could be cleansed only by participation in the churching ritual, a fact recognized and resented by some informants, one can also see the seven-to-nine-day lying-in period and the prohibitions on bread making, wetting hands, and leaving the house as rest from heavy household labour.

Women of rural Newfoundland may have cherished this break from their working routine after the physical demands of pregnancy and delivery, and recognized how engaging in heavy work too soon after childbirth could have long-term effects on their health. Churching may have been "highly valued" by the Anglicans of Newfoundland, but part of this valuing came from rural working women conscripting popular religious beliefs and official ritual into something that benefitted them physically, if not always spiritually or socially.[79] When the Canadian clergyman, the Reverend Armitage, noted the continued importance of churching for immigrant Anglicans from Newfoundland and the "mother land," his focus on ethnicity was to the neglect of other social factors. The working class or rural background of people likely to immigrate to Canada from the United Kingdom or Newfoundland at the end of the nineteenth and early twentieth centuries informed continued attachment to this religious ritual,[80] whereas for English families of the upper and middle classes, churching had been largely abandoned by the 1800s.

That being said, the messages about gender and sexuality implicit in lived Christian practices of churching cannot be ignored. Sue Morgan has criticized cultural historians for neglecting both women's agency and the impact of religion on constructions of modern sexuality, suggesting that this latter omission has stemmed largely from unquestioning acceptance among historians (for the most part) of the secularization narrative. Pointing to Foucault's analytical use of religious and confessional discourses, she concludes that "analyses that depict religion as antithetical to sexuality ... misunderstand their interdependence as modes of truth-telling and self-making."[81] Focusing on the thought and work of largely middle-class, female British writers and reformers, Morgan outlines how religious discourse was used to promote sexual purity and pleasure within heterosexual marriage, to campaign for and against birth control, to inform the social purity movement against sexual vice and venereal disease, as well as to provide language for the expression of alternative sexualities, including same-sex relationships and celibacy.[82] She concludes, "[it] was not the clerical elite but the prominent participation of laywomen as orators, writers and activists throughout the period [1800–1940] that ensured religion remained an influential arbiter of sexual behavior well into the twentieth century."[83] Morgan demonstrates how some women "by virtue of their gendered occupation of a distinctive space between ordained institutional and lay popular religious cultures" were freer to communicate on sexual matters than were ecclesiastical authorities, yet her analysis neglects somewhat the impact of class status on women's ability to communicate influentially at a national level.[84]

The Anglican women of Conception Bay likewise occupied a gendered space outside the official church where religious discourse could be applied to matters of sexuality, especially sexual purity within marriage. Within this space and religious culture, the sexual purity of a woman was understood as compromised by pregnancy and childbirth, leading to a series of prohibitions on her domestic activities, largely enforced by female kin. The tendency of female relations of a new mother, rather than clergy, to enforce twentieth-century working-class churching practices was seen also in English parishes.[85] In Conception Bay, a new mother's "uncleanness" was thought to extend especially to her ability to prepare or serve food, which included even to her being banned from sitting at the family table during mealtimes. Only after participation in the churching of women service, twinned with administration of baptism to her child, would an Anglican woman be considered cleansed and ready to assume her full household duties. Hand in hand with the restoration of domestic status went renewal of religious status as it was popularly understood that a woman was forbidden to take communion until she was churched. While some women interviewed remembered popular practices related to churching with resentment, others understood the service to be an act of thanksgiving and a blessing as the Diocese of Newfoundland's Bishop William White believed all Newfoundland Anglican women did. As with enforcement by female kin, this pattern of mixed responses to churching was mirrored in English working-class women's views of the ceremony.[86]

Different views and experiences of churching suggest variety in religious belief and practice in Conception Bay Anglican households, as well as various degrees of gender consciousness among the women who, well into the 1970s, continued to be churched after giving birth. Popular understandings of the rite, along with lying-in and the enforcement of prohibitions on newly delivered mothers, stand as examples of lived, embodied religious practice informed, yet not endorsed, by official Christianity. ●

Notes

1. *Newfoundland Churchman*, April 1968, 13.

2. The findings in this chapter form part of a broader study of interaction between women's household work in the family economy, lived religious practices and female theological culture in rural Newfoundland. See Bonnie Morgan, "Conceiving Christianity: Anglican Women and Lived Religion in Mid-Twentieth-Century Conception Bay, Newfoundland" (PhD dissertation, University of New Brunswick, 2014).

3. For a discussion of the sexual division of labour and its impact on gender relations in Newfoundland society, as well as women's work in rural Newfoundland, see Marilyn Porter, "She Was Skipper of the Shore Crew: Notes on the History of the Sexual Division of Labour in Newfoundland," in *Their Lives and Times: Women in Newfoundland and Labrador: A Collage*, ed. Carmelita McGrath, Barbara Neis, and Marilyn Porter (St. John's: Killick, 1995), 33–47; Barbara Neis, "From 'Shipped Girls' to 'Brides of the State': The Transition from Familial to Social Patriarchy in the Newfoundland Fishing Industry," *Canadian Journal of Regional Science* 16, no. 2 (1993): 185–202; Hilda Chaulk Murray, *More Than Fifty Percent: Women's Life in a Newfoundland Outport, 1900–1950* (St. John's: Breakwater, 1979); Irene Botting, "Understanding Domestic Service through Oral History and the Census: The Case of Grand Falls, Newfoundland," *Resources for Feminist Research* 28, nos. 1 and 2 (2000): 99–113; and Wileen Keough, *The Slender Thread: Irish Women on the Southern Avalon, 1750–1860* (New York: Columbia University Press, 2006).

4. Part of research completed for my doctoral dissertation, these interviews were conducted using methodology approved by the University of New Brunswick's Research Ethics Board (File #2011-011). As part of the interview process, informants quoted in this chapter agreed to be identified by name.

5. R. Marie Griffith, *Born Again Bodies: Flesh and Spirit in American Christianity* (Berkeley: University of California Press, 2004), xi, 10. The relationship between religion and the body can be seen in the history of ascetic practices, where "rituals of purification and self-denial" were "aimed at subjugating the flesh or achieving identification with the suffering, crucified Christ" as well as in Christian traditions, both Protestant and Catholic, which viewed material abundance and self-indulgence as antithetical to spiritual growth and righteousness. Ibid., 4.

6. Robert Orsi, *Between Heaven and Earth: The Religious Worlds People Make and the Scholars Who Study Them* (Princeton: Princeton University Press, 2005), 73–74.

7. Ibid., 75. In this work (chapters 1 and 3) Orsi identifies a religious culture among twentieth-century American Roman Catholics in which the bodies of children and people with disabilities were considered particularly conducive to the creation of sacred presence.

8. James Opp, *The Lord for the Body: Religion, Medicine, and Protestant Faith Healing in Canada, 1880–1930* (Montreal: McGill-Queen's University Press, 2005), 205.

9. Ibid.

10. For discussion of Reuther's theology in relation to lived religion in Newfoundland, see Darlene Brewer, "Mending Our Nets: Toward a Feminist Vision of Redemption in Dialogue with the Newfoundland Fishery" (PhD dissertation, University of Ottawa, 2008), 156–57.

11. Ibid.

12. Julie Melnyk, "Women, Writing, and the Creation of Theological Cultures," in *Women, Gender, and Religious Cultures in Britain, 1800–1940,* ed. Sue Morgan and Jacqueline deVries (New York: Routledge, 2010), 49.

13. Brigitte Enzner-Probst, "Waiting for Delivery: Counseling Pregnant Women as an Issue for the Church," *International Journal of Practical Theology* 8, no. 2 (2004): 187.

14. Natalie Knödel, "Reconsidering an Obsolete Rite: The Churching of Women and Feminist Liturgical Theology," *Feminist Theology* 5, no. 14 (1997): 106–7; Enzner-Probst, "Waiting for Delivery," 187–88.

15. Attention to churching within the Eastern Orthodox tradition is increasing. See Kathryn Wehr, "Understanding Ritual Purity and Sin in the Churching of Women: From Ontological to Pedagogical to Eschatological," *St. Vladimir's Theological Quarterly* 55, no. 1 (2011): 85–105; Matthew J. Streett, "What to Do with the Baby? The Historical Development of the Rite of Churching," *St. Vladimir's Theological Quarterly* 56, no. 1 (2012): 51–71.

16. See Susan Karant-Nunn, *The Reformation of Ritual: An Interpretation of Early Modern Germany* (London: Routledge, 1997); Paula M. Rieder, *On the Purification of Women: Churching in Northern France, 1100–1500* (New York: Palgrave, 2006); Elizabeth L'Estrange, *Holy Motherhood: Gender, Dynasty, and Visual Culture in the Later Middle Ages* (New York: Manchester University Press, 2008), 77, 94–95.

17. Paula M. Rieder, "Insecure Borders: Symbols of Clerical Privilege and Gender Ambiguity in the Liturgy of Churching," in *The Material Culture of Sex, Procreation, and Marriage in Premodern Europe*, ed. Anne L. McClanan and Karen Rosoff Encarnación (New York: Palgrave, 2002), 93, 95, 108.

18. David Cressy, *Birth, Marriage, and Death: Ritual, Religion, and the Life-Cycle in Tudor and Stuart England* (New York: Oxford University Press, 1997), 201.

19. Donna E. Ray, "A View from the Churchwife's Pew: The Development of Rites around Childbirth in the Anglican Communion," *Anglican and Episcopal History* 69, no. 4 (2000): 449, 458–59.

20. David Cressy, "Purification, Thanksgiving, and the Churching of Women in Post-Reformation England." *Past and Present* 141 (1993): 111.

21. Despite limited sources, Rieder, *On the Purification*, considered the meaning of churching for late-medieval female participants.

22. Ray, "A View," 467. Perceived unpopularity of the rite may explain why the *Oxford History of Christian Worship* included no discussion of churching practices beyond giving it as an example of an "occasional office" within the seventeenth-century church. See Bryan D. Spinks, "Anglicans and Dissenters," in Geoffrey Wainwright and Karen Westerfield Tucker, eds., *Oxford History of Christian Worship* (New York: Oxford University Press, 2006), 492–533.

23. Margaret Houlbrooke, *Rite out of Time: A Study of the Churching of Women and Its Survival in the Twentieth Century* (Donington, UK: Shaun Tyas, 2012), 65–66.

24. Ibid., 101–24.

25. Cressy, "Purification," 106–46; Sarah Williams, "Urban Popular Religion and the Rites of Passage," in *European Religion in the Age of the Great Cities, 1830–1930*, ed. Hugh McLeod (London: Routledge, 1995), 216–36; and Ray, "A View," 444–61.

26. Houlbrooke, *Rite Out of Time*, 8, 10, 13.

27. Ibid., 8, 10, 13.

28. Ray, "A View," 454–55.

29. Houlbrooke, *Rite Out of Time*, 6–7.

30. W. J. Armitage, *The Story of the Canadian Revision of the Prayer Book* (Toronto: McClelland and Stewart, 1922), 291.

31. William White, "The Bishop's Monthly Letter," *Diocesan Magazine*, March 1926, 86–87.

32. Ray, "A View," 446, 448, 450.

33. Keith Thomas, *Religion and the Decline of Magic* (New York: Penguin, 1972), 39, 60.

34. Ray, "A View," 459.

35. Armitage, *The Story*, 291.

36. Ibid.

37. Mildred (Butler) Porter, interview with the author, Conception Bay South, September 6, 2011.

38. Myra (Porter) Rideout, interview with the author, Conception Bay South, September 6, 2011.

39. The service included optional language designed to be used when a child was stillborn or died prior to the churching ceremony.

40. Houlbrooke, *Rite Out of Time*, 1.

41. L'Estrange, *Holy Motherhood*, 77.

42. As quoted in ibid., 78.

43. Ibid., 79.

44. Porter, interview.

45. Anglican Diocese of Eastern Newfoundland and Labrador, Parish of St. Peter's, Conception Bay South. *Minute Book of the CEWA, Seal Cove, 1934–39.*

46. Anglican Diocese of Eastern Newfoundland and Labrador, Parish of All Saints, Conception Bay South. *CEWA Minute Book [Long Pond], 1953–1963; 1963–1975.*

47. Renee Dowden, "Home Remedies [from Long Pond, Manuels]" (unpublished student paper, Memorial University of Newfoundland, 1988).

48. Beulah (Porter) Morgan, interview with the author, Conception Bay South, September 1, 2011.

49. Houlbrooke, *Rite Out of Time*, 111.

50. Linda Pauline Warford, "Reminiscences of a Midwife of Upper Gullies in Conception Bay South" (unpublished paper, Memorial University of Newfoundland, 1977), 1, 3.

51. Rideout, interview. Rideout was less flattering of contemporary maternity practices, noting how new mothers were "only in [hospital] a day and sometimes a few hours and then they are up and going to the supermarket, with [the baby] slung in a bag."

52. Ray, "A View," 445.

53. John K. Crellin, *Home Medicine: The Newfoundland Experience* (Montreal and Kingston: McGill-Queen's University Press, 1994), 109–10.

54. Pat (Morgan) Woolgar, interview with the author, Conception Bay South, August 17, 2011. Rachael Hennessey, born 1881, is recorded in the 1945 *Census of Newfoundland* as a widow, living alone at Kelligrews.

55. Sandra (Taylor) Tilley, interview with the author, St. John's, October 13, 2011.

56. William James Reid, "Death: In the Anglican Tradition during the 1935–40 Period in the Community of Foxtrap East Coast of Newfoundland" (unpublished paper, Memorial University of Newfoundland Folklore and Language Archives, File 73-99A, 1973), 78.

57. Mary (Petten) Porter and Enid (Porter) Haines, interview with the author, Conception Bay South, August 23, 2011.

58. Marjorie (Saunders) Dawe, interview with the author, Conception Bay South, September 21, 2011; Joyce (Andrews) Morgan, interview with the author, Conception Bay South, September 20, 2011.

59. Cressy, *Birth*, 114, 143.

60. Ibid.

61. Warford, "Reminiscences," 9.

62. For midwives and emergency baptisms in Newfoundland see An Outport Priest, "The Church's Doctrine of Holy Baptism," *Diocesan Magazine*, April 1931, 133.

63. Tilley, interview.

64. Susanna Morrill, *White Roses on the Floor of Heaven: Mormon Women's Popular Theology, 1880–1920* (New York: Routledge, 2007), 149.

65. Warford, "Reminiscences," 5, 7.

66. *Minute Book of the CEWA, Seal Cove*, February 25, 1929; March 19 and 26, 1929; April 9, 1946; May 3, 1946; January 28, 1947; December 2, 1947.

67. *CEWA Minute Book [Long Pond]*, October 14, 1953.

68. These included Eunice "Aunt Nicie" Perrin of Long Pond (b. 1877), Elizabeth "Aunt Liz" Taylor of Middle Bight (b. 1877), and Matilda Butler of Seal Cove (b. 1896). Other active Conception Bay midwives were Eliza Jane "Auntie Jen" Dawe of Upper Gullies (b. 1900), Elizabeth "Aunt Lizzie" Dawe of Long Pond, and Dorcas "Aunt Dark" Taylor of Foxtrap (b. 1899). See Warford, interview, 1, 3; Dowden, interview; Tilley, interview. Dates of birth from *Census of Newfoundland*.

69. Dowden, "Home Remedies."

70. Warford, "Reminiscences," 3. Among others, the works of Laurel Thatcher Ulrich have established women (especially midwives) as practitioners of traditional medicine in colonial North America. See Laurel Thatcher Ulrich, *A Midwife's Tale: The Life of Martha Ballard, Based on Her Diary, 1785–1812* (New York: Vintage Books, 1990), and Laurel Thatcher Ulrich, *Good Wives: Image and Reality in the Lives of Women in Northern New England, 1650–1750* (New York: Vintage, 1980).

71. Crellin, *Home Medicine*, 109.

72. Ibid.; Barbara Rieti, *Making Witches: Newfoundland Traditions of Spells and Counter-spells* (Montreal and Kingston: McGill-Queen's University Press, 2008).

73. Dawe, interview.

74. Emma (Petten) Warford, interview with the author, Conception Bay South, September 6, 2011.

75. Prudence (Morgan) Rideout and Judy (Rideout) Dawe, interview with the author, Conception Bay South, September 28, 2011.

76. Dawe, interview.

77. Tilley, interview.

78. Quoted in Ray, "A View," 461. For settlement of Conception Bay south, see *Encyclopedia of Newfoundland and Labrador*, vol. 2, s. v. "Foxtrap."

79. Churching's association with rest from agricultural work for women in rural societies was suggested by Paul Marshall, *Prayer Book Parallels: The Public Services of the Church Arranged for Comparative Study* (New York: Church Hymnal Corporation, 1989), 51.

80. For social status of immigrants to Canada from the British Isles see Rebecca J. Mancuso, "Three Thousand Families: English Canada's Colonizing Vision and British Family Settlement, 1919–39," *Journal of Canadian Studies* 45, no. 3 (2011): 5–33, and Franca Iacovetta, Michael Quinlan, and Ian Radforth, "Immigration and Labour: Australia and Canada Compared," *Labour/Le Travail* 38 (1996): 90–115.

81. Sue Morgan, "'The Word Made Flesh': Women, Religion, and Sexual Cultures," in *Women, Gender, and Religious Cultures in Britain, 1800–1940*, ed. Sue Morgan and Jacqueline deVries (New York: Routledge, 2010), 159.

82. Ibid., 161–66.

83. Ibid., 159.

84. Ibid.

85. Houlbrooke, *Rite out of Time*, 106, 109, 111, 114, 117.

86. Ibid., 105, 113.

Bibliography

Anglican Diocese of Eastern Newfoundland and Labrador, Parish of All Saints, Conception Bay South. *CEWA Minute Book [Long Pond], 1953–1963; 1963–1975.*

Anglican Diocese of Eastern Newfoundland and Labrador, Parish of St. Peter's, Conception Bay South. *Minute Book of the CEWA, Seal Cove, 1934–39.*

Armitage, W. J. *The Story of the Canadian Revision of the Prayer Book.* Toronto: McClelland and Stewart, 1922.

Botting, Ingrid. "Understanding Domestic Service through Oral History and the Census: The Case of Grand Falls, Newfoundland." *Resources for Feminist Research* 28, no. 1 and 2 (2000): 99–113.

Brewer, Darlene. "Mending Our Nets: Toward a Feminist Vision of Redemption in Dialogue with the Newfoundland Fishery." PhD dissertation, University of Ottawa, 2008.

Crellin, John K. *Home Medicine: The Newfoundland Experience.* Montreal and Kingston: McGill-Queen's University Press, 1994.

Cressy, David. *Birth, Marriage, and Death: Ritual, Religion, and the Life-Cycle in Tudor and Stuart England.* New York: Oxford University Press, 1997.

——. "Purification, Thanksgiving and the Churching of Women in Post-Reformation England." *Past & Present* 141 (1993): 106–47.

Dowden, Renee. "Home Remedies [from Long Pond, Manuels]." Unpublished student paper, Memorial University of Newfoundland Folklore and Language Archives, File 88-098, Tape C12069, 1988.

Eleventh Census of Newfoundland and Labrador [nominal], 1945.

Encyclopedia of Newfoundland and Labrador, vol. 2, s.v. "Foxtrap." St. John's: Newfoundland Book Publishers, 1988.

Enzner-Probst, Brigitte. "Waiting for Delivery: Counseling Pregnant Women as an Issue for the Church." *International Journal of Practical Theology* 8, no. 2 (2004): 185–201.

Griffith, R. Marie. *Born Again Bodies: Flesh and Spirit in American Christianity.* Berkeley: University of California Press, 2004.

Houlbrooke, Margaret. *Rite Out of Time: A Study of the Churching of Women and Its Survival in the Twentieth Century.* Donington: Shaun Tyas, 2012.

Iacovetta, Franca, Michael Quinlan, and Ian Radforth. "Immigration and Labour: Australia and Canada Compared." *Labour/Le Travail* 38 (1996): 90–115.

Karant-Nunn, Susan. *The Reformation of Ritual: An Interpretation of Early Modern Germany*. London: Routledge, 1997.

Keough, Wileen. *The Slender Thread: Irish Women on the Southern Avalon, 1750–1860*. New York: Columbia University Press, 2006.

Knödel, Natalie. "Reconsidering an Obsolete Rite: The Churching of Women and Feminist Liturgical Theology." *Feminist Theology* 5, no. 14 (1997): 106–25.

L'Estrange, Elizabeth. *Holy Motherhood: Gender, Dynasty, and Visual Culture in the Later Middle Ages*. New York: Manchester University Press, 2008.

Mancuso, Rebecca J. "Three Thousand Families: English Canada's Colonizing Vision and British Family Settlement, 1919–39." *Journal of Canadian Studies* 45, no. 3 (2011): 5–33.

Marshall, Paul. *Prayer Book Parallels: The Public Services of the Church Arranged for Comparative Study*. New York: Church Hymnal Corporation, 1989.

Melnyk, Julie. "Women, Writing, and the Creation of Theological Cultures." In *Women, Gender, and Religious Cultures in Britain, 1800–1940*, edited by Sue Morgan and Jacqueline deVries, 32–53. New York: Routledge, 2010.

Morgan, Bonnie. "Conceiving Christianity: Anglican Women and Lived Religion in Mid-20th Century Conception Bay, Newfoundland." PhD dissertation, University of New Brunswick, 2014.

Morgan, Sue. "'The Word Made Flesh': Women, Religion, and Sexual Cultures." In *Women, Gender, and Religious Cultures in Britain, 1800–1940*, edited by Sue Morgan and Jacqueline deVries, 159–87. New York: Routledge, 2010.

Morrill, Susanna Morrill. *White Roses on the Floor of Heaven: Mormon Women's Popular Theology, 1880–1920*. New York: Routledge, 2007.

Murray, Hilda Chaulk. *More Than Fifty Percent: Woman's Life in a Newfoundland Outport, 1900–1950*. St. John's: Breakwater, 1979.

Neis, Barbara. "From 'Shipped Girls' to 'Brides of the State': The Transition from Familial to Social Patriarchy in the Newfoundland Fishing Industry." *Canadian Journal of Regional Science* 16, no. 2 (1993): 185–202.

Opp, James. *The Lord for the Body: Religion, Medicine, and Protestant Faith Healing in Canada, 1880–1930*. Montreal: McGill-Queen's University Press, 2005.

Orsi, Robert. *Between Heaven and Earth: The Religious Worlds People Make and the Scholars Who Study Them*. Princeton: Princeton University Press, 2005.

An Outport Priest. "The Church's Doctrine of Holy Baptism," *Diocesan Magazine* (April 1931): 133.

Porter, Marilyn. "She Was Skipper of the Shore Crew: Notes on the History of the Sexual Division of Labour in Newfoundland." In *Their Lives and Times: Women in Newfoundland and Labrador: A Collage*, edited by Carmelita McGrath, Barbara Neis, and Marilyn Porter, 33–47. St. John's: Killick, 1995.

Ray, Donna E. "A View from the Churchwife's Pew: The Development of Rites around Childbirth in the Anglican Communion." *Anglican and Episcopal History* 69, no. 4 (2000): 443–73.

Reid, William James. "Death: In the Anglican Tradition during the 1935–40 Period in the Community of Foxtrap (East Coast of Newfoundland)." Unpublished student paper, Memorial University of Newfoundland Folklore and Language Archives, File 73-99A, 1973.

Rieder, Paula M. "Insecure Borders: Symbols of Clerical Privilege and Gender Ambiguity in the Liturgy of Churching." In *The Material Culture of Sex, Procreation, and Marriage in Premodern Europe*, edited by Anne L. McClanan and Karen Rosoff Encarnación, 93–113. New York: Palgrave, 2002.

——. *On the Purification of Women: Churching in Northern France, 1100–1500*. New York: Palgrave, 2006.

Rieti, Barbara. *Making Witches: Newfoundland Traditions of Spells and Counterspells*. Montreal and Kingston: McGill-Queen's University Press, 2008.

Spinks, Bryan D., "Anglicans and Dissenters." In *Oxford History of Christian Worship*, edited by Geoffrey Wainwright and Karen Westerfield Tucker, 492–533. New York: Oxford University Press, 2006.

Streett, Matthew J. "What to Do with the Baby? The Historical Development of the Rite of Churching." *St. Vladimir's Theological Quarterly* 56, no. 1 (2012): 51–71.

Thomas, Keith. *Religion and the Decline of Magic*. New York: Penguin, 1972.

Ulrich, Laurel Thatcher. *Good Wives: Image and Reality in the Lives of Women in Northern New England, 1650–1750*. New York: Vintage Books, 1980.

——. *A Midwife's Tale: The Life of Martha Ballard, Based on Her Diary, 1785–1812*. New York: Vintage Books, 1990.

Warford, Linda Pauline. "Reminiscences of a Midwife of Upper Gullies in Conception Bay South." Unpublished student paper, Memorial University of Newfoundland Folklore and Language Archives, File 77-247, 1977.

Wehr, Kathryn. "Understanding Ritual Purity and Sin in the Churching of Women: From Ontological to Pedagogical to Eschatological." *St. Vladimir's Theological Quarterly* 55, no. 1 (2011): 85–105.

White, William. "The Bishop's Monthly Letter." *Diocesan Magazine* (March 1926): 86–87.

Williams, Sarah C. "Urban Popular Religion and the Rites of Passage." In *European Religion in the Age of Great Cities, 1830–1930*, edited by Hugh McLeod, 215–36. London: Routledge, 1995.

3 On the Margins of Church and Society

Roman Catholic Feminisms in English-Speaking Canada

BECKY R. LEE YORK UNIVERSITY

Feminism is not the first thing people usually think of when Roman Catholicism is mentioned. In fact, quite the opposite is likely to come to mind: Roman Catholicism's seemingly outdated attitude toward, and policies regarding, women. Nevertheless, from Roman Catholicism's earliest days in Canada, feminist movements have played an active role, not only in the church, but also in Canadian society. In order to analyze their activity and influence, I will examine three feminist movements that collectively span the centuries of Roman Catholic presence in Canada: (1) women in religious communities—that is, nuns (2) the Catholic Women's League (CWL), and (3) Canadian Catholics for Women's Ordination/ Catholic Network for Women's Equality (CCWO/CNWE).

I am focusing on English-speaking Canada because, as Carolyn Sharp notes in her survey of women and Catholicism in Quebec and Canada, "relatively little historical or sociological work has been done on the history of Catholic women in English-speaking Canada," even by feminist scholars.[1] The reasons for this are to be found in the history of the European colonization of the territories today known as Canada. While Roman Catholicism played a dominant role in the religious and political history of French-speaking Canada, in English-speaking Canada, Protestantism dominated.[2]

If Roman Catholicism has been on the margins of society in English-speaking Canada, and if, as feminist scholarship of the past fifty years has demonstrated, women have been marginalized within Roman Catholicism and society generally, how can I claim that Roman Catholic feminist movements have played an active role not only in the church but also in English-speaking Canada? It is that very marginalization that has allowed them to be agents of religious and cultural change. The central insight of the feminist movements of the nineteenth and twentieth centuries is the marginal position of women in patriarchal societies. Since the 1960s, feminist theologians from various religious traditions, and later, members of those groups marginalized by Western feminism such as African American women, have claimed their position on the margins as a vantage point affording new insight, experience, and wisdom regarding their religious traditions and the cultures that they shaped and by which they have been shaped. Marginality allows the distance necessary to recognize the assumptions and prejudices that are invisible to those at the centre of the religious tradition and its surrounding culture(s).[3] African-American feminist bell hooks explains the value of this vantage point:

> Living as we did—on the edge—we developed a particular way of seeing reality. We looked both from the outside in and from the inside out. We focused our attention on the center as well as on the margin. We understood both. This mode of seeing reminded us of the existence of a whole universe, a main body made up of both margin and center. Our survival depended on an ongoing public awareness of the separation between margin and center and an ongoing private acknowledgment that we were a necessary, vital part of the whole.[4]

The marginality of Roman Catholic feminist movements in English-speaking Canada enabled them to see beyond the assumptions and prejudices of their church hierarchy and their society, and to challenge both to broader visions of what they could be.

In order to present the past and present voices of the women who have participated in women's religious communities, the CWL, and CCWO/CNWE, I have relied on archival and published documentary evidence, including audio and video media, produced by members of those movements, as well as interviews with current members. Five CWL members with varying degrees of involvement in the organization were interviewed in August and September 2012. They came from four different Ontario cities: Kitchener, Markham, Ottawa, and Toronto, and ranged in age from the late sixties to mid-eighties. Eight CCWO/CNWE members with varying degrees of involvement were interviewed in August–October 2012. They came from five different Canadian cities: Fredericton, New Brunswick; Markham, Oakville, and Toronto, Ontario; and Winnipeg, Manitoba. Also, a group of six members from the Greater Toronto Area were observed and audio recorded during a group discussion organized as part of a project to produce a promotional video intended to recruit new members. The CCWO/CNWE members ranged in age from the early thirties to mid-eighties. Most were over fifty; eight of the fourteen were over seventy. To encourage candid discussion, all those interviewed were guaranteed anonymity.

Women's religious communities came into being in the third and fourth centuries CE, long before feminism as the conscious critique of patriarchy existed. Nevertheless, women religious have subverted religious and societal gender norms and roles throughout their long history by creating an alternative to the patriarchal family, the governing paradigm of Western culture. Ironically, it was the early church fathers who made this option available to women. In their formulation of Christian doctrine, the fathers tended to favour the anti-materialism of late antiquity over the patriarchal family model presented in the Hebrew scriptures, thus valorizing asceticism, which freed the soul to follow Christ unhindered by the cares of family and material possessions. Even women, whose procreative nature ties them to the material realm, could overcome that disability by choosing to live a life of virginity dedicated to prayer and charitable works.[5] Men who choose this path stand at the centre of the Roman Catholic Church, but there has always been ambivalence toward women who have done so. Ever suspicious of the changeable nature of women evinced by their bleeding, swelling, lactating bodies, the male hierarchy has consistently worked to regulate and tame the lives of these women who obfuscate normative gender roles.[6] In church teaching and practice, they became the brides of Christ, subject to his representatives on earth, the male clerical hierarchy, who secluded them in the cloister away from men and married women, and consigned them to silence, obedience, and poverty.

In spite of the church hierarchy's ambivalence about women religious, women's religious communities have left their mark on the Roman Catholic Church in Canada and on Canadian society. Between 1639 and 1760, seven communities of religious women were established in New France. Unfettered by family ties and dedicated to lives of poverty and charity, these women were well suited to assist in creating a viable colony in the wilds of North America. Founded by women of vision and courage, including Marie de l'Incarnation, Marguerite Bourgeoys, and Marguerite d'Youville, they built hospitals and parish schools, educated French and Aboriginal girls, catechized adults, and provided whatever social services they could in Quebec City, Ville-Marie (Montreal), and Trois-Rivières.[7] They were also women of faith, dedicated to the Roman Catholic Church and its teachings. Although the exigencies of pioneer life allowed the founders of religious communities to exercise authority and to engage with men and women outside of the cloister, the constitutions or rules they drew up for their communities perpetuated their subordination to the clerical hierarchy and their seclusion from society. For this was, after all, a Roman Catholic society.

In 1627 the fathers of New France established Roman Catholicism as the religion of the colony, replicating the unity of religion and society in their European homeland.[8] When the British conquered New France in 1760, they attempted to establish Anglicanism in a similar fashion.[9] However, international treaties, the English Parliament, and the religious diversity that came to characterize North America thwarted their ambition. Roman Catholics in British North America were granted religious freedom in the Quebec Act of 1774. In 1791 Canada was divided into Upper and Lower Canada, enabling the French Catholics in Lower Canada (present-day Quebec) to run their own affairs. Protestantism dominated in Upper Canada. Although the attempt to establish the Anglican Church failed, English-speaking Protestants "conjointly asserted the Protestant identity of the new nation."[10] Consequently, women's religious communities, as well as other Roman Catholic feminist movements, were part of a religious minority in English-speaking Canada, compounding their marginalization.

"In English-speaking Canada, the establishment of women's religious [communities] was central to the creation of a Catholic minority culture that challenged Protestant domination of Canadian society while carving a space in which Catholics could thrive and flourish."[11] They came from Ireland, the United States, and Quebec at the invitation of Catholic bishops to serve the needs of the growing Catholic immigrant population. Like their compatriots in French-speaking Canada, they founded communities that soon attracted local women, organized social services, and established hospitals, orphanages, and schools. Their schools proved very influential in shaping Catholic identity in English-speaking Canada. They not only established a precedent for Catholic education in Upper Canada, which was enshrined in the British North America Act of 1867, but also fostered a distinctive Catholic identity and inculcated Catholic values in a society governed by a Protestant elite. Most importantly, in the first quarter of the nineteenth century, women's religious communities assumed a significant role in the ultramontane Catholic revival, which asserted the authority of the pope and his clerical hierarchy in spiritual and temporal matters, while at the same time insisting that the rights and privileges of the church be safeguarded within civil society.[12] The aim of this revival was to create "a sacred Catholic 'separate world' in education, marriage, communication, and social life that would defend the faithful in the face of dangers posed by the 'modern world.'"[13] That separate sphere was maintained into the twentieth century.[14] The hierarchical, anti-egalitarian world view of ultramontanism also had a significant impact on women's lives, "promot[ing] a vision of women's place in family, Church and society that emphasized their subordination to male authority."[15]

Women's religious communities in English-speaking Canada were both insiders and outsiders, simultaneously situated at the centre and at the margins of both church and society. Marta Danylewycz, in a study of women's religious communities in Quebec from 1840 to 1920, argues that the rapid expansion of religious communities during that period was due, in part, to the fact that they enabled women to realize their spiritual, intellectual, and social aspirations by allowing them to engage in "economic and political activity deemed inappropriate for 'the gentler sex.'"[16] That was equally true in English-speaking Canada. I would add that it was the marginal status of women's religious communities that enabled them to do so.

Until the twentieth century, it was unacceptable for a woman to live independent of the authority of a father or husband unless she was a widow. Women's religious communities provided a viable and respectable alternative for women who would not or could not marry. In the eyes of the church and society, they became brides of Christ, safe under the authority of the male clergy. However, as Danylewycz observes, "many ventured into religious life because convents expanded the narrow range of what was possible for women."[17] For although women's religious communities were subject to the spiritual authority of the clerical hierarchy, these communities of women were left, more or less, to manage their own administrative affairs.[18] Founding, running, and staffing educational, health care, and social service institutions afforded the members of women's religious communities some opportunities for education, careers, and career advancement not available to their secular counterparts. They held positions of power and authority normally forbidden women, giving them access to the circles of power and influence normally reserved for men.

It is doubtful that this subversion of gender roles and norms was based in a feminist consciousness, however. In all likelihood, women religious subscribed to the ultramontane ideal of women's subordination to male authority, which was also shared by their Victorian Protestant neighbours. They, and the Catholic community, would have understood their actions in spiritual terms as living out their religious vocation, a call from God that set them apart from the ordinary laity. Although they assumed an accepted and respected role in the church, that role set them apart from ordinary Catholics and the surrounding society.[19] Being consigned to living in all-female communities segregated from normal society enabled them to create an alternative lifestyle that challenged the gender roles and norms prescribed by the Roman Catholic Church and the Victorian culture of English-speaking Canada, even as they endorsed and inculcated those same gender roles and norms through their educational, health care, and social service institutions.

In the latter part of the nineteenth century, women's religious communities lost some of the independence they had experienced. This was the result of the Roman Catholic hierarchy's response to the challenges posed by modernity. Pope Pius IX called the First Vatican Council in 1869 to condemn the "errors" of modernity: rationalism, liberalism, and materialism. Religion was being undermined, and industrialization, urbanization, and immigration were changing the very nature of Western societies. In reaction to those changes, the clerical hierarchy reasserted the lines of authority within the church, including those governing women's religious communities. In that process, women's religious communities were distanced even further from ordinary society through stricter regulation of their manner of life, dress, and social interactions.[20] At the same time, however, communities dedicated to active ministry focused on serving and advocating for the marginalized, impoverished, and the casualties of industrialization were endorsed. Those communities flourished in the first half of the twentieth century.[21]

The Catholic Women's League of Canada (CWL)

DURING THE LATE NINETEENTH AND EARLY TWENTIETH CENTURIES, large numbers of Canadian women joined voluntary organizations. Roman Catholic women joined church-sponsored charitable and devotional associations.[22] The devotional associations, such as the Children of Mary, the Sodality of the Blessed Virgin Mary, and the League of the Sacred Heart, fostered an emotional piety expressed through private and public devotional rituals. That piety differentiated Roman Catholics from their Protestant neighbours while at the same time facilitating the integration of new Catholic immigrants into the Catholic community. The rituals—which included frequent reception of the sacraments, public processions, the wearing of religious medals and scapulars, the recitation of the rosary and litanies, special prayers for the intentions of the Holy Father, the pope, and visits to the church to pray before the reserved host or statues of the Blessed Virgin Mary—inculcated the separatist, hierarchical world view of ultramontanism, including the subordinate role of women.[23]

Although those associations were initiated by the clergy in order to inculcate ultramontane values, Roman Catholic charitable and devotional associations provided a forum within the parish in which women could initiate and carry out projects of their own, and from which they could participate in the larger arena of the parish. In his study of the

Irish-Catholic community in Toronto, 1850–95, Brian P. Clarke observes that women's devotional organizations were very successful at fundraising.[24] Once a bazaar, picnic, or other activity was scheduled by the local bishop or pastor, they would take over much of the organization, carry out the hands-on preparation, and run the event. Their financial contributions to the parish were essential to the building projects and maintenance of the parishes as well as to the social service establishments supported by the church. Through such activities women exercised a variety of organizational and leadership skills. Yet, because they were lay women—that is, not members of a religious community—and not men, their activism and leadership remained largely invisible, presumed to be the logical extension of their womanly role as caregiver.

That invisibility, or marginality, did have its advantages, however. Since their activities were considered women's work, women's devotional and charitable associations were allowed to conduct their activities with little male interference. The women themselves determined the internal structures of their organizations, assumed the various offices, recruited and trained new members, and developed friendships and social networks within and across their parishes. These associations provided an opportunity to develop and exercise organizational and leadership skills, a sense of identity and purpose, and a forum within which to exercise corporate initiative while being faithful members of their church.[25]

At another level, because Roman Catholic women's activism was not only located in but also focused on the parish, it remained on the margins of Protestant English-speaking Canada. That was not the case with Protestant women's religious associations. In the second half of the nineteenth century, Protestant women joined a wide variety of benevolent, missionary, and reform organizations. Their religious traditions were born out of movements of moral and social reform, and consequently fostered and legitimized activism beyond the confines of the church. Women's organizations in the Protestant traditions claimed social reform, as well as fundraising and charity, as a logical extension of their assigned maternal role.[26] First-wave feminism[27] emerged out of such organizations working for the abolition of slavery in the Americas, women's suffrage, and temperance. Nellie McClung, one of Canada's most famous early feminists, began her public-speaking career in the Women's Christian Temperance Union. A member of the Methodist Church and then the United Church of Canada, McClung crusaded for women's ordination as well as temperance and women's suffrage.[28]

Roman Catholic women in English-speaking Canada were not unaware of or immune to the social movements of their day. In 1891 Pope Leo XIII issued the encyclical *"Rerum novarum*: On Capital and Labour"* in response to the social crisis created by industrialization and the consequent rise of socialism. In it he addressed the plight of the working poor, and admonished all Christians to "true Christian charity."[29] It is the charter document of Roman Catholic social teaching, and engendered a proliferation of lay organizations across the industrialized world dedicated to addressing the needs of the working classes.[30] In Canada, a number of Catholic women's groups were formed independent of one another. Katherine Hughes of Edmonton, inspired by Miss Margaret Fletcher of England, who inaugurated a Catholic Women's League in 1906, approached her bishop in 1912 about starting a similar organization. It would assist the influx of young immigrant women arriving in Edmonton in search of domestic service positions. With the help of Abbé Casgrain, the chaplain and secretary of the Catholic Church Extension Society of Canada, an organization dedicated to preserving Roman Catholicism in remote areas and among immigrants, Hughes established a Catholic Women's League in Edmonton. Its objective was "to provide protection and support to women and girls, especially immigrants, seeking work in Edmonton."[31] One of its first acts was to set up a free job placement service and establish a residence that provided safe, affordable accommodations for unattached young women. Other groups were formed in Montreal (1917), in Toronto and Ottawa (1918), and in Halifax, Regina, and Sherbrooke (1919).

The influx of European immigrants after World War I was the impetus for creating a national Catholic Women's League. The Women's Division of the Canadian Immigration Department in Ottawa was holding consultations regarding the settlement of postwar immigrants with women's organizations from various Protestant denominations. Katherine Hughes's sister, Loretta Kneil, who was employed in the Immigration Department at the time, was asked by the minister in charge if there was a national organization of Catholic women that could be consulted. Kneil contacted

Bellelle Guerin, president of the Catholic Women's League of Montreal, who invited representatives from local Catholic women's organizations from across the country to meet in Montreal in the summer of 1920 "to consider the possibilities of federating all existing Catholic Women's Leagues in existence with a view to so standardize our aims and objects that we may become a real power for good, causing branches to spring up in every city and town of the Dominion."[32] Seven of the nine provinces were represented at that first meeting. Within the year there were a hundred branches across the country.[33] The next year there were thirty thousand members.[34]

This movement was self-consciously feminist, dedicated to the cause of improving women's lives. The invitation to the organizational meeting in 1920 began: "Believing that the time has come here in Canada when a thorough organization of Catholic women power would be of immense and far reaching value to the cause of our sex at large and the Church in particular, we, the Executive of the Catholic women's League in Montreal, extend to you a cordial invitation to consider the possibilities of federating all existing CWL organizations in existence with a view to so standardize our aims and objects [sic] that we may become a real power for good, causing branches to spring up in every city and town of the Dominion."[35]

It was also fiercely Catholic. Bellelle Guerin, who was named the first national president of the Catholic Women's League, espoused "Catholic feminism," which in her words

> should be used when facing important social problems and a woman should look at them with clear eyes, and with sound judgment decide what is best for our families and for ourselves. It is for her to direct thought, to guard morals, and to carry her influence into the scale of justice whenever righteousness demands.[36]

Unlike her Protestant sisters who criticized their churches' complicity in confining women to the domestic sphere, and valuing them only for their child-bearing and maternal instincts,[37] Guerin's Catholic feminism subscribed to the maternal nature of woman. Integral to that maternal nature, the church taught, was a heightened spiritual and moral sensibility.[38] Women's social activism, from that perspective, was an extension of a woman's role as the spiritual and moral anchor of the family. The Catholic feminism of the CWL combined that understanding of a woman's role with the social activism in the public sphere encouraged by Pope Leo XIII and his successors, and by the growing feminist movement.

From the beginning, the CWL had the support of the Canadian Roman Catholic hierarchy, although not without reservations. Father Thomas Burke, the superior-general of the Paulist Order, articulated that ambivalence in his address to the CWL in its first year. First grudgingly[39] acknowledging the necessity of women's activism on behalf of women in the "social and civic fields,"[40] he went on to caution them against "the extreme assertions made and the extreme methods employed and the extreme aims pursued by some women in their attempts to improve, as they maintain, the position of their sex."[41] Those extreme assertions, methods, and aims, he asserted, "tend rather to lower woman and to rob her of the glory and power with which Christianity has clothed her."[42]

The clerical hierarchy had nothing to fear regarding the CWL's adherence to church teachings; however, it had underestimated the independent spirit and political know-how of its founders. In the tradition of the devotional and charitable associations, these women assumed responsibility for, and the authority to, organize themselves and to carry out their agenda without interference. That agenda was to create a national organization to work for the "welfare of the nation" and for "every Catholic cause," which was summed up in the motto selected by the membership in 1921, "For God and Canada."[43] A national executive was established to oversee and facilitate the development of the organization and its work, and a magazine to facilitate communication between the groups across the country was inaugurated. In 1922, a national fund, to be built through membership fees and fundraising activities, was established "to turn resolutions into action,"[44] and in 1923 the CWL was federally incorporated. While the CWL placed itself under the patronage of the church hierarchy, and solicited the support of sympathetic bishops, the only concrete role given to the clergy in the first constitution was the assignment of a national chaplain.

Like their predecessors in the devotional and charitable associations, the women of the CWL relied upon their marginal status to avoid undue attention from the clerical hierarchy, to fly under the radar, as it were. At the Second National Convention in 1922, Archbishop Sinnott of Winnipeg thought it necessary to admonish the "ladies" to "not fritter away your time upon petty projects." Rather, he advised, they ought to "take up some work of a national character that affects into the life of the whole country." And further, "unless they united for accomplishment, their organization would come to naught."[45]

It wasn't until 1940 that the hierarchy realized how well organized the CWL was, and how far-reaching its projects. That year, Francis Carroll, bishop of Calgary, read in the newspaper that the national executive of the CWL had pledged $25,000 to the federal government for the war effort. That money was to be raised in Catholic parishes across the country.[46] He was outraged that there had been no consultation with the bishops, and that the CWL constitution not only omitted any mention of the advisory role of the bishops, but also placed funds raised within the parish setting under the sole control of the national executive: "The thing [the CWL constitution] is upside down. The women should not be deciding what is to be done, and then telling the bishops or asking the bishops' permission to do it. The bishops should tell the women what is to be done!"[47] Carroll set about trying to persuade the national executive to revise its constitution. When that failed, he canvassed Canadian bishops and found others who shared his concerns. When it became evident to the national executive that the CWL was in danger of losing the favour and support of the bishops, it initiated a process for revising its constitution. In 1947 the CWL was reorganized according to the ecclesial model, with parish units, autonomous diocesan and provincial units, and a national unit that federated the organization. The office of chaplain was replaced by that of a director. "The director was responsible for the conduct of League affairs within the territory of his title,"[48] that is, the parish priest was director of a parish group, the bishop or his appointee was director of the diocesan group, etc., so that there was clerical supervision at every level of the organization. In 1948, after this reorganization, the Canadian Conference of Catholic Bishops (CCCB) recognized the CWL as the official voice of Catholic women in Canada. Bishop Carroll had succeeded in making the CWL "a vital medium of the Lay Apostolate at the disposal of the Canadian Bishops under whose direction the League had placed itself."[49]

Bishop Carroll's outraged declaration and the CWL's ultimate capitulation to his demands points once again to the marginal position of women in Roman Catholicism and Canadian society in the first half of the twentieth century. The cost of putting itself under the direction of the CCCB was a diminishment of the CWL's independence. Nevertheless, membership continued to increase; in 1957 it was 115,000;[50] in 1990 it reached an all-time high of 124,000 members.[51] At every level of the organization—parochial, diocesan, and national—members continued to be given opportunities to develop and exercise organizational and leadership skills, to become knowledgeable about the social issues of the day, and to initiate and engage in social activism.

This women's organization also managed to keep the ears of legislators. From its beginnings, the CWL was intent upon influencing government policies, especially those that affected immigrants, women, and families. In its first recruitment drive, the newly minted national executive explained the importance of having Catholic women's voices heard:

> Why? This is the age of organization. Other bodies of women have long since become organized. Shall we remain inactive, a negligible quantity in the promotion of religious and intellectual interests, social and patriotic work? . . . Are there not public matters which affect our homes and our families in which we should have a voice? Education, Divorce, Immigration, are all questions fraught with special dangers for the future of the country.[52]

One of the decisions made at the CWL inaugural meeting in 1920 was to send a petition to the federal government asking for stricter divorce laws in Canada.[53] Numerous other petitions and letter-writing campaigns followed. The $25,000 donation to the war effort was a deliberate strategy to gain national recognition. At the 1940 national convention, Agnes Hay, the national president, recommended that the donation be made because

> while we, as Catholics, have done an enormous amount of work through the Red Cross, IODE and the Women's Institutes, our work is submerged.

Perhaps the time has come for us to go further and make a real donation in our own name and be recognized.[54]

Shortly after that, the CWL was asked to advise and assist the Canadian government in an adoption program for war orphans. Heartened by such recognition, in 1944 the CWL requested representation on both federal and provincial committees engaged in postwar reconstruction. After that, the CWL was given opportunities to present briefs to various federal legislative bodies, royal commissions, and special committees. It also began to send the resolutions from its annual conventions to the relevant government committees.[55] In 1974 the national executive started sending a delegation to Ottawa annually to present a brief of the resolutions passed at its national convention to the government. Eventually government ministers began to compile written responses to the CWL's resolutions.[56] By 1990 Cabinet ministers were meeting with CWL delegations to discuss their responses to the national convention resolutions.[57]

It took much longer to get the ear of the CCCB. The national executive of the CWL met with the executive of the CCCB for the first of their now regular meetings in 1986. No doubt, being recognized by the CCCB as the official voice of Catholic women in Canada added to the credibility of the CWL, especially among Roman Catholics. However, if the length of time it took the CCCB to commit to regular meetings with the CWL executive is any indication, the activities of this women's group remained a low priority. The discussion above suggests that the success of the CWL was due in large part to the effectiveness of the women of the CWL as recruiters, fundraisers, and social and political activists in their own right.

Outside of Roman Catholic circles, the CWL tended to be marginalized because of its loyalty to the Roman Catholic hierarchy and its teachings. Among the Protestant majority in English-speaking Canada, the ultramontane revival, with its separatist sentiments and fidelity to the pope, fuelled resentment and suspicion of the growing immigrant Catholic population. Those sentiments erupted in riots during the last quarter of the nineteenth century, and suspicions flared again in the years before and after World War I.[58] Even though it was avowedly patriotic, the determination of its founders to make the CWL a national powerhouse of Catholic social action (dedicated as it was to "unite Catholic women in the highest bonds of religion and citizenship")[59] seems to also have roused resentments and suspicions.[60] When national president Agnes Hay recommended the $25,000 donation to the war effort in 1940, she prefaced her motion with the following words: "Catholics have often been accused of lacking loyalty. Maybe it is time to demonstrate our loyalty and justify the existence of a band of women in Canada with the motto 'For God and Canada.'"[61] As we've seen, it proved an effective strategy.

The CWL's support of Roman Catholic teachings, especially its teachings regarding women's role, reproductive rights, and sexuality, also marginalized it within the feminist community. Jo Ann McNamara observes that American feminists were distrustful of Catholic nuns, considering them "the overly-effective agents of an 'unenlightened' church."[62] It is likely that English-speaking Canadian feminists held similar opinions regarding the Catholic feminism of the CWL. The CWL did not involve itself with two major issues embraced by first-wave feminism, women's suffrage, and temperance. More importantly, the CWL, in accord with Catholic teaching, actively opposed feminist initiatives regarding birth control clinics, the legalization of abortion, and easy access to divorce.[63] It was not that the women of the CWL were any less dedicated to the cause of improving women's lives than their feminist sisters. Rather, it was the League's espousal of the Roman Catholic teaching that women's welfare was tied to the welfare of the family that distanced them. In the view of the CWL, it was the other feminists who were unenlightened. Rather than being a disability, being positioned at the margins of the feminist movement motivated the CWL to bring its alternative perspective to the issues of the day, a perspective shaped by Catholic values.

In the course of the social and religious upheavals of the 1960s, the line between the CWL's Catholic values, the values of other feminists, and those of Canadian society in general became less clear. The 1960s was a decade of protest and social change characterized by the civil rights movement, anti-war demonstrations, the rejection of mainstream religions, and the second wave of feminism. A revolution also took place in the Roman Catholic Church in the 1960s after Pope John XXIII called the Second Vatican Council to renew and update the church, to build a bridge between the church and the modern world. For this discussion, the most important of the many reforms advocated by that Council was its vision of the apostolate of the laity. According to Council documents, the role of the laity was much more than praying, paying, and obeying. Lay people, by virtue of their baptism, were called to actively participate in the renewal of the Church and of the world.

It was also in the 1960s that the birth control pill became widely accessible, fuelling the sexual revolution. Birth control became a hot topic of debate within Canadian society and among Canadian Roman Catholics, for both the government and the church condoned only sexual abstinence and the rhythm method as acceptable birth control methods. Responding to the changing moral climate, the Trudeau government, in 1969, legalized artificial birth control and abortion under limited circumstances in Canada (Criminal Law Amendment Act, Omnibus Bill C-150). While introducing this bill in 1967, Trudeau, then minister of justice, famously asserted, "the state has no business in the bedrooms of the nation." The Roman Catholic Church also felt the need to respond to the changing moral climate. In 1968, when Pope Paul VI released the encyclical on birth control, *Humanae vitae*, many Catholics expected that he would remove the obstacles to using artificial contraception. The previous pope, John XXIII, had appointed a commission, in 1963, that had suggested that artificial contraception might not be intrinsically evil.[64] However, Paul VI reaffirmed the traditional church teaching on birth control and abortion.

This created a crisis within the church. The Second Vatican Council, generating great optimism among Roman Catholics, opened the door to engagement with the modern world and an active responsible role for the laity. Council documents spoke of the "primacy of conscience," asserting that the final authority in any moral decision must always be one's conscience.[65] *Humanae vitae* seemed to contradict all that the Council had promised. The response was swift and angry. Many Roman Catholic women chose to follow their own consciences when it came to birth control.

Two months after *Humanae vitae* was released, the CCCB, meeting in Winnipeg, issued a statement in response to "this hour of crisis."[66] In it, the bishops called for compassion toward those who could not make the doctrines of *Humanae vitae* their own,[67] citing the primacy of conscience as the basis of their position.[68] The conclusion of the statement reflected the optimism generated by Vatican II; it asserted that a diversity of understanding need not divide the church:

> We, the People of God, cannot escape this hour of crisis but there is no reason to believe that it will create division and despair. The unity of the Church does not consist in a bland conformity in all ideas, but rather in a union of faith and heart, in submission to God's will and a humble but honest and ongoing search for the truth. That unity of love and faith is founded in Christ and as long as we are true to Him nothing can separate us.[69]

That has not proven to be the case. Instead, Roman Catholics have become polarized over such issues.

The Winnipeg Statement was immediately met with vocal opposition from conservative Catholics and members of the pro-life movement.[70] That opposition continued up to 2012. The Rosarium of the Blessed Virgin Mary, which has recently deleted its web page, described itself as "a Canadian Catholic movement of lay people, priests, Religious, and bishops which seeks to halt and reverse the disastrous effects of the culture of death [whose foundation is contraception] in Canada, the U.S., and around the world." Until the summer of 2012, this organization was collecting signatures on a petition to the CCCB asking it to retract the Winnipeg Statement.[71]

The CWL, representing over 100,000 Catholic women, most of whom were married, also followed those events closely. As one long-time member recalls:

> I think what happened was when it was reviewed. And I've forgotten the date. And there was an encyclical? [*sic*] And all the recommendations were that contraception should be accepted and it should not be put in the same box with abortion; it's not the same thing. And all those recommendations were rejected by the pope. Who was it, Paul VI? And he rejected all those. But you know, people had studied it in the parishes. People are not stupid!

And they had followed this discussion; and they saw the recommendations. And I think people just decided to follow their own conscience.[72]

Although the CWL passed numerous resolutions regarding birth control in the 1930s when illegal contraception clinics were being prosecuted by the law, contraception appears to have quietly dropped from the CWL's list of concerns after that. As another long-time League member observes,

> I think the League would say that it does not approve of artificial contraception. But I think on the whole, in practice the League is doing what the Church is doing, and that is they leave it. They're not getting into it to any great extent. I mean, that's no longer an issue in the Church in Canada. . . . Whether that's a hypocritical way to solve the whole thing, or not, I'm not sure. But, I mean, Catholics have kind of decided themselves what they're going to do.

Nevertheless, the CWL has continued to actively support the church's positions on the related issues of abortion, the rights of the unborn, human stem cell research, euthanasia, assisted suicide, reproductive technologies, and same-sex marriage. The guiding principle behind its support is its belief in the sanctity of life from conception to natural death. However, what that means in practical terms is not always agreed upon by the members. For example, the two long-term members quoted above take different positions on abortion. One does not agree with abortion on demand, but does think that there are situations where it can be "the lesser of two evils," such as a widely publicized case where a nine-year-old girl became pregnant after having been raped. The other does not agree with abortion under any circumstances. However, she asserts that if one does not support abortion, one has to ensure that all are able to live in dignity. In her words, "Okay, if you're right-to-life, then you have to be pro-social justice. You cannot send children to school hungry, etcetera, etcetera."

Since the 1960s, liberalism, individualism, and secularism have increasingly characterized Canadian society. Prior to the 1960s, the Roman Catholic positions on moral issues like abortion, contraception, and divorce did not differ significantly from Canadian values as they were reflected in

Canadian law. Since then, the CWL and the CCCB have been unable to pre-vent further relaxation of abortion and divorce laws and the legalization of same-sex marriage, despite the fact that the CWL represents approxi-mately 100,000 Canadian women, and the CCCB represents approximately 12.8 million Canadian Catholics. Rather than being deterred by the fail-ure of Canadian legislators to heed the CWL's advice, it seems that such responses only strengthen its resolve. Convinced of the value of the alter-native perspective it brings to Canadian society, it continues to press all levels of government regarding issues concerning the sanctity of life, and regarding many others as well, including issues related to social justice, human dignity, the preservation of Christian family life, and the preferen-tial option for the poor. As one national convener stated, "we try to shape society rather than be shaped by it."[73]

Canadian Catholics for Women's Ordination/ Catholic Network for Women's Equality

FOR SOME CATHOLIC FEMINISTS, it is not only society that needs to be reformed. In their view, the Roman Catholic Church is also complicit in the systemic oppression of women and other marginalized groups. According to them, women need to participate in the decision making of the church. As Veronica Dunne explains: "issues of reproductive choice, the meanings of parenting, ways of prayer, relationships, war and peace all . . . need . . . women's insight, women's action and women's theological reflection."[74] That was the thinking of four Catholic women studying at the Toronto School of Theology, two of whom were members of religious communities. They invited Catholic women from across Canada to join them to form "a Canadian organization to work for the ordination of women in the Cath-olic Church."[75] They chose to focus on women's ordination because "for Christians, the ordination of women pushes the question of equality to its logical conclusion and draws all other injustices in the treatment of women in the Church into a firm perspective."[76] Twenty-eight women attended the inaugural meeting of the Canadian Catholics for Women's Ordination (CCWO) in July 1981.

At the time, women's ordination to the priesthood seemed within reach. In the fifteen years since the Second Vatican Council, the church had welcomed liturgical, theological, and pastoral innovation. Lay men and women were assuming liturgical roles previously reserved for ordained men. Married men were being ordained to the diaconate, and women were being admitted to schools of theology as students and instructors. Women scholars were applying a feminist critique to the teachings, structures, and actions of the church, and reinterpreting its history and scriptures from a feminist perspective.[77] In 1975 some of those scholars founded the Women's Ordination Conference (WOC) in the United States "to advance the cause of ordaining women to the Roman Catholic priesthood."[78]

As one of the founders of the CCWO commented, "things were happening, and there were people who were making things happen."[79] In Canada, the CCCB continued to be an outspoken advocate for women's rights in church and society. The Winnipeg Statement was the first of a series of pastoral letters addressing issues pertaining to women: violence against women, the eradication of poverty and violence, reproductive and genetic technologies, prostitution and pornography, child care, abortion, adult education, inclusive language, child sexual abuse, and family life.[80] In 1971 the CCCB also used its seat on the worldwide Synod of Bishops to urge the church hierarchy to consider seriously the ministries of women in the church, including "whether women too are to have a place in the sacred ministries [i.e., ordained ministries] of the Church as they now exist or as they are developing."[81] Five years later, in June 1976, an unofficial report by the Pontifical Biblical Commission was leaked to the press. The report indicated that the majority of the Catholic biblical scholars comprising the Commission agreed that the New Testament did not provide a clear answer to that question, and further "that scriptural grounds alone are not enough to exclude the possibility of ordaining women."[82]

The movement for women's ordination struck a chord with Canadian Catholic women. The next year, membership in the CCWO rose to eighty. By 1984 it had grown to two hundred. Like the CWL, the CCWO established itself as a national organization, attracting women from all walks of life and a few men from across the country. Unlike the CWL, which put itself under the patronage of the Catholic hierarchy, the mandate of the

CCWO was to challenge that hierarchy. Its first public act was to hold a press conference at the end of its inaugural meeting to issue a press release with the headline, "CCWO: Ordain Women or Stop Baptizing Them."[83] Despite the confrontational tone of that headline, the relationship between the CCWO and the CCCB was fairly congenial for the first few years. The CCCB responded to that first communication with a letter assuring the CCWO that "the CCCB shares your concern for women's full participation in the life of the Church,"[84] and quoted from its intervention at the 1980 Synod of Bishops at which the CCCB had asserted that "if there is any place where women's call for liberation should be heard, it is certainly in the Church of Jesus Christ." Representatives of the CCWO requested and were granted meetings with members of the clerical hierarchy[85] and representation in the CCCB's study of the role of women in the church conducted in 1983–84.[86] They also sent letters to members of the clerical hierarchy both commending their actions on behalf of women and criticizing them when they failed to do so.[87]

As late as 1987, the CCCB continued to be supportive of the quest for women's equality within the Roman Catholic Church. In its intervention at the Synod of Bishops that year, the CCCB argued: "the very credibility of the Church is affected if we do not actively seek out the means to assure an equitable representation of women and of men on all the levels of ecclesial life."[88] It went on to urge that women be ordained to the diaconate, which at that time had the potential to open the door to their ordination to the priesthood,[89] and reminded the assembly that "the reasoning so far to explain the reservation of Sacred Orders to men has not seemed convincing especially not to young people."[90] However, a chill toward women's quest for equality in the church had already begun to set in among the Roman Catholic clerical hierarchy. In the summer of 1986, Archbishop Ambrozic of Toronto made the news when he recommended that the teaching curriculum of the Toronto Catholic School Board emphasize traditional family life and that "girls should be impressed with the importance of motherhood."[91] That same year, the Vatican publicly acted against the Women's Ordination Conference in the United States, sending warning letters to all the heads of women's religious communities listed on the brochure for the 1986 conference. The Vatican also attempted to silence

Father Charles Curran, an outspoken North American moral theologian who was critical of the church's views toward contraception, abortion, and divorce, among other things.

The CCWO encountered hostility when it staged its first public demonstration in 1986 when Cardinal Ratzinger (later elected Pope Benedict XVI), head of the Sacred Congregation for the Doctrine of the Faith, visited Toronto. Fifteen members of CCWO distributed pamphlets and carried placards outside of Varsity Stadium, where he spoke to some five thousand Roman Catholics. What the Canadian Broadcasting Corporation neutrally reported—"They were met with mixed reactions from the waiting crowd"[92]—one member described in more graphic detail:

> We were stunned at the overt hostility of some of the thousands going into the arena. We were accused of being agents of Satan and one man thought we should be ashamed of ourselves and should be home w[h]ere we belonged![93]

Women's ordination no longer seemed imminent.

As the CCWO grew in numbers, its focus on women's ordination came into question. The experiences of the local groups, and consequently the issues they faced, differed across the country. Also, the makeup of the membership was changing as women from the local parishes joined. As one member who joined in 1986 explained:

> The women that were coming from the kind of "normal" parish life, they said, "We cannot even say the word 'women's ordination' in our place, to our priest. We need a name that is not so—forward." So they wanted something that was more benign in the title. I think that the original founders, and again, that's only my view, my impression, were mainly women academics, and they were on a different plane from the women in the parishes.

In 1988, after some soul searching, the name of the organization was changed to the Catholic Network for Women's Equality (CNWE), and the focus broadened from women's ordination to "effecting structural change in the church that reflects the mutuality and co-responsibility of women and men within the church."[94] It was hoped that this broader focus would increase membership. It appears to have worked; one year later membership reached an all-time high of 269.

Since then, the activism of CNWE groups has broadened to encompass a broad range of issues, including human trafficking, government funding of faith-based NGOs, restrictive refugee policies, affordable housing, and environmental issues. Nevertheless, much of its activism is still focused on reforming the Roman Catholic Church. A number of local groups hold annual silent vigils outside their diocesan cathedrals to protest the unequal treatment of women within the church, the protesters wearing purple stoles or scarves in emulation of the priestly vestments, symbolically claiming the rights of women to active participation in all of the ministries of the church.[95] Letters are sent to local, regional, national, and international Catholic clerics and bishops, individually and collectively, and meetings with them are requested to inform the clerical hierarchy about CNWE and to discuss its concerns. Most recently, CNWE launched a petition on its website intended for the CCCB, protesting the New Roman Missal, the prayers said at the eucharistic liturgy, because it "reflects a return to a pre–Vatican II theology of humanity and our relationship to Church and God that is narrow and unhelpful for the Catholic Church of the new millennium."[96] According to the petition, the theology of the Missal "presents humanity as largely sinful and unworthy before a monarchical God," and furthermore the language is exclusive, "thereby removing women from the language of prayer."[97]

Ellen Leonard, one of the four founding members of the CCWO, observed in an essay published in 2007 that "in spite of Vatican II's recognition of the women's movement as one of the 'signs of the times,' the Church remained a patriarchal institution. In the years following Vatican II, patriarchy has become even more entrenched."[98] Consequently, CNWE has remained on the margins of the Canadian Roman Catholic Church. However, its very marginality has allowed CNWE a more influential voice than its small membership would seem to warrant. As Anita Birt, one of the early members of CCWO, explained, "we are the group the media turn to when they want to focus on contentious issues in the church!"[99]

Fostering a relationship with the media was a deliberate strategy. The CCWO cultivated relationships with both the Catholic and the secular media, issuing press releases, advertising in Catholic newspapers and vocations supplements, and giving radio and television interviews whenever the opportunity arose.[100] As CNWE, it has continued to do so. Most recently, when worldwide attention was focused on the resignation of Pope Benedict XVI and the subsequent election of Pope Francis I, Canadian news media across the country interviewed CNWE members for their perspectives. Their voices were heard on numerous radio and television shows on local and national broadcasters, including the nationally broadcast news program *Power and Politics with Evan Solomon*, and in newspapers, including the *Toronto Star*.[101]

Some members see CNWE's marginality as a necessary step in the reform of the Roman Catholic Church. This understanding is based in the concept of women-church popularized by Rosemary Radford Ruether, Elisabeth Schüssler Fiorenza, and other American feminist theologians in the 1980s. Women-church, according to Ruether, is a community of women who come together to "collectivize their experience" and form a "critical counterculture to patriarchy" through education, social analysis, and celebration.[102] It is necessary for that group to claim some autonomy from the institutional church because its patriarchy is so pervasive that women have been unable to escape its influence in order to develop a critical culture of their own.[103] But that separate community is not an end in itself; rather, it is "a stage toward a further end in the formation of a critical culture and community of women and men in exodus from patriarchy"[104]—that is, a just, inclusive, and accountable church. This understanding is encapsulated in a theme adopted by CNWE in 2008—being the change we seek.[105]

In 2002, an event took place that brought the question of women's ordination back to the forefront of CNWE's attention. That summer, seven women were ordained to the priesthood on a ship on the Danube River by validly ordained Roman Catholic bishops. Although the Vatican refuses to acknowledge these ordinations, they are technically valid.[106] Encouraged by a small but growing number of male clergy and many other Roman Catholics, these seven women, and 123 women after them, broke what they consider to be an unjust law prohibiting women's ordination in order to change it.[107] Between 2005 and 2012, five CNWE members have been ordained; one of them, Marie Bouclin of Sudbury, Ontario, was consecrated bishop in 2011. They are very deliberately being the change they seek, offering "Catholics a renewed priestly ministry in vibrant grassroots communities where all are equal and all are welcome."[108] One CNWE member believes that it is only a matter of time before there is no longer any need for organizations like CNWE:

> It depends on how long it takes for women's ordination to be accepted. Then if there still are inequality issues, then I suppose it would go on for a bit. But, I mean, that's its goal, it's women's equality. Once women are equal, then I don't think there will be a need for CNWE anymore.

Women's ordination has become a controversial issue among CNWE members and Catholic feminists more generally.[109] Some, like the woman quoted above, believe that ordaining women will ultimately change the church. Others argue that ordaining women into the existing hierarchy will only replicate the unjust structures of the church. It is authentic women's ministry that is necessary to reconfigure the church. Before that debate is resolved, however, a more insidious form of marginalization may render the question moot. All three Roman Catholic feminist movements discussed in this chapter are having difficulty attracting new members.

Vatican II's program of renewal included far-reaching reforms of religious communities, calling them to return to the original inspiration of their founders, who were often social reformers, but also to adapt to modern times. Loosed from the restrictions of the past, these well-educated professional women played leading roles in the post–Vatican II struggle for renewal in the church.[110] At the same time, Vatican II's emphasis on the apostolate of the laity opened up new possibilities for women and men who sought to serve the church. Consequently, there was a mass exodus of women and men from religious life, and fewer young people were interested in joining religious communities. The number of women religious in Canada dropped by 52 percent between 1960 and 2000. In 2010, the average age of women religious in Canada was seventy-three.[111]

Relatively speaking, the CWL had a healthy membership of more than 92,000 members in 2012.[112] However, membership has dropped at an average of two thousand members a year since 1990, when it reached an all-time high of 124,000 members.[113] Although there was a shift to ultra-conservatism by some CWL members in the 1980s,[114] the organization as a whole embraced the reforms of Vatican II, studying its documents and changing its constitution and bylaws to reflect the challenges of the post–Vatican II world.[115] To that same end, it also played an important role in the development and study of the CCCB's discussion guide, *Women in the Church*, popularly known as "The Green Kit," designed to foster dialogue about the role of women in the church.[116] It also expanded its social activism to the developing world and beyond Catholic populations. In 2000 the CWL participated in a planning committee for the World March of Women, a worldwide women's initiative to demand that governments take action to improve the lives of women.[117] Nevertheless, the membership continues to drop, and the average age of the members continues to rise.[118]

The members of CNWE are also aging. Its membership has never been large, numbering only 269 at its height in 1989. Since then, the number of members has slowly decreased, with some fluctuation. Membership in 2012 was 145. In order to be more accessible to younger women, CNWE has moved into cyberspace, establishing an e-list and a web page and joining the social networking site, Facebook. It also revamped its newsletter so that it would "inspire, inform and support"[119] a wider readership. Those strategies have not succeeded in arresting the decline in membership. When asked why CNWE was not attracting new, young members, one member in her seventies replied, "my generation, my sisters and myself, it was important to us to get in there and act; be a part of it and do something. For them, there are too many other things in their lives."

This sentiment is shared by members of all three movements discussed in this chapter. Nevertheless, these movements are approaching this challenge as they have all the others—as an opportunity to challenge this generation within the Roman Catholic Church to a broader vision of what the church can be. Women's religious communities have developed associate programs as a way to carry on their founders' charisms, or vision and values. Through those programs, lay women and men, married and single, enter into a formal relationship with the religious community. They are instructed in the vision and values of the community, and are invited to pray with the community and to engage in the service and activism of the community in some way.[120] The CWL has just announced its plans to establish a private foundation "to train Catholic women to assume leadership roles in the church and in society."[121] It is hoped that this foundation will encourage "women of faith who are establishing careers and raising families to join the League"[122] and train them to assume leadership roles within the League and in Canadian society. CNWE has just completed a project called "Reaching Out." In order to strengthen its voice for change, it sent out teams to parts of Canada where it has few members to hold visits where they listened to women's concerns and shared with them what CNWE has learned in its thirty years "of supporting the giftedness of women and gathering in circles of prayer, learning, and action."[123]

The effectiveness of those endeavours is yet to be seen. Many of the women I spoke with felt strongly that if this generation did not succeed in breathing new life into their organization, something else more suited to the times would emerge to continue where they left off. As one CNWE member put it,

> the basis for our movement is faith. And our faith is to hope despite all odds being against us. If CNWE is really based on the Christian message, then there will always be a future. Whether the organization continues on a structural level—that's a whole other question, [but] the CNWE message will continue.

bell hooks elaborates her reflection on marginality with which I began this chapter in her essay "Choosing the Margin as a Space of Radical Openness." According to hooks, marginality "offers . . . the possibility of a radical perspective from which to see and create, to imagine alternatives, new worlds."[124] Originating in different eras in the histories of Canada and the Roman Catholic Church, the three Catholic movements—women's religious communities, the Catholic Women's League, and Canadian Catholics for Women's Ordination/the Catholic Network for Women's Equality—have all occupied positions on the margins of their society and their church—this by virtue of gender for all three and in the case of English-Canadian society, their religion. While resisting their marginality at some levels, they also embraced it. Their marginality has enabled these Roman Catholic feminist movements to see some of the assumptions and prejudices of both church and society not visible to those at their centres, and to imagine and to create alternatives that have challenged both church and society to broader visions of what they can be. ●

Notes

I wish to thank the members of the CWL and CCWO/CNWE who generously shared their reflections and experiences with me.

1. Carolyn Sharp, "Determined Builders, Powerful Voices: Women and Catholicism in Nineteenth- and Twentieth-Century Quebec and Canada," in *Encyclopedia of Women and Religion in North America*, ed. Rosemary Skinner Keller and Rosemary Radford Ruether (Bloomington: Indiana University Press, 2006), 218.

2. See also C. Thomas McIntire, "Protestant Christians," in *The Religions of Canadians*, ed. Jamie S. Scott (Toronto: University of Toronto Press, 2012), 88.

3. For a survey of the literature, see Mary Farrell Bednarowski, *The Religious Imagination of American Women* (Bloomington and Indianapolis: Indiana University Press, 1999), 21–28.

4. bell hooks, *Feminist Theory: From Margin to Center*, 2nd ed. (Cambridge, MA: South End, 2000), xvi.

5. Clarissa Atkinson, "Precious Balsam in a Fragile Glass: The Ideology of Virginity in the Later Middle Ages," *Journal of Family History* 8, no. 2 (1983): 132–33; Rosemary Radford Ruether, "Misogynism and Virginal Feminism in the Fathers of the Church," in *Religion and Sexism: Images of Woman in the Jewish and Christian Traditions*, ed. Rosemary Radford Ruether (New York: Simon and Schuster, 1974), 150–83.

6. Mary T. Malone, *Women and Christianity*, vol. 1 (Ottawa: Novalis, 2000), 144–52.

7. Sharp, "Determined Builders," 211.

8. McIntire, "Protestant Christians," 95–101; Terence J. Fay, "Catholic Christians," in *The Religions of Canadians*, ed. Jaimie S. Scott (Toronto: University of Toronto Press, 2012), 46–47.

9. William Westfall, *Two Worlds: The Protestant Culture of Nineteenth-Century Ontario* (Kingston and Montreal: McGill-Queen's University Press, 1989), 19–28.

10. McIntire, "Protestant Christians," 101.

11. Sharp, "Determined Builders," 210. I am indebted to Sharp for information presented in this section.

12. See also Jo Ann McNamara, *Sisters in Arms: Catholic Nuns through Two Millennia* (Cambridge, MA: Harvard University Press, 1996), 88. See Terence J. Fay, *A History of Canadian Catholics: Gallicanism, Romanism, and Canadianism* (Kingston and Montreal: McGill-Queen's University Press, 2002), ch. 4–7, for a detailed discussion of ultramontanism in Canada.

13. Mark G. McGowan, "Roman Catholics (Anglophone and Allophone)," in *Christianity and Ethnicity in Canada*, ed. Paul Bramadat and David Seljak (Toronto: University of Toronto Press, 2008), 64–65.

14. Fay, "Catholic Christians," 69–70.

15. Sharp, "Determined Builders," 210.

16. Marta Danylewycz, *Taking the Veil: An Alternative to Marriage, Motherhood, and Spinsterhood in Quebec, 1840–1920* (Toronto: McClelland and Stewart, 1987), 72.

17. Ibid., 105.

18. Ibid., 97.

19. McNamara, *Sisters in Arms*, 612, concurs: "Many sisters felt themselves to be privileged in their freedom from marital authority, but they did not question the authority itself." See also ibid., 625.

20. See Clarence Gallagher, "The Church and Institutes of Consecrated Life," *The Way Supplement* 50 (Summer 1984): 8.

21. See Gail Cuthbert Brandt et al., *Canadian Women: A History*, 3rd ed. (Toronto: Nelson, 2011), 181.

22. See Brian P. Clarke, *Piety and Nationalism: Lay Voluntary Associations and the Creation of an Irish-Catholic Community in Toronto, 1850–1895* (Montreal and Kingston: McGill-Queen's University Press, 1993), 62–96; Sharp, "Determined Builders," 213.

23. Clarke, *Piety and Nationalism*, 65–67.

24. Ibid., 84–85.

25. Ibid., 88–89.

26. Brandt et al., *Canadian Women: A History*, 189.

27. The terms "first-wave" and "second-wave" feminism are contested; nevertheless, they are commonly used to identify the feminisms of the late nineteenth and early twentieth centuries, and of the late twentieth century, respectively.

28. See Candace Savage, *Our Nell: A Scrapbook Biography of Nellie L. McClung* (Saskatoon: Western Producer Prairie Books, 1979), 49; Randi R. Warne, *Literature as Pulpit: The Christian Social Activism of Nellie L. McClung* (Waterloo, ON: Wilfrid Laurier University Press, 1993). See especially ch. 4.

29. Leo XIII, "Encyclical Letter, *Rerum novarum*: On Capital and Labor," *Libreria Editrice Vaticana*, 1891, para. 63.

30. Pius X, "*Il fermo proposito*: Catholic Action in Italy," *Papal Encyclicals*, 1905, para. 2, http://www.papalencyclicals.net/Pius10/p10fermo.htm. In 1905 Pius X popularized the term "Catholic Action" for those activities.

31. Valerie J. Fall, "*Except the Lord Build the House . . .*": *A History of the Catholic Women's League of Canada 1920–1990* (Winnipeg: Catholic Women's League of Canada, 1990), 5–6.

32. Quoted in Fall, *Except the Lord Build*, 6.

33. Ibid., 7–8.

34. Ibid., 22.

35. Ibid., 6.

36. *The Albany Diocesan 1919*, quoted in Sheila Ross, *Companions on the Journey: The Catholic Women's League of Canada 1990–2005* (Winnipeg: Catholic Women's League of Canada, 2007), 3, http://cwl.ca/wp-content/uploads/2013/10/Companions-on-the -Journey-1990-2005.pdf.

37. For example, see Savage, *Our Nell*, 179–81.

38. See John Paul II, "Apostolic Letter, Mulieris dignitatem: On the Dignity and Vocation of Women," *Libreria Editrice Vaticana*, 1988, para. IV.10, http://www .vatican.va/holy_father/john_paul_ii/apost_letters/documents/hf_jpi_apl _15081988_mulieris-dignitatem_en.html.

39. "The statements in regard to the lowly and degraded conditions from which women have suffered in the past have some justification," quoted in Fall, Except the Lord Build, 20.

40. Quoted in ibid., 20.

41. Ibid.

42. Ibid.

43. See ibid., 23.

44. Ibid., 25.

45. Quoted in ibid., 25.

46. See Sheila Ross, "'For God and Canada': The Early Years of the Catholic Women's League in Alberta," *CCHA, Historical Studies* 62 (1996): n.p.

47. Quoted in Ross, "For God and Canada," n.p.

48. See Ross, *Companions on the Journey*, 6.

49. Quoted in Ross, "For God and Canada," n.p.

50. Fall, *Except the Lord Build*, 56.

51. Ibid., 70.

52. Quoted in Ross, "For God and Canada," n.p.

53. Fall, *Except the Lord Build*, 7.

54. Quoted in ibid., 46–47.

55. See ibid., 53–58.

56. Ibid., 71.

57. Summaries of the meetings for 1990–2005 are recorded in Ross, *Companions on the Journey*, 10–111.

58. See John S. Moir, "Toronto's Protestants and Their Perceptions of Their Roman Catholic Neighbours," in *Catholics at the "Gathering Place": Historical Essays on the Archdiocese of Toronto 1841–1991*, ed. Mark G. McGowan and Brian P. Clarke (Toronto: Dundurn for the Canadian Catholic Historical Association, 1993), 313–27.

59. Quoted in Fall, *Except the Lord Build*, 35.

60. Ibid., 8. According to Fall in her first annual report, the honorary secretary, Mrs. Walter Armstrong, wrote: "In future years, when Canadian history shall be written, I like to think that the CWL of Canada will be an organization of such tremendous force and power that its birth in the City of Churches in June, 1920, will be chronicled among leading events."

61. Ibid., 46–47.

62. McNamara, *Sisters in Arms*, 589.

63. See CWL, "Resolutions," *The Catholic Women's League of Canada*, http://cwl.ca/resolutions-by-year/, for a comprehensive list of the CWL resolutions.

64. See Robert McClory, *Turning Point: The Inside Story of the Papal Birth Control Commission, and How* Humanae Vitae *Changed the Life of Patty Crowley and the Future of the Church* (New York: Crossroad, 1995), 76.

65. Paul VI, "*Gaudium et spes*: The Church in the Modern World," *Libreria Editrice Vaticana*, 1965, http://www.vatican.va/archive/hist_coucils/ii_vatican_council/documents/vat-ii_const_19651207_gaudium-et-spes_en.html, para. 16. "For man has in his heart a law written by God; to obey it is the very dignity of man; according to it he

will be judged." See also para. 41, 31, 43, 79, 87. See also Paul VI, "*Dignitatis humanae*: On the Right of the Person and of Communities to Social and Civil Freedom in Matters Religious," *Libreria Editrice Vaticana*, 1965, http://www.vatican.va/archive/hist_councils/ii_vatican_council/documents/vat-ii_decl_19651207_dignitatis -humanae_en.html, para. 3 and 14.

66. John Horgan, Humanae vitae *and the Bishops: The Encyclical and the Statements of the National Hierarchies* (Shannon: Irish University Press, 1972), 83, para. 34; CCCB, "Winnipeg Statement," 1968, http://www.catholic-legate.com/articles/winnipeg .html.

67. Horgan, Humanae vitae *and the Bishops*, 79, para. 17.

68. Ibid., para. 26.

69. Ibid., 83, para. 34.

70. See Catholic Legate, "Contraception," 2014, http://www.catholic-legate.com/category/contraception/.

71. A chronicle of the efforts of the Rosarium to get the "Winnipeg Statement" retracted can be found at John Pacheco, "Winnipeg Statement Index Page," Catholic Legate, 2008, http://www.catholic-legate.com/winnipeg-statement-index-page/.

72. Five CWL members with varying degrees of involvement in the organization were interviewed in August and September 2012. They came from four different Ontario cities: Kitchener, Markham, Ottawa, and Toronto. They ranged in age from the late sixties to mid-eighties. All interviews were conducted in confidentiality, and the names of interviewees are withheld by mutual agreement.

73. Fall, *Except the Lord Build*, 74.

74. Veronica Dunne, "A Force of Nature: Canadian Catholic Women Shifting the Ecclesial Landscape," in *Feminist Theology with a Canadian Accent: Canadian Perspectives on Contextual Feminist Theology*, ed. Mary Ann Beavis, Elaine Guillemin, and Barbara Pell (Ottawa: Novalis, 2008), 185.

75. CCWO, "Draft Invitation to Inaugural Meeting," CNWE, vol. 1, 1981, p. 1, Library and Archives Canada.

76. Ibid.

77. American scholars Mary Daly, Elisabeth Schüssler Fiorenza, and Rosemary Radford Ruether were particularly influential at this time.

78. "Our Story," *Women's Ordination Conference*, http://www.womensordination.org.

79. Fourteen CCWO/CNWE members with varying degrees of involvement were interviewed in August–October 2012. They came from five different Canadian

cities: Fredericton, NB; Markham, ON; Oakville, ON; Ottawa, ON; Toronto, ON; and Winnipeg, MB. They ranged in age from the early thirties to mid-eighties. Most were over fifty; eight of the fourteen were over seventy.

80. See Cathy Holtmann, "Resistance Is Beautiful: The Growth of the Catholic Network for Women's Equality in New Brunswick," in *Feminist Theology with a Canadian Accent*, ed. Mary Ann Beavis (Ottawa: Novalis, 2008), 201.

81. CCCB, *With Respect to Women: A History of CCCB Initiatives Concerning Women in the Church and Society 1971–2000* (Ottawa: CCCB Publications, 2000), 40.

82. John R. Donahue, "A Tale of Two Documents," in *Women Priests: A Catholic Commentary on the Vatican Declaration*, ed. Leonard Swidler and Arlene Swidler (Mahwah, NJ: Paulist Press, 1977), 25, http://www.womenpriests.org/classic/donahue.asp.

83. Press Release, CNWE, vol. 1, CCWO 1981, p. 1, Library and Archives Canada.

84. CCCB, "Response to CCWO," CNWE, vol. 1, CCWO 1981, p. 1, Library and Archives Canada.

85. Anita Birt, Letter to Cardinal Carter of Toronto, CNWE, vol. 1, CCWO May 3, 1982, p. 2, Library and Archives Canada; Cardinal Gerald Emmett Carter, Letter to Anita Birt, CNWE, vol. 1, CCWO June 16, 1982, p. 1, Library and Archives Canada.

86. CCWO, Correspondence re. CCCB Study: Role of Women in the Church, CNWE, vol. 1, CCWO 1984, p. 3, Library and Archives Canada.

87. CCWO, Letter to Cardinal Carter, CNWE, vol. 1, CCWO 1983, Library and Archives Canada; CCWO, Core Group Minutes, January 27, CNWE, vol. 1, CCWO 1986, p. 1, Library and Archives Canada; Jennifer Leddy, Letter to Anita Birt, February 20, CNWE, vol. 1, CCWO 1986, p. 1, Library and Archives Canada; CCWO, Letter to Cardinal Carter, CNWE, vol. 1, CCWO 1983, Library and Archives Canada.

88. CCCB, *With Respect to Women*, 51.9.

89. See Porsia Tunzi, "Media Reports Shine Light on Emerging Discussion of Women Deacons," National Catholic Reporter, November 7, 2012, http://ncronline.org/news/theology/media-reports-shine-light-emerging-discussion-women-deacons. In 2009 Pope Benedict XVI altered canon 1009 in the Code of Canon Law to make a distinction between the priesthood and the diaconate, eliminating that potential. In the revised law, only bishops and priests are understood to receive the mission and faculty of acting in the person of Christ the Head through ordination. Since deacons are no longer seen as representing Christ, it is not necessary for them to be male.

90. CCCB, *With Respect to Women*, 52.15.

91. Anita Birt, Letter to the Editor of the *Globe and Mail*, CNWE, vol. 1, CCWO August 6, 1986, p. 1, Library and Archives Canada.

92. CBC, "The Man Who Would Be Pope," *Open House*, 1986, http://www.cbc.ca/archives/.

93. "Letter to Chief Jack Marks," CNWE, vol. 1, CCWO April 15 1986, p. 1, Library and Archives Canada.

94. "Core Group Letter," CNWE, vol. 2, CCWO July 18 1987, p. 1, Library and Archives Canada. See also Anita Birt, "Conference Reflections," CNWE, vol. 2, CCWO June 2, 1987, p. 1, Library and Archives Canada; Anita Birt, Letter to Nano McConnell, CNWE, vol. 2, CCWO June 24, 1987, p. 2, Library and Archives Canada; Carol Braune, Letter to Anita Birt, CNWE, vol. 2, CCWO 1987, p. 2, Library and Archives Canada; Nano McConnell, Letter to Anita Birt, CNWE, vol. 2, CCWO June 14, 1987, p. 2, Library and Archives Canada.

95. See Sean McCarroll, "Roman Catholic Group Lobbies for Female Priests," *Telegraph-Journal*, March 23, 2005, http://dignitycanada.org/Canadian-RC-group-lobbies-for-female-priests.html; *Women's Ordination Conference*, "Action Purple Stole," http://www.womensordination.org/resources/action-purple-stole/.

96. CNWE, "CNWE Is 'Reaching Out!' In 2012–2013!" *Catholic Network for Women's Equality*, 2012, http://www.cnwe.org/news/cnwe-is-reaching-out-in-2012-2013/.

97. Mary Ellen Chown, "CNWE Petition Sent to Canadian Bishops!" *Catholic Network for Women's Equality*, 2013, http://www.cnwe.org/news/cnwe-petition-sent-to-canadian-bishops/. Over four hundred signatures were collected. In January 2013, they were sent to the English-speaking bishops of Canada with a letter outlining CNWE's issues with the New Roman Missal. Ten bishops replied. Of those, four briefly acknowledged receipt of the petition, four expressed some support, and two disagreed with CNWE's position, one at great length. See CNWE, "CNWE Is 'Reaching Out!'"; Chown, "CNWE Petition."

98. Ellen Leonard, "The Process of Transformation: Women Religious and the Study of Theology, 1955–1980," in *Changing Habits: Women's Religious Orders in Canada*, ed. Elizabeth M. Smyth (Ottawa: Novalis, 2007), 235.

99. Anita Birt, Letter to WOC, CNWE, vol. 1, CCWO October 8, 1984, p. 1, Library and Archives Canada.

100. CCWO, "Core Group Minutes," CNWE, vol. 1, CCWO September 19, 1983, Library and Archives Canada.

101. Leslie Scrivener, "Challenging the Vatican: Progressive Catholics Say Reform Must Begin with Church Governance," *Toronto Star*, February 15, 2013, http://www .thestar.com/news/insight/2013/02/15/challenging_the_vatican_progressive_ catholics_say_reform_must_begin_with_church_governance.html. See also Rosemary Ganley, "An Institution Doomed to Decline," *Peterborough Examiner*, February 19, 2013, http://www.thepeterboroughexaminer.com/2013/02/19/an-institution -doomed-to-decline. Other interviews also took place: CTV Television (Fredericton, NB), CBC Radio call-in, CBC Radio–Metro Morning (Toronto, ON), CTV TV (Hamilton, ON), CHCH TV, CBC Radio morning show syndicated to eight stations across Canada. See Mary Ellen Chown, personal communication with author, December 16, 2014.

102. Rosemary Radford Ruether, *Women-Church: Theology and Practice of Feminist Liturgical Communities* (San Francisco: Harper and Row, 1985), 60.

103. Ibid., 59.

104. Ibid., 60.

105. CNWE, "AGM Minutes," *CNWE Digital Archive 2006–12* (unpublished, 2008), motion 1. CNWE, "AGM Minutes. Being the Change," *CNWE Digital Archive 2006–12* (unpublished, 2009).

106. Although the church hierarchy refuses to recognize these ordinations, making them illicit, they are valid according to Catholic sacramental theology because the original seven women were ordained by Roman Catholic bishops who stand in apostolic succession.

107. *Roman Catholic Women Priests*, http://romancatholicwomenpriests.org.

108. Ibid.

109. See CCWO, "Core Group Minutes," CNWE, vol. 1, CCWO July 8, 1986, p. 1, Library and Archives Canada; CNWE, *SeedKeepers*, 17.1., CNWE, vol. 6, NEW 2004–05, 2005, Library and Archives Canada.

110. See Ellen Leonard, "The Emergence of Canadian Contextual Feminist Theologies," in *Feminist Theology with a Canadian Accent*, ed. Mary Ann Beavis (Ottawa: Novalis, 2008), 27; Leonard, *Changing Habits*.

111. Heidi MacDonald and Elizabeth Smyth, "Imaging *perfectae caritatis*: Viewing the Consecrated Life through the Mother House Museums of Canadian Women Religious," in *Vatican II: Experiences Canadiennes — Canadian Experiences*, ed. Michael Attridge et al. (Ottawa: University of Ottawa Press, 2011), 494.

112. CWL, Press Release, *The Catholic Women's League of Canada*, 2012, http://www.cwl
.ca/recentcorrespondence/.

113. Membership statistics for the years 1990–2006 are recorded in the annual reports
found in Ross, *Companions on the Journey*, 10–112.

114. Fall, *Except the Lord Build*, 74.

115. Ibid., 57.

116. Fay, "Catholic Christians," 266–67.

117. Ross, *Companions on the Journey*, 74–75.

118. Ibid., 112.

119. Personal communication from one of the CNWE informants.

120. For example, see "How to Be Involved," *Loretto Sisters, Canadian Province*, http://
ibvm.ca/be-involved/associate; "Your Connection: As an Associate," *Sisters of
Charity-Halifax*, http://www.schalifax.ca/category/become-an-associate/; "Join Us:
As an Associate," *Sisters of St. Joseph of Toronto*, http://www.csj-to.ca/associate.

121. "Women Leaders of Tomorrow," *The Canadian League* 88, no. 2 (2012), 7, http://www
.cwl.ca/CDN%20League/Spring%202012.pdf.

122. Ibid.

123. Patenaude, unpublished, 2012.; see also CNWE, "CNWE Is 'Reaching Out!'"

124. bell hooks, "Choosing the Margin as a Space of Radical Openness," in *Yearning:
Race, Gender, and Cultural Politics* (Toronto: Between the Lines, 1990), 150.

Archival Sources

Catholic Network for Women's Equality Digital Archive, 2006–12. Unpublished.

Library and Archives Canada, Catholic Network for Women's Equality collection.

Bibliography

Atkinson, Clarissa. "Precious Balsam in a Fragile Glass: The Ideology of Virginity in the
Later Middle Ages." *Journal of Family History* 8, no. 2 (1983): 131–43.

Bednarowski, Mary Farrell. *The Religious Imagination of American Women*. Bloomington
and Indianapolis: Indiana University Press, 1999.

Brandt, Gail Cuthbert, Naomi Black, Paula Bourne, and Magda Fahrni. *Canadian Women:
A History*. 3rd ed. Toronto: Nelson, 2011.

Catholic Legate. "Contraception." 2014. http://www.catholic-legate.com/category/
contraception/.

CBC. "The Man Who Would Be Pope." *Open House*. 1986. http://www.cbc.ca/archives/.

CCCB. "Liberating Potential: Pastoral Message on the Occasion of the 40th Anniversary of the Encyclical *Humanae vitae*." 2008. http://www.ccbi-utoronto.ca/documents/ bioethic_matters/CCCB_Liberating%20Potential_PastoralMessage_HV40thAnniv .pdf.

———. "Winnipeg Statement." 1968. http://www.catholic-legate.com/articles/winnipeg .html.

———. *With Respect to Women: A History of CCCB Initiatives Concerning Women in the Church and Society 1971–2000.* Ottawa: CCCB Publications, 2000.

Chown, Mary Ellen. "CNWE Petition Sent to Canadian Bishops!" *Catholic Network for Women's Equality.* 2013. http://www.cnwe.org/news/cnwe-petition-sent-to -canadian-bishops/.

———. Personal communication with author, December 16, 2014.

Clarke, Brian P. *Piety and Nationalism: Lay Voluntary Associations and the Creation of an Irish-Catholic Community in Toronto, 1850–1895.* Montreal and Kingston: McGill-Queen's University Press, 1993.

CNWE. "CNWE Is 'Reaching Out!' In 2012–2013!" *Catholic Network for Women's Equality.* 2012. http://www.cnwe.org/news/cnwe-is-reaching-out-in-2012-2013/.

———. "10 Bishops Respond to New Roman Missal Petition." *Catholic Network for Women's Equality.* 2013. http://www.cnwe.org/news/10-bishops-respond-to-new-roman -missal-petition/.

CWL. Press Release. *The Catholic Women's League of Canada.* 2012. http://www.cwl.ca/ recentcorrespondence/.

———. "Resolutions." *The Catholic Women's League of Canada.* n.d. http://cwl.ca/resolutions -by-year/.

Danylewycz, Marta. *Taking the Veil: An Alternative to Marriage, Motherhood, and Spinsterhood in Quebec, 1840–1920.* Toronto: McClelland and Stewart, 1987.

Donahue, John R. "A Tale of Two Documents." In *Women Priests: A Catholic Commentary on the Vatican Declaration,* edited by Leonard Swidler and Arlene Swidler, 25–34. Mahwah, NJ: Paulist Press, 1977. http://www.womenpriests.org/classic/donahue.asp.

Dunne, Veronica. "A Force of Nature: Canadian Catholic Women Shifting the Ecclesial Landscape." In *Feminist Theology with a Canadian Accent: Canadian Perspectives on Contextual Feminist Theology,* edited by Mary Ann Beavis, Elaine Guillemin, and Barbara Pell, 179–99. Ottawa: Novalis, 2008.

Fall, Valerie J. *"Except the Lord Build the House . . .": A History of the Catholic Women's League of Canada 1920–1990.* Winnipeg: The Catholic Women's League of Canada, 1990.

Fay, Terence J. "Catholic Christians." In *The Religions of Canadians,* edited by Jaimie S. Scott, 33–74. Toronto: University of Toronto Press, 2012.

——. *A History of Canadian Catholics: Gallicanism, Romanism, and Canadianism.* Montreal and Kingston: McGill-Queen's University Press, 2002.

Gallagher, Clarence. "The Church and Institutes of Consecrated Life." *The Way Supplement* 50 (Summer 1984): 3–15. http://www.theway.org.uk/back/s050Gallagher.pdf.

Ganley, Rosemary. "An Institution Doomed to Decline." *Peterborough Examiner,* February 19, 2013. http://www.thepeterboroughexaminer.com/2013/02/19/an-institution-doomed-to-decline.

Holtmann, Cathy. "Resistance Is Beautiful: The Growth of the Catholic Network for Women's Equality in New Brunswick." In *Feminist Theology with a Canadian Accent,* edited by Mary Ann Beavis, 200–219.

hooks, bell. "Choosing the Margin as a Space of Radical Openness." *Yearning: Race, Gender, and Cultural Politics,* 145–53. Toronto: Between the Lines, 1990.

——. *Feminist Theory: From Margin to Center.* 2nd ed. Cambridge, MA: South End, 2000.

Horgan, John. *Humanae vitae and the Bishops: The Encyclical and the Statements of the National Hierarchies.* Shannon: Irish University Press, 1972.

"How to Be Involved." *Loretto Sisters, Canadian Province.* http://ibvm.ca/be-involved/associate.

John Paul II. "Apostolic Letter. Mulieris dignitatem: On the Dignity and Vocation of Women." *Libreria Editrice Vaticana.* 1988. http://www.vatican.va/holy_father/john_paul_ii/apost_letters/documents/hf_jp-ii_apl_15081988_mulieris-dignitatem_en.html.

"Join Us: As an Associate." *Sisters of St. Joseph of Toronto.* http://www.csj-to.ca/associate.

Leo XIII. "Encyclical Letter. Rerum novarum: On Capital and Labor." *Libreria Editrice Vaticana.* 1891. http://w2.vatican.va/content/leo-xiii/en/encyclicals/documents/hf_l-xiii_enc_15051891_rerum-novarum.html.

Leonard, Ellen. "The Emergence of Canadian Contextual Feminist Theologies." In *Feminist Theology with a Canadian Accent,* edited by Mary Ann Beavis, 23–38. Ottawa: Novalis, 2008.

——. "The Process of Transformation: Women Religious and the Study of Theology, 1955–1980." In *Changing Habits: Women's Religious Orders in Canada,* edited by Elizabeth M. Smyth, 230–46. Ottawa: Novalis, 2007.

MacDonald, Heidi, and Elizabeth Smyth. "Imaging *perfectae caritatis*: Viewing the Consecrated Life through the Mother House Museums of Canadian Women

Religious." In *Vatican II: Experiences Canadiennes—Canadian Experiences*, edited by Michael Attridge, Catherine E. Clifford, and Gilles Routhier, 476–94. Ottawa: University of Ottawa Press, 2011.

Malone, Mary T. *Women and Christianity*. Vol. 1. Ottawa: Novalis, 2000.

McCarroll, Sean. "Roman Catholic Group Lobbies for Female Priests." *Telegraph-Journal*, March 23, 2005. http://dignitycanada.org/Canadian-RC-group-lobbies-for-female-priests.html.

McClory, Robert. *Turning Point: The Inside Story of the Papal Birth Control Commission, and How Humanae Vitae Changed the Life of Patty Crowley and the Future of the Church*. New York: Crossroad, 1995.

McGowan, Mark G. "Roman Catholics (Anglophone and Allophone)." In *Christianity and Ethnicity in Canada*, edited by Paul Bramadat and David Seljak, 49–100. Toronto: University of Toronto Press, 2008.

McIntire, C. Thomas. "Protestant Christians." In *The Religions of Canadians*, edited by Jamie S. Scott, 75–130. Toronto: University of Toronto Press, 2012.

McNamara, Jo Ann. *Sisters in Arms: Catholic Nuns through Two Millennia*. Cambridge, MA: Harvard University Press, 1996.

Moir, John S. "Toronto's Protestants and Their Perceptions of Their Roman Catholic Neighbours." In *Catholics at the "Gathering Place": Historical Essays on the Archdiocese of Toronto 1841–1991*, edited by Mark G. McGowan and Brian P. Clarke, 313–27. Toronto: Dundurn for the Canadian Catholic Historical Association, 1993.

Pacheco, John. "Winnipeg Statement Index Page." The Catholic Legate. 2008. http://www.catholic-legate.com/winnipeg-statement-index-page/.

Patenaude, Rita. "Reaching Out." Unpublished document. November 11, 2012.

Paul VI. "*Dignitatis humanae*: On the Right of the Person and of Communities to Social and Civil Freedom in Matters Religious." *Libreria Editrice Vaticana*. 1965. http://www.vatican.va/archive/hist_councils/ii_vatican_council/documents/vat-ii_decl_19651207_dignitatis-humanae_en.html.

——. "*Gaudium et spes*: The Church in the Modern World." *Libreria Editrice Vaticana*. 1965. http://www.vatican.va/archive/hist_councils/ii_vatican_council/documents/vat-ii_const_19651207_gaudium-et-spes_en.html.

——. "*Humane vitae*: On the Regulation of Birth." *Libreria Editrice Vaticana*. 1968. http://www.vatican.va/holy_father/paul_vi/encyclicals/documents/hf_p-vi_enc_25071968_humanae-vitae_en.html.

Pius X. "*Il fermo proposito*: Catholic Action in Italy." *Papal Encyclicals.* 1905. http://www
.papalencyclicals.net/Pius10/p10fermo.htm.

Power and Politics with Evan Solomon. *Power and Politics with Evan Solomon.* CBC News
Network, February 26, 2013.

Roman Catholic Womenpriests. http://romancatholicwomenpriests.org.

Ross, Sheila. *Companions on the Journey: The Catholic Women's League of Canada 1990–
2005.* Winnipeg: Catholic Women's League of Canada, 2007. http://cwl.ca/wp
-content/uploads/2013/10/Companions-on-the-Journey-1990-2005.pdf.

——. "'For God and Canada': The Early Years of the Catholic Women's League in
Alberta." *CCHA, Historical Studies* 62 (1996): 89–108. http://www.cchahistory.ca/
journal/CCHA1996/Ross.htm#_ftnref57.

Ruether, Rosemary Radford. "Misogynism and Virginal Feminism in the Fathers of the
Church." In *Religion and Sexism: Images of Woman in the Jewish and Christian Traditions,* edited by Rosemary Radford Ruether, 150–83. New York: Simon and Schuster, 1974.

——. *Women-Church: Theology and Practice of Feminist Liturgical Communities.* San Francisco: Harper and Row, 1985.

Savage, Candace. *Our Nell: A Scrapbook Biography of Nellie L. McClung.* Saskatoon: Western Producer Prairie Books, 1979.

Scrivener, Leslie. "Challenging the Vatican: Progressive Catholics Say Reform Must
Begin with Church Governance." *Toronto Star,* February 15, 2013. http://www
.thestar.com/news/insight/2013/02/15/challenging_the_vatican_progressive
_catholics_say_reform_must_begin_with_church_governance.html.

Sharp, Carolyn. "Determined Builders, Powerful Voices: Women and Catholicism in
Nineteenth- and Twentieth-Century Quebec and Canada." In *Encyclopedia of
Women and Religion in North America,* vol. 1, edited by Rosemary Skinner Keller and
Rosemary Radford Ruether, 209–18. Bloomington: Indiana University Press, 2006.

Tunzi, Porsia. "Media Reports Shine Light on Emerging Discussion of Women Deacons."
National Catholic Reporter, November 7, 2012. http://ncronline.org/news/theology/
media-reports-shine-light-emerging-discussion-women-deacons.

Warne, Randi R. *Literature as Pulpit: The Christian Social Activism of Nellie L. McClung.*
Waterloo, ON: Wilfrid Laurier University Press, 1993.

Westfall, William. *Two Worlds: The Protestant Culture of Nineteenth-Century Ontario.*
Kingston and Montreal: McGill-Queen's University Press, 1989.

"Women Leaders of Tomorrow." *The Canadian League* 88, no. 2 (2012): 6–7. http://wp.dol
.ca/webportal/uploads/Spring_2012.pdf.

Women's Ordination Conference. http://www.womensordination.org.

"Your Connection: As an Associate." *Sisters of Charity-Halifax.* http://www.schalifax.ca/
category/become-an-associate/.

4 Unveiling Leah

Examining Women's Voices in Two Canadian Jewish Worship Services

AVIVA GOLDBERG YORK UNIVERSITY

In the past forty years, women have been transforming the face of Jewish practice. They have redefined and reconfigured synagogue leadership, liturgy, and ritual. By 2006, there were 829 women rabbis in the Reform, Reconstructionist, and Conservative movements.[1] These rabbis have "compelled their congregations to embrace religious and spiritual innovation."[2] Innovations in the liberal movements have included counting women toward the *minyan*, the quorum often needed for a complete prayer service; allowing women to wear the prayer shawl and skull caps normally reserved for men; women reading regularly from the Torah; women learning Hebrew and the skills necessary to lead worship services; and creating life cycle rituals that celebrate women's experiences from childbirth to menopause. Simultaneous to these changes, women have embraced higher education in all areas of Jewish studies, thereby increasing their ability to add their standpoint to biblical analysis, rabbinic law, Jewish history, and literature. As Pamela Nadell notes, "today no subfield of Jewish studies—Bible, rabbinics, history, sociology, anthropology, literature—remains untouched by [women's scholarly] work."[3]

Concomitant with these changes within liberal Judaism, there has been a gradual, yet monumental, movement for greater learning and a demand for increased rights within the Orthodox milieu. Orthodox women and their male sympathizers are challenging the paternalistic rabbinic observations (which may have held true under certain socioeconomic circumstances, but do not apply universally today) and even subjecting these to empiric examination . . . voicing their refusal to allow male judgements about their nature to play a determining role in halakhic [sic] deliberations.[4]

As part of this challenge, a small group of women, headed by Orthodox Jewish feminist Blu Greenberg, established the Jewish Orthodox Feminist Alliance (JOFA) in 1997. In the twenty-six years since its founding, it has grown to over five thousand members. JOFA has hosted several international conferences and created a journal. Their board members represent various regions in the United States and their general membership is active in such countries as Israel, England, Germany, and Australia. JOFA's goal is "to expand the spiritual, ritual, intellectual and political opportunities for women within the framework of halakha." The group advocates meaningful participation and equality for women in family life, synagogues, houses of learning, and Jewish communal organizations to the full extent possible within Halacha (rabbinic law).[5] As activists for women's participation in ritual life at home and in the synagogue, within Halachic parameters, JOFA has created several resources such as the *Ta Shma Halakhic Source Guides*. One such guide, *Women and Men in Communal Prayer: Halakhic Perspectives*, explores the Halachic ways in which women can "reconcile the competing values of tradition and human dignity."

The question of human dignity is crucial to contemporary Orthodox perspectives and to *responsa* (authoritative replies by rabbis on Halachic questions), which focus on women's participation in worship services. According to Orthodox Rabbi Daniel Sperber, there are basic values that permeate rabbinic law. He has written that "compassion and sensitivity are the hallmarks of classical normative halacha [sic], and that is why they were the catalysts for creative and innovative problem solving."[6] Sperber asserts that this sensitivity is expressed in the principle of *kevod haberiyot* (human dignity). It is this principle that supersedes many of the restrictions classical rabbis put on women's participation in worship. In this regard, Tamar Ross notes that Orthodox women's appreciation of less formalistic considerations extends to the nature of Halacha itself. She asserts that women's entry into Halachic discourse "may eventually serve the function of restoring to the *halakhah* [*sic*] some of the flexibility that once characterized its method, in placing moral and spiritual considerations over and above . . . the adherence to formal rules."[7]

Since the 1970s, Orthodox women have been creating women-only *tefillah* (prayer) groups. Supporters of these groups considered them to be cutting edge. However, more radical changes were yet to come. In 2009 Yeshivat Maharat was founded in New York. It is the first institution to ordain Orthodox women as spiritual leaders and Halachic authorities. As its website states: "through a rigorous curriculum of Talmud, *halakhic* decision-making (*psak*), pastoral counseling, leadership development, and internship experiences, our graduates will be prepared to assume the responsibility and authority to be *poskot* (legal arbiters) for the community."[8]

There is a great deal of controversy regarding all of the above attempts by Orthodox Jewish women to have equality and shared leadership within synagogue worship. The Rabbinic Council of America, which represents affiliated Orthodox congregations in the United States, does not support these initiatives. They released the following statement in response to the ordination of the first Orthodox women by Yeshivat Maharat:

> In light of the opportunity created by advanced women's learning, the Rabbinical Council of America encourages a diversity of *halachically* and communally appropriate professional opportunities for learned, committed women, in the service of our collective mission to preserve and transmit our heritage. Due to our aforesaid commitment to sacred continuity, however, we cannot accept either the ordination of women or the recognition of women as members of the Orthodox rabbinate, regardless of the title. The RCA views this event as a violation of our *mesorah* (tradition) and regrets that the leadership of the school has chosen a path that contradicts the norms of our community.[9]

It is, in fact, only unaffiliated Orthodox synagogues and groups that are able to offer Orthodox women a place for leadership and shared worship. This is the reality in Canada, Toronto included.

In order to situate the position of women's worship in two unaffiliated synagogues in Toronto, it is first necessary to understand the particular character of Toronto's affiliated Orthodox and Conservative synagogues. According to the North American Jewish Data Bank, there are approximately 375,000 Jews living in Canada. Over one-third of Canadian Jews, approximately 130,000, live in Toronto. The National Synagogue Directory notes in its 2011–12 listing of synagogues in Ontario that there are over eighty synagogues in Toronto. The following is a breakdown of these synagogues according to denominations: sixty-one Orthodox (this includes those that are Sephardim and Chabad),[10] two Modern Orthodox, one "mixed seating" Orthodox, eight Reform, fifteen Conservative, one Reconstructionist, one Traditional (Egalitarian), one Liberal, and three unaffiliated. Congregation Shir Libeynu is one of these unaffiliated congregations. As the unaffiliated Toronto Partnership Minyan was created after these statistics were recorded, it was not included in this data. Additionally, in 2012 the City Shul, a new Reform synagogue, opened its doors in downtown Toronto, increasing the number of Reform synagogues to nine.

It is important to identify aspects of Conservative, Orthodox, and what is termed Modern Orthodox worship services in Toronto, particularly in relation to women's participation. There are several similarities in the observances of many of Toronto's Conservative, Orthodox, and Modern Orthodox synagogues. Historically, the Conservative denomination saw Judaism as an unfolding religion emphasizing organic continuity.[11] Like some aspects of Orthodox Judaism, Conservative Judaism combines an acceptance of critical secular scholarship regarding Jewish sacred texts with a commitment to Jewish observance. In most Conservative synagogues, aspects of the tradition "have been modified in response to changing social realities."[12] In Toronto, however, the Conservative movement is less liberal than its counterpart south of the border. As a recent article in the *Jewish Tribune* noted, "an estimated 80% of Conservative congregations in the United States feature some form of egalitarianism, but Toronto congregations have towed [sic] a more traditional line."[13] Indeed there are only two fully egalitarian Conservative congregations in Toronto, Beit Rayim and B'nai Shalom Congregation. The issue of full ritual inclusion is a complex one. As Kapustin notes,

Torah egalitarianism [allowing women to participate in all aspects of the Torah service] is one of four options for women's ritual inclusion in the movement, which also include no egalitarianism, "minyan egalitarianism" (which, more liberal than Torah egalitarianism, counts women for a quorum in services) but doesn't allow them to lead all services and full egalitarianism.[14]

Despite the fact that the Conservative denomination's Jewish Theological Seminary in New York has been ordaining women since 1985, there are no women rabbis in any Toronto Conservative congregation. The newly formed Canadian Council of Conservative Synagogues reflects this more traditional ethos. It consists of four of the largest Conservative synagogues in Toronto. Three out of the four congregations left the New York–based United Synagogues of Conservative Judaism, which is the umbrella group for about seven hundred Conservative congregations in North America. Some of the major reasons for this split were theological differences, including the fact that the American movement's Jewish Theological Seminary's rabbinical program recognizes and admits openly gay students to its rabbinic programs.[15]

Of importance as well in understanding women's role in synagogue life in Toronto is the formation of the Canadian Yeshiva and Rabbinical School. It is the "fully halachic yet modern . . . home of Classical Judaism." According to its website, Classical Judaism derives from certain forms of Orthodox Judaism and traditional Conservative Judaism. It defines itself as "representing everlasting Judaism, the modern continuation of pre-denominationalism, rooted in the past, fructifying the present, seeding the future." Further, the website notes that "with some forms of Orthodoxy rapidly moving rightward and with some forms of Conservative Judaism rapidly moving leftward, Classical Judaism cries for a sense of common Jewish destiny."[16] Their sense of a common Jewish destiny, however, does not include women's destiny as the seminary will not ordain women. Women may attend the school, however, and receive a degree in Jewish theology. Interestingly, there are three women listed as members of the Canadian Yeshiva and Rabbinical School's School of Hebrew Letters and two women faculty members in their School of Professional Practice.

As the above implies, it would appear that the majority of Toronto's Jewish synagogue attendees reflect this small-"c" conservative, traditionalist attitude espoused in this newly formed Canadian rabbinical seminary. This conservatism is most obviously reflected in the fact that the number of Orthodox synagogues in Toronto far outweighs those of the other denominations.

It is most difficult to define the variety of philosophies of Toronto's Conservative movement. Similarly, there is difficulty in explaining what a synagogue means when it identifies as Modern Orthodox as opposed to Orthodox. Samuel C. Heilman suggests that "to add the adjective modern to the identity Orthodox is somehow to invite the inference that this implies modification in the attachment to tradition."[17]

Borrowing the term "contrapuntal" from British anthropologist Mary Douglas, he describes two types of Orthodoxy today—contrapuntal and enclavist—the latter being his original term. Heilman asserts that "contrapuntalism allows people to belong to multiple institutions and cultures simultaneously, but also grants them some modicum of autonomy in making and establishing those affiliations." Modern Orthodox, contrapuntal Jews endow "the general civilization ... with ontological meaning and cultural value, even as they remain attached to Jewish tradition and law (Halacha)."[18] They follow what Rabbi Samson Raphael Hirsch called *Torah im derech eretz*, Torah Judaism combined with the surrounding culture.[19] Although, as noted above, only two Orthodox synagogues in Toronto defined themselves as Modern Orthodox in the National Synagogue Directory, this does not mean that the others fall into the category of what Heilman calls enclavist. According to him, the goal is "not to fit Orthodoxy to the surrounding culture but rather to ensure that all insiders conform to the religious behaviour and worldview that predominate within the enclave culture, no matter how retrograde it may seem."[20] What is important to realize is that this sectarian stance is the approach of increasingly visible Orthodox Jewish groups not only in the United States, but also, I contend, in Toronto. Particularly in the past ten to twenty years, there has been a move by the Toronto Orthodox communities to "the heroic retreat from ... fragmentation—from engagement in plural life-worlds seeking instead the haven of religious insularity in their enclaves."[21] As

Heilman suggests, within the current ideological battle between the different understandings of Orthodoxy the *"frum is giving way to frummer"* and the *frum* are losing the battle.[22] That is to say, the observant are giving way to the more observant and Modern Orthodoxy is losing the battle.

As the core of this chapter is a discussion of women and worship, it is beyond its scope to enter into a discussion of all the complexities of Orthodox life. I am not suggesting that the majority of those synagogues in Toronto that go by the title "Orthodox" understand that it is necessary for adherents to insulate themselves from secular life, or that they are all enclavists. Nonetheless, from my own observations of the changes in Orthodoxy in Toronto in the past twenty years, I would submit that the influence of enclavists is evident not only in synagogues but in the general cultural norms of Toronto Orthodox Jewry today.[23] Thirty years ago, for example, it was rare for an Orthodox Jewish wedding to have separate seating, yet today it is quite prevalent. Similarly, thirty years ago, mixed seating was the norm for all Jewish funerals. This has changed dramatically and it is so much the norm now that when families use the chapels of the two major funeral homes in Toronto, unless the officiant is a Reform rabbi, they must request mixed seating rather than the other way around.[24] It is within this most conservative milieu that the Toronto Partnership Minyan resides.

In order to situate my standpoint and the character of this chapter, it is necessary to explicate the significance of the main title of this chapter, "Unveiling Leah," and its relevance and significance to the principles of Congregation Shir Libeynu and the Toronto Partnership Minyan. Additionally, it is necessary to explain the various methodologies I shall be using in my analysis.

It is my contention that the strength of Leah, hidden and veiled in the biblical narrative, corresponds to the hidden strengths of contemporary Jewish women both Modern Orthodox and liberal. The conflicting readings of the Leah narrative by the rabbis, readings in which the rabbis present Leah in either a positive or negative light, are concomitant with the attitudes of rabbis today with regard to women's synagogue rights and rites. What are these differing, conflicting readings of Leah?

Leah is the eldest daughter of Laban, the uncle and eventually the father-in-law of the patriarch Jacob. Genesis 29:16–30 relates the story of Jacob, Laban, and his daughters Leah and Rachel. Jacob, we are told, loves Rachel and works for her father for seven years in order to marry her. But on the evening of what was to be the consummation of their marriage, Laban tricks Jacob and substitutes Leah for Rachel. It was not until the morning when he actually sees with whom he has slept that Jacob realizes it was Leah and not Rachel. "And it was in the morning and here she was: Leah! And he [Jacob] said to Laban, 'what is this you've done to me? Didn't I work with you for Rachel? And why have you deceived me'" (Genesis 29:25)? The rabbis ask how it is that Jacob could not tell Rachel and Leah apart. One Midrash (biblical commentary) suggests that in fact Rachel was aware of her father's deception and warned Jacob of Laban's plans. According to *Midrash Eichah Rabbah*, Jacob and Rachel had agreed upon a sign to allow Jacob to distinguish between the sisters, but at the last minute Rachel did not wish her sister to be shamed and so abandoned the plan and aided in her sister's deception.[25] Others suggest that Leah was so heavily veiled that Jacob did not recognize her.

If one were to take the events in the text at face value, it would seem that Leah is a trickster and purposely defrauded Jacob. To support this perspective, the narrative states that Jacob hates Leah: "And YHWH saw that Leah was hated and He opened her womb" (Gen. 29:31). One of the leading sixteenth-century commentators, Sfornos, explains that when Jacob saw that Leah was barren, he hated her. Therefore God, taking pity on her, "opened her womb." The thirteenth-century commentator Nachmanides goes further and states that Jacob would have divorced Leah for deceiving him and "also for taking what . . . rightfully belonged to Rachel," but when Leah gave birth, he changed his mind.[26] Thus for some rabbinic authorities, Leah is a weak and despised woman. Yet other rabbinic sources present a more positive and sympathetic understanding of Leah. They assert that the term "hated" actually means less loved and therefore the implication is that Jacob preferred Rachel, but did not hate Leah. Additionally, they give Leah the honour of being called a prophetess who knew even before the subsequent events that Jacob was to have twelve sons by four wives and that she would be the one to give birth to six of them.[27]

Similarly, a reading of the text in relationship to ritual reveals the various misconceptions regarding veiling and the misogynistic attitudes of some rabbinic *minhagim* (customs), attitudes that are prevalent today in rabbinic discussions of women and ritual. Many connect the Jewish marriage ritual of veiling, the *badeken*, with this story.[28] *Badeken* is a Yiddish word related to the words *dekens*, meaning "to cover"; *deknomen*, which means "alias" (literally "cover name"); and *dektikhl*, which means "veil." It refers to the custom where the groom, or in some cases the rabbi, covers the face of the bride just before the marriage ceremony before the couple stand beneath the *chuppah* (bridal canopy).[29]

There is little doubt that Leah was heavily veiled so that Jacob would not know it was she and not her sister. However, if one were to use this particular narrative as the source of the custom of *badeken*, the husband should be unveiling his bride under the *chuppah* just before pronouncing the marriage vow. This would guarantee that the groom would not find himself in the same position as Jacob did with Leah. A more likely origin narrative for the *badeken* ritual is the biblical story about the matriarch Rebekah. When she saw Isaac for the first time, she "took a veil and covered herself" (Gen. 24:65). In fact, the custom is that once the groom has veiled his bride, the accompanying rabbi and gathered assembly pronounce a blessing on her, the very same blessing invoked on Rebecca in this biblical narrative: "And they blessed Rebekah and said to her, 'you're our sister. Become thousands of ten thousands'" (Gen. 24:60).

Regardless of the origins of *badeken*, the entire issue of veiling is a contentious and sexist subject for Jewish women. One of the reasons given for covering the bride's face with a veil is so that the "husband conceals his bride from the eyes of others."[30] It emphasizes that once the bride is married, gazing at her is forbidden.[31] As the *Shulchan Aruch* (Code of Jewish Law), a compilation of Jewish laws and customs, notes, it is forbidden to look at a bride's face.[32] Isaac Klein explains that there are a number of interpretations for this custom, two of which are that it is an indication of modesty and piety, and that it serves to distinguish the "virtues of Jewish womanhood; the bride's beauty is reserved for her husband."[33] It is obvious that the aforementioned rabbinic interpretations have, as their basis, an understanding that women are the property of their husbands. In order to understand Jewish women today and their place in the synagogue, particularly those women who consider themselves to be Modern Orthodox, it is necessary to realize that Halachic and Midrashic rabbinic views are "neither fixed nor monolithic."[34] To paraphrase Leah Leila Bronner, the interaction between the rabbinic and contemporary society, Midrashic method, individual sensibilities, and an awe and reverence for the text casts the role of women in Judaism in a variety of ways.[35]

Biblical exegesis is an ongoing process within Judaism. The tradition of Torah interpretation and the creation of narratives that fill the gaps in the sacred text (Midrash) are embodied in a large mass of writings going back to antiquity.[36] As Gerald L. Bruns suggests, "the Bible always addresses itself to the time of interpretation."[37] In the past almost four decades women are adding to rabbinic Midrash. They are doing so by creating new feminist Midrash that gives meaning to the often neglected women of the Hebrew Bible. It is women's time for interpretation.

In this vein, it is conceivable to view the Leah narrative not only through a variety of rabbinic commentaries as above, but as well through a feminist lens. The latter can be done by creating an imaginative Midrash, one that is grounded in classical rabbinic exegesis. In the following feminist Midrash, which I have created, Leah agrees to Laban's ruse, neither because she is evil nor crafty but rather because, as a prophetess, she knows that this subterfuge is necessary to assist in fulfilling Jacob's destiny to be the patriarch of the twelve tribes of Israel. She knows in her prophetic vision that she will give birth to six of these sons and take care of two more. Her revelation of these twelve tribes makes her face glow with a "Divine glare." As Moses veiled his face when speaking to the people of Israel after his encounter with the Divine on Mount Sinai,[38] similarly Leah must veil her face. She covers her head while under the marriage canopy in order to hide both the aura of the prophetess that surrounds her and the brightness of the *Shechinah* (feminine emanation of the Divine), which shines forth from her face.

As I shall demonstrate in this chapter, both the Toronto Partnership Minyan and Congregation Shir Libeynu offer women the opportunity to unveil Leah and to assert her true, multifaceted identity through their eyes and their experience. They do so in an unaffiliated synagogue milieu that is not confined to denominational edicts and that allows for a broader, freer scope of interpretation and ritual participation.

In order to discuss the ritual participation by women in these two worship settings, it is important to explicate four different yet related methodologies within my analysis. First, from a feminist religious studies perspective, I shall employ what Ursula King describes as a gynocritical approach, a process in which "women scholars analyze and interpret religious phenomena specifically associated, experienced, articulated and described by women." My concerns are to see "women as *writers*, that is women as their own agents [creating] their own structures of meaning."[39] In this regard, I shall be implementing King's methodological paradigm in which I admit to a reflexive and openly subjective position of inquiry. Within this paradigm, I am acknowledging Sandra Harding's standpoint theory that "the subject-agent of feminist knowledge is multiple, heterogeneous and frequently contradictory in a way that mirrors the situation of women."[40]

Second, related to the above feminist subjective position of inquiry, I am drawing upon the ethno-hermeneutical approach of participant-observer. Ethno-hermeneutics is a postmodern hermeneutic that "overcomes the oppositional poles of positivist and hermeneutic inquiry by locating and making explicit the perspectives of both researcher and subject of inquiry in the production and the presentation of knowledge."[41] My unique role as the ritual leader of and participant in worship services at Congregation Shir Libeynu, and my upbringing in a Modern Orthodox home, which allows me to evaluate and discuss the worship service of the Toronto Partnership Minyan, position me as both an insider and outsider. Thus, I am combining two perspectives that Armin W. Geertz describes as "[1] the reflection of the student of religion and [2] the reflection of the indigenous student of religion. Two hermeneutical endeavours brought together, but located in personal, social and historical contexts."[42] In employing a participant-observer approach, I acknowledge what Barbara Tedlock describes as the observation of participation. In this modified participant-observation, the participant reflects on and critically engages with her own participation within the ethnographic frame.[43] As Tedlock explains, "the philosophical underpinnings of this discourse lie in the domains of critical, feminist, poststructuralist and postmodern theories, with their comparative, interruptive, non-universalistic modes of analysis."[44] Consequently, I am locating my subjective position in the worship services I shall be discussing. Nonetheless, I am asserting that it is possible to situate these observations in both the personal and participatory through reflection and critical engagement.

Third, in relating my observations of both worship groups, I shall be noting the theoretical work of two major ritual experts, Tom F. Driver and Leslie Northup. Though I shall discuss in greater detail these theorists later on in this chapter, the following is a brief summary of their respective perspectives. Driver's discussion of one of the modes of ritual performance—the self-revelatory or confessional—is most relevant when examining women ritualizing. Similarly, Northup's definitions of women's ritualizing and what she describes as emerging patterns in women's ritualizing categories are important when analyzing women in worship.

Finally, in my discussion of the participation of women in both worship groups, I am referring to two of the four categories of feminist theology that Johanna Stuckey articulates in *Feminist Spirituality: an Introduction to Feminist Theology in Judaism, Christianity, Islam, and Feminist Goddess Worship*. These categories or classifications of feminist theological concerns are revisionist and revolutionary.

Congregation Shir Libeynu—Participant-Observation

CONGREGATION SHIR LIBEYNU (SONG OF OUR HEARTS) is an unaffiliated, inclusive, and liberal non-Halachic synagogue in downtown Toronto. It has been in existence for sixteen years, initially holding only High Holy Day services.[45] Four years after its founding, it expanded its mandate and began to include other types of worship services during the course of the year: the occasional Sabbath day service and Friday night service and some festival services. Attendance at the High Holy Day services has grown from about seventy participants to over 320 in September 2012.[46] Its mission is as follows:

We are a liberal, egalitarian, and participatory congregation, unaffiliated with any particular stream of Judaism. Our goals are to joyfully celebrate and experience all aspects of Jewish life spiritually within an environment of inclusiveness, innovation and intellectual challenge. We welcome new rituals and liturgy whilst recognizing and affirming the many paths our tradition offers.[47]

Approximately six years ago, Congregation Shir Libeynu entered into a partnership with the Miles Nadal Jewish Community Centre (MNJCC) and conducts Sabbath services once a month in its Michael Bernstein chapel. This chapel holds approximately seventy-five people and is at capacity for most of these monthly Sabbath services. It is quite a beautiful setting with one wall of stained glass windows, and comfortable seats arranged around the Torah stand and facing the Torah ark. This is the traditional custom in Jewish prayer settings; to face east is to face in the direction of Jerusalem. Although the ark is shared with the Paul Penna downtown day school, which is housed in the MNJCC, the Torah belongs to the congregation and both the Torah mantel and the Torah pointer have been donated by members.[48]

A typical Sabbath morning service runs for about an hour and a half. I facilitate the majority of these Sabbath services, while others are led by members of the congregation. The congregation does not have a rabbi. *Chazzanut*, or cantorial duties, are shared by both men and women. Both men and women chant the Torah portion and equally share all *aliyot* (the recitations of the blessings before and after a section of the Torah scroll is read). It should be noted here that participation in all ritual areas is inclusive of the LGBTQ community.

Congregation Shir Libeynu follows the rabbinic dictate: "better a little supplication with kavanah, than much without it."[49] Rather than reciting all of the prayers for the Sabbath morning, the importance is the *kavanah* (intention) while reciting the prayers. As Henry Glazer points out, "because prayer is an almost internal act, the intentionality, the thought or feeling levels accompanying the recital of words are vital to the prayerful experience."[50] The individual who is leading the service selects prayers from the prayer book, *Siddur Eit Ratzon*. Joseph G. Rosenstein, the author of the English translations, commentaries, and meditations in this prayer book, describes it as a "traditional prayerbook [sic] designed for those who seek spirituality and meaning beyond what they have found in conventional prayerbooks [sic]."[51] *Siddur Eit Ratzon* also provides a line-by-line transliteration of the entire Hebrew text. This is important to members of Congregation Shir Libeynu as many are not fluent in reading Hebrew. Relevant also to the feminist perspective of this congregation is that all of the translations of the Hebrew prayers are non-sexist. As Rosenstein points out, the prayer book "refers to God using contemporary English terms that are relevant to our experience, and addresses God primarily in the second person, so that the prayers are more personal as well as gender-neutral."[52] Additionally, Rosenstein has added the names of the matriarchs in the *Amidah* (Standing) prayer while traditional prayer books list only the patriarchs.

At each Sabbath service, there is a two- to four-page handout that includes English prose, alternative translations of prayers and poetry. Many of these readings differ from month to month and most are read aloud by volunteers during the course of the service. These handouts also contain various contemporary chants in Hebrew and English and some songs not found in the prayer book. Again, in keeping with the participatory nature of the congregation, members of the congregation often submit readings they feel may be appropriate for the service handouts. Depending on the Sabbath, the readings in these handouts reflect specific themes such as pride in the June service, Passover in the spring service, and Holocaust remembrance in November when the Toronto Jewish community holds a Holocaust education week during which synagogues, churches, and community agencies host speakers, films, special performances, and exhibits.

When the Sabbath falls during or just before the week-long celebration of Passover, for example, the handout may include "Miriam's Song," composed and written by the late contemporary liturgist and song writer Debby Friedman. This song celebrates the liberating actions of Miriam as recounted in the book of Exodus. The final verse and refrain is as follows:

> And the women dancing with their timbrels followed Miriam as she sang her song. Sing a song to the One whom we've exalted. Miriam and the women danced and danced the whole night long.... And Miriam the prophet took her timbrel in her hand, and all the women followed her

just as she had planned. And Miriam raised her voice in song. She sang with praise and might, "We've just lived through a miracle: We're going to dance tonight!"[53]

Another liturgical innovation includes repeating chants for the purposes of contemplation. One such a chant uses the words from Psalm 65, "*L'cha dumiya tehilla*, For You silence is praise," which is repeatedly sung in both Hebrew and English before the full reciting of the *Amidah* (standing) prayer. Often, the repetition of this chant precedes a silent meditation, which replaces the actual reciting of the full *Amidah* prayer.

Depending on the service, members of the congregation who play instruments often accompany specific songs or chants with drums, guitar, and flute. It is obvious by the exuberant participation of congregants in the singing and chanting that they are involved with and find meaning in this manner of worship. Similarly, the silence and focus of members during the contemplative aspects of the service demonstrates their appreciation of this alternative form of Jewish prayer.

As noted above, *aliyot* are recited by either men or women, or there may be group *aliyot* that reflects a particular theme from the Torah section that has been read. For example, if the Torah portion is the Genesis narrative regarding the conflict between the brothers Esau and Jacob and their eventual reconciliation, congregants are asked to come up to the Torah for an *aliyah* when asked to consider their own sibling rivalries and their desire for resolution. Similarly there are group *aliyot* for healing, be it emotional, spiritual, or physical. Again, depending on who is leading the service, congregants may also be asked, just before this healing *aliyah*, to silently think of the name or publically say the name of an individual in their lives who is in need of healing. After this *aliyah*, the congregation sings the following alternative healing blessing or *Misheberach*:

> *Misheberach avotaynu m'kor habracha l'imoteinu.* May the source of strength who blessed the ones before us; Help us find the courage to make our lives a blessing, and let us say Amen. *Mi sheberach imotainu, m'kor habracha l'avoteinu.* Bless those in need of healing with *refuah shelayma*, the renewal of body, the renewal of spirit and let us say Amen.[54]

In accordance with the tradition, the leaders of the service wear prayer shawls and skull caps. Of the seventy or so congregants who attend services on a typical Sabbath, about half wear prayer shawls and skull caps. Of these, many are women. However, no one is forced to either cover their heads or wear a tallit (prayer shawl) at any time during the service. In general the dress code is casual. Some women wear slacks and it is rare for men to wear suits.

Often the leader of the service presents a *dvar* torah or speech commenting on the Torah portion being read that day. Sometimes this speech is a dialogic one, in which the person presents some points about the section and asks the congregants to share their own ideas on a point or theme. At other times, a member of the congregation gives a speech centring on an important event in her or his life, such as the anniversary of the death of a loved one.

Although children of all ages are welcome in the service, child care is provided with arts and crafts activities and storytelling, often related to an upcoming Jewish holy day. At most services when children are present, they are invited to come into the sanctuary at the end of the service to join in front of the congregation and say the blessing over the wine and challah.

Immediately after the service there is a communal kiddush, a reception for congregants where food and drinks are served in a large room down the hall from the sanctuary. Volunteers as well as paid staff set up the kiddush meal, which is often sponsored and paid for by a member of the community who may be celebrating an event in her or his life. Tables and chairs are arranged around the room and people sit in groups eating and talking, often for more than an hour after the actual service is over.

In concluding this participant-observation description of Congregation Shir Libeynu's Sabbath services, I must reiterate my own subjective stance. Not only am I one of the founders of the synagogue, I am also the ritual leader. Although there is a board of directors, many of the decisions regarding liturgy and ritual are mine. As can be seen by the description above, leadership is often shared and though those leading the services may use the same elements of the service as I do, they are autonomous as to what they add or remove from the service.

As well, during the course of the year, I speak with members of the congregation both formally and informally to receive feedback on the services. At the annual congregation's day- long retreat, congregants' and board members' suggestions, critiques, and reflections are discussed, weighed, and acted upon.

Analysis

The wearing of prayer shawls and skullcaps, the shared egalitarian leadership and shared egalitarian rituals such as the *aliyot*, and the use of non-gendered prayers all demonstrate what Stuckey would call the revisionist category of feminist theology. According to Stuckey, revisionists centre their perspective on what they understand as correct interpretations of biblical and rabbinic texts, arguing that this will reveal "the liberating message at the core of the tradition."[55] As will be noted, this perspective is also central to women within the Toronto Partnership Minyan. However, it is most closely linked to women of Congregation Shir Libeynu.

Additionally it should be noted that the liturgical additions of alternative songs and prayers that focus on feminine heroes and narratives in the Bible represent a theology that reflects Stuckey's revolutionary category. The position of those who hold revolutionary attitudes is one that advocates "pushing a tradition to its limits."[56]

These innovations, including the use of chanting and drumming, are elements of what Northup describes as the ritual action of women. As she points out, "chanting promotes solidarity and a sense of community, [and has] a powerful austerity that enhances spirituality, and can be performed with little training or practice."[57] Another aspect of the liturgy, which Northup considers an element in women's ritualizing, is the healing *aliyah*. As Northup states, "women's healing rituals easily cross the boundaries between pagan, Jewish, Christian, and Asian women's groups."[58] She notes that "the age-old expertise of women as healers, midwives, nurses, and herbalists is claimed or reclaimed in many women's rituals." She further states that women are not only bringing back ancient healing practices but inventing new ones.[59]

The sense of community is also present in the healing *aliyah*. These rituals, as well as the ability of congregants to share their stories when giving sermons and when discussing their personal reflections on the Torah narratives, reflect what Driver calls the confessional mode of ritual performance. "Confession," as Driver notes, "denotes disclosure of identity." He suggests that the confessional mode bridges the gap between institutional and personal religion. As he states, "the confession finds, or perhaps makes, its community, so that the situation of the individual comes to be seen as something the community shares and the community is legitimated as the necessary complement of the individual."[60]

Northup suggests that reflexivity is a ritual action specific to women. She asserts that reflection on the rituals being performed is part of an "egalitarian approach to the process of ritual creation."[61] I would concur and add that this element is integral to the structure of Congregation Shir Libeynu.

Finally, it is imperative to realize that the participants at Sabbath services at Congregation Shir Libeynu come from all denominations of Judaism. Many, like me, have Orthodox upbringings. Several come from Conservative backgrounds. Others who have joined the congregation were Reform or in some cases secular Jews. What is important to note, however, is that the worship services at Congregation Shir Libeynu give voice to manifold theological perspectives. As its mission statement attests, the synagogue welcomes new rituals and liturgy while recognizing and affirming the many paths the tradition offers. Its unaffiliated structure allows for no denominational restrictions in the area of liturgy, ritual, and women's full and equal participation in all areas of leadership, worship, and decision making.

Toronto Partnership Minyan—Participant-Observation

THE TORONTO PARTNERSHIP MINYAN held its first service in November 2008. Its mission statement declares the following:

> Our community strives to set in motion a shift towards greater spirituality and openness, within the confines of halachah, in the modern Orthodox/observant Jewish community in the Greater Toronto Area, through participatory prayer, study and other aspects of communal religious life. Our community follows the approach of those Orthodox rabbis who have argued that the dignity of human beings (kevod ha-beriyot) is a crucial

halachic value that permits us, and in fact obligates us, to expand the roles of women, particularly in the area of Torah reading and aliyot.[62]

The group meets twice a month at two different locations: the Reena Centre, which is located in Thornhill, a suburban neighbourhood in the northern part of the Greater Toronto Area, and at Beit Habonim in Toronto. The Toronto Partnership Minyan has two different locations because many, if not all, of the members are Orthodox and do not drive on the Sabbath. Therefore, they need to have services within walking distance of their homes. As Toronto's Jewish community spans a large area from mid-town Toronto to the suburbs, two different sites are necessary. Although the service is lay-led, Rabbi Dr. Martin Lockshin serves as the Halachic adviser and rabbi for the community. As of this writing, the group, which is unaffiliated, has not held High Holy Day services. In fact, of those who attend services, most belong to an Orthodox or Conservative congregation in Toronto where services are more frequent.[63]

I attended a Sabbath service at the Beit Habonim site in March 2013. The service began around 9:30 a.m. and continued for about two and a half hours. The room was set up with chairs facing the east. There were about seventy people. The congregation was evenly divided between men and women. Several quite small children were milling about and sitting on the floor at the back of the room with their parents. The room was quite large and utilitarian with a curtain running the width of the room. This floor-to-ceiling curtain divided the area where worship took place from the area where food was served for the after-service kiddush. In the centre of the worship space there was a low *mechitza* (partition), separating the men and women. The *mechitza* was about waist high and made of a white curtain. At approximately the centre of this partition, there was a table on which stood a small wooden ark holding the Torah. In front of the first row of chairs, there was a space where the *mechitza* ended and this is where those leading the prayers stood.

When I entered the room, the service had just begun. A woman wearing a prayer shawl and a hat was standing at the front of the room in the centre where there was no partition. She was leading the *chazzanut* for the morning blessings. About one half hour or so into the service, a man took over the singing of the prayers. The same woman who began the services also led the Torah service.

The Toronto Partnership Minyan uses the Modern Orthodox *Koren-Sacks* prayer book, which has the order of the service in Hebrew with an English translation and various commentaries on the prayers. All the prayers, however, were sung in Hebrew. The only prayers read in English took place at the end of the service and were the Prayer for Israel and the Prayer for the Welfare of the Government. It was obvious that the members of the congregation were able to follow the service in Hebrew and all joined exuberantly in the singing. The atmosphere of the service was relaxed and welcoming.

In fact, when I first sat down, I was approached by a woman who welcomed me and asked me if I would like to come up to the Torah for an *aliyah*. It is the custom to give a newcomer this honour. When I said that I would do so, she handed me a small piece of paper on which the *aliyah* prayers were written in Hebrew with an English transliteration. The paper also noted the number of my *aliyah*. When I was called up for the fifth of the seven *aliyot*, I was asked my Hebrew names and the Hebrew names of my parents and was called formally for this *aliyah* by this nomenclature.

The reading of the Torah was shared by both men and women, as were the *aliyot*. A woman also had the role of the *gabbai*, the person who calls people up for an *aliyah* and blesses them afterwards. When the Torah processional took place, a woman carried it first around the women's section and then handed it over the partition to a man, who carried it around the men's section. There was also a young woman who chanted the *Haftorah* (the selection from the Prophets that thematically connects to the Torah portion) after the Torah reading.

Only the women leading sections from the service wore prayer shawls. Most of the men wore prayer shawls and all wore skull caps. Many of the women wore hats or some form of head covering, though not skull caps. The dress code appeared rather formal as most of the men wore suits and all the women wore dresses or skirts.

As their rabbinic adviser, Rabbi Dr. Lockshin was present for this service and was giving a class a little later that afternoon; he gave a short speech concerning the upcoming Passover holy days. I was told that at other services, male or female members deliver the sermons on a variety of topics concerning either the portion of the Torah that is read or an upcoming festival.

At the conclusion of the service, people shared a small kiddush and mingled. As noted earlier, the atmosphere was very open and friendly. Several individuals introduced themselves to me, asked me how I had heard about the Toronto Partnership Minyan, and invited me to come back and attend services more often.

In concluding this participant-observation description of the Toronto Partnership Minyan's Sabbath services, I should note that I attended only one of their bimonthly services. Additionally, the methodology I used does not include formal interviews. However, it is my contention that this discussion, though partial and somewhat speculative, provides a contrast to the style of worship for women as seen in Congregation Shir Libeynu. As well, as will be noted in the following analysis, it does suggest that women have power in the worship at the Toronto Partnership Minyan.

Analysis

The limitations put on women's participation in the Toronto Partnership Minyan follow the Halachic guidelines that Elitzur A. and Michal Bar-Asher Siegal delineate in their *Guide for the Halachic Minyan*.[64] Essentially, decisions of what men and women can do are based on the premise that where there is no Halachic obligation for men, women are allowed to lead. In practice, therefore, the *barchu* (the call to worship), *shacharit* (the morning service that includes the *Amidah*), and *musaf* (the additional service for the Sabbath) are all led by men. As noted, women do read from the Torah and have *aliyot*. Both men and women serve as the *gabbai* and both women and men read the Sabbath *Haftorah* selection. The Toronto Partnership Minyan neither calls itself nor understands itself as egalitarian. As Rabbi Dr. Lockshin stated in an interview, "our goal is not to make Orthodoxy egalitarian, but it can take steps to make women and men have a partnership feeling by having services where some roles are played by men and others by women."[65] In light of these restrictions, the service fits Stuckey's revisionist category.

The non-hierarchical, lay-led aspects of the service can be considered a characteristic of women's ritual practice. As Northup suggests, the lack of emphasis on formal leadership is a way that "consciously seeks to avoid distinctly hierarchical styles of worship."[66] Additionally, the calling up of men and women for an *aliyah* using their names and the names of both their mothers and fathers (Orthodox synagogues use only the father's name in this ritual) is an example of what she calls reverencing our ancestors. This is an element of women's rituals in which the narrative emphasizes honouring and remembering female ancestors.[67] As Northup explains, there is a "common understanding that women must remember their own heroes, leaders and prophets [and deceased family members] or they will be forgotten by history and that this process must be ritualized." She notes that "the image of the past re-enlivened through the process of active memory is common in women's ritualizing."[68]

The fact that Orthodox women play an important role in leadership can also be said to be an element of the confessional and ethical mode of ritual performance. One woman told me that the Toronto Partnership Minyan serves her spiritual needs much more effectively than would a traditional Orthodox synagogue where she would have to watch men lead services. She continued by saying that it was important to her that her son and daughters see women having an active role in the service, one that approaches men's level of participation.[69]

Having attended an Orthodox synagogue well into my teens, I can attest to the reality of her words. The Toronto Partnership Minyan service resonated with me, bringing back positive memories of my childhood and of sitting in the men's section of the sanctuary with my father when I was a little girl. However, as I grew into a young adult, I too became uncomfortable sitting in the women's section watching the men but being unable to participate fully. Despite the fact that as an adult I have chosen to move away from Orthodox practice, I could not help but be moved by seeing and being a participant in an Orthodox service where women took on so many leadership roles. For me personally, the above reflects what Driver describes as ritual performance in which "members of human communities make known to each other, as best they can, the often veiled truths of their existence."[70]

Liturgically, the choice of the *Koren-Sacks* prayer book is an important one. In 2009, JOFA officially endorsed this prayer book. The Alliance felt that it presented a more modern rather than "ultra" Orthodox nature.[71] The prayer book includes prayers for the birth of a daughter, and for women to recite upon returning to synagogue after giving birth. Some of the prayers following the rules of Hebrew grammar note the correct feminine verb form that would be appropriate to be used by a woman, alongside the correct masculine verb form to be used by men. These quite minor changes and additions are not found in the *Artscroll* prayer book, which most Toronto Orthodox synagogues have been using for more than a decade.

Although this prayer book is more progressive than other Orthodox prayer books, in informal conversations with several of the women who were at the service, I learned that some have difficulties with aspects of the liturgy. This is particularly so in the morning blessings where a verse read by men states that they are thankful they were not made a woman. Many Orthodox rabbis state that these words are meant to emphasize a man's gratitude for being able to partake in all ritual obligations as opposed to the lesser ritual responsibilities of women. They emphasize that the prayer is not meant to denigrate women. Nonetheless, having it in the prayer book is offensive to some women and to some progressive men.

Finally, as noted in the opening section of this chapter, the Toronto Partnership Minyan truly follows the approach of Orthodox rabbis who understand the expansion of women's roles in the synagogue to be a matter of *kevod haberiyot* (the dignity of human beings). Orthodox Rabbi Sperber asserts that to not allow women greater participation in the synagogue service causes women hardship. As he has written, "the absence of such a change will be a source of pain and suffering to an important segment of the community [women]."[72]

It is difficult to predict the direction that Toronto's affiliated Conservative and Orthodox synagogues will take in the future. It would appear that as of this writing, these synagogues are not only enclavist but entrenched in their conservative approach to women's worship. Though Congregation Shir Libeynu is quite radical in its approach to liturgical change, and in its egalitarianism in all aspects of synagogue worship in comparison to the Modern Orthodox Toronto Partnership Minyan, both unaffiliated groups allow and encourage women's leadership in worship settings. It may be that in the future, Jewish women and men will choose to create their own unaffiliated places of worship and not be confined or limited by the oligarchic control of the establishment Orthodox and Conservative institutions. ●

Notes

My gratitude goes to Rabbi Dr. Martin Lockshin and to Dr. Tziporah Cohen, both of whom patiently answered my many queries about the Toronto Partnership Minyan. My thanks go as well to the members of Congregation Shir Libeynu who continue to help me grow as a human being and as a Jew, and to the Toronto Partnership Minyan for their courageous and welcoming spirit.

1. Pamela S. Nadell, "Women and American Judaism," in *Women and Judaism: New Insights and Scholarship*, ed. Frederick E. Greenspan (New York: New York University Press, 2009), 166.

2. Ibid. In 2013, eight of the nine graduates of the Reconstructionist Rabbinical Seminary were women; fifteen out of thirty-one graduates of Hebrew Union Colleges (in Los Angeles, New York, and Cincinnati), the Reform movement's rabbinic seminary, were women; and twenty men and women (I do not have the breakdown of these graduates according to gender) were ordained by the Conservative movement's Jewish Theological Seminary. See Gerhard Falk, "Female Rabbis, *Jewish Buffalo on the Web*, jbuff.com/c090607.htm.

3. Pamela S. Nadell, *Women and Judaism: New Insights and Scholarship*, ed. Frederick E. Greenspan (New York: New York University Press, 2009), 169.

4. Tamar Ross, *Expanding the Palace of Torah: Orthodoxy and Feminism* (Lebanon, NH: Brandeis University Press, 2004), 230.

5. "Who We Are," *JOFA: Jewish Orthodox Feminist Alliance*, http://www.jofa.org/Who _We_Are/about.

6. Daniel Sperber, "On Sensitivity and Compassion in *Pesak Halakha*," *Jewish Orthodox Feminist Alliance Journal* 5, no. 2 (2004): 2.

7. Ross, *Expanding the Palace*, 242.

8. *Yeshivat Maharat*, http://yeshivatmaharat.org.

9. Linda Zlatkin, "Orthodox Women Charting New Course at Montreal Shul," *Jewish Tribune*, May 14, 2013, http://www.jewishtribune.ca/.../orthodox-woman-charting -new course-at-montreal-shul.

10. Chabad actually stands for Chabad-Lubavitch. As their main website states: "Chabad-Lubavitch is a major movement within mainstream Jewish tradition with its roots in the Chassidic movement of the eighteenth century. Chabad is an 'Orthodox' Jewish movement because it adheres to Jewish practice and observance within the guidelines of Talmudic law and its codifiers." See Cabad.org. Sephardic Jews (Sephardim) include Jews who come from North Africa, Iraq, Syria, Greece, Turkey, and the Iberian Peninsula in general. As Jeff Malka notes, Sephardic Jewry is not divided into the religious denominations of those who are descended from eastern European Jewry. Rather, Sephardim are largely homogeneous in and "more traditionally religious in what for lack of a better term is called Orthodox." Jeff Malka, www.jewishgen.org/Sephardic/SEPH_who.HTM.

11. John L. Esposito, *World Religions Today* (Don Mills, ON: Oxford University Press, 2006), 98.

12. Alan F. Segal, "Jewish Traditions," in *A Concise Introduction to World Religions*, 2nd ed., ed. Willard G. Oxtoby and Alan F. Segal (Don Mills, ON: Oxford University Press, 2012), 123.

13. Shlomo Kapustin, "Conservative Shuls Run Gamut from Egalitarian to Traditional in GTA," *Jewish Tribune*, March 20, 2012, http://www.jewish tribune.ca/features/2012/03/20/conservative-shuls-run-gamut-from-egalitarianism-to-traditional-in-gta.

14. Ibid.

15. Ibid.

16. *Canadian Yeshiva and Rabbinical School*. http://www.cdnyeshiva.org.

17. Samuel C. Heilman, *Sliding to the Right: The Contest for the Future of American Jewish Orthodoxy* (Berkeley: University of California Press, 2006), 19.

18. Ibid., 3.

19. Cited in ibid., 19.

20. Ibid., 4.

21. Heilman, *Sliding to the Right*, 13.

22. Ibid.

23. It is, of course, impossible in this chapter to discuss all aspects of Orthodox practice in Canada. Although there is no doubt that Toronto's Orthodox community fits the description I have given, this appears different in Montreal. In June 2013, the unaffiliated Modern Orthodox Congregation Shaar Hashomayim of Montreal hired Rachel Kohl Finegold, one of the first women graduates of the Modern

Orthodox seminary, Yeshivat Maharat. Finegold is the "first woman to be hired as a member of the clergy" in any Modern Orthodox synagogue in Canada. Zlatkin, "Orthodox Women," Jewish Tribune, May 14, 2013, http://www.jewishtribune.ca/religion/2013/05/14/orthodox-woman-charting-new-course-at-montreal-shul.

24. When my father, an Orthodox Jew, passed away over twenty years ago, it was understood by the funeral home that we wished mixed seating. Almost twenty years later, when my mother-in-law, an Orthodox Jew, passed away, another Jewish funeral home, to our surprise, presumed that we wanted separate seating as she was Orthodox. Without notifying us, they directed men and women to separate sides of the chapel for the service. In retrospect, this was quite ironic as we not only had women speak at her funeral but her granddaughter sang, neither of which would normally occur in an Orthodox Jewish funeral in Toronto today.

25. Tamara Cohn Eskenazi and Andrea L. Wiess, eds., *The Torah: A Women's Commentary* (New York: URJ Press, 2008), 177.

26. A. Cohen, *The Soncino Chumash* (London: Soncino Press, 1956), 172.

27. Ibid.

28. I have not only heard several rabbis refer to this biblical narrative when explaining the *badeken* at weddings, but also have seen it noted in one Internet source concerning customs for Jewish weddings. *Jewish Federations,* www.jewishfederations.org.

29. *Encyclopaedia Judaica,* "Badeken" (Jerusalem: Keter Publishing House, 1972), http://go.galegroup.com/ps/retrieve.do?sgHitCountType=None&sort=RELEVANCE&inPS=true&prodId=GVRL&userGroupName=imcpl1111&tabID=T003&searchId=R1&resultListType=RESULT_LIST&contentSegment=&searchType=BasicSearchForm&currentPosition=1&contentSet=GALE%7CCX2587513338&&docId=GALE|CX2587513338&docType=GALE.

30. Shemu'el Pinhas Gelbard, *Rite and Reason: 1050 Jewish Customs and Their Sources* (Jerusalem: Feldheim Publishers, 1998), 618.

31. Ibid.

32. Solomon Ganzfried, *Code of Jewish Law,* trans. Goldin Hyman (New York: Hebrew Publishing Company, 1961), 4:6.

33. Isaac Klein, *A Guide to Jewish Religious Practice* (New York: Ktav Publishing, 1979), 401.

34. Leila Leah Bronner, *From Eve to Esther: Rabbinic Reconstructions of Biblical Women* (Louisville, KY: Westminster John Knox Press, 1994), xiv.

35. Ibid.

36. Nicholas de Lange, *An Introduction to Judaism* (Cambridge: Cambridge University Press, 2000), 50.

37. Gerald L. Bruns, "Midras and Allegory: The Beginning of Scriptural Interpretation," in *The Literary Guide to the Bible*, ed. Robert Alter and Frank Kermode (Cambridge, MA: Harvard University Press, 1987), 633.

38. This is one of the explanations that rabbis give for the veiling of the bride under the *chuppah*. As Rabbi Aron Moss notes, "when the bride and groom stand under the *chuppah*, they are in an elevated state, as they are about to unite as one. In the bride, this elevated state is more revealed. She radiates a special holiness; the Divine Presence (Shechinah), the feminine aspect of G-d, shines through the face of the bride. This light is so intense that it must be veiled, just as the light emanating from Moses' face had to be covered," http://www.chabad.org/library/article_cdo/aid/267679/jewish/Why-Does-a-Bride-Wear-a-Veil.htm/mobile/false.

39. Ursula King, "Gender and the Study of the Religion," in *Religion and Gender*, ed. Ursula King (Oxford: Blackwell Publishers, 1995), 19.

40. Sandra Harding, "Rethinking Standpoint Epistemology: What Is Strong Objectivity?" in *Feminist Epistemologies*, ed. Linda Alcoff and Elizabeth Potter (New York: Routledge, 1993), 59.

41. Bonnie Glass-Coffin, "The Meaning of Experience: Theoretical Dilemmas in Depicting a Peruvian *Curandera's* Philosophy of Healing," in *Perspectives on Method and Theory in the Study of Religion: Adjunct Proceedings, International Association for the Study of Religions Congress*, ed. Armin W. Geertz and Russell T. McCutcheon (Leiden and Boston: E. J. Brill, 2000), 227.

42. Armin W. Geertz, "Global Perspectives on Methodology in the Study of Religion," in *Perspectives on Method and Theory in the Study of Religion: Adjunct Proceedings, International Association for the Study of Religions Congress*, ed. Armin W. Geertz and Russell T. McCutcheon (Leiden and Boston: E. J. Brill, 2000), 71.

43. Barbara Tedlock, "From Participant Observation to the Observation of Participation: Emergence of Narrative Ethnography," *Journal of Anthropological Research* 47, no. 1 (1991): 69.

44. Barbara Tedlock, "The Observation of Participation and the Emergence of Public Ethnography," in *Strategies of Qualitative Inquiry*, ed. Norman K. Denzin and Yvonna S. Lincoln (Thousand Oaks, CA: Sage Publications, 1998), 151.

45. For a detailed discussion of the rituals for High Holy Day services at Congregation Shir Libeynu, see Aviva Goldberg, "Re-Awakening Deborah: Locating the

Feminist in the Liturgy, Ritual and Theology of Contemporary Jewish Renewal" (PhD dissertation, York University, 2002).

46. After the first service, which was held in an auditorium of the Ontario Institute of Studies in Education, services were moved to the Cecil Street Community Centre. As attendance increased, it was necessary in 2009 to again move the High Holy Day services to a larger venue, the First Unitarian Congregation's building in midtown Toronto, where the congregation continues to hold High Holy Day services.

47. Congregation Shir Libeynu, *High Holy Day Supplement 2001–5762*. Personal papers and publicity promotions re. congregation Shir Libeynu.

48. In keeping with the participatory nature of Congregation Shir Libeynu, the ark that the congregation uses for the High Holy Days was made by a member of the congregation, as was the stand on which the Torah lies when it is read on the High Holy Days.

49. Henry Glazer, *I Thank Therefore I Am: Gateways to Gratefulness* (Dartford, UK: Xlibris Corporation, 2012), 105.

50. Ibid.

51. Joseph G. Rosenstein, *Siddur Eit Ratzon* (Highland Park, NJ: Shiviti Publications, 2003), ii.

52. Ibid.

53. Debby Friedman, "Miriam's Song," *Debbie Friedman at Carnegie Hall*, audiovisual media (San Diego: Sounds Write Productions, 1996).

54. Debby Friedman, "Mi Shebeirach," *Renewal of Spirit*, audiovisual media (San Diego: Sounds Write Productions, 1995).

55. Johanna H. Stuckey, *Feminist Spiritually: An Introduction to Feminist Theology in Judaism, Christianity, Islam, and Feminist Goddess Worship* (Toronto: Centre for Feminist Research, York University, 1998), 17.

56. Ibid.

57. Leslie A. Northup, *Ritualizing Women* (Cleveland: Pilgrim Press, 1997), 41.

58. Ibid., 40.

59. Ibid., 39.

60. Tom F. Driver, *Liberating Rites: Understanding the Transformative Power of Ritual* (Boulder, CO: Westview Press, 1998), 118.

61. Northup, *Ritualizing Women*, 18.

62. *Toronto Partnership Minyan*, http://www.torontopartnershipminyan.com.

63. Rabbi Dr. Martin Lockshin, personal conversation with the author, March 2013.

64. Elitzur A. Siegal and Michal Bar-Ashar, *Guide for the Halachic Minyan,* http://upload .kipa.co.il/media-upload/kulech/1214602.PDF.

65. Francis Kraft, "Orthodox Minyan Has Torah Honours for Women," *Canadian Jewish News,* November 6, 2008, http://www.cjnews.com/node/82072.

66. Northup, *Ritualizing Women,* 46.

67. Ibid., 42.

68. Ibid., 35.

69. Dr. Tziporah Cohen, email correspondence with the author, May 2013.

70. Driver, *Liberating Rites,* 119.

71. Rebecca Honig Friedman, "JOFA Endorses Koren-Sacks Siddur," *T. J. C. Newsdesk,* May 19, 2009, newsdesk.tjctv.com/2009/05/jofa-endorses-koren-sacks-siddur.

72. Daniel Sperber, "Congregational Dignity and Human Dignity: Women and Public Torah Reading," *Edah Journal* 3, no. 2 Elul 5763 (2002): 14.

Bibliography

Bronner, Leila Leah. *From Eve to Esther: Rabbinic Reconstructions of Biblical Women.* Louisville, KY: Westminster John Knox Press, 1994.

Bruns, Gerald L. "Midrash and Allegory: The Beginning of Scriptural Interpretation." In *The Literary Guide to the Bible,* edited by Robert Alter and Frank Kermode, 627–33. Cambridge, MA: Harvard University Press, 1987.

Canadian Yeshiva and Rabbinical School. www.cdnyeshiva.org.

Chabad-Lubavitch Media Center. www.chabad.org.

Cohen, A. *The Soncino Chumash.* London: Soncino Press, 1956.

Cohen, Dr. Tziporah. Email correspondence with the author, May 2013.

Congregation Shir Libeynu, *High Holy Day Supplement.*

De Lange, Nicholas. *An Introduction to Judaism.* Cambridge: Cambridge University Press, 2000.

Driver, Tom F. *Liberating Rites: Understanding the Transformative Power of Ritual.* Boulder: Westview Press, 1998.

Encyclopaedia Judaica. Jerusalem: Keter Publishing House, 1972.

Eskenazi, Tamara Cohn, and Andrea L. Wiess, eds. *The Torah: A Women's Commentary.* New York: URJ Press, 2008.

Esposito, John L. *World Religions Today.* Don Mills, ON: Oxford University Press, 2006.

Falk, Gerhard. "Female Rabbis," *Jewish Buffalo on the Web.* jbuff.com/c090607.htm.

Friedman, Debby. "Miriam's Song." *Debbie Friedman at Carnegie Hall.* Audiovisual media. San Diego: Sounds Write Productions, 1996.

——. "Mi Shebeirach" *Renewal of Spirit.* Audiovisual media. San Diego: Sounds Write Productions, 1995.

Friedman, Rebecca Honig. "JOFA endorses Koren-Sacks Siddur." *T. J. C. Newsdesk.* May 19, 2009. newsdesk.tjctv.com/2009/05/jofa-endorses-koren-sacks-siddur.

Ganzfried, Solomon. Code of Jewish Law. Translated by Hyman Goldin. New York: Hebrew Publishing Company, 1961.

Geertz, Armin. "Global Perspectives on Methodology in the Study of Religion." In *Perspectives on Method and Theory in the Study of Religion: Adjunct Proceedings, International Association for the Study of Religions Congress,* edited by Armin W. Geertz and Russell T. McCutcheon, 49–74. Leiden and Boston: E. J. Brill, 2000.

Gelbard, Shemu'el Pinhas. *Rite and Reason: 1050 Jewish Customs and Their Sources.* Jerusalem: Feldheim Publishers, 1998.

Glass-Coffin, Bonnie. "The Meaning of Experience: Theoretical Dilemmas in Depicting a Peruvian *Curandera's* Philosophy of Healing." In *Perspectives on Method and Theory in the Study of Religion: Adjunct proceedings, International Association for the Study of Religions Congress,* edited by Armin W. Geertz and Russell T. McCutcheon, 226–38. Leiden and Boston: E. J. Brill, 2000.

Glazer, Henry. *I Thank Therefore I Am: Gateways to Gratefulness.* Dartford, UK: Xlibris Corporation, 2012.

Goldberg, Aviva. "Re-Awakening Deborah: Locating the Feminist in the Liturgy, Ritual, and Theology of Contemporary Jewish Renewal." PhD dissertation, York University, 2002.

Grimes, Ronald L. *Beginnings in Ritual Studies.* Washington, DC: University Press of America, 1982.

Harding, Sandra. "Rethinking Standpoint Epistemology: What Is Strong Objectivity?" In *Feminist Epistemologies,* edited by Linda Alcoff and Elizabeth Potter, 49–83. New York: Routledge, 1993.

Heilman, Samuel C. *Sliding to the Right: The Contest for the Future of American Jewish Orthodoxy.* Berkeley: University of California Press, 2006.

Kapustin, Shlomo. "Conservative Shuls Run Gamut from Egalitarian to Traditional in GTA." *Jewish Tribune,* March 20, 2012. http://www.jewishtribune.ca/features/2012/03/20/conservative-shuls-run-gamut-from-egalitarianism-to-traditional-in-gta.

King, Ursula. "Gender and the Study of Religion." In *Religion and Gender,* edited by Ursula King, 1–41. Oxford: Blackwell Publishers, 1995.

Klein, Isaac. *A Guide to Jewish Religious Practice.* New York: Ktav Publishing, 1979.

Kraft, Francis. "Orthodox Minyan Has Torah Honours for Women." *Canadian Jewish News,* November 6, 2008. http://www.cjnews.com/node/82072.

Lockshin, Rabbi Dr. Martin. Personal conversation with author, March 2013.

Malka, Jeff. *Who Are the Sephardim?* www.jewishgen.org/Sephardic/SEPH_who.HTM.

Nadell, Pamela S. "Women and American Judaism." In *Women and Judaism: New Insights and Scholarship,* edited by Frederick E. Greenspan, 155–81. New York: New York University Press, 2009.

Northup, Leslie A. *Ritualizing Women.* Cleveland: Pilgrim Press, 1997.

Rosenstein, Joseph G. *Siddur Eit Ratzon.* Highland Park, NJ: Shiviti Publications, 2003.

Ross, Tamar. *Expanding the Palace of Torah: Orthodoxy and Feminism.* Lebanon, NH: Brandeis University Press, 2004.

Segal, Alan F. "Jewish Traditions." In *A Concise Introduction to World Religions,* 2nd ed., edited by Willard G. Oxtoby and Alan F. Segal, 80–140. Don Mills, ON: Oxford University Press, 2012.

Siegal, Elitzur A., and Michal Bar-Asher. *Guide for the Halachic Minyan,* 2011. http://upload.kipa.co.il/media-upload/kulech/1214602.PDF.

Sperber, Daniel. "Congregational Dignity and Human Dignity: Women and Public Torah Reading." *Edah Journal* 3, no. 2 Elul 5763 (2002): 1–14.

——. "On Sensitivity and Compassion in *Pesak Halakha.*" *Jewish Orthodox Feminist Alliance Journal* 5, no. 2 (2004): 1–3.

Stuckey, Johanna H. *Feminist Spirituality: An Introduction to Feminist Theology in Judaism, Christianity, Islam, and Feminist Goddess Worship.* Toronto: Centre for Feminist Research, York University, 1998.

Tedlock, Barbara. "From Participant Observation to the Observation of Participation: The Emergence of Narrative Ethnography." *Journal of Anthropological Research* 47, no. 1 (1991): 69–94.

——. "The Observation of Participation and the Emergence of Public Ethnography." In *Strategies of Qualitative Inquiry,* edited by Norman K. Denzin and Yvonna S. Lincoln, 151–71. Los Angeles: Sage Publications, 1998.

Toronto Partnership Minyan. www.torontopartnershipminyan.com/.

"Who We Are." *JOFA: Jewish Orthodox Feminist Alliance.* http://www.jofa.org/WhoWe Are/About.

Yeshivat Maharat. http://yeshivatmaharat.org.

Zlatkin, Linda. "Orthodox Women Charting New Course at Montreal Shul." *Jewish Tribune,* May 14, 2013. http://www.jewishtribune.ca/religion/2013/05/14/orthodox -woman-charting-new-course-at-montreal-shul.

Part B

New Religions in Canada

5   Charity Chicks

A Discourse-Analysis of Religious
Self-Identification of Rural Canadian
Mormon Women

KATE POWER UNIVERSITY OF BRITISH COLUMBIA

1. Introduction

For much of the twentieth century, the dominant public discourse about religion in Western industrialized societies pitted modernization and religion against each other as "a zero-sum phenomenon."[1] Often touted as a product of the Enlightenment, this perspective asserts that "the sum of modernization and religion is always zero: the more religion, the less modernization; and especially the reverse: the more modernization, the less religion."[2] More recently, the significance of religion has been increasingly recognized by both media and scholarly commentators. Yet, religion itself is still commonly regarded as a "problem" and "a reaction to the modern world," rather than "simply a way of being modern."[3]

Consequently, considerably more attention has been paid to religious violence and fundamentalism than to the everyday practices of religious individuals and groups.[4] Public and scholarly analyses of The Church of Jesus Christ of Latter-Day Saints (hereafter the LDS Church), for example, often highlight the controversial practice of polygamy, which, although maintained by a small number of "shadow fundamentalist churches,"[5] was officially abandoned by the LDS Church in 1890.[6]

The present study is one attempt to redress this imbalanced representation of religion, and the LDS Church in particular, by privileging the voices of Mormon women over those who might talk or write about them. Based on interviews and group discussions conducted in the rural

Canadian town of Claresholm, southern Alberta, it uses membership categorization analysis (MCA) and stance analysis[7] to examine how members of the LDS Church's Relief Society produce a sense of their own religious identities in "talk-in-interaction,"[8] both by talking explicitly about their religious tradition and categorizing themselves in relation to it, and by using, questioning, reinterpreting, even subverting various public discourses, including discourses associated with their own religious tradition. As André Droogers has observed in relation to religious people more generally, Mormon women demonstrably "do not behave in a consistent manner, despite the official, more or less homogeneous and integrated version of their religion, as represented by its religious figureheads."[9] Nor are they merely the "animators" of pre-existing religious discourses. On the contrary, as this chapter illustrates, Mormon women are also active, creative "authors"[10] who craft and convey a sense of their own religious identities by drawing on and combining various religious and other public discourses.[11]

2. LDS Women in Southwestern Alberta

BECAUSE THIS CHAPTER FOCUSES on how Mormon women construct a sense of their own religious identities, I will not attempt here to describe comprehensively either the LDS Church or its Relief Society, rather only to provide sufficient background to contextualize my informants' talk.

The LDS Church was established in the United States by Joseph Smith in 1830, with the Relief Society also being founded by Smith on March 17, 1842, as a women's organization. Its purpose was "not only to relieve the poor, but [also] to save souls."[12] The status of the LDS Church as a Christian denomination has long been a matter of dispute, but the church has grown from its origins as a small, controversial group—opposed by others as much for its endorsement of polygamy as for its unconventional doctrines[13]—into a well-established religion with over fourteen million members internationally.[14] Membership in the Church's Relief Society, which includes all female Saints eighteen years of age and over, as well as any married women and single mothers younger than eighteen years,[15] now stands at "over five and a half million . . . sisters in 170 countries."[16] Yet, the LDS Church is still often considered both socially and doctrinally deviant.[17]

In taking their gospel outside the United States, LDS missionaries went first to Upper Canada (what is now southern Ontario).[18] Mormon immigrants to Canada, however, favoured southwestern Alberta, where the first permanent Canadian LDS community was established in 1887 as a sanctuary for Saints fleeing American opposition to polygamy, and the first LDS stake (an administrative unit resembling a diocese in the Anglican and Catholic churches) outside the United States was founded in 1895.[19] The dedication of the Alberta Temple in Cardston in 1923 also contributed to southern Alberta becoming "a Canadian Mormon core or heartland ... analagous [sic] to Utah for the United States."[20]

Since those times, the largest proportion of Canadian Mormons has lived in Alberta, peaking at 60 percent in 1941,[21] and now just under 50 percent.[22] Consequently, the province, and southwestern Alberta in particular, is widely regarded as "Mormon Country."[23] The first LDS settlers in Alberta met with a mixed reception. On the one hand, Canadian government officials coveted Mormon agricultural experience and industry for the still sparsely settled prairie province. On the other hand, public opinion and most local newspapers strongly opposed Mormon polygamy.[24] More recently, too, hostility toward the LDS Church has been noted in southern Alberta, particularly among disaffected Mormons, religiously active conservative Protestants, and individuals with few or no Mormon acquaintances.[25]

Southern Alberta is a politically and socially conservative area, noted for its American-style populism and public prominence of religious discourse and practice.[26] In terms of their political leanings, "Alberta Mormons are as typically Albertan as are the adherents of any religious group in the province."[27] Socially, Canadian Mormons also resemble their non-Mormon counterparts in several respects. Mormons are employed in professional occupations at approximately the same rate as the general population. LDS women work outside the home at close to the national average, although more often in part-time positions. Mormon educational attainment is considerably above that of the general population, as are both LDS fertility levels (particularly in western Canada) and life expectancy. Mormon women also marry younger, are more likely to be currently divorced or separated, and lone parent at a higher rate than other Canadian women. In western Canada most Mormons are "born into LDS families."[28]

Officially, the LDS Church in Canada is a Canadian church.[29] Yet, the church's Correlation Program (administered from Salt Lake City, Utah), under which the activities and structures of all LDS congregations internationally have been both centralized and standardized,[30] means not only that southern Albertan Mormons are "firmly under the wing of the central church,"[31] but also that their initially female-governed Relief Society now falls under the auspices of the LDS Church's all-male "priesthood."[32]

Several scholars have noted this "erosion in the equality and power of [Mormon] women as far as ecclesiastical policy is concerned,"[33] an erosion that has taken place despite the fact that LDS women are typically the backbone of their church's lay-led wards (i.e., local congregations)[34] and Mormon marriages are more often egalitarian than patriarchal in nature.[35] Scholars have also described both an early form of Mormon feminism (evident during the nineteenth century) and a relatively brief moment of modern LDS feminist critique in the 1970s and 1980s, both of which

> made use of a unique and little-known Mormon doctrine about a female deity or Heavenly Mother, much to the consternation of church authorities, who have been reluctant to see that doctrinal idea developed outside their control or applied to modern issues.[36]

For the most part, however, Mormon women seem hesitant to critique the patriarchal rhetoric of their religious tradition—a woman's place "is in the home"[37] and the feminist movement is "a major threat to the integrity of Mormon institutions"[38]—perhaps because, within LDS organizational culture, "criticism of the prophet is not popular."[39] Within this framework, the Relief Society remains "the official body of Mormon women,"[40] but chiefly involves weekly meetings devoted to worship, doctrinal instruction, and the promotion of homemaking skills.[41]

The study on which this chapter is based involved individual and group interviews with eight members of the Claresholm LDS Relief Society (aged in their mid-thirties to mid-sixties). Home to just over 3,500 people, almost 90 percent of whom are Canadian-born and more than 90 percent

English-only speakers,[42] Claresholm is by no means a model of cultural, racial, or linguistic diversity. It does boast some interesting religious diversity, however, hosting churches representing ten Christian denominations (including Jehovah's Witnesses and the LDS Church), as well as three Hutterite colonies. Unlike some neighbouring towns, Claresholm is not a predominantly Mormon community, but the LDS Church is the largest religious group in town, with approximately four hundred members and an average weekly attendance at worship services of two hundred people. Yet, the LDS Church is excluded from Claresholm's Ministerial Association, under the banner of which Catholic, evangelical, mainline, and charismatic clergy jointly provide spiritual and other services to the town, including the publication of a weekly religion column in the Claresholm *Local Press*.

3. Religious Identity: Self-Categorization and Self-Representation

IDENTITY IS A WORD USED SO FREQUENTLY within scholarly circles today that Mary Bucholtz and Kira Hall maintain "it is no overstatement to assert that the age of identity is upon us, not only in sociocultural linguistics but also in the human and social sciences more generally."[43] Yet, *identity* is also a word that suffers from overuse.[44] Rogers Brubaker and Frederick Cooper observe that "'identity' ... tends to mean too much (when understood in a strong sense), too little (when understood in a weak sense), or nothing at all (because of its sheer ambiguity)."[45] They therefore propose dispensing with the term altogether and replacing it with alternatives such as

1. *identification/categorization*, both of which connote "particular acts ... performed by particular identifiers and categorizers,"[46] and
2. *self-representation/self-identification*, both of which "suggest at least some degree of explicit discursive articulation."[47]

This proposal clearly reflects the emergent scholarly view of identity not as a "pre-discursive construct,"[48] that is, as a pre-existing, unitary, and fixed or essential categorization, but rather as something constructed by individuals who negotiate their own and others' category memberships in diverse contexts via linguistic and other social practices.[49] For Mary Bucholtz, such negotiation involves both positive and negative practices: "'Negative identity practices' are those that individuals employ to distance themselves from a rejected identity, while 'positive identity practices' are those in which individuals engage in order actively to construct a chosen identity."[50] Both positive and negative identity practices potentially include "the social positioning of self and other."[51] Just as positioning can be both "reflexive" and "interactive" without necessarily being "intentional,"[52] so, too, can social (including religious) identity be both a label assigned by individuals to themselves, as well as a label assigned to them by others.[53]

As mentioned earlier, this chapter draws on MCA and stance analysis to show how LDS women construct a sense of their own religious identities via specific discursive acts of (positive and negative) self-categorization (Section 4) and self-representation (Section 5). My analysis therefore begins with a brief overview of MCA.

4. Religious Self-Categorization

MCA IS A CONVERSATION ANALYTIC TOOL that builds on Harvey Sacks's early work in which he examined how people and "social configurations"[54] are categorized in specific contexts.[55] As such, it has been used repeatedly to investigate discursive constructions of identity.[56] In contrast to cognitive approaches to both categorization and social identity,[57] MCA treats category memberships not as the "immutable properties of persons,"[58] but rather as discursive accomplishments.[59] Moreover, it focuses on how "the actual speakers and hearers who are the parties to the talk"[60] in question invoke, orient to, and make sense of social identity categories. In the discussion that follows, I will show how LDS women employ "the resources of membership categorization"[61] to identify themselves as both belonging to (Section 4.1), and not belonging to (Section 4.2) specific religious identity categories. I will also examine how they engage with categorizations assigned to them by others (Section 4.3).

4.1 Belonging

Perhaps the most obvious self-categorization strategy employed by the LDS women who participated in this study was the use of religious membership categories (RMCs) explicitly to identify themselves as members of a specific form of institutional religion, what Lena Jayyusi calls a "self-organized" group with "a proper [name]."[62] In Excerpt 1 below,[63] Olive[64] uses the category "label,"[65] "a member of Relief Society" (lines 1–2), to identify herself with the LDS Church's official women's group. A similarly explicit religious self-categorization is also found in Excerpt 2, where Gail identifies herself, along with other Relief Society members, using a RMC drawn from the "membership categorization device,"[66] *religious job descriptions* ("Visiting Teachers," line 1).

Excerpt 1:	1	Olive	I'm Olive Johnston I've been a member since I was eighteen **a**
	2		**member of Relief Society** um it's pretty much the same story I
	3		although you join Relief Society when you're eighteen **it's**
	4		**something that you grow into yourself** [. . .]

Excerpt 2:	1	Gail	all of us are **Visiting Teachers** and we all have a beat we call
	2		Visiting Beats

Both of these speakers are engaging in person-categorization, which is the primary concern of most MCA work.[67] Yet, Relief Society members also conflate *religious person-* and *religious collectivity*-categorization. In Excerpt 3 below, Wendy's repeated "self-repair"[68] in line 1, replacing "everyone," first with "it" and then "we," effectively categorizes not only the LDS Church as a collectivity of record-keepers, but also herself (and unnamed others) as belonging to that collectivity (*"we*'re a real record keeping church," lines 1–2).

Excerpt 3:	1	Wendy	within the Church **everyone is it we're a real record keeping**
	2		**church** and so there are records that they will send from where
	3		we lived before someone will forward those on so they know
	4		that you're coming and //they know how many of you there are

Excerpt 3 also points to a further strategy with which LDS women identify themselves as belonging to a specific religious group, namely by **depicting their own behaviour and/or attributes**—including "knowledge, belief[s], entitlements, obligations and other characteristics"[69]—**as the "category-bound"[70] "predicates"[71] of a particular group**. In excerpts 4 and 5 below, for example, three LDS informants depict *sameness* as a key feature of both Relief Society and LDS identity ("the exact same outlook," Excerpt 4, line 3; "the same lesson," Excerpt 5, lines 2–3; "the lessons are the same," Excerpt 5, lines 3–4; "the same lesson," Excerpt 5, line 6; see also "the unity," Excerpt 4, line 5; "common goal," Excerpt 4, line 7).

Excerpt 4:	1	Sally	the support is just incredible and to be able to walk into a room
	2		a Relief Society room anywhere in the world and know that
	3		those women in there have the exact same outlook on life that
	4		you do is a real phenomenal feeling really I don't even know
	5		how you can describe it **the unity** that is there and the support
	6		it's just incredible
	7	Wendy	**common goal** that you're all working towards

Excerpt 5:	1	Gail	so if I was to go like we went and traveled in the States this
	2		year so if I went to California **they'd be having the same**
	3		**lesson in California that we would be having here so the**
	4		**lessons are the same** our children's **lessons are the same** and
	5		so when we go home we're able to discuss that now the men
	6		meet in Priesthood and they have **the same lesson** as we have
	7		so that's great so when you're come home for dinner you can
	8		say hey what did you think of the lesson today and so it
	9		stimulates conversation

Similarly, in Excerpt 6 below, both Leisl and Wendy self-identify as being older than eighteen ("that would be about twenty years ago," lines 8–9; "when I was eighteen," line 13), marking that age as the point of entry into Relief Society for females born into the LDS Church ("when you're eighteen they kind of bump you out of there and you get to go with the the women," lines 4–6; "when I was eighteen and I was moved up into Relief

Society," lines 13–14). Strikingly, in both cases, LDS young women are depicted not as actively seeking membership in Relief Society, but rather as passively receiving a religious identity assigned to them by unnamed others (*"they* kind of bump you," lines 4–5; "I *was moved* up," line 13).

Excerpt	1	Leisl	same thing I was **born in the church** my mother was born into
6:	2		the church from it goes back about probably five
	3		generations of members of the church so same thing you go to
	4		youth things and then **when you're eighteen they kind of**
	5		**bump you out of there and you get to go with the**
	6		**women**
	7	All	[laughter]
	8	Leisl	being yeah join them so yeah same thing **that would be about**
	9		**twenty years ago** [laughter]
	10		[. . .]
	11	Wilma	Wilma and same thing I was ah well my mum was a member
	12		of this church my dad wasn't he you know he joined later but
	13		um so **when I was eighteen and I was moved up into Relief**
	14		**Society** but since then I've actually spent more time in the
	15		youth group just because I was called to be a leader with them
	16		so I've probably spent more time in the youth group than in
	17		Relief Society on Sundays but then we have our weekday um
	18	Nola	activities
	19	Wilma	activities for for the women so I go to those

In Excerpt 1 above, by contrast, Olive represents identification with Relief Society as something requiring agency on the part of LDS young women ("it's something that you grow into yourself," lines 3–4). That some LDS young women hesitate to join Relief Society was noted by more than one of my informants. In Excerpt 7 below, both Gail and Olive observe that Relief Society membership is often associated primarily not only with female adulthood, but also with elderliness ("grey-haired older people," line 4) and traditional forms of female domesticity ("crocheting and making casseroles," lines 7–8; "making quilts," line 10).

Excerpt 7:	1	Gail	[. . .] **I think it is hard for sometimes for eighteen-year-old**
	2		**girls to think that it's fun to come at first** and so [laughter]
	3	Olive	well you've kind of watched your **mother** and your
	4		**grandmother** and //**grey-haired older people which I am**
	5		**now**
	6	All	//[laughter]
	7	Olive	at the time you think oh they're just **crocheting and making**
	8		**casseroles**
	9	All	[laughter]
	10	Olive	and **making quilts** and you're not quite there yet but ah there's
	11		other aspects that include you and make you feel part of it

In this excerpt, both Gail and Olive display their own (and others') "common-sense knowledge"[72] about the religious group with which they self-identify, namely, that it is geared more for "mother[s]" and "grandmother[s]" (lines 3–4; see also Olive's "which I am now," lines 4–5) than for "eighteen-year-old girls" (lines 1–2). In doing so, they effectively reproduce and transmit a particular perspective on LDS culture. As Stokoe and Smithson observe, different "people draw upon different versions of common-sense knowledge" when invoking identity categories.[73] Consequently, what the members of one religious group consider a category-bound activity or attribute may differ significantly from the category-bound predicates perceived by members of other religious groups.[74] As the following two excerpts illustrate, this difference is particularly salient when religious behaviour is invoked as a warrant for category membership, that is, as the grounds for establishing particular religious identities.[75]

Excerpt 8:	1	Nola	**we are Christians** and we love to tell people that **we are truly**
	2		**Christians** //He is
	3	Olive	//**well every prayer we pray** //**in the name of Jesus Christ**
	4		you know
	5	Nola	//yes in the name of Jesus Christ and that that is where we're
	6		often misunderstood so definitely **we are Christians**

Excerpt	1	Dave	[. . .] to me it's about Jesus and so I don't have any problems
9:	2		with the Anglicans with the Lutherans with the Catholics with
	3		the ah Pentecostal I mean it goes around I do have a huge
	4		problem with like the Jehovah's Witness or the Mormons
	5		because to me **they're not worshipping the same Jesus that I**
	6		**am**
	7	Kate	although they do talk about Jesus don't they and um present **to**
	8		**be Christian**
	9	Dave	yes **but their theology makes Jesus out to be something**
	10		**different than what I believe He is**

In Excerpt 8 above, Olive offers a description of LDS religious practice ("every prayer we pray in the name of Jesus Christ," line 3) in support of Nola's claim that members of the LDS Church are "truly Christians" (lines 1–2). In Excerpt 9, by contrast, Dave, a non-Mormon religious leader who participated in the larger study from which this chapter is drawn, rejects claims by Mormons (and Jehovah's Witnesses) "to be Christian" (lines 7–8) on the grounds that (1) "they're not worshipping the same Jesus that [Dave is]" (lines 5–6) and (2) "their theology makes Jesus out to be something different than what [Dave] believe[s] He is" (lines 9–10). In other words, both Olive and Dave invite inferences about the religious category membership of Mormons based on LDS worship of Jesus Christ, although they clearly disagree about whether or not that behaviour warrants the categorization "Christian."[76]

Finally, LDS women categorize themselves as belonging to a particular religious group by **likening their own religious group to mainstream Canadian religious norms**. In Excerpt 8 above, Nola repeatedly makes explicit claims to be "Christian" (lines 1–2 and 6), Christianity long having been Canada's "shadow establishment"[77] and its unofficial benchmark for "normal" religion.[78] Similarly, in Excerpt 10 below, LDS women self-categorize in terms of religion by likening one LDS religious group to another religious identity.

Excerpt	1	Wendy	**Young Women's**
10:	2	Gail	um that would be our young women that are aged twelve to
	3		eighteen and that's just a group of women that they meet
	4		weekly like we meet weekly for Relief Society with **it would**
	5		**be like a youth group at another church**

Here Gail explains Wendy's reference to the LDS Church's "Young Women's" group (line 1) by likening it to "a youth group at another church" (line 5), thus simultaneously (1) indicating awareness that her church's organizational structures may not be familiar to the interviewer; (2) identifying a comparable structure in another religious group, which she thereby construes as more readily recognizable; and (3) depicting her own church as akin, if not identical, to that other group.

4.2 Non-belonging

In addition to categorizing themselves as *belonging to* a specific religious tradition (and subgroup within that tradition), Claresholm Relief Society members also employ negative identity practices[79] to represent themselves as *not belonging to* various religious identity categories, both within and outside their own tradition. In Excerpt 11 below, Sally, who arrived late for a focus group discussion, categorizes herself as "the convert" (lines 10 and 12). In doing so, she implicitly self-identifies as belonging to the LDS Church. By using the definite article "the," however, she also simultaneously marks herself as the sole incumbent of the "convert" category, thereby differentiating herself from other Relief Society members, most of whom had already claimed to have been "born in the church" (e.g., Excerpt 6, line 1).

Excerpt	1	Gail	//this is Sally
11:	2	Wendy	//this is Sally
	3	All	//[laughter]
	4	Gail	this is Sally Bacon
	5	Kate	//Sally chip in
	6	Wendy	//say hello
	7	Gail	[unclear] all about tonight
	8	Sally	I completely forgot I apologize
	9	Kate	that's alright
	10	Sally	**I'm the convert**
	11	Kate	oh [laughter]
	12	Sally	**I am the convert**

Similarly, in Excerpt 12 below, Barbara distinguishes herself from other LDS women by **owning a RMC that indexes *non*-affiliation**. That is, she categorizes herself as previously having been unaffiliated with the LDS Church by appending the prefix *non-* to the RMC *Mormon* ("being non-Mormon," line 3; see also "I was once of of a different religion," line 1). In doing so, Barbara identifies herself as one party of a "contrast pair," which Carolyn Baker defines as a categorization of any two people or entities different from one another with respect to a particular feature or set of features, for example, "good kids, plodders."[80] In Barbara's case, she contrasts herself as a former "non-Mormon" (line 3) to unnamed others who "[have] been born into my church and . . . always been LDS or Mormons" (lines 9–11).

Excerpt	1	Barbara	**I was once of of a different religion** so I was once on the
12:	2		outside looking in I was actually um in a a predominantly
	3		Mormon community **being non-Mormon** so I was on the
	4		outside looking in and now I'm in a community that's
	5		predominantly non-Mormon and I'm the one so I'm always on
	6		the outside [laughter] looking in for some reason
	7	Kate	yeah yeah
	8	Barbara	but ah so it's it's interesting I have sort of a both sides of the
	9		story that **someone who has been born into my church** and
	10		you know since their great great grandfather **they've always**
	11		**been LDS or Mormons** um they don't have that perspective

As both of the previous two excerpts illustrate, some of my informants categorized themselves as different from other members of Relief Society, but LDS women also routinely use category-bound activities and/or attributes to mark themselves as different from non-Mormons. In Excerpt 13 below Teresa produces a contrast pair ("my neighbour across the street," line 6, and "the sisters," line 7) and explicitly assigns to the latter party "the same standards ... concerns that I have" (lines 7–8), while using reported speech ("oh yeah don't worry about it," lines 6–7) implicitly to depict the former party as not sharing those same standards or concerns.

Excerpt	1	Teresa	without a spouse at home to discuss a lot of the issues that I
13:	2		have um with my children that you would go to your husband
	3		and say okay this is this is what's come up I know that I can go
	4		to any one of the sisters and discuss what it is that that I need
	5		help making a decision knowing what their standards are if I
	6		go just to **my neighbour across the street** they may say **oh**
	7		**yeah don't worry about it** you know but **the sisters have the**
	8		**same standards they have the same concerns that I have** so
	9		I can go to them any number of them

LDS religious identity is thus associated with "hav[ing]" (lines 7 and 8) a particular category-bound predicate (i.e., specific concerns about one's children), but it can also be rooted in the *non*-performance of activities bound to other identity categories. In Excerpt 14 below, Sally depicts tea drinking as an activity bound to her "Scottish" heritage (line 6), which she "gave up" (line 5) upon joining the LDS Church. Similarly, Gail implicitly links Mormon identity to (1) wearing "modest clothing instead of . . . revealing plunging necklines and the bikini bellies" (Excerpt 15, lines 3–4) and (2) "[not] just go[ing] to church on Sunday" (Excerpt 17, line 1). In each case, LDS women rehearse, and thereby reproduce, their perspective on LDS culture.

Excerpt 14:	1	Sally	I'm thinking specifically my parents I certainly don't throw it
	2		in their faces but I'm more um comfortable about saying no I
	3		won't do that or no I don't want that or you know that kind of
	4		stuff and they're more accepting of me doing that instead of
	5		making a judgment for the fact that ah yeah **I gave up tea**
	6		**coming from a Scottish family** and all **gave up tea was hard**
	7		**even for them to deal with**

Excerpt 15:	1	Gail	I know in in the past we've had ah little fashion shows with
	2		modest clothing and how girls can look just as cute in
	3		**modest clothing instead of you know revealing plunging**
	4		**necklines and the bikini bellies**

Finally, "it is possible to infer"[81] a negative self-categorization from a speaker's disavowal not only of particular behaviour, but also of category-bound attributes. In this study, LDS women routinely represent themselves as different from religious others by **disavowing specific religious attributes**, including (1) qualities they claim not to *be* ("it's not just a Sunday church," Excerpt 16, line 1), and (2) properties they claim not to *have* ("no haloes," Excerpt 17, lines 6 and 9).

| Excerpt 16: | 1 | Barbara | yeah oh absolutely this church **it's not just a Sunday church** |
| | 2 | | that's for sure [laughter] |

Excerpt 17:	1	Gail	**we don't just go to church on Sunday** we try we're all trying
	2		to live our religion every day and some days we do better at
	3		that than others and ah so yeah **we don't want to look at like**
	4		**we're these [laughter] glowing people**
	5	All	[laughter]
	6	Wendy	**no haloes**
	7	Gail	yeah
	8	All	[laughter]
	9	Gail	**no haloes**

Gail and Wendy's jocular claims not to have "haloes" (Excerpt 17, lines 6 and 9) invoke commonsense knowledge of haloes as the exclusive and de rigueur couture of angels and saints and thus implicitly categorize both women as neither angels nor saints. It is worth noting that this kind of negative religious self-categorization functions routinely as a way of avoiding (being perceived to be) boasting. In Excerpt 17 above, Gail claims that Relief Society members "don't want to look like we're these [. . .] glowing people" (lines 3–4). Indeed, my LDS informants appear acutely aware of how their religious self-categorizations might be perceived by others and repeatedly avoid claims that might subject them to charges of claiming to be better than others. One can only speculate, of course, as to why they might do so, but I would propose that this pattern is likely informed by social norms of both modesty (within religious circles) and respecting religious diversity (within the context of Canadian multiculturalism).

4.3 Engaging with Other-Categorization

In addition to categorizing themselves and their church, the LDS women in this study also engage with category labels assigned to them by others, both within and outside the research interview setting. In Excerpt 19 below, Gail reports two RMCs assigned to LDS women by unnamed others outside the interview ("we quite often will get the label Relief Society Sisters," lines 1–2; "Charity Chicks," lines 5 and 9).

Excerpt 19:	1	Gail	I think too **we quite often will get the label Relief Society Sisters which is what we are //right**
	2		
	3	?	//**yep**
	4	?	//**yep**
	5	Gail	right yeah [laughter] **Charity Chicks**
	6	?	Charity Chicks
	7	Kate	//Charity Chicks
	8	All	//[laughter]
	9	Gail	//that's our **that's our latest label Charity Chicks**
	10	Leisl	that's not a bad one
	11	All	//[laughter]
	12	Gail	//no that's not a bad one yeah
	13	Wendy	**I'll take it**
	14	Leisl	**we'll take it** [laughter]

Both Gail and her interlocutors explicitly accept the RMCs assigned to them by others in this excerpt ("which is what we are right," line 2; "yep," lines 3 and 4; "I'll take it," line 13; "we'll take it," line 14), but other categorizations of LDS women meet with a more mixed response. In Excerpt 20 below my informants display varied responses to the categorization *Mormon*: Gail (lines 4, 6, and 17) and Wendy (lines 7–10 and 18) both accept, but find fault with it; Nola (line 19) signals partial readiness to adopt it; Leisl and others (lines 20–22) claim to have used it previously, but apparently no longer do so; while Tracy rejects it outright ("we aren't Mormons," line 32), preferring the self-categorization "members of the Church of Jesus Christ of Latter-Day Saints" (lines 32–33).

Excerpt	1	Kate	you mentioned Mormon before that it's kind of a phrase that
20:	2		gets applied to people from your church that maybe isn't a
	3		good fit but um //how else would
	4	Gail	//**I'm okay with that**
	5	Olive	**oh yeah**
	6	Gail	**it doesn't really //[unclear] who we are**
	7	Wendy	I //[unclear] yeah I think **it just gives people the false**
	8		**impression** that we worship Mormon //[57 words omitted] and
	9		so I think **being called a Mormon just gives people the**
	10		**wrong impression** of what we do believe
	11	Wilma	//that that's the name
	12	Olive	it's not offensive though //by any means
	13	Wendy	//no no not at all
	14	Kate	would you use it with reference to yourselves or not like if
	15		someone said to you oh what religion are you //would you say
	16		I'm a Mormon
	17	Gail	//**I would say sure**
	18	Wendy	**sure I would say //I'm a Mormon**
	19	Nola	//**sometimes**
	20	Leisl	**when I was growing up I always said that**
	21	All	**yeah**
	22	Leisl	**we were Mormons**
	23	Tracy	actually **I taught my kids to make um to tell people that**
	24		**they are a member of the Church of Jesus Christ of Latter-**
	25		**Day Saints and when they get the blank look then you say**
	26		**the Mormons**
	27	[unclear]	//okay
	28	[unclear]	//aha
	29	All	[laughter]
	30	Kate	and why did you //why did you teach them that
	31	[unclear]	//aha
	32	Tracy	because **we aren't Mormons we are members of the Church**
	33		**of Jesus Christ of Latter-Day Saints**

In this excerpt, Tracy indirectly depicts the RMC *Mormons* as a non-members' category ("when they get the blank look then you say the Mormons," lines 25–26), thus corroborating Sacks's observation that some categories are used differently by incumbents and non-incumbents of the category in question. In doing so, Tracy also implicitly aligns herself with the official position of the LDS Church hierarchy.[82]

As Excerpts 21 and 22 below illustrate, LDS women also resist religious categorizations assigned to them by others by (1) negatively evaluating, and thus implicitly distancing themselves from, the proposed categorization (Excerpt 21: "it's disappointing when people will say that we aren't Christians," lines 1–2; "that's kind of frustrating," lines 2–3); (2) owning a redefined, and thus seemingly more acceptable, version of the proposed categorization (Excerpt 21: "which I guess technically we are [. . .] the definition of a cult is following a single person," lines 7 and 10–11); and (3) acknowledging, but providing alternate explanations for, behaviour that either does or might give rise to negative categorizations by others (Excerpt 22: "they may think we're snobs," lines 10–11; "but they don't realize," lines 11–12; "sometimes we do tend to be cliquey or look cliquey but," lines 15–16; "we don't mean to be," lines 18 and 19; "it's just," line 20; "and we're just," line 21).

Excerpt	1	Leisl	[. . .] **it's disappointing when people will say that we**
21:	2		**aren't Christians** [52 words omitted] I guess **that's kind**
	3		**of frustrating** sometimes
	4	Kate	//so
	5	Tracy	//**or that or that we are a cult**
	6	All	yeah [general murmuring agreement]
	7	Tracy	**which I guess technically we are** because we follow
	8		[laughter] Christ
	9	All	[laughter]
	10	Tracy	//**the cult the definition of a cult is following a single**
	11		**person right**

Excerpt 22:	1	Gail	I think it's very healthy for us to have all different kinds of
	2		friends not just to stay in a group which is really hard for us
	3		because if we meet each other on the street
	4	All	//[laughter]
	5	Gail	//we're just going to yatter yatter yatter and if somebody's
	6		walking by they're going to think oh those Mormon kids
	7		they // you know they
	8	All	//[laughter]
	9	Gail	and the same thing if we were to go to maybe a school
	10		production and there was two or three of us there **they may**
	11		**think we're snobs** because we're all talking together **but**
	12		**they don't realize** on Sunday we really don't have a lot
	13		of time to chat so at other than at Enrichment we don't get
	14		together a lot maybe on the telephone or whatever so
	15		**sometimes we do tend to be cliquey or look cliquey**
	16		**but** I don't //the majority of us are
	17	Tracy	//[unclear]
	18	Gail	**we don't mean to be**
	19	Wendy	**we don't mean to be**
	20	Gail	**it's just** we have a common thread that pulls us together and
	21		but yeah I thought //it was unique growing up==
	22	Wendy	//and **we're just** excited to see ya

5. Attitudinal Stance-Taking on Matters Other Than Religion

FINALLY, MY RESEARCH INDICATES that LDS women also convey a sense of their own religious identities, not only via overt self-categorization and engagement with categorizations assigned to them by others, but also by discussing matters other than religion. In this section, therefore, I will discuss how one LDS woman represents her own Mormon identity via attitudinal stance-taking on Canadian multiculturalism.

By stance-taking I mean the "dialogical and intersubjective activity"[83] of "simultaneously *evaluating* objects, *positioning* subjects ... and *aligning* with other subjects with respect to any salient dimension of the sociocultural field."[84] Several scholars have noted a relationship between stance/stance-taking and identity.[85] Elinor Ochs argues that both affective and epistemic stances can be indirectly constitutive of social identity.[86] Likewise, Richard Fitzgerald and William Housley maintain that by taking a stance on a specific topic, and particularly on controversial topics, individuals "can be seen to move into and personally occupy what may be called a 'topic-opinion category' in which their opinion locates them on either one side of the debate or the other."[87] In other words, attitudinal stances can function as the "known-in-common"[88] or category-bound attributes of specific social identities.

It is important to note that the binding of predicate to category in academic studies of religion is done by the scholar, not by a member of a religious group. Despite recognizing that "the diversity of women's lives means that any attempt to categorize them will, to some extent, fail to capture the nuances of the ways in which they negotiate boundaries," Lori Beaman categorizes her LDS informants as "Molly Mormons," "Moderates," and "Mormon feminists."[89] In this section, however, I do not mean to suggest that LDS women project particular attitudinal stances on multiculturalism because they have a particular religious identity, or that their linguistic stance-taking behaviour is determined by their religious affiliation. Rather, I will argue that (1) attitudes about multiculturalism can "carry symbolic importance . . . as a signal to others" of LDS women's religious identities;[90] (2) given the local conventional associations that pertain to particular attitudinal stances and particular stereotypical religious identities, stance-taking on matters other than religion is one way in which LDS women can enact and/or recast those identities; and (3) Canadian LDS women both construct and critique their own religious identities via attitudinal stance-taking on multiculturalism.

In Excerpt 23 below, Barbara recollects Canada's 1990 "turban affair," in which more than 200,000 Canadians protested a decision by the Royal Canadian Mounted Police (RCMP) to allow Sikh Mounties to don turbans in lieu of the traditional Stetson hat.[91] The protestors argued that the turban, as a religious symbol, would undermine "the non-religious nature of the force," violating other Canadians' "constitutional right to a secular state free of religious symbols."[92] Their claims were rejected by the Supreme Court of Canada, but more than two decades later, the controversy around this issue still reverberates in the Canadian public consciousness, as Barbara's comments illustrate.

Excerpt 23:

Excerpt	1	Kate	do you have any insight at all as to how a country like Canada
23:	2		can accommodate the different religious perspectives of its
	3		people in public life
	4	Barbara	well that's tricky **I mean I remember** one particular
	5		**argument over you know the Sikhs being able to wear their**
	6		**TURBANS** and how that's not a part of **our** UNIFORMS so
	7		**we** change **OUR** traditions to incorporate THEIR
	8		religious beliefs **that's tricky you know in one way you want**
	9		**to be able to include people but you also don't want to**
	10		**water down what is Canadian you know** and and what does
	11		that mean to be Canadian [laughter]

In this excerpt, Barbara projects an ambivalent stance on the accommodation of non-Christian religions by Canada's public institutions ("in one way you want ... but you also don't want," lines 8–9). She begins by using the comment clauses "I mean" and "I remember" (both line 4) to "launch"[93] her remarks, which signal opposition to multiculturalism on the grounds that it threatens Christianity's "shadow establishment" status in Canada.[94] This is a stance that indirectly positions Barbara within a topic-opinion category[95] stereotypically associated with conservative Christianity.[96]

None of the other pronouns used in this excerpt encode specific personal reference. Instead, Barbara relies on "you" (line 8), used "impersonally for generic reference,"[97] to project a "more distanced, less personal" stance.[98] Barbara's "we" and "our/OUR" (lines 6 and 7) both have ambiguous referents and her exaggerated prosodic realization of "OUR" (line 7) suggests a measure of parody on Barbara's part, rendering it unclear whether she intends to speak as "author" or merely "animator"[99] of the "argument" against "the Sikhs being able to wear their turbans" (line 5).

Barbara also repeatedly uses the comment clause "you know" to invoke "meta-knowledge about what is generally known" (line 5),[100] to attribute knowledge to her interlocutor (line 8)[101] and to appeal "to the listener for reassuring feedback" (line 10).[102] In each case, "you know" seems to "[appeal] to the hearer's shared knowledge or experience for the acceptance"[103] of Barbara's remarks thus serving to align Barbara's stance on Canadian multiculturalism with "the [presumed] beliefs"[104] of her interlocutor. By shifting from using the personal and specific pronoun "I" to the generic "you" in this way, Barbara marks the topic of conversation as being in some way problematic,[105] while signalling both her own disaffiliation from parties opposed to multiculturalism[106] and her positive alignment with Canadian social norms and the presumed stance of her interlocutor thereby arguably representing her own religious identity as less conservative than other (stereotypical) forms of Canadian Christianity.

Again, in Excerpt 24 below, Barbara distinguishes herself from religious others, although here the others from whom she dissociates herself are her co-religionists. The excerpt begins with Barbara's positive evaluation of a brief statement attributed to Ovide Mercredi (national chief of the Assembly of First Nations in Canada between 1991 and 1997), which opposed assimilation and prioritized respect for differences and the promotion of diversity (line 1).

Excerpt	1	Barbara	mm **I like the one by ah Ovide Mercredi** [70 words omitted]
24:	2		**I think that's that's sort of what I believe in a nutshell** right
	3		there
	4	Kate	right there that's interesting
	5	Barbara	yeah that **sort of** sums it up for me um **I think**
	6		**assimilation is wrong I think that people need to look at**
	7		**other people's ideas and to recognize and affirm them um I**
	8		**heard a quote once that said ah oneness is is boring**
	9	Kate	[laughter]
	10	Barbara	[laughter]
	11		you know I mean there's unity is different if everyone were the
	12		same and had the same ideas you don't progress you don't go
	13		anywhere you know it takes **two heads are better than one**
	14	Kate	right [laughter]

Continued . . .

15		mhm mhm and is that kind of perspective is that something
16		that um sits comfortably with the religious tradition that
17		you're part of or they wouldn't sort of view it
18		quite the same way
19	Barbara	ah I think and this is my own personal opinion [laughter]
20	Kate	[laughter]
21	Barbara	because I do have you know judgments on my own religion
22		and and question some of the ways they do things but
23		assimilation is a big part of what they do I think I mean um
24		but I think it's almost unconscious sometimes you know
25		they don't really realize that's in fact what they're doing
26		and they'd be shocked to know [laughter] you know our
27		Prophet right now President Hinckley I I really agree with
28		a lot of things he says and he said you know we should
29		never belittle or make fun of anyone else's religion we
30		should show them what we have and be willing to share
31		with them but not you know tell them that they're wrong
32		or they're bad or that their beliefs are you know recognize
33		the good in everybody and and that's how I feel I think a lot
34		of people um like I said because we're a proselyting church
35		and and we believe that the whole world should be we
36		believe we we're right and everyone else is wrong
37		[laughter]
38	Kate	[laughter]
39	Barbara	basically [laughter] I guess if it boils down to that right um I
40		think people need to lose not lose sight of that but to to look
41		at the good in everybody and I think then the Mormon
42		church would be more accepted among the general
43		population

Comparisons with the United States frequently serve as a touchstone for Canadian identity, and critique of assimilation, in particular, routinely functions as the *via negativa* of Canadian multicultural discourse. Barbara's appraisals of assimilation, in terms of "affect"[107] (I *like* the one by," line 1) and "social sanction"[108] ("I think assimilation is *wrong*," lines 5–6), can thus be heard as endorsing multiculturalism. This endorsement is mitigated somewhat by both the "epistemic phrase"[109] "I think" (lines 2, 5, and 6) and the epistemic "stance adverbial"[110] "sort of" (lines 2 and 5). Barbara's appropriation of Canadian multicultural discourse also takes other linguistic forms including *modulation* expressing obligation to behave in accordance with multicultural principles ("people *need* to," line 6), *lexicalizations* drawn from the Canadian Multiculturalism Act, encoding key principles of multiculturalism ("recognize," line 7), and *intertextual* references supportive of multiculturalism ("I heard a quote once that said," lines 7–8; "two heads are better than one," line 13).

Jackie Abell and Greg Myers observe that commonplaces are often used when "closing off an interactionally problematic topic,"[111] and Barbara's introduction of both the quotation "oneness is is boring" (line 8) and the commonplace "two heads are better than one" (line 13) summate her appraisal of the Mercredi statement and of assimilation more generally. In both cases, Barbara rounds off her turn with laughter, which is echoed in the first case by collaborative laughter from the interviewer. In the second, however, the interviewer withholds laughter, instead reopening the topic with a two-part move that (1) invites evaluation of the Mormon position on diversity (Barbara having earlier identified with the LDS Church), and (2) alludes to the LDS Church's notoriously racist past.[112] At the same time, the interviewer positions Barbara squarely within that religious group[113] by referring to "the religious tradition that you're part of" (lines 16–17).

Although mitigated somewhat by hedging ("sort of," line 17; "quite," line 18), the interviewer's implicit suggestion of a discrepancy between Barbara's views and those of her church seems to constitute what Penelope Brown and Stephen Levinson call a "face threatening act."[114] Erving Goffman observes that individuals can lose face as a result of their association with a stigmatized (religious) group. In such cases, he maintains that

[a] stigmatized individual may exhibit identity ambivalence when he obtains a close sight of his own kind behaving in a stereotyped way. . . . The sight may repel him, since after all he supports the norms of the wider society, but his social and psychological identification with these

offenders holds him to what repels him.... In brief, he can neither embrace his group nor let it go.[115]

It would seem that, for Barbara, such a threat to face arose with the interviewer's question about her church's position. Brown and Levinson argue that "people can be expected to defend their faces if threatened, and in defending their own to threaten others' faces."[116] Barbara's response supports that observation as she both dissociates herself from her fellow Mormons (whom she allows multicultural discourse to critique) and represents herself as an independent critical thinker, supportive of multiculturalism. For example, by delaying briefly before answering, using the holding adjunct "ah" followed by the familiar disclaimer "and this is my own personal opinion" (both line 19), accentuated by an altered tone of voice and punctuated with laughter (echoed again by the interviewer's own laughter), Barbara displays a measure of distance from her own religious group. This is reinforced by her claim to "have you know judgments on my own religion and and question some of the ways they do things" (lines 21–22), as well as by her framing of assimilation as "a big part of what *they*" [i.e., not 'we' or 'I'] do" (line 23).

Barbara's response here is complex, illustrating the "ideological dilemma"[117] faced by many religious Canadians who seek simultaneously to uphold the credo of multiculturalism while adhering to exclusivist religions. Barbara allows multicultural discourse to critique her religious group while exonerating herself. The *I* who thinks and has judgments contrasts sharply with the *they* who *do* assimilation. Yet, Barbara's co-religionists are by no means simply sacrificial lambs on the altar of her positive self-presentation. She is quick to shield them from her own negative judgment, proffering as measures in their defence both lack of awareness and good intentions ("they don't really realize . . . and they'd be shocked to know," lines 25–26).

Barbara's quotation of Gordon B. Hinckley is also important in this regard since it offsets the critique of her co-religionists by providing a fresh construal of her religious group with which she can and does identify. Maggie Charles observes in relation to academic writing that authors "select sources which they consider to be persuasive within the context of their own discipline and study."[118] I would argue that the same holds true for speakers who quote religious leaders and/or texts as backing for their own attitudinal stances; whom (or what) one chooses to quote in this way can be suggestive of whom (or what) one considers authoritative or convincing. Thus Barbara signals the convergent alignment of her own stance with that of President Hinckley via both the "prefatory gloss"[119] with which she introduces his speech ("I really agree with a lot of things he says," line 27–28), and the commentary that follows hard upon his remarks ("and that's how I feel," line 33).

In her analysis of Christian fundamentalist rhetoric in the United States, Suzanne Harding identifies a pattern of "speech mimesis," whereby

> church-people ... borrow, customize, and reproduce the ... speech of their preachers and other leaders in their daily lives. Preachers appropri-ate each other's sermons piecemeal and wholesale, while church people assimilate their preachers' language at the level of grammar, semantics and style.[120]

Speech mimesis is particularly evident here in Barbara's use of pronouns: President Hinckley's reported in-group ("*we* should never belittle ... *we* should show them what *we* have," lines 28–30) soon becomes Barbara's ("*we*'re a proselyting [sic] church and and *we* believe that the whole world should be *we* believe *we we*'re right," lines 34–36) and his out-group ("any-one else," line 29) likewise becomes hers ("everyone else," line 36).

Through quoting President Hinckley and her subsequent alignment of her pronoun use with his, Barbara construes herself as part of "a prose-lyting [sic] church" (line 34), the members of which "believe we we're right and everyone else is wrong" (line 36). (This quotation is allocated and does not indicate endorsement of the views expressed in it.) Yet, her laughter (lines 37 and 39) and extended hedge ("basically ... I guess if it boils down to that," line 39) imply discomfort with this confession. The interviewer meets Barbara's laughter with her own (line 38), suggesting recognition that this construal of the LDS Church positions Barbara awkwardly with respect to both her religious group and the "horizontal space" proposed by Canadian multicultural discourse, which allows "no theoretical or analytical room for social relations of power and ruling."[121] Thus, religious and multicultural discourses seem to vie for dominance in Barbara's self-presentation in this excerpt. I would argue that it is in precisely this combination and contention of discourses—in the warp and weft of her ideological dilemma—that Barbara's identity as a Canadian Mormon is simultaneously discursively construed and critiqued.

An important macro-topic of Canadian multicultural discourse that appears in this excerpt concerns the nature and extent of recognition afforded religious groups in Canada, particularly religious minorities. Richard Day observes that "the theory of recognition has an important place in modern political philosophy, in general, and in Canadian multiculturalist philosophy, in particular" even though "the official discourse is not faithful to this lineage."[122] According to Day, the Canadian government recognizes the existence of different groups and grants a range of "differentiated citizenship rights" without recognizing the value or equality of such groups.[123] My research, however, raises somewhat different questions concerning the reciprocity of recognition between individuals and groups with different religious affiliations. In Excerpt 24 Barbara depicts the LDS Church as lacking acceptance "among the general population" (lines 41–42). Earlier in this same interview (not shown here), she referred to "the persecution there was in the beginning years of the church," some of which she claimed "is still there," evident in "animosity between other religions and the LDS faith." Barbara also mentioned the lack of LDS representation on the Claresholm Ministerial Association, explaining that "a lot of people believe that we're not Christian" (see also Excerpts 8, 9, and 21). Indeed, it is "to correct that misconception," Barbara maintained, that "the church leadership wants us to say our name as the Church of Jesus Christ of Latter-Day Saints" (see also Excerpt 20).

The macro-topic of recognition is unmistakable in these comments, but Barbara's focus is her religious group's ability to secure recognition from other individuals and groups. In Theo van Leeuwen's terms, she represents non-Mormon social actors here in terms of "aggregated indetermination" ("the general population," "a lot of people"), "differentiation" ("other religions"), and "collectivization" ("the Ministerial Society") thus construing the predicament of her group as both vague and vast.[124] The

LDS Church is set against a generalized other, from whom only *"mis*recognition"[125] is said to be forthcoming.

Hans Mol suggests that religion is one means of promoting "coherence within and separation without."[126] Mary Douglas observes further that the exaggeration of difference "between within and without, above and below, male and female, with and against" allows for the creation of "a semblance of [social] order."[127] In Excerpt 24, Barbara depicts the LDS Church as provoking differentiation between within and without, with and against. However, the order thereby obtained is not construed as desirable. On the contrary, Barbara's comments suggest that the LDS project is rather to conflate difference; her co-religionists seek to assimilate others within their cultural ambit, while her leaders seek recognition for their church *as a Christian religion* by promoting the use of its full name. For Barbara, however, the LDS Church's capacity to secure recognition from others is contingent upon her co-religionists' ability to pull off the discursive juggling act she herself attempts, namely, "recogniz[ing] the good in everybody" (lines 32–33), while "not [losing] sight of" (line 40) the notion that "we're right and everyone else is wrong" (line 36). Barbara thus articulates a dilemma faced not only by the LDS Church, but also by other strands of exclusivist Christianity—indeed all exclusivist religion—namely, the challenge of finding "ways of both retaining its identity and uniqueness and opening up itself to the reality and value of religious plurality."[128]

6. Interactional Uses of Religious Self-Identification

AS MY ANALYSIS THUS FAR DEMONSTRATES, religious self-identification is more complex than a simple matter of belonging or non-belonging.[129] First, it involves both explicit and implicit forms of self-categorization, including engagement with categorizations assigned by others, which can serve a variety of interactional functions. Schegloff observes that "terms from membership categorization devices are mostly used as resources for identifying, describing, formulating, etc., persons" (as in Excerpts 1, 2, and 19 above),[130] but other interactional goals achieved via categorization include: (1) "imputing motives, contesting explanations and providing for the intelligibility of particular actions,"[131] as in Excerpts 3, 6, 7, and 11; (2) justifying "subsequent predicates and moral claims,"[132] as in Excerpts 5 and 12; (3) pre-empting, countering, and/or foreclosing challenges, including alternate categorizations,[133] as in Excerpts 8, 20, 21, and 22; (4) presenting oneself and one's behaviour in terms of particular socio-cultural expectations,[134] as in Excerpt 10; and (5) avoiding referring to specific individuals and/or groups,[135] as in Excerpts 12 and 13.

Second, the resources of religious self-identification also include various forms of self-representation, notably via attitudinal stance-taking on matters other than religion. That Canada's 1988 Multiculturalism Act was the first such law passed anywhere in the world is a point of pride for many Canadians, and my research indicates that LDS women work hard linguistically to represent their own religious identities as resonant with Canada's dominant cultural milieu, even when their religious views diverge from multicultural principles. By thus drawing on public sphere discourses as a resource for religious self-identification, LDS women effectively reject "the marginal and privatized role which theories of modernity as well as theories of secularization had reserved for them," simultaneously "forc[ing] modern societies to reflect publicly and collectively upon their normative [religious] structures," even "forc[ing themselves] to confront and possibly come to terms with modern [non-religious] normative structures."[136]

7. Conclusion

IN IDENTIFYING VARIOUS DISCURSIVE STRATEGIES USED BY LDS WOMEN to construct a sense of their own religious identities, this study highlights an important difference between religious self- and other-identification. The second of these acts is the stock-in-trade of fiction and the mainstream media, as well as much of the scholarly literature about religious identity. By contrast, this study argues for the scholarly prioritization of religious self-identifications and ongoing critical reflection on a priori assumptions about the known-in-common[137] attributes and activities of specific religious identity categories. It also demonstrates the relevance of close linguistic analysis to academic religion inquiries, inviting both a more nuanced examination of diverse religious identities and faith-based stances on controversial social issues, and ongoing critical evaluation of different analytical frameworks for investigating the discursive construal of religious identity within the context of multiculturalism. ●

Notes

1. Talcott Parsons, "The Distribution of Power in American Society," in *Structure and Process in Modern Societies*, ed. Talcott Parsons (Glencoe, IL: Free Press, 1960), 219.

2. Lieven Boeve, "Religion after Detraditionalisation: Christian Faith in a Post-Secular Europe" (Manchester: University of Manchester Department of Religions and Theology 2004), 14, http://www.art.man.ac.uk/reltheol. See Peter L. Berger, *The Desecularization of the World: Resurgent Religion and World Politics* (Grand Rapids, MI: William B. Eerdmans, 1999); Richard J. Neuhaus, *The Naked Public Square: Religion and Democracy in America* (Grand Rapids, MI: William B. Eerdmans, 1984) for discussions about the relationship of modernization, religion, and the Enlightenment.

3. Grace Davie, "The Future of Religion and Its Implications for the Social Sciences," in *Playful Religion: Challenges for the Study of Religion*, ed. A. von Harskamp, M. Klaver, J. Roeland, and P. Versteeg (Delft: Eburon, 2006), 139.

4. Paul Bramadat, "Re-Visioning Religion in the Contemporary Period: The United Church of Canada's Ethnic Ministries Unit," *Canadian Diversity* 4, no. 3 (2005): 59–62.

5. Claudia L. Bushman, *Contemporary Mormonism: Latter-Day Saints in Modern America* (Westport, CT: Praeger Publishers, 2006), 51.

6. See Lawrence Foster, *Women, Family, and Utopia: Communal Experiments of the Shakers, the Oneida Community, and the Mormons* (New York: Syracuse University Press, 1991); Jessie L. Embry, *Mormon Polygamous Families: Life in the Principle* (Salt Lake City: University of Utah Press, 1987); Richard S. Van Wagoner, *Mormon Polygamy: A History* (Salt Lake City, UT: Signature Books, 1986); B. Carmon Hardy, *Solemn Covenant: The Mormon Polygamous Passage* (Urbana: University of Illinois Press, 1992); Wendy Stueck and Justine Hunter, "B.C. Court Upholds Anti-Polygamy Law as Constitutional," *Globe and Mail*, November 23, 2011, http://www.theglobe andmail.com/news/national/british-columbia/bc-politics/bc-court-upholds-anti -polygamy-law-as-constitutional/article2246238/; Jeff Lee, "B.C. Polygamy Ban Won't Face any Further Appeals, Province Says," *National Post*, March 26, 2012, http://news.nationalpost.com/2012/03/26/b-c-polygamy-ban-wont-face-any

-further-appeals-province-says/; D. Michael Quinn, "Plural Marriage and Mormon Fundamentalism, " in *Fundamentalisms and Society: Reclaiming the Sciences, the Family, and Education,* ed. Martin E. Marty and R. Scott Appleby (Chicago: University of Chicago Press, 1993), 240–93; Lori Beaman, "Church, State, and the Legal Interpretation of Polygamy in Canada," *Nova Religio: The Journal of Alternative and Emergent Religions* 8, no. 1 (2004): 20–38, for discussions on how polygamy is treated as a controverial practice.

7. For membership categorization analysis, see Georgia Lepper, *Categories in Text and Talk* (London: Sage, 2000); Stephen Hester and Peter Eglin, "Membership Categorization Analysis: An Introduction," in *Culture in Action: Studies in Membership Categorization Analysis,* ed. Stephen Hester and Peter Eglin (Lanham, MD: International Institute for Ethnomethodology and Conversation Analysis and University Press of America, 1997), 1–24; Emmanuel A. Schegloff, "A Tutorial on Membership Categorization," *Journal of Pragmatics* 39, no. 3 (2007): 462–82; Lena Jayyusi, *Categorization and the Moral Order* (Boston: Routledge and Kegan Paul, 1984); Harvey Sacks, "Hotrodder: A Revolutionary Category," in *Everyday Language: Studies in Ethnomethodology,* ed. George Psathas (New York: Irvington Press, 1979), 7–14; Harvey Sacks, *Lectures on Conversation,* vol. 1, ed. Gail Jefferson (Oxford and Cambridge, MA: Basil Blackwell, 1992); Harvey Sacks, "On the Analyzability of Stories Told by Children," in *Directions in Sociolinguistics: The Ethnography of Communication,* ed. John J. Gumperz and Dell Hymes (1972; Oxford: Basil Blackwell, 1986), 325–45. For stance analysis, see Paul Kockelman, "Stance and Subjectivity," *Journal of Linguistic Anthropology* 14, no. 2 (2004): 127–50; Alexandra Jaffe, ed. *Stance: Sociolinguistic Perspectives* (Oxford: Oxford University Press, 2009); John W. Du Bois, "The Stance Triangle," in *Stancetaking in Discourse: Subjectivity, Evaluation, Interaction,* ed. Robert Englebretson (Amsterdam: John Benjamins, 2007), 139–82; Robert Englebretson, ed., *Stancetaking in Discourse: Subjectivity, Evaluation, Interaction* (Amsterdam and Philadelphia: John Benjamins, 2007).

8. Emanuel A. Schegloff, "Between Micro and Macro: Contexts and Other Connections," in *The Micro-Macro Link,* ed. Jeffrey C. Alexander, B. Giesen, R. Munch, and N. J. Smelser (Berkeley: University of California Press, 1987), 207.

9. André Droogers, "Identity, Religious Pluralism, and Ritual in Brazil: Umbanda and Pentecostalism, " in *Playful Religion: Challenges for the Study of Religion,* ed. Anton von Harskamp, Mirander Klaver, Johan Roeland, and Peter Versteeg (1995; Delft: Eburon, 2006), 29.

10. Erving Goffman, "Footing," in *Forms of Talk*, ed. Erving Goffman (Philadelphia: University of Pennsylvania Press, 1981), 144.

11. As Roz Ivanič points out, identity construction often involves the interweaving of multiple discourses. Roz Ivanič, *Writing and Identity: The Discoursal Construction of Identity in Academic Writing* (Amsterdam and Philadelphia: John Benjamins, 1998).

12. Smith, as quoted in Dallin H. Oaks, "The Relief Society and the Church," *Ensign* (May 1992): 34–37.

13. See Merlin B. Brinkerhoff and Elaine Grandin, "Contemporary Reactions to Mormonism: A Case Study from Rural Alberta," *Canadian Journal of Sociology* 16, no. 2 (1991): 165–85, for a discussion of the opposition the LDS Church faced because of its endorsement of polygamy. See Douglas J. Davies, *An Introduction to Mormonism* (Cambridge: Cambridge University Press, 2003) for a discussion of opposition because of its unconventional doctrines.

14. "Basic Facts about the Church," *The Church of Jesus Christ of Latter-Day Saints*, http://www.lds.org/church/facts?lang=eng.

15. "Introduction to Relief Society," *The Church of Jesus Christ of Latter-Day Saints*, http://www.lds.org/pa/display/0,17884,4689-1,00.html.

16. "Relief Society—History," *The Church of Jesus Christ of Latter-Day Saints*, http://www.lds.org/pa/display/0,17884,4748-1,00.html.

17. As noted by Annette P. Hampshire and James A. Beckford, "Religious Sects and the Concept of Deviance: The Mormons and the Moonies," *British Journal of Sociology* 34, no. 2 (1983): 226.

18. George K. Jarvis, "Demographic Characteristics of the Mormon Family in Canada," in *The Mormon Presence in Canada*, ed. Brigham Y. Card, Herbert C. Northcott, John E. Foster, Howard Palmer, and George K. Jarvis (Edmonton: University of Alberta Press, 1990), 281–301.

19. Dean R. Louder, "Canadian Mormons in Their North American Context: A Portrait," *Social Compass* 40, no. 2 (1993): 271–90; Leslie Alm and Leah Taylor, "Alberta and Idaho: An Implicit Bond," *American Review of Canadian Studies* 33, no. 2 (2003): 197–218.

20. Brigham Y. Card et al., *The Mormon Presence in Canada* (Edmonton: University of Alberta Press, 1990), xx.

21. Louder, "Canadian Mormans."

22. Canada, Statistics Canada, *2001 Census Analysis Series: Religions in Canada* (Catalogue Number 96F0030XIE2001015) (Ottawa: Statistics Canada, 2003).

23. Card et al., *The Mormon Presence*, xix. See also Peter S. Morris, "Charles Ora Card and Mormon Settlement on the Northwestern Plains Borderlands," in *The Borderlands of the American and Canadian Wests*, ed. Sterling Evans (Lincoln and London: University of Nebraska Press, 2006), 172–82.

24. Lawrence B. Lee, "The Mormons Come to Canada, 1887–1902," *Pacific Northwest Quarterly* 59, no. 1 (1968): 11–22; Howard Palmer, "The Reaction to Mormons in Canada, 1887–1923," in *The Mormon Presence in Canada*, ed. Brigham Y. Card, Herbert C. Northcott, John E. Foster, Howard Palmer, and George K. Jarvis (Edmonton: University of Alberta Press, 1990), 1–59.

25. Brinkerhoff and Grandin, "Contemporary Reactions."

26. Robert V. Bartlett, "Political Culture and the Environmental Problematique in the American West," in *Environmental Politics and Policy in the West*, ed. Zachary Smith (Dubuque, IA: Kendall/Hunt Publishing, 1993), 101–16; Alm and Taylor, "Alberta and Idaho"; Tom Flanagan, "From Riel to Reform (and a Little Beyond): Politics in Western Canada," *American Review of Canadian Studies* 31, no. 4 (2001): 623–38.

27. David K. Elton, "Political Behavior of Mormons in Canada," in *The Mormon Presence in Canada*, ed. Brigham Y. Card, Herbert C. Northcott, John E. Foster, Howard Palmer, and George K. Jarvis (Edmonton: University of Alberta Press, 1990), 277. See also Jeffrey C. Fox, "A Typology of LDS Sociopolitical Worldviews," *Journal for the Scientific Study of Religion* 42, no. 2 (2003): 279–89.

28. Jarvis, "Demographic Characteristics," 299. The details and statistics in this paragraph have been drawn from Tim B. Heaton, "Sociodemographic Characteristics of Religious Groups in Canada," *Sociological Analysis* 47, no. 1 (1986): 54–65, and Jarvis, "Demographic Characteristics."

29. L. J. Arrington, "Crisis in Identity: Mormon Responses in the Nineteenth and Twentieth Centuries," in *Mormonism and American Culture*, ed. Marvin S. Hill and James B. Allen (New York: Harper and Row, 1972), 181. See also O. Kendall White Jr., "Mormonism in America and Canada: Accommodation to the Nation-State," *Canadian Journal of Sociology* 3, no. 2 (1978): 161–81.

30. "An Era of Correlation and Consolidation," in *Church History in the Fulness of Times Student Manual*, 562–78, The Church of Jesus Christ of Latter-Day Saints. https://www.lds.org/manual/church-history-in-the-fulness-of-times-student-manual/chapter-forty-three-an-era-of-correlation-and-consolidation?lang=eng.

31. White Jr., "Mormanism in America," 179.

32. Lori Beaman, "Molly Mormons, Mormon Feminists, and Moderates: Religious Diversity and the Latter Day Saints Church," *Sociology of Religion* 62, no. 1 (2001): 80.

33. A. L. Mauss, *The Angel and the Beehive: The Mormon Struggle with Assimilation* (Chicago: University of Illinois Press, 1994), 203. See also Foster, *Women, Family, and Utopia*; Marie Cornwall, "The Institutional Role of Mormon Women," in *Contemporary Mormonism: Social Science Perspectives*, ed. Marie Cornwall, Tim B. Heaton, and Lawrence A. Young (Chicago: University of Illinois Press, 1994), 239–64.

34. Bushman, *Contemporary Mormonism*.

35. A. L. Mauss, "Flowers, Weeds, and Thistles: The State of Social Science Literature on the Mormons," in *Mormon History*, ed. R. W. Walker, D. J. Whittaker, and J. B. Allen (Urbana and Chicago: University of Illinois Press, 2001), 153–97.

36. Ibid., 173. See O. Kendall White Jr., "A Feminist Challenge: 'Mormons for ERA' as an Internal Social Movement," *Journal of Ethnic Studies* 13, no. 1 (1985): 29–37, and O. Kendall White Jr., "Mormonism and the Equal Rights Amendment," *Journal of Church and State* 31, no. 2 (1989): 249–67, for a discussion of Mormon feminisms.

37. Bushman, *Contemporary Mormanism*, 113.

38. Gary Shepherd and Gordon Shepherd, *Mormon Passage: A Missionary Chronicle* (Urbana and Chicago: University of Illinois Press, 1998), 422.

39. Bushman, *Contemporary Mormanism*, 118.

40. Maureen Ursenbach Beecher, "Mormon Women in Southern Alberta: The Pioneer Years," in *The Mormon Presence in Canada*, ed. Brigham Y. Card, Herbert C. Northcott, John E. Foster, Howard Palmer, and George K. Jarvis (Edmonton: University of Alberta Press, 1990), 224.

41. Bushman, *Contemporary Mormanism*, 121.

42. Canada, Statistics Canada, *2001 Community Profiles* (Catalogue Number 93F0053XIE) (Ottawa: Statistics Canada, 2002).

43. Mary Bucholtz and Kira Hall, "Identity and Interaction: A Sociocultural Linguistic Approach," *Discourse Studies* 7, no. 4–5 (2005): 608.

44. Thomas Meyer, *Identity Mania* (London: Zed Books, 2001); Héctor Grad and Luisa Martín Rojo, "Identities in Discourse: An Integrative View," in *Analysing Identities in Discourse*, ed. Rosana Dolón and Júlia Todolí (Amsterdam and Philadelphia: John Benjamins, 2008), 3–28.

45. Rogers Brubaker and Frederick Cooper, "Beyond 'Identity,'" *Theory and Society* 29, no. 1 (2000): 1.

46. Ibid., 17.

47. Ibid., 18.

48. Bethan Benwell and Elizabeth Stokoe, *Discourse and Identity* (Edinburgh: Edinburgh University Press, 2006), 26.

49. See Anna Triandafyllidou and Ruth Wodak, "Conceptual and Methodological Questions in the Study of Collective Identities: An Introduction," *Journal of Language and Politics* 2, no. 2 (2003): 205–23; Bucholtz and Hall, "Identity and Interaction."

50. Mary Bucholtz, "'Why Be Normal?': Language and Identity Practices in a Community of Nerd Girls," *Language in Society* 28, no. 2 (1999): 211.

51. Bucholtz and Hall, "Identity and Interaction," 586.

52. Bronwyn Davies and Rom Harré, "Positioning: The Discursive Production of Selves," *Journal for the Theory of Social Behaviour* 20, no. 1 (1990): 48.

53. Margaret Wetherell, ed., *Identities, Groups, and Social Issues* (London: Sage, 1996), 34.

54. Jeff Coulter, "Remarks on the Conceptualisation of Social Structure," *Philosophy of the Social Sciences* 12, no. 1 (1982): 36.

55. Sacks, "Hotrodder"; Sacks, *Lectures on Conversation*; Sacks, "On the Analyzability of Stories."

56. D. R. Watson, "Categorisation, Authorisation, and Blame-Negotiation in Conversation," *Sociology* 12, no. 1 (1978): 105–13; Elizabeth Stokoe, "Mothers, Single Women, and Sluts: Gender, Morality, and Membership Categorization in Neighbour Disputes," *Feminism and Psychology* 13, no. 3 (2003): 317–44. See, for example, T. J. Berard, "Evaluative Categories of Action and Identity in Non-Evaluative Human Studies Research: Examples from Ethnomethodology," *Qualitative Sociology Review* 1, no. 1 (2005): 5–30; Schegloff, "Between Micro and Macro"; Stephen Hester and R. Fitzgerald, "Category, Predicate, and Task: Some Organisational Features in a Radio Talk Show," in *Media Studies: Ethnomethodological Approaches, SECA, No. 5*, ed. Paul Jalbert (Lanham, MD: University Press of America, 1999), 171–93; Richard Fitzgerald and William Housley, "Identity, Categorization, and Sequential Organization: The Sequential and Categorial Flow of Identity in a Radio Phone-In." *Discourse and Society* 13, no. 5 (2002): 579–602; Peter Eglin, "Members' Gendering Work: 'Women,' 'Feminists,' and Membership Categorization Analysis," *Discourse and Society* 13, no. 6 (2002): 819–25; Peter Eglin and Stephen Hester, *The Montreal Massacre: A Story of Membership Categorization Analysis* (Waterloo, ON: Wilfrid Laurier University Press, 2003); Elizabeth Stokoe, "On Ethnomethodology, Feminism, and the Analysis of Categorial Reference to Gender in Talk-in-Interaction," *Sociological*

Review 54, no. 3 (2006): 467–94; Elizabeth Stokoe, "Categories and Sequences: Formulating Gender in Talk-in-Interaction," in *Gender and Language Research Methodologies*, ed. Kate Harrington, Lia Litosseliti, Helen Saunston, and Jane Sunderland (London: Palgrave Macmillan, 2009); Maria T. Wowk, "Blame Allocation, Sex, and Gender in a Murder Interrogation," *Women's Studies International Forum* 7, no. 1 (1984): 75–82; D. R. Watson and T. Weinberg, "Interviews and the Interactional Construction of Accounts of Homosexual Identity," *Social Analysis* 11, no. 1 (1982): 56–78; Stephen Hester and William Housley, *Language, Interaction, and National Identity: Studies in the Social Organisation of National Identity in Talk-in-Interaction* (Aldershot, UK: Ashgate, 2002); P. Jalbert, "Categorisation and Beliefs: News Accounts of Haitian and Cuban Refugees," in *The Interactional Order: New Directions in the Study of Social Order*, ed. D. T. Helm, W. T. Anderson, A. J. Meehan, and A. W. Rawls (New York: Abingdon, 1989); Paul Drew, "Accusations: The Occasioned Use of Members' Knowledge of 'Religious Geography' in Describing Events," *Sociology* 12, no. 1 (1978): 1–22.

57. For categorization, see Carolyn B. Mervis and Eleanor Rosch, "Categorization of Natural Objects," *Annual Review of Psychology* 32 (1981): 89–115. For social identity, see Henri Tajfel, *Human Groups and Social Categories: Studies in Social Psychology* (Cambridge: Cambridge University Press, 1981); John C. Turner et al., *Rediscovering the Social Group* (Oxford: Blackwell, 1987). For cognitive approaches, see Michael Hogg and Craig McGarty, "Self-Categorization and Social Identity," in *Social Identity Theory: Constructive and Critical Advances*, ed. Dominic Abrams and Michael Hogg (London: Harvester Wheatsheaf, 1990), 10–27; John C. Turner, "Social Categorization and the Self-Concept: A Social-Cognitive Theory of Group Behaviour," in *Advances in Group Processes: Theory and Research*, ed. Edward J. Lawler (Greenwich, CT: JAI Press, 1985), 77–122.

58. Mark Rapley, "'Just an Ordinary Australian': Self-Categorization and the Discursive Construction of Facticity in 'New Racist' Political Rhetoric," *British Journal of Social Psychology* 37, no. 3 (1997): 328.

59. See Charles Antaki et al., "Social Identities in Talk: Speakers' Own Orientations," *British Journal of Social Psychology* 35 (1996): 473–92; Derek Edwards and Jonathan Potter, *Discursive Psychology* (London: Sage, 1992); Jonathan Potter, *Representing Reality: Discourse, Rhetoric, and Social Construction* (London: Sage, 1996); Jonathan Potter and Margaret Wetherell, *Discourse and Social Psychology* (London: Sage, 1987).

60. Lepper, *Categories in Text*, 15.

61. Carolyn D. Baker, "Membership Categorization and Interview Accounts," in *Qualitative Research: Theory, Method, and Practice*, ed. David Silverman (London: Sage, 2004), 174.

62. Jayyusi, *Categorization*, 23.

63. The transcription symbols used in this chapter (listed below) are a simplified version of the transcription system developed by Gail Jefferson. See J. M. Atkinson and J. Heritage, *Structures of Social Action: Studies in Conversation Analysis* (Cambridge: Cambridge University Press, 1984). Conventional spelling has been used throughout, but other elements of natural speech (including minimal response tokens and false starts) have been included.

?	Speaker not able to be identified.
//	Double obliques indicate the beginning of overlapping or simultaneous speech.
==	Double equal signs denote contiguous or "latched" utterances.
(.)	One period inside parentheses signals a pause (these have not been timed).
–	Dashes mark a false-start or truncated word.
[. . .]	Square brackets contain my commentary on the transcript, including explanations of the conversational setting and notations of omitted material.
HOORAY	Upper-case letters signal vocal emphasis.
Mormon	Bold font marks features of interest to the analyst.

64. All names are pseudonyms.

65. Michale Moerman, *Talking Culture. Ethnography, and Conversation Analysis* (Philadelphia: University of Pennsylvania Press, 1988), 90.

66. Sacks, *Lectures*, 246.

67. Coulter, "Remarks," 37.

68. Emanuel Schegloff et al., "The Preference for Self-Correction in the Organization of Repair in Conversation," *Language* 53, no. 2 (1977): 361.

69. Maria T. Wowk and Andrew P. Carlin, "Depicting a Liminal Position in Ethnomethodology, Conversation Analysis, and Membership Categorization Analysis: The Work of Rod Watson," *Human Studies* 27, no. 1 (2004): 72.

70. Sacks, "On the Analyzability," 335.

71. D. R. Watson, "The Presentation of 'Victim' and 'Motive' in Discourse: The Case of Police Interrogations and Interviews," *Victimology: An International Journal* 8, no. 1/2 (1983): 41; Watson, "Categorization."

72. Emanuel Schegloff, *Sequence Organization in Interaction: A Primer in Conversation Analysis* (Cambridge and New York: Cambridge University Press, 2007), 476.

73. Elizabeth Stokoe and Janet Smithson, "Making Gender Relevant: Conversation Analysis and Gender Categories in Interaction," *Discourse and Society* 12, no. 2 (2001): 226. See also Sacks, *Lectures*; Schegloff, *Sequence Organization*.

74. It is important to note, however, that intra-religious group differences may exceed inter-religious group differences in this regard.

75. Some activities are widely regarded as criterial for membership in particular RMCs, e.g., being ordained is often considered a requirement for membership in the category *priest*. However, different religious groups have established different criteria in this regard, e.g., the LDS Church categorizes all male members as *priests*. Conversely, Sarah J. Schubert et al., "'ADHD Patient' or 'Illicit Drug User'? Managing Medico-Moral Membership Categories in Drug Dependence Services," *Discourse and Society* 20, no. 4 (2009): 511, observe that some social membership categories (such as "illicit amphetamine user" and "adult ADHD patient") have "overlapping predicates," which are "interactionally exploitable," such that members of the first category can present themselves strategically as belonging to the second category (and thus gain access to the entitlements of membership in that category) by owning those predicates.

76. Both members' categories and the predicates to which they are bound are susceptible to social change. See Pam Nilan, "Membership Categorization Devices under Construction: Social Identity Boundary Maintenance in Everyday Discourse," *Australian Review of Applied Linguistics* 18, no. 1 (1995): 69–94. This is a fact that can work to the advantage of minority groups. See Wowk, "Blame Allocation." For a discussion of how particularization can be used both to establish and to defend category memberships, see Michael Billig, "Prejudice, Categorization, and Particularization: From a Perceptual to a Rhetorical Approach," *European Journal of Social Psychology* 15, no. 1 (1985): 93–94.

77. David Martin, "Canada in Comparative Perspective," in *Rethinking Church, State, and Modernity: Canada Between Europe and America*, ed. D. Lyon and Marguerite Van Die (Toronto: University of Toronto Press, 2000), 23.

78. Beaman, "Church, State," 25.

79. Bucholtz, "Why Be Normal?" 211.

80. Baker, "Membership Categorization," 170.

81. Stephen Hester, "Recognising References to Deviance in Referral Talk," in *Text in Context: Contributions to Ethnomethodology*, ed. Graham Watson and Robert M. Sieler (Newbury Park: Sage, 1992), 165.

82. This position was made explicit by LDS Church hierarchy in the lead-up to the 2002 Winter Olympic Games in Salt Lake City. It "specifically requested that the common labels 'Mormon Church,' the 'Latter-day Saints Church' and the 'LDS Church' not be used." See Bushman, *Contemporary Mormonism*, xiii.

83. Pentti Haddington, "Stance Taking in News Interviews," *SKY Journal of Linguistics* 17 (2004): 101.

84. Du Bois, "The Stance Triangle," 163; emphasis added.

85. See Penelope Eckert, *Linguistic Variation as Social Practice* (New York and London: Teachers College Press, 2000); Scott F. Kiesling, "Variation, Stance, and Style: Word-final -*er*, High Rising Tone, and Ethnicity in Australian English," *English World Wide* 26, no. 1 (2005): 1–42; Barbara Johnstone, "Linking Identity and Dialect through Stancetaking," in *Stancetaking in Discourse*, ed. Robert Englebretson (Amsterdam and Philadelphia: John Benjamins, 2007), 49–68.

86. Elinor Ochs, "Linguistic Resources for Socializing Humanity," in *Rethinking Linguistic Relativity*, ed. John J. Gumperz and Stephen C. Levinson (Cambridge: Cambridge University Press, 1996), 407–37; Elinor Ochs, "Indexing Gender," in *Rethinking Context: Language as an Interactive Phenomenon*, ed. A. Duranti and C. Goodwin (Cambridge: Cambridge University Press, 1992), 335–58; Elinor Ochs, "Constructing Social Identity: A Language Socialization Perspective," *Research on Language and Social Interaction* 26, no. 3 (1993): 287–306.

87. Fitzgerald and Housley, "Identity," 592.

88. Wowk, "Blame Allocation," 76.

89. Beaman, "Molly Mormons," 74.

90. Frank Bechhofer et al., "Constructing National Identity: Arts and Landed Elites in Scotland," *Sociology* 33, no. 3 (1999): 527.

91. Bhikhu Parekh, *Rethinking Multiculturalism: Cultural Diversity and Political Theory* (Basingstoke: Macmillan, 2000).

92. Ibid., 244.

93. Douglas Biber et al., *The Longman Grammar of Spoken and Written English* (London: Longman, 1999), 1003.

94. Martin, "Canada," 23.

95. Fitzgerald and Housley, "Identity," 592.

96. John Biles and Humera Ibrahim, "Religious Diversity in Canada: In the Shadow of Christian Privilege," *Canadian Diversity* 4, no. 3 (2005): 67–70; John G. Stackhouse Jr., "Bearing Witness: Christian Groups Engage Canadian Politics since the 1960s," in *Rethinking Church, State, and Modernity: Canada between Europe and America*, ed. D. Lyon and Marguerite Van Die (Toronto: University of Toronto Press, 2000), 113–28.

97. Ruth A. Berman, "Introduction: Developing Discourse Stance in Different Text Types and Languages," *Journal of Pragmatics* 37, no. 2 (2005): 109.

98. Janet G. van Hell et al., "To Take a Stance: A Developmental Study of the Use of Pronouns and Passives in Spoken and Written Narrative and Expository Texts in Dutch," *Journal of Pragmatics* 37, no. 2 (2005): 243.

99. Goffman, "Footing," 144.

100. Deborah Schiffrin, *Discourse Markers* (Cambridge and New York: Cambridge University Press, 1987), 268.

101. The use of "you know" to position one's interlocutor as possessing shared knowledge was noted by Janet Holmes. Janet Holmes, "Hedges and Boosters in Women's and Men's Speech," *Language and Communication* 10, no. 3 (1990): 189.

102. Ibid.

103. Biber et al., "The Longman Grammar," 1077.

104. Joanne Scheibman, "Subjective and Intersubjective Uses of Generalizations in English Conversation," in *Stancetaking in Discourse*, ed. Robert Englebretson (Amsterdam and Philadelphia: John Benjamins, 2007), 132.

105. That shifts from "I" to generic "you" can signal discomfort was noted by Lisa Abney. Lisa Abney, "Pronoun Shift in Oral Folklore, Personal Experience and Literary Narratives, or 'What's Up with *You*?'" *SECOL Review* 20, no. 2 (1996): 203–26.

106. The use of generic "you" to distance oneself from a particular position was noted by Scheibman, "Subjective," 2007.

107. James R. Martin, "Beyond Exchange: APPRAISAL Systems in English," in *Evaluation in Text: Authorial Stance and the Construction of Discourse*, ed. Susan Hunston and G. Thompson (Oxford: Oxford University Press, 2000), 159.

108. Ibid., 155.

109. Elise Kärkkäinen, *Epistemic Stance in English Conversation: A Description of Its Interactional Functions, with a Focus on I Think* (Amsterdam and Philadelphia: John Benjamins, 2003), 20.

110. Susan Conrad and Douglas Biber, "Adverbial Marking of Stance in Speech and Writing," in *Evaluation in Text*, ed. Susan Hunston and Geoff Thompson (Oxford: Oxford University Press, 2000), 65.

111. Jackie Abell and Greg Myers, "Analyzing Research Interviews," in *Qualitative Discourse Analysis in the Social Sciences*, ed, Ruth Wodak and Michał Krzyżanowski (Basingstoke, UK: Palgrave Macmillan, 2008), 154.

112. Armand Mauss observes that, whereas other denominations in the United States officially relinquished racial discrimination during the 1960s, the Church of Jesus Christ of Latter-Day Saints "retained an anachronistic nineteenth-century policy of excluding members of black African ancestry from its male lay priesthood" until the late 1970s. According to Mauss, "this situation left the Mormons conspicuously unique among major denominations in their policy toward African Americans." See Mauss, "Flowers," 171.

113. Mary Douglas and A. Wildavsky, *Risk and Culture: An Essay on the Selection of Technological and Environmental Dangers* (Berkeley: University of California Press, 1983).

114. Penelope Brown and Stephen C. Levinson, "Universals in Language Usage: Politeness Phenomena," in *Questions and Politeness*, ed. Esther N. Goody (Cambridge: Cambridge University Press, 1978), 11.

115. Erving Goffman, *Stigma: Notes on the Management of Spoiled Identity* (New York: Simon and Schuster, 1963), 107–8.

116. Brown and Levinson, "Universals," 61.

117. Michael Billig, *Ideology and Opinions* (London: Sage, 1991); Michael Billig, *Banal Nationalism* (London and Thousand Oaks, CA: Sage, 1995); Michael Billig et al., *Ideological Dilemmas: A Social Psychology of Everyday Thinking* (London: Sage, 1988).

118. Maggie Charles, "The Construction of Stance in Reporting Clauses: A Cross-Disciplinary Study of Theses," *Applied Linguistics* 27, no. 3 (2006): 494.

119. Elizabeth Holt, "Reporting and Reacting: Concurrent Responses to Reported Speech," *Research on Language and Social Interaction* 33, no. 4 (2000): 438.

120. Susan F. Harding, *The Book of Jerry Falwell: Fundamentalist Language and Politics* (Princeton, NJ: Princeton University Press, 2000), 12.

121. Himani Bannerji, "The Paradox of Diversity: The Construction of a Multicultural Canada and 'Women of Colour,'" *Women's Studies International Forum* 23, no. 5 (2000): 555.

122. Richard Day, *Multiculturalism and the History of Canadian Diversity* (Toronto: University of Toronto Press, 2000), 197.

123. Ibid., 209.

124. Theo van Leeuwen, "The Representation of Social Actors," in *Texts and Practices: Readings in Critical Discourse Analysis*, ed. C. R. Caldas-Coulthard and M. Coulthard (London: Routledge, 1996), 32–71.

125. Charles Taylor, "The Politics of Recognition," in *Multiculturalism and the Politics of Recognition*, ed. Amy Gutmann (Princeton, NJ: Princeton University Press, 1992), 25; emphasis mine.

126. Hans Mol, "Theory and Data on Religious Behaviour of Migrants," *Social Compass* 26, no. 1 (1979): 37.

127. Mary Douglas, *Purity and Danger: An Analysis of Concepts of Pollution and Taboo* (London and New York: Routledge, 2001), 4.

128. Parekh, *Rethinking Multiculturalism*, 33.

129. Indeed, religious studies scholars have identified various models of religious *half-belonging*. See Abby Day, "Believing in Belonging: An Ethnography of Young People's Constructions of Belief," *Culture and Religion* 10, no. 3 (2009): 263–78. See also Grace Davie, *Religion in Britain since 1945: Believing without Belonging* (Oxford: Blackwell, 1994).

130. Emanuel Schegloff, "Categories in Action: Person-Reference and Membership Categorization," *Discourse Studies* 9, no. 4 (2007): 456.

131. Eglin and Hester, *The Montreal Massacre*, 94. See also Carolyn D. Baker and Peter Freebody, "'Constituting the Child' in Beginning School Reading Books," *British Journal of Sociology of Education* 8, no. 1 (1987): 55–76.

132. D. Winiecki, "The Expert Witnesses and Courtroom Discourse: Applying Micro and Macro Forms of Discourse Analysis to Study Process and the 'Doings of Doings' for Individuals and for Society," *Discourse and Society* 19, no. 6 (2008): 770.

133. Carolyn D. Baker, "The "Search for Adultness': Membership in Adolescent-Adult Talk," *Human Studies* 7, no. 3/4 (1984): 301–24; Susan A. Speer and Jonathan Potter, "The Management of Heterosexist Talk: Conversational Resources and Prejudiced Claims," *Discourse and Society* 11, no. 4 (2000): 543–72.

134. Stokoe, "Mothers," 2003.

135. Schegloff, "Categories."

136. José Casanova, *Public Religions in the Modern World* (Chicago: University of Chicago Press, 1994), 5, 228.

137. Wowk, "Blame Allocation," 76.

Bibiography

Abell, Jackie, and Greg Myers. "Analyzing Research Interviews." In *Qualitative Discourse Analysis in the Social Sciences*, edited by Ruth Wodak and Michał Krzyżanowski, 145–61. Basingstoke: Palgrave Macmillan, 2008.

Abney, Lisa. "Pronoun Shift in Oral Folklore, Personal Experience, and Literary Narratives, or 'What's Up with *You*?'" *SECOL Review* 20, no. 2 (1996): 203–26.

Alm, Leslie, and Leah Taylor. "Alberta and Idaho: An Implicit Bond." *American Review of Canadian Studies* 33, no. 2 (2003): 197–218.

Antaki, Charles, Susan Condor, and Mark R. Levine. "Social Identities in Talk: Speakers' Own Orientations." *British Journal of Social Psychology* 35 (1996): 473–92.

Arrington, L. J. "Crisis in Identity: Mormon Responses in the Nineteenth and Twentieth Centuries." In *Mormonism and American Culture*, edited by Marvin S. Hill and James B. Allen, 168–84 New York: Harper and Row, 1972.

Atkinson, J. Maxwell, and John Heritage. *Structures of Social Action: Studies in Conversation Analysis.* Cambridge: Cambridge University Press, 1984.

Baker, Carolyn D. "Membership Categorization and Interview Accounts." In *Qualitative Research: Theory, Method, and Practice*, edited by David Silverman, 162–76. London: Sage, 2004.

——. "The 'Search for Adultness': Membership in Adolescent-Adult Talk." *Human Studies* 7, no. 3/4 (1984): 301–24.

Baker, Carolyn D., and Peter Freebody. 1987. "'Constituting the Child' in Beginning School Reading Books." *British Journal of Sociology of Education* 8, no. 1 (1987): 55–76.

Bannerji, Himani. "The Paradox of Diversity: The Construction of a Multicultural Canada and 'Women of Colour.'" *Women's Studies International Forum* 23, no. 5 (2000): 537–60.

Bartlett, Robert V. "Political Culture and the Environmental Problematique in the American West." In *Environmental Politics and Policy in the West*, edited by Zachary Smith, 101–16. Dubuque, IA: Kendall/Hunt Publishing, 1993.

"Basic Facts about the Church." *The Church of Jesus Christ of Latter-Day Saints.* http://www.lds.org/church/facts?lang=eng.

Beaman, Lori. "Church, State, and the Legal Interpretation of Polygamy in Canada." *Nova Religio: The Journal of Alternative and Emergent Religions* 8, no. 1 (2004): 20–38.

——. "Molly Mormons, Mormon Feminists, and Moderates: Religious Diversity and the Latter Day Saints Church." *Sociology of Religion* 62, no. 1 (2001): 65–86.

Bechhofer, Frank, David McCrone, Richard Kiely, and Robert Stewart. "Constructing National Identity: Arts and Landed Elites in Scotland." *Sociology* 33, no. 3 (1999): 515–34.

Beecher, Maureen Ursenbach. "Mormon Women in Southern Alberta: The Pioneer Years." In *The Mormon Presence in Canada*, edited by Brigham Y. Card, Herbert C. Northcott, John E. Foster, Howard Palmer, and George K. Jarvis, 211–30. Edmonton: University of Alberta Press, 1990.

Benwell, Bethan, and Elizabeth Stokoe. *Discourse and Identity*. Edinburgh: Edinburgh University Press, 2006.

Berard, T. J. "Evaluative Categories of Action and Identity in Non-evaluative Human Studies Research: Examples from Ethnomethodology." *Qualitative Sociology Review* 1, no. 1 (2005): 5–30.

Berger, Peter L. *The Desecularization of the World: Resurgent Religion and World Politics*. Grand Rapids: William B. Eerdmans, 1999.

Berman, Ruth A. "Introduction: Developing Discourse Stance in Different Text Types and Languages." *Journal of Pragmatics* 37, no. 2 (2005): 105–24.

Biber, Douglas, Stig Johansson, Geoffrey Leech, Susan Conrad, and Edward Finegan. *The Longman Grammar of Spoken and Written English*. London: Longman, 1999.

Biles, John, and Humera Ibrahim. "Religious Diversity in Canada: In the Shadow of Christian Privilege." *Canadian Diversity* 4, no. 3 (2005): 67–70.

Billig, Michael. *Banal Nationalism*. London and Thousand Oaks, CA: Sage, 1995.

———. *Ideology and Opinions*. London: Sage, 1991.

———. "Prejudice, Categorization, and Particularization: From a Perceptual to a Rhetorical Approach." *European Journal of Social Psychology* 15, no. 1 (1985): 79–103.

Billig, Michael, Susan Condor, Derek Edwards, Mike Gane, Dai Middleton, and Alan Radley. *Ideological Dilemmas: A Social Psychology of Everyday Thinking*. London: Sage, 1988.

Boeve, Lieven. "Religion after Detraditionalisation. Christian Faith in a Post-Secular Europe." Manchester: University of Manchester Department of Religions and Theology, 2004. http://www.art.man.ac.uk/reltheol.

Bramadat, Paul. "Re-Visioning Religion in the Contemporary Period: The United Church of Canada's Ethnic Ministries Unit." *Canadian Diversity* 4, no. 3 (2005): 59–62.

Brinkerhoff, Merlin B., and Elaine Grandin. "Contemporary Reactions to Mormonism: A Case Study from Rural Alberta." *Canadian Journal of Sociology* 16, no. 2 (1991): 165–85.

Brown, Penelope, and Stephen C. Levinson. "Universals in Language Usage: Politeness Phenomena." In *Questions and Politeness*, edited by Esther N. Goody, 56–289. Cambridge: Cambridge University Press, 1978.

Brubaker, Rogers, and Frederick Cooper. "Beyond 'Identity.'" *Theory and Society* 29, no. 1 (2000): 1–47.

Bucholtz, Mary. "'Why Be Normal?': Language and Identity Practices in a Community of Nerd Girls." *Language in Society* 28, no. 2 (1999): 203–23.

Bucholtz, Mary, and Kira Hall. "Identity and Interaction: A Sociocultural Linguistic Approach." *Discourse Studies* 7, no. 4–5 (2005): 585–614.

Bushman, Claudia L. *Contemporary Mormonism: Latter-Day Saints in Modern America.* Westport, CT: Praeger Publishers, 2006.

Canada. Statistics Canada. *2001 Census Analysis Series: Religions in Canada* (Catalogue Number 96F0030XIE2001015). Ottawa: Statistics Canada, 2003.

———. *2001 Community Profiles* (Catalogue Number 93F0053XIE). Ottawa: Statistics Canada, 2002.

Card, Brigham Y., Herbert C. Northcott, John E. Foster, Howard Palmer, and George K. Jarvis, eds. *The Mormon Presence in Canada.* Edmonton: University of Alberta Press, 1990.

Casanova, José. *Public Religions in the Modern World.* Chicago: University of Chicago Press, 1994.

Charles, Maggie. "The Construction of Stance in Reporting Clauses: A Cross-Disciplinary Study of Theses." *Applied Linguistics* 27, no. 3 (2006): 492–518.

Conrad, Susan, and Douglas Biber. "Adverbial Marking of Stance in Speech and Writing." In *Evaluation in Text*, edited by Susan Hunston and Geoff Thompson, 56–73. Oxford: Oxford University Press, 2000.

Cornwall, Marie. "The Institutional Role of Mormon Women." In *Contemporary Mormonism: Social Science Perspectives*, edited by Marie Cornwall, Tim B. Heaton, and Lawrence A. Young, 239–64. Chicago: University of Illinois Press, 1994.

Coulter, Jeff. "Remarks on the Conceptualisation of Social Structure." *Philosophy of the Social Sciences* 12, no. 1 (1982): 33–46.

Davie, Grace. "The Future of Religion and its Implications for the Social Sciences." In *Playful Religion: Challenges for the Study of Religion*, edited by A. von Harskamp, M. Klaver, J. Roeland, and P. Versteeg, 137–49. Delft: Eburon, 2006.

———. *Religion in Britain since 1945: Believing without Belonging.* Oxford: Blackwell, 1994.

Davies, Bronwyn, and Rom Harré. "Positioning: The Discursive Production of Selves." *Journal for the Theory of Social Behaviour* 20, no. 1 (1990): 43–63.

Davies, Douglas J. *An Introduction to Mormonism*. Cambridge: Cambridge University Press, 2003.

Day, Abby. "Believing in Belonging: An Ethnography of Young People's Constructions of Belief." *Culture and Religion* 10, no. 3 (2009): 263–78.

Day, Richard J. F. *Multiculturalism and the History of Canadian Diversity*. Toronto: University of Toronto Press, 2000.

Douglas, Mary. *Purity and Danger: An Analysis of Concepts of Pollution and Taboo*. London and New York: Routledge, 2001.

Douglas, Mary, and A. Wildavsky. *Risk and Culture: An Essay on the Selection of Technological and Environmental Dangers*. Berkeley: University of California Press, 1983.

Drew, Paul. "Accusations: The Occasioned Use of Members' knowledge of 'Religious Georgraphy' in Describing Events." *Sociology* 12, no. 1 (1978): 1–22.

Droogers, André. "Identity, Religious Pluralism, and Ritual in Brazil: Umbanda and Pentecostalism." In *Playful Religion: Challenges for the Study of Religion*, edited by Anton von Harskamp, Mirander Klaver, Johan Roeland, and Peter Versteeg, 27–45. Delft: Eburon, 2006. First published in 1998 by The Scarecrow Press.

Du Bois, John W. "The Stance Triangle." In *Stancetaking in Discourse: Subjectivity, Evaluation, Interaction*, edited by Robert Englebretson, 139–82. Amsterdam: John Benjamins, 2007.

Eckert, Penelope. *Linguistic Variation as Social Practice*. New York and London: Teachers College Press, 2000.

Edwards, Derek, and Jonathan Potter. *Discursive Psychology*. London: Sage, 1992.

Eglin, Peter. "Members' Gendering Work: 'Women,' 'Feminists,' and Membership Categorization Analysis." *Discourse and Society* 13, no. 6 (2002): 819–25.

Eglin, Peter, and Stephen Hester. *The Montreal Massacre: A Story of Membership Categorization Analysis*. Waterloo, ON: Wilfrid Laurier University Press, 2003.

Elton, David K. "Political Behavior of Mormons in Canada." In *The Mormon Presence in Canada*, edited by Brigham Y. Card, Herbert C. Northcott, John E. Foster, Howard Palmer, and George K. Jarvis, 260–78. Edmonton: University of Alberta Press, 1990.

Embry, Jessie L. *Mormon Polygamous Families: Lfe in the Principle*. Salt Lake City: University of Utah Press, 1987.

Englebretson, Robert, ed. `Stancetaking in Discourse: Subjectivity, Evaluation, Interaction*. Amsterdam and Philadelphia: John Benjamins, 2007.

"An Era of Correlation and Consolidation." In *Church History in the Fulness of Times Student Manual*, 2003, 562–78. The Church of Jesus Christ of Latter-Day Saints. https://www.lds.org/manual/church-history-in-the-fulness-of-times-student-manual/chapter-forty-three-an-era-of-correlation-and-consolidation?lang=eng.

Fitzgerald, Richard, and William Housley. "Identity, Categorization, and Sequential Organization: The Sequential and Categorial Flow of Identity in a Radio Phone-In." *Discourse and Society* 13, no. 5 (2002): 579–602.

Flanagan, Tom. "From Riel to Reform (and a Little Beyond): Politics in Western Canada." *American Review of Canadian Studies* 31, no. 4 (2001): 623–38.

Foster, Lawrence. *Women, Family, and Utopia: Communal Experiments of the Shakers, the Oneida Community, and the Mormons.* New York: Syracuse University Press, 1991.

Fox, Jeffrey C. "A Typology of LDS Sociopolitical Worldviews." *Journal for the Scientific Study of Religion* 42, no. 2 (2003): 279–89.

Goffman, Erving. "Footing." In *Forms of Talk*, edited by Erving Goffman, 124–59. Philadelphia: University of Pennsylvania Press, 1981.

——. *Stigma: Notes on the Management of Spoiled Identity.* New York: Simon and Schuster, 1963.

Grad, Héctor , and Luisa Martín Rojo. "Identities in Discourse: An Integrative View." In *Analysing Identities in Discourse*, edited by Rosana Dolón and Júlia Todolí, 3–28. Amsterdam and Philadelphia: John Benjamins, 2008.

Haddington, Pentti. "Stance Taking in News Interviews." *SKY Journal of Linguistics* 17 (2004): 101–42.

Hampshire, Annette P., and James A. Beckford. "Religious Sects and the Concept of Deviance: The Mormons and the Moonies." *British Journal of Sociology* 34, no. 2 (1983): 208–29.

Harding, Susan F. *The Book of Jerry Falwell: Fundamentalist Language and Politics.* Princeton, NJ: Princeton University Press, 2000.

Hardy, B. Carmon. *Solemn Covenant: The Mormon Polygamous Passage.* Urbana: University of Illinois Press, 1992.

Heaton, Tim B. "Sociodemographic Characteristics of Religious Groups in Canada." *Sociological Analysis* 47, no. 1 (1986): 54–65.

Hester, Stephen. "Recognising References to Deviance in Referral Talk." In *Text in Context: Contributions to Ethnomethodology*, edited by Graham Watson and Robert M. Sieler, 156–74. Newbury Park, UK: Sage, 1992.

Hester, Stephen, and Peter Eglin. *Culture in Action: Studies in Membership Categorization Analysis, Studies in Ethnomethodology, and Conversation Analysis*. Lanham, MD: International Institute for Ethnomethodology and Conversation Analysis and University Press of America, 1997.

———. "Membership Categorization Analysis: An Introduction." In *Culture in Action: Studies in Membership Categorization Analysis, Studies in Ethnomethodology, and Conversation Analysis*, edited by Stephen Hester and Peter Eglin, 1–24. Lanham, MD: International Institute for Ethnomethodology and Conversation Analysis and University Press of America, 1997.

———. "The Reflexive Constitution of Category, Predicate, and Context in Two Settings." In *Culture in Action: Studies in Membership Categorization Analysis, Studies in Ethnomethodology, and Conversation Analysis*, edited by Stephen Hester and Peter Eglin, 25–48. Lanham, MD: International Institute for Ethnomethodology and Conversation Analysis and University Press of America, 1997.

Hester, Stephen, and R. Fitzgerald. "'Category, Predicate and Task: Some Organisational Features in a Radio Talk Show.'" In *Media Studies: Ethnomethodological Approaches. SECA*, no. 5, edited by Paul Jalbert, 171–93. Lanham, MD: University Press of America, 1999.

Hester, Stephen, and William Housley. *Language, Interaction, and National Identity: Studies in the Social Organisation of National Identity in Talk-in-Interaction*. Ashgate, UK: Aldershot, 2002.

Hogg, Michael, and Craig McGarty. "Self-Categorization and Social Identity." In *Social Identity Theory: Constructive and Critical Advances*, edited by Dominic Abrams and Michael Hogg, 10–27. London: Harvester Wheatsheaf, 1990.

Holmes, Janet. 1990. "Hedges and Boosters in Women's and Men's Speech." *Language and Communication* 10, no. 3 (1990): 185–205.

Holt, Elizabeth J. "Reporting and Reacting: Concurrent Responses to Reported Speech." *Research on Language and Social Interaction* 33, no. 4 (2000): 425–54.

Hyland, Ken. *Disciplinary Discourses: Social Interactions in Academic Writing*. London: Longman, 2000.

"Introduction to Relief Society." *The Church of Jesus Christ of Latter-Day Saints*. http://www.lds.org/pa/display/0,17884,4689-1,00.html.

Ivanič, Roz. *Writing and Identity: The Discoursal Construction of Identity in Academic Writing*. Amsterdam and Philadelphia: John Benjamins, 1998.

Jaffe, Alexandra, ed. *Stance: Sociolinguistic Perspectives*. Oxford: Oxford University Press, 2009.

Jalbert, P. "Categorisation and Beliefs: News Accounts of Haitian and Cuban Refugees." In *The Interactional Order: New Directions in the Study of Social Order,* edited by D. T. Helm, W. T. Anderson, A. J. Meehan, and A. W. Rawls, 231–48. New York: Abingdon, 1989.

Jarvis, George K. "Demographic Characteristics of the Mormon Family in Canada." In *The Mormon Presence in Canada,* edited by Brigham Y. Card, Herbert C. Northcott, John E. Foster, Howard Palmer, and George K. Jarvis, 281–301. Edmonton: University of Alberta Press, 1990.

Jayyusi, Lena. *Categorization and the Moral Order*. Boston: Routledge and Kegan Paul, 1984.

Johnstone, Barbara. "Linking Identity and Dialect Through Stancetaking." In *Stancetaking in Discourse,* edited by Robert Englebretson, 49–68. Amsterdam and Philadelphia: John Benjamins, 2007.

Kärkkäinen, Elise. 2003. *Epistemic Stance in English Conversation: A Description of Its Interactional Functions, with a Focus on I Think*. Amsterdam and Philadelphia: John Benjamins, 2003.

Kiesling, Scott F. "Variation, Stance, and Style: Word-final *-er*, High Rising Tone, and Ethnicity in Australian English." *English World Wide* 26, no. 1 (2005): 1–42.

Kockelman, Paul. "Stance and Subjectivity." *Journal of Linguistic Anthropology* 14, no. 2 (2004): 127–50.

Lee, Jeff. "B.C. Polygamy Ban Won't Face Any Further Appeals, Province Says." *National Post*, March 26, 2012. http://news.nationalpost.com/2012/03/26/b-c-polygamy-ban-wont-face-any-further-appeals-province-says/.

Lee, Lawrence B. "The Mormons Come to Canada, 1887–1902." *Pacific Northwest Quarterly* 59, no. 1 (1968): 11–22.

Lepper, Georgia. *Categories in Text and Talk*. London: Sage, 2000.

Louder, Dean R. "Canadian Mormons in Their North American Context: A Portrait." *Social Compass* 40, no. 2 (1993): 271–90.

Martin, David. "Canada in Comparative Perspective." In *Rethinking Church, State, and Modernity: Canada between Europe and America,* edited by D. Lyon and Marguerite Van Die, 23–33. Toronto: University of Toronto Press, 2000.

Martin, James R. "Beyond Exchange: APPRAISAL systems in English." In *Evaluation in Text: Authorial Stance and the Construction of Discourse*, edited by Susan Hunston and G. Thompson, 142–75. Oxford: Oxford University Press, 2000.

Mauss, A. L. *The Angel and the Beehive: The Mormon Struggle with Assimilation*. Chicago: University of Illinois Press, 1994.

———. "Flowers, Weeds, and Thistles: The State of Social Science Literature on the Mormons." In *Mormon History*, edited by R. W. Walker, D. J. Whittaker, and J. B. Allen, 153–97. Urbana and Chicago: University of Illinois Press, 2001.

Mervis, Carolyn B., and Eleanor Rosch. "Categorization of Natural Objects." *Annual Review of Psychology* 32 (1981): 89–115.

Meyer, Thomas. *Identity Mania*. London: Zed Books, 2001.

Moerman, Michael. *Talking Culture. Ethnography, and Conversation Analysis*. Philadelphia: University of Pennsylvania Press, 1988.

Mol, Hans. "Theory and Data on Religious Behaviour of Migrants." *Social Compass* 26, no. 1 (1979): 31–39.

Morris, Peter S. "Charles Ora Card and Mormon Settlement on the Northwestern Plains Borderlands." In *The Borderlands of the American and Canadian Wests*, edited by Sterling Evans, 172–82. Lincoln and London: University of Nebraska Press, 2006.

Neuhaus, Richard J. *The Naked Public Square: Religion and Democracy in America*. Grand Rapids, MI: William B. Eerdmans, 1984.

Nilan, Pam. "Membership Categorization Devices under Construction: Social Identity Boundary Maintenance in Everyday Discourse." *Australian Review of Applied Linguistics* 18, no. 1 (1995): 69–94.

Oaks, Dallin H. "The Relief Society and the Church." *Ensign* (May 1992): 34–37.

Ochs, Elinor. "Constructing Social Identity: A Language Socialization Perspective." *Research on Language and Social Interaction* 26, no. 3 (1993): 287–306.

———. "Indexing Gender." In *Rethinking Context: Language as an Interactive Phenomenon*, edited by A. Duranti and C. Goodwin, 335–58. Cambridge: Cambridge University Press, 1992.

———. "Linguistic Resources for Socializing Humanity." In *Rethinking Linguistic Relativity*, edited by John J. Gumperz and Stephen C. Levinson, 407–37. Cambridge: Cambridge University Press, 1996.

Palmer, Howard. "The Reaction to Mormons in Canada, 1887–1923." In *The Mormon Presence in Canada,* edited by Brigham Y. Card, Herbert C. Northcott, John E. Foster, Howard Palmer, and George K. Jarvis, 1–59. Edmonton: University of Alberta Press, 1990.

Parekh, Bhikhu C. *Rethinking Multiculturalism: Cultural Diversity and Political Theory.* Basingstoke, UK: Macmillan, 2000.

Parsons, Talcott. "The Distribution of Power in American Society." In *Structure and Process in Modern Societies,* edited by Talcott Parsons, 199–225. Glencoe, IL: Free Press, 1960.

Potter, Jonathan. *Representing Reality: Discourse, Rhetoric, and Social Construction.* London: Sage, 1996.

Potter, Jonathan, and Margaret Wetherell. *Discourse and Social Psychology.* London: Sage, 1987.

Quinn, D. Michael. "Plural Marriage and Mormon Fundamentalism." In *Fundamentalisms and Society: Reclaiming the Sciences, the Family, and Education,* edited by Martin E. Marty and R. Scott Appleby, 240–93. Chicago: University of Chicago Press, 1993.

Rapley, Mark. "'Just an Ordinary Australian': Self-Categorization and the Discursive Construction of Facticity in 'New Racist' Political Rhetoric." *British Journal of Social Psychology* 37, no. 3 (1997): 325–44.

"Relief Society—History." *The Church of Jesus Christ of Latter-Day Saints.* http://www.lds.org/pa/display/0,17884,4748-1,00.html.

Sacks, Harvey. "Hotrodder: A Revolutionary Category." In *Everyday Language: Studies in Ethnomethodology,* edited by George Psathas, 7–14. New York: Irvington Press, 1979.

——. *Lectures on Conversation,* vol. 1, edited by Gail Jefferson. Oxford and Cambridge, MA: Basil Blackwell, 1992.

——. "On the Analyzability of Stories Told by Children." In *Directions in Sociolinguistics: The Ethnography of Communication,* edited by John J. Gumperz and Dell Hymes, 325–45. Oxford: Basil Blackwell, 1986. First printed in 1972 by Holt, Rinehart and Winston.

Schegloff, Emanuel A. "Between Micro and Macro: Contexts and Other Connections." In *The Micro-Macro Link,* edited by Jeffrey C. Alexander, B. Giesen, R. Munch, and N. J. Smelser, 207–34. Berkeley: University of California Press, 1987.

——. "Categories in Action: Person-Reference and Membership Categorization." *Discourse Studies* 9, no. 4 (2007): 433–61.

——. *Sequence Organization in Interaction: A Primer in Conversation Analysis*. Cambridge and New York: Cambridge University Press, 2007.

——. "A Tutorial on Membership Categorization." *Journal of Pragmatics* 39, no. 3 (2007): 462–82.

Schegloff, Emanuel A., Gail Jefferson, and Harvey Sacks. "The Preference for Self-Correction in the Organization of Repair in Conversation." *Language* 53, no. 2 (1977): 361–82.

Scheibman, Joanne. "Subjective and Intersubjective Uses of Generalizations in English Conversation." In *Stancetaking in Discourse*, edited by Robert Englebretson, 111–82. Amsterdam and Philadelphia: John Benjamins, 2007.

Schiffrin, Deborah. *Discourse Markers*. Cambridge and New York: Cambridge University Press, 1987.

Schubert, Sarah J., Susan Hansen, Kyle R. Dyer, and Mark Rapley. "'ADHD Patient' or 'Illicit Drug User?' Managing Medico-Moral Membership Categories in Drug Dependence Services." *Discourse and Society* 20, no. 4 (2009): 499–516.

Shepherd, Gary, and Gordon Shepherd. *Mormon Passage: A Missionary Chronicle*. Urbana and Chicago: University of Illinois Press, 1998.

Speer, Susan A., and Jonathan Potter. 2000. "The Management of Heterosexist Talk: Conversational Resources and Prejudiced Claims." *Discourse and Society* 11, no. 4 (2000): 543–72.

Stackhouse, John G., Jr. "Bearing Witness: Christian Groups Engage Canadian Politics since the 1960s." In *Rethinking Church, State and Modernity: Canada between Europe and America*, edited by D. Lyon and Marguerite Van Die, 113–28. Toronto: University of Toronto Press, 2000.

Stokoe, Elizabeth. "Categories and Sequences: Formulating Gender in Talk-in-Interaction." In *Gender and Language Research Methodologies*, edited by Kate Harrington, Lia Litosseliti, Helen Saunston, and Jane Sunderland, 139–57. London: Palgrave Macmillan, 2009.

——. "Mothers, Single Women, and Sluts: Gender, Morality, and Membership Categorization in Neighbour Disputes." *Feminism and Psychology* 13, no. 3 (2003): 317–44.

——. "On Ethnomethodology, Feminism, and the Analysis of Categorial Reference to Gender in Talk-in-Interaction." *Sociological Review* 54, no. 3 (2006): 467–94.

Stokoe, Elizabeth, and Janet Smithson. 2001. "Making Gender Relevant: Conversation Analysis and Gender Categories in Interaction." *Discourse and Society* 12 (2): 217–44.

Stueck, Wendy, and Justine Hunter. "B.C. Court Upholds Anti-Polygamy Law as Constitutional." *Globe and Mail*, November 23, 2011. http://www.theglobeandmail .com/news/national/british-columbia/bc-politics/bc-court-upholds-anti-polygamy -law-as-constitutional/article2246238/.

Tajfel, Henri. *Human Groups and Social Categories: Studies in Social Psychology*. Cambridge: Cambridge University Press, 1981.

Taylor, Charles. "The Politics of Recognition." In *Multiculturalism and the Politics of Recognition*, edited by Amy Gutmann, 25–73. Princeton, NJ: Princeton University Press, 1992.

Triandafyllidou, Anna, and Ruth Wodak. "Conceptual and Methodological Questions in the Study of Collective Identities: An Introduction." *Journal of Language and Politics* 2, no. 2 (2003): 205–23.

Turner, John C. "Social Categorization and the Self-Concept: A Social-Cognitive Theory of Group Behaviour." In *Advances in Group Processes: Theory and Research*, edited by Edward J. Lawler, 77–122. Greenwich, CT: JAI Press, 1985.

Turner, John C., Michael A. Hogg, P. J. Oakes, S. D. Reicher, and Margaret Wetherell. *Rediscovering the Social Group*. Oxford: Blackwell, 1987.

van Hell, Janet G., Ludo Verhoeven, Marjan Tak, and Moniek van Oosterhout. 2005. "To Take a Stance: A Developmental Study of the Use of Pronouns and Passives in Spoken and Written Narrative and Expository Texts in Dutch." *Journal of Pragmatics* 37, no. 2 (2005): 239–73.

van Leeuwen, Theo. "The Representation of Social Actors." In *Texts and Practices: Readings in Critical Discourse Analysis*, edited by C. R. Caldas-Coulthard and M. Coulthard, 32–71. London: Routledge, 1996.

Van Wagoner, Richard S. *Mormon Polygamy: A History*. Salt Lake City, UT: Signature Books, 1986.

Watson, D. R. "Categorisation, Authorisation and Blame-Negotiation in Conversation." *Sociology* 12, no. 1 (1978): 105–13.

——. "The Presentation of 'Victim' and 'Motive' in Discourse: The Case of Police Interrogations and Interviews." *Victimology: An International Journal* 8, no. 1/2 (1983): 31–52.

Watson, D. R., and T. Weinberg. "Interviews and the Interactional Construction of Accounts of Homosexual Identity." *Social Analysis* 11, no. 1 (1982): 56–78.

Wetherell, Margaret, ed. *Identities, Groups, and Social Issues*. London: Sage, 1996.

White, O. Kendall, Jr. "A Feminist Challenge: 'Mormons for ERA' as an Internal Social Movement." *Journal of Ethnic Studies* 13, no. 1 (1985): 29–37.

———. "Mormonism in America and Canada: Accommodation to the Nation-State." *Canadian Journal of Sociology* 3, no. 2 (1978): 161–81.

———. "Mormonism and the Equal Rights Amendment." *Journal of Church and State* 31, no. 2 (1989): 249–67.

Winiecki, D. "The Expert Witnesses and Courtroom Discourse: Applying Micro and Macro Forms of Discourse Analysis to Study Process and the Doings of Doings for Individuals and for Society." *Discourse and Society* 19, no. 6 (2008): 765–81.

Wowk, Maria T. "Blame Allocation, Sex, and Gender in a Murder Interrogation." *Women's Studies International Forum* 7, no. 1 (1984): 75–82.

Wowk, Maria T., and Andrew P. Carlin. "Depicting a Liminal Position in Ethnomethodology, Conversation Analysis, and Membership Categorization Analysis: The Work of Rod Watson." *Human Studies* 27, no. 1 (2004): 69–89.

6 "The Whole World Opened Up"

Women in Canadian Theosophy

GILLIAN MCCANN NIPISSING UNIVERSITY

Introduction

Even though many Theosophical women were among the most radical and socially engaged women of their time, their history in the Canadian context has remained largely unwritten. There are a number of reasons for this lacuna. Histories of alternative religions are few and far between in Canadian scholarship despite a burgeoning field of study in the United States and England. Also, little work has been done on women in non-Christian religious movements in Canada, which means that the information on them tends to be fragmentary. The evidence available to us, however, indicates that, as in countries like England, Australia, and the United States, Theosophy created an open and accepting space for women outside the mainstream in Canada.

An examination of the lives of Theosophical women offers an alternative lens through which to observe social and religious change in Canada. Feminist thinkers have emphasized how viewing society from the margins can offer a fuller and more accurate picture and help recognize the ways in which "gender constitutes experience."[1] The challenges faced by Theosophical women highlight the key issues at play as women struggled to attain equality in the political, social, and religious spheres.

My discussion in this has benefited from recent works such as the biographies of Rose Henderson and Helen Gutteridge, both Canadian women who were active in public life and interested in alternative religions, including Theosophy. As Peter Campbell notes when attempting to explain Henderson's free fall into obscurity, those who were members of a variety of causes such as labour, woman's suffrage, and education reform often remain "hidden from history," and are not documented by the historians of any of these movements. In *Rose Henderson: A Woman for the People*, Campbell asserts that Canadian historians have not been much interested in "histories of the left" or of women, and as a result radicals like Henderson have tended to be ignored within Canadian historiography.[2] For many of these women, political and religious experimentation went hand and hand, and both were viewed as contributing to a spiritually based society anchored in social justice and equity.

This chapter focuses on women in the Toronto Theosophical Society (TTS) and places them in a larger international context in an attempt to understand what attracted them to the movement. The chapter also examines whether or not these women participated in the rise of Theosophical feminism as developed in England and Australia, and as documented by scholars Joy Dixon and Jill Roe. The chapter then looks at two oral histories that offer an important perspective on the reasons why Theosophy appealed to Canadian women. It concludes with a consideration of the impact of Theosophy in terms of Canadian styles of religiosity.

The inclusion of oral history offers an emic perspective that recognizes the self-understanding of the practitioner. As Cort notes, this approach allows new and unexpected data to emerge rather than have it "relegated to a marginal position if it does not correspond to the model."[3] The use of personal narrative also recognizes the "activities of actual living individuals as the ontological ground of social science."[4]

The challenge involved in ensuring that these protean women find their proper place in the historical record has also been noted by historians of the Theosophical movement other than Campbell. Dixon has argued that the histories of socialism in Britain have written out women who were involved in alternative religions such as Theosophy despite their prominence. Theosophical women have often fallen afoul of the Enlightenment paradigm that renders the idea of a progressive form of religiosity largely unthinkable. From this point of view, all religion is essentially regressive and oppressive for women. Marxist feminists, for example, have often espoused this position; for them, rejecting religion entirely is the only road forward for women. This understanding does not take into consideration the multivalent nature of religion that can "both unsettle and stabilize."[5]

In attempting to discern whether or not Theosophy functioned as an empowering religious tradition for women, Mary Farrell Bednarowski's *Outside the Mainstream* offers useful schemata. Bednarowski argues that religions that foster female leadership and participation tend to possess four characteristics: first, a perception of the divine that de-emphasizes the masculine either by means of a bisexual divinity or an impersonal, non-anthropomorphic divine principle; second, a tempering or denial of the doctrine of the Fall; third, a denial of the need for traditional ordained clergy; and finally, a view of marriage that does not stress the married state and motherhood as the proper sphere for women and their only means of fulfillment.[6] According to Bednarowski's model, Theosophy emerges as a paradigmatic case of a positive religion for women.

While Theosophy was popular among many members of what Webb[7] has termed the occult underground, it was, according to feminist scholars, particularly appealing to women. As Alex Owen writes, women found "a unique sociospiritual environment offering personal validation and an intellectual rapport" in occult organizations.[8] Catherine Wessinger and Robert Ellwood have argued that the lack of a theological barrier to equality in Theosophy contributed to an openness to an enlarged role for women in the movement, and that Theosophy has "consistently affirmed and practiced gender equality and has provided a spiritual home for many actively feminist women."[9]

Given its theological openness, it is not surprising that the Theosophical movement produced many influential women leaders such as its founder Helena Blavatsky, Annie Besant, Katherine Tingley, Rukmini Devi, and Charlotte Despard. In her work on the utopian community of Point Loma developed under the leadership of Katherine Tingley, Penny Waterstone describes the community as a "limited feminine commonwealth."[10] She goes on to say that Point Loma allowed women a degree of independence without overtly challenging Victorian/Edwardian gender constructions. More overt demonstrations of an egalitarian ethos can be seen in the many Theosophical lodges that opened up leadership positions and provided opportunities to speak in public and to write for the array of Theosophical publications.

An overview of the religious beliefs of Theosophical women reveals a tendency on their part to ignore denominational boundaries and many moved across several in their lifetimes.[11] While she was never a Theosophist, the life trajectory of Alice Chown is instructive in understanding the ways in which the lives of some Canadian women were changing by the mid-nineteenth century. Chown was born in Kingston, Ontario, in 1866, into a devoutly Methodist family and was among the first Canadian women to receive a university education.[12] After her mother's death, Chown became active in a wide number of causes, including women's rights, labour, and pacifism, much to the dismay of her establishment family.[13] This pattern was also true of Rose Henderson, who started her life as a Methodist, became a Theosophist, and ended her life as a Quaker.[14]

The tenets of Theosophy appealed to those New Women who had begun to question traditional ideas about women's abilities and their roles in society. By the end of the Victorian era, these women were experiencing dissatisfaction with their political, social, familial, and religious roles, and their numbers began to grow in North America by the late nineteenth century. As Smith-Rosenberg writes, in "rejecting conventional female roles and asserting their right to a career, a public voice, to visible power, [women] laid claim to the rights and privileges customarily accorded bourgeois men."[15] The dropping birth rate in countries like Canada, and the education of women and their consequent entry into public and professional life contributed to a call for the re-evaluation of the place of women in society. This questioning of women's political position developed in tandem with the questioning of their role in the religious realm.

In her introduction to *Women's Religious Experience*, Pat Holden states that in the nineteenth century men controlled all aspects of mainstream religious traditions.[16] She notes that in traditional Christianity men "perform the important rituals, formulate the dogma, and hold the pens that write the sacred 'divinely inspired' texts. They control the powers of female reproductivity and dictate the social and cultural roles of women." While Christian sects like the Quakers and Shakers challenged the unequal status of women, most Christian denominations, by the latter part of the nineteenth century, were losing intelligent and energetic women to Spiritualism, Christian Science, and Theosophy. Holden argues that the purpose of Theosophy coincided with those of feminism and socialism, making it extremely appealing to politically radical New Women, offering them a new and broader arena for self-expression largely denied to them in the rest of society.[17]

Jill Roe, a scholar of Theosophy in Australia, notes that many Theosophical women disputed the "orthodox Christian doctrine of a male deity, a male clergy and female depravity" as well as "rigid attitudes to marriage and sex roles."[18] Theosophical women often lived outside the social norms of the time and were divorced, separated, widowed, or single. Many who were married espoused the ideal of "companionate marriage," a marriage of equal partners.[19]

In their willingness to both live and think differently, Theosophical woman were part of the avant-garde introducing new ideas about the potential of women into mainstream discourse. A number of talented women in the Theosophical movement were able to carve out a space for themselves from which to speak. Under the auspices of the Society, they were able to write and express themselves publicly on a wide variety of issues, including the position of women in society, in the political realm, and within the family.

Annie Besant, who was elected president of the international Society in 1907, is a paradigmatic example of a Theosophical woman. Besant had been a rebel long before she converted to Theosophy under the influence of Helena Blavatsky. Fleeing an abusive marriage to a clergyman, Besant had made the rights of women a central part of her political activism, and agitated for expanded property rights for women and access to birth control. The latter almost landed her in jail in 1877 for her work in publishing and distributing a pamphlet on contraception.[20] Besant, in looking back on her failed marriage, described herself as "indifferent to home details, impulsive, very hot tempered, and proud as Lucifer."[21] Besant, like Blavatsky before her, offered a new and expanded template and mentored women, encouraging them to participate in public life.[22] Her unorthodox views did not go unpunished and she lost custody of her children and was accused of abandoning her "Christian home and the faith of her fathers."[23]

For many New Women, this restless seeking can be attributed to the desire to find a philosophy that would be expansive enough to shelter their various programs and interests. With its synthetic theology/philosophy, Theosophy was appealing to many who experienced the Victorian crisis of faith. As Linklater writes of Charlotte Despard's diverse political, religious, and social interests, "only when she discovered Theosophy were these disparate enthusiasms drawn into one undivided vision."[24] Many Theosophical women found within the movement an open space that allowed them to experiment with a variety of approaches to spirituality and to try out different ideas related to their position in society.

For many women who were dissatisfied with their roles in mainstream Christianity, Theosophy also offered what McKay refers to as a "realm of freedom" where they could think through complex religious questions.[25] Dixon argues that Theosophical women were the precursors of feminist spirituality in their engagement with ideas about the relationship between divinity and the feminine.[26] The Theosophical Society also offered what Nelson refers to as an "epistemological community" in which new forms of thought and knowledge could be developed.[27] The question of "gendering the divine" continues to be central to feminist spirituality into the present day. Theosophists were among the first in the Western world to seriously question the idea of the gender of God. Theosophical women addressed the problem from a variety of angles, including positing the idea of the Divine Hermaphrodite and embracing the divine as both male and female or Father/Mother God.

The Theosophical belief in reincarnation also destabilized categories such as race and gender. As Theosophists believed that a person might be male in one lifetime and female another, it could be argued that gender was not a fixed or essential part of human identity. Theosophist Eva Gore-Booth argued that the true self was spirit, and therefore neither male nor female in an argument that "enabled a radical rethinking of gender relations and sexuality that drew more directly on Theosophical debates about reincarnation."[28] On the more extreme end of the Theosophical spectrum were the ideas of Frances Swiney, who turned Aristotle on his head and argued that men were merely imperfect women.[29] She posited that eventually male births would cease as the human race became perfected. Not surprisingly, her ideas were attacked by both Theosophists and those outside the movement. However, the nature of these ideas indicates the freedom of thought and expression that was possible for women within the Theosophical Society when discussing theology and the nature of the divine.

While Dixon has established a direct connection between philosophical/theological speculation and gender politics, little scholarly work has been done on the New Woman in a Canadian context. However, in looking at the history of women in the pivotal period from the 1880s to the 1920s, Kealey notes the connection between an interest in dress reform, bicycle riding, spiritualism, and reform movements.[30] Sea changes in the Canadian economy and rapid urbanization and industrialization were directly impacting the lives of women, and by the 1880s women and children constituted one-third of the labour force in Toronto.[31] By the time the Toronto Theosophical Society was founded in 1891, some Canadian women had begun to make their way into the public sphere and were addressing a variety of social reform issues. Looming problems of urban poverty were becoming apparent, and many New Women threw themselves into a variety of ameliorative movements.

For many Canadians in the nineteenth century who were committed to building religious communities, their efforts were largely directed at creating some form of continuity with their European past. This deployment of religion continues within contemporary diasporic communities where religion becomes a rallying point and serves as psychic protection in a new country.[32] In nineteenth-century Ontario, traditional forms of Christianity, Roman Catholicism and Protestantism, formed an "unofficial, yet extremely powerful, moral establishment."[33] However, according to Grant, the existence of Mormons, Seventh Day Adventists, and Theosophists was indicative of changes occurring in the religious topography of the province.[34]

In the case of new religious movements like Theosophy, the efforts of members were directed toward building a new and better social order rather than cementing a pre-existing one. Theosophy was one of the many religious movements emerging from the larger occult revival that functioned as a countercultural movement. Central to the concern of many to build a better world was the creation of an expanded social role for women. Alternative religious movements like Theosophy, Spiritualism, and Christian Science functioned as social laboratories in which different approaches and roles could be tested.

To understand the appeal of Theosophy to women, some background is necessary. The Theosophical Society was founded in New York City in 1875 by Helena Petrovna Blavatsky, a Russian émigré and former medium; Henry Steel Olcott, a lawyer and journalist interested in the occult; and William Quan Judge, an Irish lawyer living in New York. Blavatsky was the movement's primary ideologue, and she set the template for the maverick and rebellious women who would be attracted to Theosophy. Blavatsky was born into the Russian aristocracy, but at an early age rejected her society's ideas about the role of women, and at the age of seventeen ran away from her marriage to a man many years her senior. Blavatsky appears to have been interested in the occult and mysticism already in childhood and also liked to "joke, tease and cause a commotion."[35]

After living a bohemian life that included extensive travel, Madame Blavatsky settled in the United States in 1873 and helped to found the Theosophical Society. The stated objectives of the Theosophical Society were to "form the nucleus of a Universal Brotherhood of Humanity, without distinction of race, creed, sex, caste or colour, to encourage the study of comparative religion, philosophy and science, and to investigate the powers latent in man."[36] Theosophists were part of a larger neo-Romantic movement that questioned the hegemony of both science and mainstream religion. They were interested in a wide variety of forms that King refers to as "rejected knowledge," including astrology, alchemy, and systems of divination such as tarot cards.[37] Theosophy has been belatedly recognized as one of the primary influences on the renaissance of astrology in the Western world.[38]

In his preface to *The Theosophical Enlightenment*, a work that examines the history of esoteric and occult movements in the English-speaking world, Godwin states that Theosophy held a "crucial position as the place where all these currents temporarily united, before diverging again."[39] While these occult practices were often dismissed then as they are now,

Alex Owen has argued that they were a vital part of a resistance to the process of "disenchantment" most fully described by sociologist Max Weber.[40]

The role of Theosophists as cultural ambassadors has increasingly been recognized by scholars. Theosophists were especially interested in Hinduism and Buddhism, and it is now widely accepted that they were one of the most important forces for introducing Hindu philosophical concepts into the Western world.[41] The Theosophical movement grew rapidly, chartering lodges around the globe and eventually moving its headquarters to Adyar in south India in 1882, where it remains to the present. Poised as they were between East and West, Theosophists understood themselves to be translators of Eastern ideas to a Western audience. Annie Besant, the international president from 1907 to 1933, declared that the Theosophical concept of combining the best philosophical ideas of East and West would result in the "blended ideal of the future."[42]

The idea that religions like Hinduism had something to contribute to Western society was a radical one in the Victorian and Edwardian eras at a time when missionaries flooded the subcontinent in an attempt to gain converts to Christianity. Theosophists were viewed with suspicion by the English in India, and their belief in the equality of all cultures and religions put them at cross-purposes with both missionaries and imperialists. Seeing Theosophists as traitors and in opposition to the work of Christian missionaries, many British imperialists "were particularly appalled by the 'treachery' of Westerners 'going native.'"[43] In Canada, Theosophists like Albert Smythe not only defended the traditions of Buddhism and Hinduism, but also the practices of First Nations peoples. Smythe criticized the Department of Indian Affairs and argued for the right of Aboriginal communities to continue to practise their traditional religion.[44]

As Ellwood has noted, those interested in alternative religion in general tended to be "Anglo-Saxon, middle class, well educated and *female*."[45] The fact that so many of those who were "turning East" were women was not lost on those in the establishment and was greeted with alarm. In 1891 the year of the founding of the Toronto Theosophical Society, writers for *The Christian Guardian*, a Methodism paper, criticized those who sought to "glorify heathen traditions."[46] In a column called "Notes and News from India," which was dedicated to missionary work in India, the columnist wrote: "We learn with regret that the wife of one of the most distinguished Editors and citizens of New York has been led so far astray by Madame Blavatsky's spiritualism as to lose her head."[47]

A number of societal fears vied against one another as prominent women became interested in Eastern religions such as Hinduism. As Stefanie Syman points out, there was also a fear of actual physical contact between Anglo-Saxon women and Indian men, and threats to the nuclear family as women became "victims of Hindu mysticism."[48] While a growing minority of women was increasingly dissatisfied with mainstream religious denominations, Theosophical women tended to be the most experimental in their approach to theology.

Theosophy allowed many women who were questioning their own religious traditions to retain a religious world view without resorting to either materialism or fundamentalism. The milieu in which these women moved is described by Henry James in his novel *The Bostonians* (1885) as one of "witches, wizards, mediums, and spirit rappers and roaring radicals."[49] This underground world with its mixture of esotericism, politics, and radicalism existed in Canada, the United States, and Great Britain in the late nineteenth century. In his work on Spiritualism in Canada, Stan McMullin notes that, because of its emphasis on individual experience, women in the movement could bypass the need for male clergy.[50] Spiritualism offered an opportunity for women to take positions of leadership as men and women were considered to be equal in Spiritualist practice and theology. Scholarship on the women involved in the occult organization, Order of the Golden Dawn, reveals that they developed a wide variety of oscillating roles for themselves.[51]

The beginning of 1899 marked the publication of Fred Bury's *Journal of New Thought* and *The Realm*. That same year, *The Journal of Psychosophy* was launched. The articles in these publications ranged in topic from health, animal rights, labour, to New Thought and Spiritualism; they featured advertisements for magnetic healers, clairvoyants, and massage therapists. Despite Toronto's reputation for both religious and political conservatism, these publications in circulation in Toronto at the end of the Victorian era indicate that an audience for occult topics and the creation of what Morrisson calls a "counter-public sphere" existed.[52]

The Toronto Theosophists launched their own paper, *The Lamp*, in 1894. Articles in *The Lamp* were eclectic and covered a variety of topics, including biographies of leaders of the Theosophical movement, astrology, vegetarianism, and readings from Hindu scripture such as the *Bhagavad Gita* and *Vishnu Purana*. In its pages, editor and president of the TTS, Albert Smythe, recognized the Theosophical affinity with other reform movements, including the Salvation Army and the Socialist League.[53]

While many Theosophists clearly emerged from the occult milieu of the Victorian and Edwardian eras, discerning the religious backgrounds of Theosophical women is challenging. Theosophy had soft boundaries and one could be both a Theosophist and a professing Christian. Theosophical women often moved from Protestant denomination to Protestant denomination showing very little interest in these traditional demarcations. In this they were like their American cousins who practised what Ahlstrom refers to as "harmonial religions," which represent a "highly diffuse religious impulse that cuts across all the normal lines of religious division."[54] While this approach to religiosity was typical of the United States with its "free market religious economy," as described by Finke and Stark, by the late Victorian period it was becoming increasingly common in Canada as well.[55]

Likely because they did not have to choose between Christianity and Theosophy, the movement attracted women from a variety of Protestant denominations. These women brought with them their activist skills honed in voluntary organizations that had sprung up across Ontario. The activist impulse, particularly strong in Methodism, resulted in "the growth of voluntary associations and created a public function for women."[56] Groups like the Women's Christian Temperance Union (WCTU) evolved into a sophisticated and well-organized lobby group, and the WCTU was the first mainstream organization to support the movement for women's suffrage.[57]

The charter members of the TTS were congruent with the membership of other Theosophical societies. The founders were Albert Ernest Stafford Smythe, Algernon Blackwood, Ethel Day MacPherson, and Dr. Emily Stowe and Dr. Augusta Stowe-Gullen. All had roots in liberal Protestantism and/or had radical political backgrounds and many were journalists.

The composition of the group reveals clearly that Theosophy was attractive to the New Women of Toronto.

Ethel Day MacPherson was a suffragette and women's editor of *The Labor Advocate*, a socialist weekly.[58] In an article she wrote for *The Labor Advocate*, she explained the connection between occultism and reform as she saw it, emphasizing self-reliance:

> The law of karma is the law of action and reaction—of cause and effect, and teaches that each thought, word and deed, of our present life, is a cause that produces effect in the next reincarnation that, in short, we are the creators of our own destiny.[59]

In her article, MacPherson also advocated for the "Brotherhood of Man" and called for a society oriented toward a more noble principle of association than that of competition.

Founding members Emily Stowe and her daughter Augusta Stowe-Gullen were also New Women, and both were well-known medical doctors and advocates of women's suffrage. Becoming a doctor in 1867, Stowe was the first woman to practise medicine in Canada. Catherine Cleverdon, historian of the suffrage movement in Canada, writes:

> Largely owing to Dr. Stowe's efforts, the University of Toronto opened its doors to women in 1886, and professional schools began to let down their bars. Dr. Stowe also strove to secure factory and health laws, a better Married Women's Property Act, and above all, the political enfranchisement of women, for she rightly felt this would act as a powerful lever in opening the door to other reforms.[60]

Augusta-Stowe Gullen followed in her mother's footsteps, both as a doctor and as an activist, and was the first woman to receive a medical degree from a Canadian university.[61] She was an advocate of women's rights and succeeded her mother as president of the Dominion Women's Enfranchisement Association in 1903.[62] Stowe-Gullen also offered her resources to the fledgling TTS, hosting the first Theosophical meetings at her house on Spadina Avenue.[63]

Lelia Davis was another early member of the TTS who was active in a wide variety of reform movements, was also a member of the WCTU, and wrote a pamphlet on dress reform.[64] Davis went on to become one of the founding members of the Socialist League along with five other Theosophists.[65] Many Theosophists internationally were sympathetic to socialism and viewed capitalism as fundamentally opposed to their values of cooperation and universal brotherhood. While Theosophists drew the line at violent revolution, they tended to be sympathetic to programs that allowed for the redistribution of wealth and that encouraged socialist legislation such as old age pension and welfare.

One of the most remarkable women to join the TTS, and a person almost wholly obscured within the mainstream narrative of Canadian history, is Flora MacDonald Denison. Denison joined the TTS in 1918 and was one of the prime movers of the Committee for Social Reconstruction, which operated under the auspices of the TTS. The group was focused on the postwar issues of labour, soldiers, and "food problems."[66] Her participation in the Theosophical movement reveals the continuing appeal of Theosophy to feminist and activist Canadian women. Like Emily Stowe and Augusta Stowe-Gullen, with whom she was friends, Denison was dedicated to the suffrage movement and had been elected president of the Canadian Suffrage Association in 1911.[67]

Denison's full biography remains to be written, but some of her history can be gleaned from her unpublished autobiographical novel, *Mary Melville Psychic* (1900), which tells the story of her unorthodox family, and her testimony in Austin's, *Why I Converted to Spiritualism*. Denison's connection with Theosophy came about through her meeting TTS president, Albert Smythe, while working for the Toronto paper, *The World*, in which she often wrote on topics related to women's rights.[68] Denison spoke on women's suffrage in Canada, the United States, and Europe and knew many of the key players in the women's movement, including Susan B. Anthony and Emmeline Pankhurst.[69]

Denison was a successful businesswoman and a radical feminist who supported the accessibility of divorce, birth control, and "even attacked the sanctity of the nuclear family."[70] She maintained a pacifist stance throughout World War I despite, or perhaps because of, her own son fighting in the conflict.[71] In her pamphlet, "War and Women," which was originally delivered as a speech at the Biennial Meeting of the Canadian Suffrage Association, Denison denounced militarism.[72] She asserted the essentially constructive nature of women and tied it to maternity. Denison went on to assert that the women of England had no quarrel with the women of Germany, and "every man who ever went to battle meant that some woman had gone down into the shadow of the valley of suffering to give him birth."[73] She linked the issue of war to that of suffrage, stating that without the vote women were powerless to impact the course of events that would affect their families. Then, taking a more philosophical perspective, she argued that "there is no democracy while women are a disenfranchised class."[74]

Along with the fight for the vote and her commitment to pacifism, Denison was also involved in the cause of labour. She was concerned with the working conditions of the needle trade workers, then the largest industry in Toronto, and wrote on the topic of their abuse in publications like *Saturday Night* magazine.[75] Denison offered concrete support to the movements she championed, for example, paying the rent for the headquarters of the Canadian Suffrage Association on Yonge Street in Toronto.[76] Denison's political views, which included support of birth control, went far beyond that of the maternal feminism of many middle-class suffragettes, and she was eventually removed from a position of power in the Canadian Suffrage Association because of them.[77]

Another influential woman affiliated with the TTS, although not an official member, was Emma Goldman, who was in exile from her adopted American homeland throughout the 1930s. The anarchist and feminist lived in Toronto from 1926 to 1928, 1933 to 1935, and 1939 to 1940.[78] Deemed the "most dangerous woman in the world," she was not permitted to speak at the University of Toronto, but appeared numerous times at the Theosophical Hall at 52 Isabella Street.[79] She lectured on a variety of topics, including education, modern drama, and the thought of George Bernard Shaw.[80] In her memoir, *Living My Life*, Goldman had few positive things to say about Toronto, complaining about the difficulty of finding the books that she needed.[81] She also commented that "both Catholic and Anglican churches hold the city by the throat, and mould the habits and the opinions of the people of Toronto."[82]

It is clear that the TTS, like Theosophical lodges around the world, attracted powerful, self-determined women such as founding members Emily Stowe and Augusta Stowe-Gullen. Despite this fact, men outnumbered women substantially in the early years of the TTS,[83] and almost all the top executive positions were held by men. Women in the TTS rarely held positions of authority, except for a brief period when an effort was made to recruit women for these positions.[84]

In this the Toronto Theosophists differed from their counterparts in England and Australia. Roe speculates that many of the Australian lodges adopted a more traditional religious focus that emphasized devotionalism and that this led to the development of "theosophic feminism."[85] The TTS, however, rejected this model, advocated by international president Annie Besant, and maintained its original bureaucratic structure as a Victorian voluntary society that organized lectures, printed pamphlets, and held regular meetings. Dixon notes that this style of occultism was essentially a man's world, emerging as it did from the British model of the man's private club.[86] A parallel can be seen in the Arts and Letters Club, which was another cultural centre of Toronto in the early twentieth century, and one that had many Theosophists as members. The club was exclusively for men and the president August Bridle writes with outrage of a visiting Italian opera singer who dared to bring his wife.[87]

As a result of not adopting a more traditional religious form as advocated by Besant, the "feminization" of Theosophy did not happen in the case of the TTS. The publications of the society, *The Lamp* and *The Canadian Theosophist*, had little to say about women, and when women did contribute, it was generally on philosophical subjects such as yoga, and did not touch on the role of women specifically.[88] Women participated in the ladies auxiliary of the Toronto lodge, but it wielded little direct political or economic power.

The roles for women in the TTS were largely supportive, and analogous to those held by women in mainstream Christian churches. Men dominated as lecturers and in holding positions of executive power on key committees, and at no time did a woman hold the position of president of the lodge. Women served in traditional roles such as librarians, running the Children's Lotus Circle, or as secretary to the president. The women of the TTS were often vital to the financial survival of the lodge, especially during the Depression, but this did not result in any more power being granted to them.

The topics addressed in Theosophical lectures and in *The Lamp* and *Canadian Theosophist* were similar to those of Theosophical societies elsewhere; favourite subjects included astrology, vegetarianism, Indian philosophy such as yoga, the concepts of karma and reincarnation, and particularly in the 1930s, economics and pacifism. As with other Theosophical lodges, the lecture and article topics reveal an interest in comparative religion, including Hinduism, Sikhism, and Judaism. The position of women seems to have rarely been the actual topic of discussion; although there were numerous female speakers that addressed the TTS, they do not seem to have spoken on subjects related directly to women.

Some of the reasons for the relative lack of power wielded by women in the TTS can likely be laid at the feet of the TTS president Albert Smythe, who was the defining figure in Canadian Theosophy up until World War II. While Smythe was extremely progressive in many of his political views, his views on women appear to have remained resolutely Victorian and conventional. His daughter remembers his exhortation to her to remember that she was "a lady," which appears to have meant that she should be polished, refined, and not work outside the home.[89] Smythe groomed men such as Roy Mitchell and Frederick Housser for executive positions, but did not do this for women. The women in the TTS who worked alongside him were always maintained in purely supportive roles, and had little decision-making power about the direction of the Society. That being said, Smythe's grandson remembers him in his eighties still teaching a class of mostly women.[90]

Despite the lack of political power, women continued to be attracted to the Theosophical Society and two oral histories offer insights into why this may have been the case. While a variety of analyses can be utilized in looking at the position of women in the TTS, allowing the women to speak about their own experience helps to avoid what Smith refers to as the "magisterial forms of objective discourse."[91] Sarah Lakin and Ruth Playle, who are the focus of the second part of this chapter, were not public figures such as the women discussed above. As a result they help illuminate the experience of female members drawn from the rank-and-file of the movement. Their comments can offer insight into what appealed to Canadian women about Theosophical ideas and institutions.

Sarah Lakin
"Joining Was the Biggest Moment of My Life"

SARAH LAKIN, whom I interviewed in her apartment at a retirement home in Toronto, has a great deal to contribute to an understanding of the history of Theosophy in Canada. Lakin, who was in her eighties when I interviewed her, began attending the Hamilton lodge meetings in 1936. She remembered the society as a refuge from the difficulties of her life, having · grown up in a poverty-stricken family. Born in 1914 in Hamilton, Ontario, to British parents, Lakin remembered her family struggling to survive during the Depression when all the men in the family were out of work. At fifteen she found a job at Real Silk Hosiery, and supported her entire family on $6 a week. Although Lakin worked full time, she continued to educate herself despite her family's lack of support. Although Lakin's family was nominally Christian and she attended the United Church as a child, she felt no affinity with the denomination.

In her late teens, Lakin developed an interest in Spiritualism. She began to attend séances conducted by medium Tom Lacey, who was active in Hamilton and Kitchener-Waterloo.[92] Lakin said of this experience:

> Tom Lacey probably was a good medium at one time and was genuine . . .
> when he gave a talk there was a big circle of people: chiropractors and
> businessmen, all kinds of different people from Hamilton. . . . This is
> where I heard about reincarnation and guess where Tom Lacey got all
> this stuff? From *The Secret Doctrine*. Reincarnation was the only answer
> for me because of my unhappy childhood.

When Lacey suggested that she become his mistress, Lakin became disillusioned with Spiritualism and moved on to the study of Theosophy. This movement from Spiritualism to Theosophy was typical and can be seen in the trajectory of other Toronto Theosophists like Flora MacDonald Denison.

Lakin described joining the Society and meeting Albert Smythe as the turning point in her life and remembers in detail going to the Templar's Hall in Hamilton.

> I often go over it even though it was many years ago. I go over the first day that I went in because the world just opened up when I heard the objects of the Society. I nearly fainted with excitement and then he started to lecture on higher and lower *manas* and I had never heard a Sanskrit word in my life. It was so ignorant in our house, we had no music, no books, they were so poor and it took all their time to make a living and keep things going.

Although Smythe does not seem to have prepared women for executive positions, it is clear that his personality was one of the reasons Lakin was attracted to the Society. Lakin also noted the disapproval of her family: "When I first joined my family thought that I had gone to a cult. Eventually though my mother told me many years later that she used to read all the books I brought home." The attitude expressed by Lakin's family was typical of mainstream society toward Theosophy, and in 1940 Albert Smythe wrote that "relations are often hostile to the student of Theosophy."[93]

Lakin remembers that the Theosophical Society had difficulty obtaining meeting space due to prejudice against the Society fostered by the negative press in *The Hamilton Spectator.* She recalled that the group would often disguise its identity when trying to obtain a room. Despite this Lakin remembers the meetings as being peopled by the wealthy as it was "the stylish thing to do."

The role that Theosophy played in continuing education, especially for women, has not really been examined in histories of the Theosophical Society. Lakin stated that:

> If it hadn't been for the TS I would never have been able to hold my own in a discussion group. I was so terribly shy and my education was so limited. So you see I was completely self-educated through the society . . . if I was president or vice-president [of groups she belonged to] I always

made sure there was a good chairman and knew how to set up an organization and how to advertise.

At that time, lodges would have been some of the only institutions offering
teachings in comparative religion, which has since become typical of university offerings post-1960s. Lakin was invited by Smythe to attend a study
class in his home in north Hamilton. She recalled that Smythe spoke about
India favourably while "we'd always been told that Indians were pagans."

Lakin emphasized that as a member of the Theosophical Society, she
was treated with respect, and that no one inquired about her background.
Through the Society, she encountered alternative approaches to health
and healing as well as being exposed to Indian philosophy. When she was
struck with debilitating arthritis after the birth of her son, Lakin believed
that she was able to cure herself with the help of a fellow Theosophist
who was a chiropractor and iridologist. Lakin recalled that a number of
her friends ended up in jail in the 1940s for practising iridology and using
herbal remedies. As a result of her experience with alternative medicine,
Lakin made a link between attitudes and illness that now characterize
many beliefs that have emerged from the New Age movement. She said, "I
had to change my eating patterns and my attitude to relatives."

Sarah Lakin was reconciled with her mother through her belief in
karma and remembered that Albert Smythe advised her to be thankful
for her karma as otherwise she would have been a "milquetoast." "I hated
my mother," she said, "but as time went on I understood. And as the years
went by we had a wonderful relationship and Peter [her son] really loved
her."

Lakin's attitudes were also shaped by a relationship with a fellow
Theosophist who was homosexual and who would "read me poetry, take
me to concerts, and not hassle me at the door." She felt that this relationship contributed to her positive attitude toward her son's homosexuality. It
would appear that the Theosophical Society also offered a more welcoming environment for those who were non-normative either in their sexuality or politics.

Lakin remained active throughout her life as a member of the Theosophical Society and the Consumer Health Organization, and stated that

the confidence to be an active participant came from her experience organizing and participating in Theosophical events. Becoming a member of the Theosophical Society for Lakin was a transformative experience that helped her deal with a difficult childhood by providing a coherent philosophical framework that reframed suffering within the context of greater meaning. The TTS contributed to her further education and provided her with the skills and confidence to become active as a public citizen. For a working-class woman whose family could not afford secondary education, the TTS provided much of the training that would have come from a university education. The moment of her discovery of Theosophy and her meeting Albert Smythe remained indelibly imprinted in her memory as pivotal; she declared, "joining was the biggest moment of my life."

Ruth Playle
Silver Tea Sets during the Depression

WHEN I INTERVIEWED RUTH PLAYLE at a Tim Hortons in Toronto, she was ninety years old. In fine health, and a lifelong vegetarian, she was living independently and still taking classes on astrology. Playle was born in 1910 to English parents in Nelson, British Columbia. Her father was an Anglican and her mother was Baptist. Upon the death of her mother when Ruth was five years old, the family moved to Toronto, where her paternal grandfather was a successful businessman. While the family did not want materially, and Ruth attended Moulton College, a private school at Bloor and Yonge, her family life was far from happy.

Playle's home life, which she described as dysfunctional, deteriorated quickly upon their move east. After her father's remarriage, Playle lived part of the time with a maternal aunt, a devout Baptist. Remembering her childhood, Playe said that from the age of seven, "when I knew what meat was," she was a strict vegetarian. An excellent student, Ruth was awarded a math scholarship that allowed her to attend McMaster University, then located in Toronto. Because the scholarship covered only the first three years of her degree, and Ruth had not been assured of her father's support, she worked in the summer to pay her fourth-year fees. In 1931 she graduated and began looking for a job.

Playle knew that there were few jobs available, particularly for women, but she was determined to make an independent living. That same year she worked for three months without pay at the Neighbourhood Workers, a social work agency at St. Clair and Oakwood in Toronto, which assisted people who needed affordable housing. At the age of twenty-five Ruth moved into her own apartment and worked at a series of temporary jobs in lawyers' offices and then permanently as secretary to a socially minded lawyer named Malcolm Wallace McCutcheon. After six years in this position she decided to return to school to get an education degree.

Early in the 1940s, Playle came across a notice board for the Toronto Theosophical Society outside its building at 52 Isabella Street. Although she did not go in when she first saw the notice, she began to take note of the lecture topics being advertised:

One day I looked and the subject was reincarnation by Dudley Barr and I never missed his lectures for years after. He was just marvelous. I just wandered in on a Sunday and an elderly man with a lot of vitality, Felix Belcher, came up to me. It turned out he knew my grandfather, John Playle, who had been an early member. Many of them were middle-aged so they were delighted to see a young person. I was very much interested in philosophy, I studied it at McMaster and Theosophy sounded mystical and mysterious.

Playle began attending regularly both the lectures and social events such as the monthly tea put on by the women's committee, where vegetarian food was served along with tea in a "shining sterling silver tea set."

After a period in which her interest in Theosophy grew, Playle formally became a member, and attended the talks of visiting lecturers such as Clara Codd and Madeleine Hindsley. Hindsley was an English woman who had lived in India and knew both Gandhi and Nehru. Clara Codd, in her seventies, was also English, and Playe said of her, "she was perfection, an intellectual and a great writer and lecturer on Theosophy." Codd had been an active suffragette in England, spending a month in Holloway women's prison as a result of her work on behalf of the Women's Social and Political Union.[94] Like Annie Besant, she became dissatisfied with a purely political approach to the issues of the time and quit the Union to join the Theosophical Society. Codd retained her belief in the equality of the sexes and lectured on the Hindu concept of feminine power as understood in the concept of Shakti.[95]

While the more material impacts of Theosophy are evident in terms of social connections, one should not underestimate the appeal of Theosophical teachings, which promote a more esoteric approach to religion. This especially interested Playle:

> The mystical always enticed me and I have had an interest in the unexplained. I was never a member of a church. I believe in reincarnation and for twenty-five years I have been studying astrology. I have never been as fascinated by any subject as I have been by astrology. I am eternally grateful to Theosophy for bringing astrology to me.

Playle became a high school teacher, and taught English, drama, commercial shorthand, and typing at Leaside Public School. She remained a member of the Toronto Theosophical Society and in the 1970s she went on a world tour that included India, where she attended the World Vegetarian Conference as a delegate. She then travelled to Japan, Afghanistan, Greece, Egypt, and Turkey and said of the experience, "I am an independent person and as I soon as I could save up enough money and time, I was off." While in India, Playle visited Adyar, where she attended the Annual Theosophical Conference. At the Theosophical headquarters, she met a young man whom she sponsored to live in Canada. He subsequently moved to the United States, but Playle remained in touch with him and his family.

Sarah Lakin and Ruth Playle reveal certain interesting commonalities. Both came from unhappy families and had English backgrounds, and both were particularly attracted to the Theosophical idea of reincarnation. Both women were also working at a time when it was still unusual for women to have careers and were committed to self-education. These characteristics are in harmony with the overall pattern within the Theosophical movement that attracted independently minded, philosophical women who ventured beyond the religious traditions of their families. While neither would identify herself as a feminist, they were both clearly independent and self-determining. In her work on Shakers, Marjorie Procter-Smith emphasizes the need to exercise caution in reading back modern ideas of feminism onto the past.[96] However, she does acknowledge the empowering elements women found within new religious movements like Shakerism. This was often true also in the case of Theosophy regardless of whether or not the women aligned themselves publicly with issues of women's rights.

Sarah Lakin, being from a working-class background, also sought to enlarge her knowledge of the world and derived new self-confidence from her work in Theosophy. Ruth Playle, while from a middle-class background, was seeking a different way of life from that of her aunts whom she felt were in unhappy marriages arranged by family members. The two women shared a determination to inhabit roles outside the traditionally sanctioned ones of wife and mother. Lakin did marry and have a family, but she maintained her Theosophical activities.

Through Theosophy both women were also exposed to South Asian thought and culture, and this led to a lifelong interest in the subcontinent, Playle as evinced by her visit to India and Lakin through her work with an Indian orphanage. In interviewing these women it was clear to me that even if they did not identify as feminists, a term that came into common parlance when both were already older, they were unusual women who had sought a more expanded type of life that moved them beyond traditional expectations of women.

Conclusion

THEOSOPHY WORLDWIDE reached its peak in 1928 with 45,098 members. By 1930 membership had begun to decline rapidly.[97] Some of the reasons given for the decline include lack of leadership, financial depression, and competition from similar spiritual groups.[98] Another reason was the changing social landscape after World War II. While membership in the TTS remained steady until the 1960s, numbers began to drop again steeply in the 1970s. A new type of counterculture, the hippie movement, was developing during this period that eschewed the Victorian/Edwardian values that had shaped the Theosophical Society. Hippies did, however, retain an interest in Eastern religions while rarely recognizing a link with the movements, such as Theosophy, that had gone before them.

Another reason for the decline of the Theosophical Society was no doubt the fact that South Asians, including teachers and swamis, began to arrive in countries like Canada as a result of liberalized immigration laws.[99] The role of Theosophists as translators of Hindu and Buddhist ideas to the West became redundant as those interested could seek out Indian teachers.

The role of the Theosophical Society in preparing the ground for this interest in Asian religion is only now beginning to be fully appreciated as is its contribution to a broader understanding of religious pluralism.[100] Far ahead of their time, many members of the Theosophical Society recognized the equality of all religious traditions. Writers in the *Canadian Theosophist* spoke out on a variety of issues, including the rights of the First Nations in Canada, and in defence of the Jews in Germany in the 1930s. This was expressed firmly in the sectional publication in which a writer stated: "humans love their prejudices more than truth. In Theosophical circles, however, anti-Semitism has no place ... [the Jews] are part of the Universal Brotherhood and have their own contribution to make."[101]

These sentiments, however, largely fell on deaf ears as the Canadian government resolutely refused to take its share of Jewish refugees. In an article entitled "Fifty Years of Theosophy," C. Jinarajadasa, international vice-president of the Theosophical Society, noted the impact of Theosophy on issues of religious and racial tolerance writing that racism had become largely unacceptable in the Western world.[102]

In the fluid identity and sometimes restless shifting of Theosophists across religious boundaries, we can see the precursor of both the New Age and feminist spirituality movements. What Sutcliffe has called the "discourse of New Age spirituality" can be traced directly to the Theosophical Society, and founder Helena Blavatsky has been referred to as the Mother of the New Age.[103] One of the hallmarks of New Age spirituality is an interest in the East; this is clearly a contribution of Theosophy. The Theosophical concept of the seeker who is on a road to spiritual truth was taken up by the counterculture beginning in the 1960s. For those practising this new style of religiosity, the search was often as important, if not more so, than the destination.[104]

In his book *Spiritual, but Not Religious,* Fuller discusses the increasing number of people—up to 20 percent of Americans—who perceive themselves as neither atheists or materialists but who are "unchurched."[105] This lack of interest in institutional religion can be seen in the approach of the Theosophists, who emphasized the personal search for truth. As part of the larger counterculture, Theosophists developed ideas about religion that eventually entered into the mainstream. As Eisler argues, what she refers to as "peripheral isolates" can "sometimes with relative rapidity and unpredictability become the nuclei for the buildup of a whole new system."[106]

The continuing expansion of feminist spirituality and the many books written on the subject also indicate that this field, partly pioneered by Theosophical women, is here to stay. In her essay on the feminist spirituality movement, Eller makes a direct connection between contemporary movements such as neo-paganism and goddess-centred religion and earlier movements such as Theosophy, Spiritualism, and Christian Science.[107] Eller argues that groups like Theosophy made primary conceptual contributions to the development of religion that was empowering for women, namely, the rejection of the connection between women and original sin, the idea that women are somehow more "bodily" than men, and the need for permission to have "an autonomous will, the free use of intellectual gifts, and the ability to transcend bodily existence in communion with the divine."[108] The influence of Theosophy is also clear in the women-centred new religions emerging from the upheavals of the 1960s with their attempts to establish a "new model for ritual and social organization."[109]

The Canadian women who joined the Theosophical Society were originators of styles of religiosity that were welcoming to women and to individualized approaches to the sacred. Like those who participated in the New Age movement that followed, they were often interested in alternative approaches to health and healing, vegetarianism, and to ideas about the creation of a more egalitarian and just society.[110] This chapter, however, is only a first effort aimed at understanding the activities of women in Canadian Theosophy. Knowing that there were large and active

Theosophical lodges across the country in cities like Winnipeg, Ottawa, Montreal, and Vancouver means that this chapter presents just a fragment of the total story that still remains to be written.

In this preliminary investigation of women in Canadian Theosophy, it becomes immediately evident that Theosophy attracted some of the most unusual and creative Canadian women in the late-Victorian period up to World War II. Women appear to have been attracted to the TTS for a variety of reasons. Some were political radicals who wanted to see their religious world view reflected in political and social programs. Others, like Sarah Lakin, were mentored within the group and trained in public speaking and organizing. Many appear to have developed an abiding interest in the religions of India, astrology, alternative health, and vegetarianism.

Although access to direct executive power for women was not encouraged, the TTS appears to have provided an ideologically open space where new concepts and ideas could be considered, discussed, and developed. While women in the TTS did not seem to have participated directly in the rise of Theosophical feminism, they were often active in women's causes outside the Society. Subject to the sweeping changes taking place in their society, many Canadian women found in the Theosophical Society a safe harbour that contributed to their ability to lead unorthodox and productive lives. ●

Notes

1. Bat-Ami Bar-On, "Marginality and Epistemic Privilege," in *Feminist Epistemologies*, ed. Linda Alcoff and Elizabeth Potter (New York: Routledge, 1993), 83.
2. Peter Campbell, *Rose Henderson: A Women for the People* (Montreal: McGill-Queen's University Press, 2010), 276. For a biography of Helena Gutteridge, see Irene Howard, *The Struggle for Social Justice in British Columbia: Helena Gutteridge the Unknown Reformer* (Vancouver: UBC Press, 1992).
3. John E. Cort, "Models for the Study of the Jains," *Methods and Theory in the Study of Religion* 2, no. 1 (1990): 42–71.
4. Dorothy E. Smith, *The Conceptual Practices of Power: A Feminist Sociology of Knowledge* (Grand Rapids: Northeastern University Press, 1990), 38.
5. Fiona Bowie, "Anthropology of Religion," in *The Blackwell Companion to the Study of Religion*, Robert A. Segal (Oxford: Blackwell Publishing, 2006), 4.

6. Mary Farrell Bednarowski, "Outside the Mainstream: Women's Religions and Women Religious Leaders in Nineteenth-Century America," *Journal of the American Academy of Religion* 48, no. 2 (1980): 207–31.

7. James Webb, *The Occult Underground* (LaSalle: Open Court, 1974).

8. Alex Owen, *The Place of Enchantment: British Occultism and the Culture of the Modern* (Chicago: University of Chicago Press, 2004), 90.

9. Robert Ellwood and Catherine Wessinger, "The Feminism of 'Universal Brotherhood': Women in the Theosophical Movement," in *Women's Leadership in Marginal Religions: Explorations Outside the Mainstream*, ed. Catherine Wessinger (Chicago: University of Illinois Press, 1993), 82.

10. Penny Waterstone, "Domesticating Universal Brotherhood: Feminine Values and the Construction of Utopia" (PhD dissertation, University of Arizona, 1995), 339.

11. Toronto Theosophist Flora MacDonald Denison is typical in that she was born a Protestant, became interested in Spiritualism, Theosophy, and then the philosophy of Walt Whitman. Anglo-Irish Theosophist Charlotte Despard began her life as a Protestant, became interested in Theosophy, and ended her life as a Catholic/Communist.

12. Alice A. Chown, *The Stairway* (Toronto: University of Toronto Press, 1988), xiv. First published in 1921 by University of Toronto Press. Citations refer to the University of Toronto edition.

13. See Chown, *The Stairway* and Campbell, *Rose Handerson*.

14. Campbell, *Rose Handerson*.

15. Carroll Smith-Rosenberg, *Disorderly Conduct: Visions of Gender in Victorian America* (New York: Oxford University Press, 1985), 176.

16. Pat Holden, "Introduction," in *Women's Religious Experience*, ed. Pat Holden (London: Croom Helm, 1983), 2.

17. Ibid., 6.

18. Jill Roe, *Beyond Belief* (Kensington: New South Wales University Press, 1986), 167.

19. Diana Burfield, "Theosophy and Feminism: Some Explorations in Nineteenth-Century Religious Biography," in *Women's Religious Experience*, ed. Pat Holden (London: Crooms Helm, 1983), 50. Companionate marriage allowed for use of birth control and divorce for childless couples if there was mutual consent.

20. Ellwood and Wessinger, "Feminism," 77.

21. Annie Besant, *Annie Besant: An Autobiography* (Adyar: Theosophical Publishing House, 1995), 64. First published in 1893 by Unwin.

22. G. Sundari Adyar, interview with author, December 1997.

23. J. N. Farquhar, *Modern Religious Movements in India* (New York: Macmillan, 1915), 21.

24. Andro Linklater, *An Unhusbanded Life: Charlotte Despard Suffragette, Socialist, and Sinn Feiner* (London: Hutchison and Co., 1980), 158.

25. Ian McKay, *Rebels, Reds, Radicals: Rethinking Canada's Left History* (Toronto: Between the Lines, 2005), 1–21.

26. Joy Dixon, *Divine Feminine* (Baltimore: The John Hopkins University Press, 2001), 183.

27. Lynn Hankinson Nelson, "Epistemological Communities," in *Feminist Epistemologies*, ed. Linda Alcoff and Elizabeth Potter (New York: Routledge, 1993), 121–59.

28. Dixon, *Divine Feminine*, 193.

29. Ibid., 168.

30. Linda Kealey, "Introduction," in *A Not Unreasonable Claim: Women and Reform in Canada, 1880s–1920s*, ed. Linda Kealey (Toronto: Women's Educational Press, 1979), 1.

31. Ibid., 4.

32. Steven Vertovec, *The Hindu Diaspora: Comparative Patterns* (London: Routledge, 2000), 18.

33. John Webster Grant, *A Profusion of Spires: Religion in Nineteenth-Century Ontario* (Toronto: University of Toronto Press, 1988), 224–25.

34. Ibid., 219.

35. Sylvia Cranston, *H. P. B. The Extraordinary Life and Influence of Helena Blavatksy, Founder of the Modern Theosophical Movement* (New York: Jeremy P. Tarcher/Putnam, 1993), 35.

36. Josephine Ransom, *A Short History of the Theosophical Society, 1875–1938* (Adyar: Theosophical Publishing House, 1938), 551–52.

37. Francis King, *Satan and Swastika: The Occult and the Nazi Party* (St. Alban's: Mayflower, 1976), 32.

38. Jutta Lehmann, "The Influence of the Theosophical Movement on the Revival of Astrology in Great Britain and North America in the Twentieth Century" (PhD dissertation, Concordia University, 1998); Gordon J. Melton, "The Revival of Astrology in the United States," in *Religious Movements: Genesis, Exodus, and Numbers*, ed. Rodney Stark (New York: Paragon House Publishers, 1985).

39. Joscelyn Godwin, *The Theosophical Enlightenment* (Albany: State University of New York Press, 1994), xi.

40. Owen, *The Place of Enchantment*, 1–16.

41. Sydney E. Ahlstrom, *A Religious History of the American People* (New Haven: Yale University Press, 1972), 1040.

42. *The Canadian Theosophist* 2, no. 9 (1921): 129.

43. Kumari Jayawardena, *The White Woman's Other Burden* (New York: Routledge, 1995), 132.

44. *The Canadian Theosophist* 12, no. 12 (1932): 6

45. Robert S. Ellwood, "The American Theosophical Synthesis," in *The Occult in America: New Historical Perspectives*, ed. Howard Kerr and Charles K. Crow (Urbana: University of Illinois Press, 1983), 23–24.

46. *The Christian Guardian*, April 22, 1891.

47. *The Christian Guardian*, May 27, 1891.

48. Stefanie Syman, *The Subtle Body: The Story of Yoga in America* (New York: Farrar, Straus and Giroux, 2010), 78.

49. Henry James, *The Bostonians* (1885; New York: Bantam Books, 1984), 3.

50. Stan McMullin, *Anatomy of a Séance: A History of Spirit Communication in Central Canada* (Montreal: McGill-Queen's University Press, 2004), 24–25.

51. Mary K. Greer, *Women of the Golden Dawn: Rebels and Priestesses* (Rochester: Park Street Press, 1995), 11–20.

52. Mark Morrisson, "The Periodical Culture of the Occult Revival: Esoteric Wisdom, Modernity, and Counter-Public Spheres," *Journal of Modern Literature* 31, no. 2 (2008): 1–22.

53. *The Lamp* 1, no. 3 (1894): 32.

54. Ahlstrom, *Religious History*, 1020.

55. See Roger Finke and Rodney Stark, *The Churching of America, 1776–1990: Winners and Losers in Our Religious Economy* (New Brunswick, NJ: Rutgers University Press, 1992).

56. Sharon Anne Cook, *Through Sunshine and Shadow: The Women's Christian Temperance Union: Evangelicalism and Reform in Ontario, 1874–1930* (Montreal: McGill-Queen's University Press, 1995), 12.

57. Catherine Cleverdon, *The Woman Suffrage Movement in Canada* (1950; Toronto: University of Toronto Press, 1978), 11.

58. Michele Lacombe, "Theosophy and the Canadian Idealist Tradition: A Preliminary Exploration," *Journal of Canadian Studies* 17, no. 2 (1982): 100–117.

59. Ethel Day MaPherson, *Labor Advocate*, February 13, 1891.

60. Cleverdon, *The Woman Suffrage Movement*, 19–20.

61. Carlotta Hacker, *The Indomitable Lady Doctors* (1974; Halifax, NS: Formac Publishing Group, 1984), 29.

62. *Encyclopedia Canadiana*, s.v. "Carlotta Hacker, Ann Augusta Stowe Gullen," http://www.thecanadianencyclopedia.com/en/article/ann-augusta-stowe-gullen/.

63. Toronto Theosophical Society Minutes, March 26, 1891.

64. Lelia A. Davis, *Woman's Dress: A Question of the Day* (Toronto: Department of Hygiene and Heredity, 1894).

65. Samuel Eldon Charles Wagar, "Theosophical Socialists in the 1920s Okanagan: Jack Logie's Social Issues Summer Camps" (MA thesis, Simon Fraser University, 2005), 17.

66. Toronto Theosophical Society Minutes, June 19, 1918.

67. Cleverdon, *The Woman's Suffrage Movement*, 29.

68. Greg Gatenby, *Toronto: A Literary Guide* (Toronto: McArthur and Company, 1999), 114.

69. Phillipa Schmeigelow, "Canadian Feminists in the International Arena: A Retrospective," *Canadian Woman Studies* 17, no. 2 (1997): 85–87.

70. Deborah Gorham, "Flora MacDonald Denison: Canadian Feminist," in *A Not Unreasonable Claim: Women and Reform in Canada 1880s–1920s*, ed. Linda Kealey (Toronto: Women's Educational Press, 1979), 49.

71. John Campbell, *The Mazinaw Experience: Bon Echo and Beyond* (Toronto: Natural Heritage/Natural History, 2000), 92.

72. Flora MacDonald Denison, *War and Women* (Toronto: Canadian Suffrage Association, 1914), 5.

73. Ibid., 6.

74. Ibid., 7.

75. Gorham, *Flora MacDonald Denison*, 54.

76. Ibid.

77. Ibid., 68.

78. Albert Moritz and Theresa Moritz, *The World's Most Dangerous Woman: A New Biography of Emma Goldman* (Vancouver: Subway Books, 2001), 2.

79. Richard Drinnon, *Rebel in Paradise: A Biography of Emma Goldman* (Chicago: University of Chicago Press, 1982), 261. First published in 1961 by University of Chicago Press.

80. *The Canadian Theosophist* 8, no. 10 (1928): 229; *The Canadian Theosophist* 8, no. 4 (1927): 70–71.

81. Emma Goldman, *Living My Life*, vol. 2, (1931; New York: Dover, 1970), 991.

82. Drinnon, *Rebel in Paradise*, 261.

83. In 1895 the records show that of thirty-three members listed, twenty-one were men and twelve were women. See Minutes of the Toronto Theosophical Society, May 15, 1895.

84. Toronto Theosophical Society Minutes, February 23, 1900; February 22, 1901.

85. Roe, *Beyond Belief*, 170.

86. Dixon, *Divine Feminine*, 67.

87. Augustus Bridle, *The Story of the Club* (Toronto: Ryerson Press, 1945), 15.

88. Mrs. Walter Tibbitts, *Canadian Theosophist* 2, no. 10 (1921): 37; *Canadian Theosophist* 3, no. 3 (1922): 37. In her discussion of yoga, Tibbitts talks about the "cruel crude Calvinism" of her youth, but says nothing about her experience as a woman specifically.

89. Moira Davis, interview with author, Ottawa, November 2001.

90. Hugh Smythe, interview with author, Toronto, December 2000.

91. Smith, *The Conceptual Practices of Power*, 4.

92. McMullin, *Anatomy of a Séance*, 161.

93. *Canadian Theosophist* 21, no. 6 (1940): 164.

94. Dixon, *Divine Feminine*, 177.

95. Ibid.

96. Marjorie Procter-Smith, "In the Line of the Female: Shakerism and Feminism," in *Women's Leadership in Marginal Religions: Explorations Outside the Mainstream*, ed. Catherine Wessinger (Urbana: University of Chicago Press, 1993), 30.

97. Ransom, *A Short History*, 507.

98. Annual General Report, Toronto Theosophical Society, 1934, 11.

99. David R. Hughes and Evelyn Kaller, *The Anatomy of Racism: Canadian Dimensions* (Montreal: Harvest House, 1974), 113.

100. See Kathy Phillips, *The Spirit of Yoga* (London: Cassell Illustrated, 2001); Phillip C. Almond, *The British Discovery of Buddhism* (Cambridge: Cambridge University Press, 1988).

101. *Canadian Theosophist* 15, no. 11 (1935): 349–50.

102. *Canadian Theosophist* 6, no. 7 (1925): 97.

103. Steven J. Sutcliffe, *Children of the New Age: A History of Spiritual Practices* (London and New York: Routledge, 2003), 213; Cranston, *H. P. B.*, 521–34.

104. Christopher Partridge, *The Re-Enchantment of the West*, vol. 1 (London: T and T Clark International, 2004), 33.

105. Robert C. Fuller, *Spiritual, but Not Religious: Understanding Unchurched America* (New York: Oxford University Press, 2001), 1–12.

106. Riane Eisler, *The Chalice and the Blade* (New York: HarperCollins Publishers, 1987), 136.

107. Cynthia Eller, "Twentieth-Century Women's Religion as Seen in the Feminist Spirituality Movement," in *Women's Leadership in Marginal Religions: Explorations Outside the Mainstream,* ed. Catherine Wessinger (Chicago: University of Illinois Press, 1993), 189.

108. Ibid.

109. Sarah M. Pike, *New and Neopagan Religions in America* (New York: Columbia University Press, 2004), 119.

110. Peter C. Emberley, *Divine Hunger: Canadians on Spiritual Walkabout* (Toronto: Harper-Collins, 2002).

Interviews

Moira Davis, Ottawa, ON, November 2001 (four hours)

Sarah Lakin, Toronto, ON, November 2000 (three hours)

Ruth Playle, Toronto, ON, June 2000 (two two-hour interviews)

Hugh Smythe, Toronto, ON, December 2000 (four hours)

G. Sundari, Adyar, India, December 1997 (one and a half hours)

Bibliography

Ahlstrom, Sydney E. *A Religious History of the American People.* New Haven: Yale University Press, 1972.

Almond, Phillip C. *The British Discovery of Buddhism.* Cambridge: Cambridge University Press, 1988.

Bar-On, Bat-Ami. "Marginality and Epistemic Privilege." In *Feminist Epistemologies,* edited by Linda Alcoff and Elizabeth Potter, 83–100. New York: Routledge, 1993.

Bednarowski, Mary Farrell. "Outside the Mainstream: Women's Religions and Women Religion Leaders in Nineteenth-Century America." *Journal of the American Academy of Religion* 48, no. 2 (1980): 207–31.

Besant, Annie. *Annie Besant: An Autobiography.* Adyar: Theosophical Publishing House, 1995. First published in 1893 by Unwin.

Bowie, Fiona. "Anthropology of Religion." In *The Blackwell Companion to the Study of Religion,* edited by Robert A. Segal, 3–24. Oxford: Blackwell Publishing, 2006.

Bridle, Augustus. *The Story of the Club.* Toronto: Ryerson Press, 1945.

Burfield, Diana. "Theosophy and Feminism: Some Explorations in Nineteenth-Century Religious Biography." In *Women's Religious Experience,* edited by Pat Holden, 27–55. London: Crooms Helm, Totowa, Barnes and Noble, 1983.

Campbell, John. *The Mazinaw Experience: Bon Echo and Beyond.* Toronto: Natural Heritage/ Natural History, 2000.

Campbell, Peter. *Rose Henderson: A Woman for the People.* Montreal: McGill-Queen's University Press, 2010.

Chown, Alice A. *The Stairway.* Toronto: University of Toronto Press, 1988.

Cleverdon Catherine. *The Woman Suffrage Movement in Canada.* Toronto: University of Toronto Press, 1978. First published in 1950 by University of Toronto Press.

Cook, Sharon Anne. *Through Sunshine and Shadow. The Women's Christian Temperance Union: Evangelicalism and Reform in Ontario, 1874–1930.* Montreal: McGill-Queen's University Press, 1995.

Cort, John E. "Models of and for the Study of the Jains." *Method and Theory in the Study of Religion* 2, no. 1 (1990): 42–71.

Cranston, Sylvia. *H. P. B: The Extraordinary Life and Influence of Helena Blavatsky, Founder of the Modern Theosophical Movement.* New York: Jeremy P. Tarcher/Putnam, 1993.

Davis, Lelia A. *Woman's Dress: A Question of the Day.* Toronto: Department of Hygiene and Heredity, 1894.

Denison, Flora MacDonald. "War and Women." Toronto: Canadian Suffrage Association, 1916.

Dixon, Joy. *Divine Feminine.* Baltimore: Johns Hopkins University Press, 2001.

Drinnon, Richard. *Rebel in Paradise: A Biography of Emma Goldman.* Reprinted 1982. Chicago: University of Chicago Press, 1982. First published in 1961 by University of Chicago Press.

Eisler, Riane. *The Chalice and The Blade.* New York: HarperCollins Publishers, 1987.

Eller, Cynthia. "Twentieth-Century Women's Religion as Seen in the Feminist Spirituality Movement." In *Women's Leadership in Marginal Religions: Explorations Outside the Mainstream,* edited by Catherine Wessinger. Chicago: University of Illinois Press, 1993.

Ellwood, Robert S. "The American Theosophical Synthesis." In *The Occult in America: New Historical Perspectives,* edited by Howard Kerr and Charles K. Crow, 111–34. Urbana: University of Illinois Press, 1993.

Ellwood, Robert, and Catherine Wessinger. "The Feminism of 'Universal Brotherhood': Women in the Theosophical Movement." In *Women's Leadership in Marginal Religions: Explorations Outside the Mainstream,* edited by Catherine Wessinger, 55–67. Chicago: University of Illinois Press, 1993.

Emberley, Peter C. *Divine Hunger: Canadians on Spiritual Walkabout.* Toronto: HarperCollins, 2002.

Farquhar, J. N. *Modern Religious Movements in India.* New York: Macmillan, 1915.

Finke, Roger, and Rodney Stark. *The Churching of America, 1776–1990: Winners and Losers in Our Religious Economy.* New Brunswick, NJ: Rutgers University, 1992.

Fuller, Robert C. *Spiritual, but Not Religious: Understanding Unchurched America.* New York: Oxford University Press, 2001.

Gatenby, Greg, *Toronto: A Literary Guide.* Toronto: McArthur and Company, 1999.

Godwin, Joscelyn. *The Theosophical Enlightenment.* Albany: State University of New York Press, 1994.

Goldman, Emma. *Living My Life,* vol. 2. New York: Dover Publications, 1970. First published in 1931 by Alfred A. Knopf.

Gorham, Deborah. "Flora MacDonald Denison: Canadian Feminist." In *A Not Unreasonable Claim: Women and Reform in Canada, 1880s–1920s,* edited by Linda Kealey, 47–70. Toronto: Women's Press, 1979.

Grant, John Webster. *A Profusion of Spires: Religion in Nineteenth-Century Ontario.* Toronto: University of Toronto Press, 1988.

Greer, Mary K. *Women of the Golden Dawn: Rebels and Priestesses.* Rochester: Park Street Press, 1995.

Hacker, Carlotta. *The Indomitable Lady Doctors.* Halifax, NS: Formac Publishing Group, 1984. First published in 1974 by Clarke Irwin & Company.

———. "Ann Augusta Stow Gullen." *Encyclopedia Canadiana.* http://www.thecanadian encyclopedia.com/en/article/ann-augusta-stowe-gullen/.

Hanegraf, Wouter. "Forbidden Knowledge: Anti-Esoteric Polemics and Academic Research." *Aries* 15, no. 2 (2005): 225–54.

Holden, Pat. "Introduction." In *Women's Religious Experience,* edited by Pat Holden, 1–14. London: Croom Helm and Totowa: Barnes and Noble, 1983.

Howard, Irene. *The Struggle for Social Justice in British Columbia: Helena Gutteridge the Unknown Reformer.* Vancouver: UBC Press, 1992.

Hughes, David R., and Evelyn Kaller. *The Anatomy of Racism: Canadian Dimensions.* Montreal: Harvest House, 1974.

James, Henry. *The Bostonians*. New York: Bantam Books, 1984. First published in 1885–86 in *The Century Magazine*.

Jayawardena, Kumari. *The White Woman's Other Burden*. New York: Routledge, 1995.

Kealey, Linda. "Introduction." In *A Not Unreasonable Claim: Women and Reform in Canada, 1880s–1920s*, edited by Linda Kealey, 1–14. Toronto: Women's Educational Press, 1979.

King, Francis. *Satan and Swastika: The Occult and the Nazi Party*. St. Albans: Mayflower, 1976.

Lacombe, Michele. "Theosophy and the Canadian Idealist Tradition: A Preliminary Exploration." *Journal of Canadian Studies* 17, no. 2 (1982): 100–117.

Lehmann, Jutta. *The Influence of the Theosophical Movement on the Revival of Astrology in Great Britain and North America in the 20th Century*. PhD dissertation, Concordia University, 1998.

Linklater, Andro. *An Unhusbanded Life: Charlotte Despard: Suffragette, Socialist, and Sinn Feiner*. London: Hutchison and Co., 1980.

McCann, Gillian. "A Pilgrim Forever: The Life and Thought of Albert Smythe." *Journal of Canadian Studies* 44, no. 1 (Winter 2010): 184–201.

——. *Vanguard of the New Age: The Toronto Theosophical Society 1891–1945*. Kingston and Montreal: McGill-Queen's University Press, 2012.

McKay, Ian. *Rebels, Red, Radicals: Rethinking Canada's Left History*. Toronto: Between the Lines, 2005.

McMullin, Stan. *Anatomy of a Séance: A History of Spirit Communication in Central Canada*. Montreal: McGill-Queen's University Press, 2004.

Melton, Gordon J. "The Revival of Astrology in the United States." In *Religious Movements: Genesis, Exodus, and Numbers*, edited by Rodney Stark, 279–96. New York: Paragon House Publishers, 1985.

Moritz, Albert, and Theresa Moritz. *The World's Most Dangerous Woman: A New Biography of Emma Goldman*. Vancouver: Subway Books, 2001.

Morrisson, Mark. "The Periodical Culture of the Occult Revival: Esoteric Wisdom, Modernity, and Counter-Public Spheres." *Journal of Modern Literature* 31, no. 2 (2008): 1–22.

Nelson, Lynn Hankinson. "Epistemological Communities." In *Feminist Epistemologies*, edited by Linda Alcoff and Elizabeth Potter, 121–59. New York: Routledge, 1993.

Owen, Alex. *The Place of Enchantment: British Occultism and the Culture of the Modern*. Chicago: University of Chicago Press, 2004.

Partridge, Christopher. *The Re-Enchantment of the West*, vol. 1. London: T and T Clark International, 2004.

Phillips, Kathy. *The Spirit of Yoga*. London: Cassell Illustrated, 2001.

Pike, Sarah M. *New Age and Neopagan Religions in America*. New York: Columbia University Press, 2004.

Procter-Smith, Marjorie. "'In the Line of the Female': Shakerism and Feminism." In *Women's Leadership in Marginal Religions: Explorations Outside the Mainstream*, edited by Catherine Wessinger, 23–40. Urbana and Chicago: University of Illinois Press, 1993.

Ransom, Josephine. *A Short History of the Theosophical Society, 1875–1938*. Adyar, India: Theosophical Publishing House, 1938.

Roe, Jill. *Beyond Belief: Theosophy in Australia, 1879–1939*. Kensington: New South Wales University Press, 1986.

Schmeigelow, Phillipa. "Canadian Feminists in the International Arena: A Retrospective." *Canadian Woman Studies* 17, no. 2 (1997): 85–87.

Smith, Dorothy E. *The Conceptual Practices of Power: A Feminist Sociology of Knowledge*. Grand Rapids: Northeastern University Press, 1990.

Smith-Rosenberg, Carroll. *Disorderly Conduct: Visions of Gender in Victorian America*. New York: Oxford University Press, 1985.

Sutcliffe, Steven J. *Children of the New Age: A History of Spiritual Practices*. London and New York: Routledge, 2003.

Syman, Stefanie. *The Subtle Body: The Story of Yoga in America*. New York: Farrar, Straus and Giroux, 2010.

Vertovec, Steven. *The Hindu Diaspora: Comparative Patterns*. London: Routledge, 2000.

Wagar, Samuel Eldon Charles. *Theosophical Socialists in the 1920s Okanagan: Jack Logie's Social Issues Summer Camps*. MA thesis, Simon Fraser University, 2005.

Waterstone, Penny. *Domesticating Universal Brotherhood: Feminine Values and the Construction of Utopia*. PhD dissertation, University of Arizona, 1995.

7 Belief, Identity, and Social Action in the Lives of Bahá'í Women

LYNN ECHEVARRIA YUKON COLLEGE

Introduction

This chapter draws on data from a life history study of twenty older Bahá'ís in Canada and the lives of three women in particular.[1] It provides an overview of Canadian Bahá'í history, a discussion of the origin of the religion, its central figures and major teachings, and then takes a narrative turn by presenting the story of an early woman disciple who holds a significant place as a role model for contemporary followers. The rest of the chapter explores excerpts from the above-mentioned life histories and how these people responded to Bahá'í teachings and were moved to act upon them in the public realm.

Who am I as author, you may wonder? I am a researcher who is a long-term member of the Bahá'í Faith. In sociological theory this would be called a committed member and the phenomena under study.[2] My fifty-plus years of acquired knowledge of Bahá'í community life as an "insider" means that I know something about the features of Bahá'í group life, the practices assumed, the vocabulary of understandings, the structure of Bahá'í institutions, and the rhythm of community life.[3]

My study is also informed by the symbolic interactionist sociological perspective that emphasizes the individual as social actor and agent, and prescribes participant observation and open-ended interviewing. It promotes discovering, first-hand, the participants' subjective understandings and their social interactions in daily life. Using this framework,

I examine how women make meaning of the Bahá'í teachings and translate that into action.

A scholarly history about Canadian Bahá'í women is still embryonic.[4] In order to contribute a small measure to the lessening of this lacuna, I concentrate only on how these women construct their religious identity and explain their activities and interpersonal relations.[5]

Canadian Beginnings

NORTH AMERICANS first heard public mention of Bahá'u'lláh, the prophet-founder of the Bahá'í Faith, in 1893 at the World Parliament of Religions in Chicago.[6] A young woman, Edith Magee, and her mother, sister, and two aunts, joined the religion in 1898 and formed the first Canadian Bahá'í group in London, Ontario.[7] In the same year, oceans away, a group of Western people made a pilgrimage to the Holy Land (Acre, Israel, then Palestine), to visit Bahá'u'lláh's family. May Ellis-Bolles, an American by birth, living in Paris, was one of these pilgrims. She was destined to play a unique and key role in the development of the European and Canadian Bahá'í communities. These pilgrims, and the many to follow, brought knowledge of Bahá'í teachings and stories about the early believers back to the Western world. In 1902, the Maxwell/Ellis-Bolles family (May and her husband, Canadian architect W. Sutherland Maxwell) moved to Montreal. Their home became the centre for Bahá'í activity and May provided the impetus for the growth of the Bahá'í Faith in Canada. She is considered the founder of the Canadian Bahá'í community.

The Bahá'í Faith is a transplanted, non-Western religion. Its followers did not come to Canada in a major immigration, nor did they form a "spontaneous frontier movement" or block settlement.[8] May Maxwell and the Bahá'ís of Montreal figured prominently in the dispersion of travelling teachers across the nation and, at the beginning, attracted people of independent means, mostly from a Protestant religious background. Recruits were sought from the host society, and after establishing local groups, Bahá'ís were directed to expand the religion on a national scale, rather than build up local congregations or ideal, self-contained communities. The same orientation characterized Bahá'í activity in other countries.

Canadian and American women and men voluntarily travelled individually, as teams, or with Bahá'í spouses to promote the religion through informal talks, study classes, and formal lectures at public meetings. There was a high percentage of women (66–71 percent), and those without direct family responsibilities were able to make regional and national moves throughout Canada. They worked to support themselves, and were able to devote their extra time and energy to assist the small groups and eventual local Spiritual Assemblies (governing councils).[9]

The community did not have distinctive boundary markers, such as esoteric language, ascetic lifestyle, distinct clothing, or geographic separation, and believers were encouraged to maintain and promote family, personal, and community ties wherever possible. Gradually markers emerged as more Bahá'í sacred writings became available in English. Additional guidance was given from the Bahá'í World Centre regarding the existence of a Bahá'í Calendar, how to make contributions to the Bahá'í Funds, and the holding of, and participation in, the Nineteen-Day Feast[10]—the last two restricted to Bahá'ís only.[11] Members kept in touch with one another through extensive personal correspondence and visits. Eventually, connections were also made through annual events, such as conferences, conventions, and summer schools, and through the national and international news magazines and bulletins that were regularly published in the United States and, later, in Canada. These newsletters and other correspondence also shared news from Bahá'ís around the world, as well as directives for plans to expand the Bahá'í World Centre in Haifa, Israel. Guidance from this Centre was vital in nurturing a sense of history and social memory for Canadian Bahá'ís. The articulation of the Canadian community's national identity linked it with other national communities as sisters—members of a world family, and directly connected its spiritual heritage to the early history of the Bahá'ís of Iran.[12]

In this regard, McMullen describes the Bahá'í faith as a universalizing movement that inspires, within its members, a collective consciousness with a universal message and identity. He explains that participation in democratically elected local Bahá'í governance brings Bahá'ís into alignment with the national and globalized authority structures. Frequent consultations through a global network of grassroots communities facilitate this linkage, and reflexively mould the religious identity of Bahá'ís as world citizens.[13]

The process of institutionalization in the Bahá'í community's first hundred years resulted in the election of many local Spiritual Assemblies in Canada, and in 1948, its national governing body.[14] There is no clergy or system of elders in the Bahá'í Faith because, according to Bahá'u'lláh's "Covenant,"[15] authoritative guidance and spiritual inspiration were to be invested in the sacred texts and teachings and the administrative system rather than in any individual.[16] Also, and importantly, the theological assertions of equality (for women and minority peoples) are embedded in the Constitution of the Spiritual Assemblies, and ratified through an Act of Parliament (1949).[17] Interestingly, through the routinization of the religion, there has been an increase in and diversification of the roles that women can assume.[18] What the historical record shows is that the rights of women and their equality with men were safeguarded and protected by the Covenant as actualized in the administrative order.[19] Later in this chapter I discuss how the believers themselves viewed equality.

Three significant demographic processes occurred in the Bahá'í community after 1948: an influx of indigenous peoples and young people of varied backgrounds in the 1960s–70s, and the immigration of Iranian Bahá'í refugees in the 1980s to whom the Canadian government had granted asylum because they faced possible death if they remained in Iran due to the persecution of Bahá'ís there. The National Spiritual Assembly of the Bahá'ís of Canada initiated a settlement program to assist several thousand Iranian Bahá'ís to move to most of the major centres in Canada, and some of the rural areas as well.[20] A living Iranian-Bahá'í history and older social memory of the Bahá'í Faith, as well as different manifestations of cultural and religious behaviours of the Iranians, First Nations Bahá'ís, and emergent Bahá'í youth presence, would all contribute to diversify the Canadian community.

Historical Background of the Bahá'í Faith

A RELIGIOUS RENAISSANCE EMERGED IN PERSIA IN 1844 with the advent of the spiritual revelation of the Báb (1819–50). He claimed to be the new Messenger of God awaited by Islam and he founded an independent religion with its own community and scriptures.[21] The Báb was a harbinger preparing the way for the prophet-founder of the Bahá'í Faith, Bahá'u'lláh (1817–92).[22]

The Bahá'í faith is an independent religion, and has been described, sociologically, as a world religion and a new religious movement.[23] Bahá'u'lláh's daughter, Bahíyyih Khánum (1846–1932) is the foremost woman of the Bahá'í Faith. She played a key role in the administration and leadership of the religion, part of which was to communicate with Bahá'ís globally, including the Canadian Bahá'ís, whom she encouraged, rallied, educated, and inspired.[24] Bahá'u'lláh's son, 'Abdu'l-Bahá (1844–1921), was named by Bahá'u'lláh as the source of authority upon his passing and the exemplar of his teachings.[25] His visit to North America in 1912 was a singular event in the lives of the early Bahá'ís, and in the Bahá'í history of Canada. He travelled to Quebec, central Canada, and the United States to lecture on Bahá'u'lláh's teachings. The topics of the oneness of humanity, world peace and justice, racial harmony, and the equality of women and men were central to his presentations. 'Abdu'l-Bahá returned home to Haifa in 1913, and for the rest of his ministry guided the Bahá'ís from Israel.

The Story of Táhirih
A Disciple and a Champion of Equality

IN THIS SECTION I PRESENT THE STORY OF TÁHIRIH. I take the opportunity to share this narrative for several reasons: she is the most important woman in Bahá'í history next to Bahíyyih Khánum; her life is central to the beginnings of Bahá'í history, and she holds a unique place as a female disciple, a herald of the new religion, and a champion for the advancement of women's equality. Táhirih's qualities of courage, activism, and piety are upheld as exemplary in Bahá'í literature, and her story is a foundational part of Bahá'í social memory that recognizes the potential of women to be social actors. This account, therefore, helps to illustrate that there is a legacy of social activism across time and place, and that a tangible relationship exists between a leading historic figure and the Canadian women in this chapter.

Zarrín-Táj (Crown of Gold) (1817–52), later named Táhirih, was born and brought up in Qazvin, Persia, in a strict religious Muslim family. Her father was a famous cleric[26] who provided an education for his daughter, which was unusual for the time.[27] At the young age of thirteen she was married off and subsequently had three children. Later she would become known as a poet and scholar of religion.[28]

One night Táhirih had a vision of a holy being reciting a prayer she had not heard before. Later, when she came across the teachings of the Báb, she immediately recognized his words as those from her vision, and accepted his claim as the latest messenger of God. Táhirih was chosen as a disciple by the Báb, and collaborated with Bahá'u'lláh, recognizing him as the "exalted bearer" of his as yet undisclosed mission.[29]

In the face of extreme danger to herself and the Bábí community, Táhirih travelled from city to city to promote the Báb's teachings. She met with the leading clerics, and preached to many women as well.[30] She confounded "the Shí'ah, Sunni, Christian, and Jewish notables of Baghdad who had endeavoured to dissuade her from her avowed purpose of spreading the tidings of the new Message."[31] Her oratory, poetry, devotion, and leadership in the new cause attracted many followers, women and men alike.

At a chosen moment Táhirih arose to take on the role of herald. Publicly removing her veil at a conference of Bábís, she announced, "I am the Word that the Qá'im[32] is to utter, the Word which shall put to flight the chiefs and nobles of the earth!"[33] Thereby she demonstrated the revolutionary character of the new religion, which was a complete break from Islam or more precisely was "permanently divorced from the laws and institutions of Islam"[34] Those Bábís present were shocked by her audacious demonstration, and because of it they regarded Táhirih as unchaste and scandalous. The Báb and Bahá'u'lláh responded by upholding her reputation of purity and chastity, and endorsed for her the title, Táhirih (The Pure One).[35] Táhirih also incited the wrath of the Muslim clergy because of her skill in theological debate and "her unveiled threat to their power." She was passionate in her claims, and attracted large audiences and adherents everywhere she travelled.[36] Eventually she was placed under house arrest.[37]

On July 9, 1850, the Sháh of Persia (Násiri'd-Din-Sháh) ordered that the Báb be executed, and Táhirih was accused of heresy in the ensuing persecutions of the Bábís. She was taken before the Sháh, who offered her a proposal of marriage if she would recant her faith, but she would not and was thereby sentenced to death.[38] "One night aware that the hour of her death was at hand, she put on the attire of a bride and anointed herself with perfume.... She closeted herself in her chambers and awaited in prayer and meditation, the hour." At her death she uttered these words: "you can kill me as soon as you like, but you cannot stop the emancipation of women." She was then strangled, thrown into a well, and covered with stones.[39] A tribute from a renowned Turkish poet, Sulaymán Nazím Bey, movingly reflects upon her nobility of character: "O Táhirih you are worth a thousand Násiri'd-Din-Sháhs."[40]

Bahá'í literature acclaims Táhirih's "remarkable intellectual ability," "piety," "beauty," "courage," "holiness," "love of God,"[41] her "audacity in her acts," "rank of apostleship in the new dispensation," "captivating eloquence," "unorthodox views," "indomitability of spirit," and "bold heroism."[42] The spiritual virtues and qualities she acquired are upheld in Bahá'í writings and used as a transformative model to which both women and men aspire.[43] This orientation was started by 'Abdu'l-Bahá, who promoted the stories of the early women believers as role models of women's leadership. The story of Táhirih's life is shared globally in conferences, seminars, and study classes for children and adults.[44] Her life story remains close to the hearts of Canadian believers as demonstrated in the lives of Clara and Ethel, two women discussed in this chapter.

The advancement of religious truth, for which Táhirih gave her life, is the animating force in the Revelation of Bahá'u'lláh. Central to his teachings is the principle of oneness—the oneness of God, religion, and humankind.[45] In this next section we briefly explore this principle and then continue on to meet the Canadian women of my study.

The Principle of Oneness

BAHÁ'U'LLÁH TAUGHT that "the earth is but one country and mankind its citizens."[46] "World citizenship," as envisioned in Bahá'í teachings, "encompasses the principles of social and economic justice, both within and among nations; non-adversarial decision making at all levels of society; equality of the sexes; racial, ethnic, national and religious harmony."[47] It can be achieved only, the BIC states, through the complementary principle of unity in diversity, which necessitates recognizing and honouring differences such as culture, gender, race, and individuality. Unity in diversity is a necessary complement to the concept of oneness, for without it conformity results.[48] Far more than a utopian vision or "a spirit of goodwill," oneness implies "an organic change in the structure of present-day society."[49] The blueprint for building this new structure—an administrative system— is laid out in Bahá'í teachings, which state that this system will "embody" oneness, "demonstrate its validity, and perpetuate its influence."[50]

Women in Contemporary Times

HOW DID WOMEN INTERACT with this new system and set of beliefs? We now turn to the life histories of three women—Ethel, Ruth, and Clara—in order to gain some understanding of how members of this religion live their lives.[51] My focus is on women's activity in the public realm, not on private devotional practices or social processes that can occur in Bahá'í family life and formal activities.[52] It must also be kept in mind that these narratives are from people who were young and at the height of their involvement in the Bahá'í Faith from the 1940s to the 1960s. Their lives were subject to the many social forces in Canadian society during the midtwentieth century. One's personal experience of those years would depend on many diverse factors, such as where one lived in Canada or one's age, class, race, and ethnic and religious background. However, one can generally state that the end of the Depression and the war years, the rise of middle-class single and married women in the labour force, the gradual opening up of jobs, and the influx of new consumer goods and housing all combined to influence this generation of women with hopes for a better material life and future, in contrast to their mothers' generation. Notwithstanding these positive developments, traditional values still defined women's roles narrowly and constrained their participation in every field of endeavour. Ambition, independence, agency, and achievement in the public realm were still qualities and activities associated with men. Even though over the first fifty years of the last century women had formed bonds of solidarity through work, political activism, co-operatives, and focus groups, it was not until the 1960s that gender discrimination was seriously questioned in society at large. Furthermore, it was not until the 1970s with the Royal Commission on the Status of Women that their issues and concerns became legitimized in Canada.[53]

The religious backgrounds of the women in this chapter were Christian. Both Ruth and Ethel had an Anglican background, and Clara was raised in a residential school, although she also had a legacy of spiritual teachings from her clan. Knowledge of Christian teachings and familiarity with women's participation in Christian churches was the heritage of these women. They grew up in Christian families and/or were immersed in the Christianized culture of pre-war and postwar Canada. My participants, for example, were well aware that racial prejudices and practices, and institutionalized racism abounded. Beliefs about the unequal nature of women and men persisted, reinforcing the separate spheres ideology, and influencing Christian women's work in the church and in their communities. They could see that men needed women to work alongside them in Christian community building and to provide Christian education, yet women were generally viewed, publicly and privately, as men's inferior. They knew that church doctrine supported women's self-sacrifice and self-denial as normative. They appreciated that the organizations and societies developed by Catholic and Protestant women, both within and without the church, provided needed outreach and education to girls and women, in Canada and overseas.[54] Certainly Ruth, Ethel, and other people of my larger study were recipients of fellowship, friendship, and that very education, as we shall now examine.

Dr. Ethel Martens (1916–98)

ETHEL WAS BORN IN A LOG CABIN in The Pas, Manitoba. Her mother, from Hull, Yorkshire, was a pianist and singer, and brought her music and Anglican Sunday school to the rural North. Ethel took great pleasure in recounting the remarkable story of her mother's emigration from Britain. A family mishap caused her to miss taking the *Titanic* and she was forced to wait in Liverpool for the next ship sailing. Biding her time, she attended a talk by 'Abdu'l-Bahá, who was unknown to her prior to this event.

(Interestingly, 'Abdu'l-Bahá had declined an invitation to sail on the *Titanic* and instead took the SS *Cedric*.)[55] After this encounter, Ethel's mother would teach in her future Sunday school classes that all religions were one. Ethel's father, an Oxford-educated Londoner, moved to Canada and learned to farm successfully. Ethel and her two siblings attended a rural French Canadian school, and later she earned a teacher's certificate. Ethel first came in contact with the Bahá'ís in 1947. Although a staunch Anglican, she earnestly studied the new religion and attended many Bahá'í events in Australia, England, and Canada. In 1953 she "got off the fence and joined," as did her mother and brother at a later time. When she turned fifty she earned her PhD—"I wanted to be a doctor, not marry a doctor"—and she indeed never married. Ethel became a pioneer in the health field, and a public health scholar and educator.

Ruth Eyford, née Monk (1930–95)

RUTH WAS BORN IN SYDNEY, CAPE BRETON, and brought up in a high Anglican family in a small conservative community. Her narrative highlights the fact that she struggled for many years to overcome a fear of making mistakes and taking risks—a fear that she traced to the tensions of living with a stern, authoritarian father. She moved to Halifax and then to Montreal to pursue training in psychiatric nursing. Later she became involved in YWCA women's programming on the Prairies. In 1957, after meeting Bahá'ís and studying the literature, she decided she wanted to join the faith: "I saw Bahá'u'lláh as the return of Christ, you know. The [Bahá'í] teachings did that for me; they spoke to me as coming from the same Source." She recalls that her father said,

> "Ruth, what would you want to bother and do a thing like that for?" because he saw no reason to stand out, to be counted, to be different, for something like a religious belief. And that meant sort of trouble in terms of being different, being criticized, of not being socially the same as others. And my mother said, "Ruth, if you could live by some or most of those teachings, you can't go wrong."

Ruth married a Bahá'í, had two children, and went on to become an educator and distinguished Bahá'í administrator.

Clara Schinkel, née Johns (1935–2006)

SÀTLÈNDÙ.O AND D'ESADLI, CLARA, daughter of Agnes and Peter Johns, was of Tagish-Tlingit heritage, and was born in her grandparents' hunting cabin in Carcross (Caribou Crossing), southern Yukon Territory. Clara began her narrative with a family genealogy, and then related her experience of a traditional childhood living on the land. Clara was taken from her people at age five and put into a mission school, where for seven years she and her siblings suffered terribly. When she came of age she spoke out and rejected membership in the church. She married and had five children. Her clan, Dakhl'awèdí, had a powerful inheritance of elders' dreams, visions, and prophecies that foretold that a new religion would come to their land to nurture the people and promote unity. In 1959 Clara met a Bahá'í First Nations Tlingit, Jim Walton, from Alaska. He showed her prophecies in the Bible about the Bahá'í Faith. She read Bahá'í books and recognized that their teachings concurred with clan laws and the elders' visions. Clara was the first of her family to join the Bahá'í community, followed by 103 other family members. Being a lover of history and passionate about the agency of women (her own great-grandmother was a powerful shaman, Tudeshgiá.ma'), she was moved to name her second daughter Táhirih. After earning an education degree, Clara devoted her life to working for Yukon First Nations, as well as the Bahá'í Faith.

Foundational Bahá'í Teachings and Creative Applications

SINCE THERE IS NO ECCLESIASTICAL STRUCTURE OR PRIESTHOOD in the Bahá'í religion, individuals are responsible for their own spiritual development. The women of my study were exponents of a new world view, working within a social system unlike anything they had experienced before, and they had to endeavour to live their lives in accordance with their new beliefs. When people become aware of certain features of community life, they develop a conceptual framework of definitions, and perceive themselves and others in the context of these meanings.[56] For example, during her first year as a member of the Bahá'í Faith, Ruth was able to take things in her stride—she was "comfortable" with the basic interactions of Bahá'í life. After this initial period, Ruth wanted to become more involved with the religion, and she found that, in order to take the next steps toward a higher level of commitment, she had to move out of her comfort zone and align her thoughts and actions with her new beliefs:

> And I walked in and I just sort of floated along and took part. And it wasn't easy for me, but it wasn't difficult, either. It's different from anything else you've done before, because there is no other pattern that is set up exactly like a Bahá'í community, where there is so much opportunity for an individual to participate, so much encouragement to be independent in your thinking, and to share your thinking. I found I could take part according to my own comfort level. I was very quiet but I just learned by observing, by reading a little bit as I went along, and certainly by my fellow Bahá'ís asking me to join them in their deepening [study] activities and their social activities, and going to Bahá'í Holy Days and Feasts together. They just sort of took me under their wing and made sure that I knew things were going on, that I had the opportunity to attend, and that I understood what I was going to. And to me that's very important for any new Bahá'í.

Bahá'í theology describes living a Bahá'í life as a transformative process that involves elements of knowledge, volition, and action.[57] The practice of acquiring knowledge is made dynamic through a process of individual daily study, prayer, and meditation on the sacred writings, which are then translated, alone or with others, into service, as Ruth describes:

> Before you can learn something you have to know its basic laws and principles. Then you have to be given the tools in order to put it into practice, and the support while you're putting it into practice. Throughout my Bahá'í life, there has always been this important transition from knowing [the teachings] and putting them into practice, so that it becomes a visible expression and testimony.

The will to undertake action is explained in the Bahá'í writings as a key dynamic: "the attainment of any object is conditioned upon knowledge, volition and action. Unless these three conditions are forthcoming there is no execution or accomplishment."[58]

Ruth shared her heartfelt feelings about making a change in her spiritual orientation, which reflected her conscious desire to "make it happen"—to will it. "I wanted to make myself more submissive to the will of God. I wanted to put myself into the protection of God, and open myself to the will of God. I was new and I had so much to learn. But also that you wanted to change. And the emphasis for me was on that."

According to the Bahá'í World Centre, social action "seeks to apply the teachings and principles of the [Bahá'í] Faith to improve some aspect of the social or economic life of a population, however modestly."[59] From the beginnings of the religion in Canada, Canadian Bahá'ís took seriously Bahá'í writings, which directed people to facilitate women's participation in community life, particularly in the arena of governance and decision making. Clara explained how she was able to enter into this type of service, and how she gained self-confidence as she worked hand in hand with others:

> In 1960, April, I was [elected] on the Assembly. I don't know the first thing about administration, but I learned. It's just like you have on-the-job training. And that's the best way, because it's good to learn by books, but by doing it—that's the way the Indian people learn. That's how they teach, by doing things. And the Bahá'í law is to teach [share the message, but not proselytize, about the religion] and I accepted it wholeheartedly.

Whether they felt capable or not, women found that they were expected to be active participants in consultation and elected and appointed roles. The stories of the first women heroes and teachers of the religion (like Táhirih and May Maxwell) were shared to inspire individuals about women's participation and activism, as Ethel described:

Well, I think it was important for us to know that women were active [in the Bahá'í Faith] and were playing a role that is remembered. Cause many of the roles women play [in general society] are forgotten when it comes to telling stories. But, you know, we would talk about Táhirih, and talk about some of the other prominent Bahá'í women ... and the prominent figures in the Faith.

While Ethel was highly unusual in the type and scope of work she would carry out for Bahá'í institutions and government agencies, she was very similar to other women and men of her time in the variety of services she undertook:

Well, I suppose I played a pretty active role in any community. And each time you are doing something different you're learning. You can't give without receiving. I became a Baha'i in February, and in April I was elected to the local Spiritual Assembly, and in 1954 [a year later] I was chairman of the Assembly, and I was secretary of the [Bahá'í] National Teaching Committee. I had a fireside [an informal meeting to share the Bahá'í teachings] every week in my home, and at the university I organized [Bahá'í] meetings. I was in Hull, Quebec, 1970–73 in a home front goal [part of a teaching plan to expand the religion]. I was combining Bahá'í work, and [Royal] Commission [on the Status of Women] work, and trips across Canada to evaluate the [government] Community Health Care Program, and I was writing my dissertation.

For many women, these new fields of service included ways of interacting that they were not used to. They needed to develop or enhance certain self-definitions and virtues, such as courage and acumen. Their learning would take place through the principle of consultation.

True consultation is spiritual conference in the attitude and atmosphere of love. But spiritual conference and not the mere voicing of personal views is intended. He who expresses an opinion should not voice it as correct and right but set it forth as a contribution to the consensus of opinion. Before expressing his own views he should carefully consider the views already advanced by others. If he finds that a previously expressed opinion is more true and worthy, he should accept it immediately and not willfully hold to an opinion of his own. By this excellent method he endeavors to arrive at unity and truth.[60]

In the course of sharing her life story, Ruth gave a very thoughtful, detailed, and helpful analysis of the process of learning to take on activity in Bahá'í community life, and particularly in expressing herself verbally. She was, at the beginning, very nervous and insecure about speaking but she was able to act upon her other strengths, such as a skill for organization and team work. Later she struggled to understand consultation, but step by step, she acted upon her desire to become competent in this process:

> I was very active. I would arrange things for the firesides [home gatherings], I'd call people up, and Glen [her husband] could do the talking and the presentation. I didn't come into the Faith with those gifts. I hadn't developed, or hadn't had the opportunity to develop, the skills of expressing myself on intellectual matters, on taking part in discussion, on speaking in public, of expressing myself with different views. It was a challenge of participation at that time, either in saying a prayer or reading a writing [sacred verse], or giving an opinion during the consultative portion of the deepenings [study sessions] or the Feasts. And I'd often pass or I'd half finish something, my knees would quiver, my voice would shake. I could very seldom finish a sentence. Together we'd be an okay team.
>
> Understanding what it meant to consult [was difficult] because our understanding then was so limited. All that we knew of consultation came from an adversarial method, although we didn't know it at the time. When you are consulting [according to Bahá'í principle you pray, consult the facts] you share, you put forth your views, and you look at the person with a kindly face, and you try to understand their point of view. It's not competitive, it's not adversarial. And that was easy enough to say, but it was difficult to do, because we didn't know how to do it, but we believed in doing it. So acquiring knowledge and tools and skills to do it, and the practicing of it so that it becomes a force of attraction as well as changes the competence level of the individual—that is a sort of

education. That's what education's all about, I think. Isn't it? And then when you're able to put it into action, then it becomes a force of attraction and is a silent teacher in its own way. When you are able to consult, people say, "What is this, you are doing something different?" [So you say] what we're seeing before us is consultation.

People negotiate meanings from the social worlds they occupy, and construct reality according to the prevailing discourses of their society, thus engaging in a continuous lifelong reflectivity. This learning, and also sharing the new information, is a key way in which the Bahá'í identity is further incorporated into the self, as Ethel's and Clara's narratives illustrate:

ETHEL: I suppose I grew in it myself, while you are helping others you grow too. You may not be conscious of the growth but still it is there. The Bahá'í Faith has meant a lot to me in my development, I had the principles to stand by. You get deeper into the principles and you are teaching them and you try to live by them. In medical services they knew I was a Bahá'í, and I was not only the first woman to be appointed into medical services in the government, but the first Bahá'í too to hold any position of stature like that. It was a good declaration for the Bahá'í, I didn't hide the fact that I was a Bahá'í but I didn't use it, I didn't abuse my position to promote the Bahá'í Faith, I just tried to live the life and let everybody know I was a Bahá'í and what the Bahá'í principles were. And of course in the [government] training program [I developed and led] I had the opportunity to put them all into action.

CLARA: One of the things I know is that I'm a Dakhl'awèdí, and I have my grandchildren, and they have to know the truth of who they are. Not only as Bahá'ís but as human beings, and as First Nation people. And what we've done is incorporate the Bahá'í teachings into our way. So that's my responsibility, to see that my children know about it, and my grandchildren. And I tell them stories, all the time, about 'Abdu'l-Bahá, Bahá'u'lláh. Also, my sisters and brothers, my nieces and nephews, come to me for guidance. We can't lose our identity, you know, because our identity makes us who we are. And I can truly say I'm a Bahá'í. And it's part of me and it's grown in me, and has made me who I am. The teachings have made me who I am.

The societal discourses that were opposed to women's or minority's advancement certainly influenced the self-identity of both Bahá'í women and men. The gender norms of the times in the wider society encouraged women's domesticity and deference to men, and discouraged extra-domestic achievements. The cohort of people I interviewed said that they had to construct new definitions of their roles as they worked in collaboration with, or in resistance to, others in the secular as well as the Bahá'í communities. Ethel remarked that there were men "who liked their role, the masculine role and although they were Bahá'ís, they weren't prepared to give up that old world masculine role." In contrast, a Bahá'í man with four daughters and a wife who was very active in the public realm, pointed out that women just went ahead anyway. He was not aware of the men he knew deliberately stopping women in any way.[61]

Whatever the individual circumstances were in the 1940s–60s and thereafter, the administrative and propagation needs of the Bahá'í community facilitated additional opportunities for women to take their place in the public realm in governance, educational activities, public speaking, the holding of meetings, and so on. This demonstration of women's capacity, the opportunities afforded them, and the desire to serve their religion encouraged more women to act, and made more men take them seriously, as the following excerpt illustrates.

Bill Carr, a Bahá'í from Ethel's and Ruth's cohort, observed that focusing on gender equality was, in some sense, seen as unnecessary in the consciousness of the community, since women were so active in all areas of the religion anyway:

I know on the Calgary Assembly, for several years, there were eight women and one man. And so I think that, with eight women and one man on an Assembly, you don't talk too much about the equality of men and women. I think the women were just in there, really doing the work, heroic share of the work. It was a part of everyday life. It's something you mentioned at every public meeting—that the Bahá'ís believe in the equality of men and women. And perhaps we thought that the women had obtained equality at that time. Or certainly I would think that the women in the 40s and 50s thought they were much better off than they had been at the turn of the century. And so I don't think it was a big issue in the faith . . . but that's only a man speaking.[62]

In all fields of service in community life (governance, devotions, finances, and in the production and dissemination of knowledge) the community knew that, according to the sacred texts, women had the right to participate, and it was part of Bahá'u'lláh's Covenant. But my male participants freely shared that though they recognized the equality of women and men in principle, it took many years for them to comprehend that equality was more than rights—it was also about positive attitudes, behaviours, and actions of men, and it took time for them to internalize and attempt to actualize that understanding.[63]

For the women in this study, alternate definitions about women's potential in the Bahá'í texts, and the presence of a number of enthusiastic, active women believers, were potent forces of encouragement and support. As Ethel and others mentioned, there were many men who did work alongside women, collaborating and supporting them in their endeavours.[64]

Ruth recalls how input from her husband Glen, and positive religious and secular discourses, worked together to socialize her. In turn, she was able to help the Bahá'í Assemblies in developing local community:

I had been elected to different local Spiritual Assemblies and appointed to many committees. My committee work locally developed and flowed into being appointed to national committees. The one that I really liked a lot was Assembly development work which fitted in with my learning about program development. I learned so much about women's programming from YWCA. And I was confirmed by people like Glen, who knew community development in theory [Glen had been to University of Berkeley, CA, to learn about group process when they first started courses in it 1952/53]. I made great use of it in my future years in service to the faith. Assembly development work was a very big highlight in my life because you formed in teams and you met with Assemblies. You helped them identify areas where they would like to develop their skills, and knowledge related to the work of local Spiritual Assembly. And so we had to study those [principles] and become so familiar with them that we could help an Assembly identify the need in a community and consider ways of applying them.

In the 1970s Ruth was elected to the National Spiritual Assembly of the Bahá'ís of Canada. By that time she had grown into a respected and skilled administrator. She would become the first female chairperson of this Assembly. In this capacity, also together with her husband, she gave distinguished service in administration and community building to the Bahá'ís in Iceland, India, and Canada. Ruth wrote scholarly articles and curricula on various Bahá'í topics. She became a much sought after counsellor and workshop leader, and an inspiring speaker on the topics of community development, marriage, and consultation.[65]

Travelling teachers/speakers were a very important resource for the early Bahá'í community. They offered different perspectives on the Bahá'í teachings, and they shared news of Bahá'ís in other provinces and countries. Their movement from place to place engendered a national and transnational orientation, as well as a global vision. The connections they made between people contributed to the formation of friendship networks. These "spiritual kinfolk" were the family who supported, loved, and encouraged the fledgling Bahá'ís. Through their informal and formal talks and meetings, travelling teachers were also one means by which the Bahá'í message was spread.[66]

Aboriginal Bahá'ís who participated in these travel opportunities were, according to the historical record, active agents of their own accord. They evinced, in their physical presence, the concept of equality—that the religion encouraged and facilitated the participation of minorities in the administrative order,[67] and that they were contributing to and advancing the religion. As Clara averred:

I was quite involved in the faith . . . in all aspects—as delegate at [National] Bahá'í Conventions, took part in gatherings—just travelled to every gathering. All my Bahá'í life I have travelled and taught. I travelled all over Yukon, Alaska, I went to Kodiak Island and to the Northwest Territories, and in 1963, down through Alberta to Saskatchewan [to visit Native and other communities].

She also felt it was important to share stories about numinous experiences from her travels. Using dreams to teach others is a Yukon First Nations traditional practice, and Clara described a time when a vision brought people together in the dream and earthly realms:

The air was just really generating the power of the Word. I remember we were going into this one reserve, and Jim [Walton] was driving. So this man was sitting beside the road, an elder, and Jim got out, and that man looked at him, and looked again, and he stood up and he said, "You finally got here. Waited three days for you." He had dreamt about Jim. Jim had a message to tell him. And he sat by the road for three days waiting for Jim. And it was meetings like this that we went on to all over.

Ethel was often called upon to work with the Bahá'í administrative order on national and international levels. One unusual project, which she agreed to undertake, was the development of a Canadian Bahá'í agency that would contribute to change in the health profession. The Bahá'í precept she knew that could be fittingly applied to this endeavour was "work as worship." In Bahá'í writings it is described thus:

In the Bahá'í Cause arts, sciences and all crafts are [counted as] worship . . . all effort . . . prompted by the highest motives and the will to do service to humanity this is worship. To serve mankind and to minister to the needs of the people. Service is prayer. A physician ministering to the sick, gently, tenderly, free from prejudice and believing in the solidarity of the human race, he is giving praise.[68]

In order to develop the agency, Ethel reflected on her experience in the public health field working with doctors and nurses in Canada and abroad. Her understanding of their struggles to maintain an ethical outlook and behaviour in the face of a materialistic society informed her approach:

I was asked if I would develop the Bahá'í International Health Agency [BIHA]. So I came back to Ottawa to do that in 1983. The goal of the agency was to spiritualize the health profession, and to get them to serve mankind and not their profession. And we had to find out where the doctor and health professionals were around the world. The first order of Bahá'ís is to serve humanity—that's the most important thing. Doctors didn't always serve humanity; they served doctors, they served their profession. They would put their profession first before they would put humanity first. That is part and parcel of the medical profession, and, Bahá'ís had to be different. What we did is we had a bulletin, we wrote articles and searched the Bahá'í writings for quotes on Bahá'í health, and sent it out, and had a conference once a year. I organized four or five conferences.

Ethel was well known inside and outside the Canadian Bahá'í community for her long and distinguished service. In 1998 she was officially recognized by the Canadian government with the Order of Canada for "being a pioneer in the field of primary health care, and empowering disadvantaged people in Canada, Africa, and Asia, to improve their lives."[69]

The final example of how spiritual beliefs are transformed into action pertains to the directive in the Bahá'í writings that indigenous culture and language be maintained—a characteristic of unity in diversity. This orientation encourages and upholds indigenous peoples' right to take pride in and develop their own identity, culture, and language.[70] Clara's first pilgrimage to the Bahá'í World Centre in January 1973 was influential in her decision to adopt this calling, and her efforts had long-term, far-reaching consequences. This narrative opens with her providing personal context to what she saw happening with First Nations peoples in Yukon, and then how she set about to make change, beginning with herself and then with her family:

> Everybody that went to the mission school came to Whitehorse because we didn't fit in at home anymore, couldn't speak our language, punished for speaking Indian, you know. They didn't even know what clan they belonged to, and so everyone was drinking. And these are the ones that

are lost. I've been there, you know. I went through that. I went through the struggles. I think the Bahá'í teachings came and took this young, lost person and formed me.

The Tagish language was dying out. It's going to get lost, everything was dying out. I told Auntie Angela [Sidney] about what the Guardian [Shoghi Effendi] said about our culture and the language. You know, the Guardian recommended that the First Nations should keep their traditional ways. Like, keep their language, keep their traditional customs. So we started language [classes] in Carcross and then it went into dancing. It was mostly my family that was there. We were all Bahá'ís. We started using the Bahá'í principles to teach. And like I say, the clan system was very, very familiar [congruent] with the Bahá'í Teachings . . . the Bahá'í laws. So it was easy to teach them. And that's how the dance group got started. Finally the principal [of the school where they were practising] got involved. And we started, you know, talking about the traditional ways. So we got the language started in Carcross. This was in 1973. And I took them to Haines, Alaska, at a celebration. They had a celebration there, and our dance group danced there, and that that was the beginning—The Tagish Nation dancers. [Later] when I first went to work for Council of the Yukon Indians, it was in cultural education and I was the Director of Cultural Education then, so I got a lot of traditional camps started. Then at the same time I was working with the Education Minister here [Whitehorse] and I was telling them how important the language is. I talked to a lot of people and finally we had a meeting, and talked about the language and how we can start it, how we can keep going. And then it just built up from that. From that we got the Language Centre at the College [Yukon Native Language Centre].

The dance group comprised members of Clara's family. Her sister, Bahá'í Doris McLean, also participated in forming the Inland Tlingit children's dance group, and later her daughter, Bahá'í Marilyn Jensen (Clara's niece), would go on to found the Dakhká Khwáan Dancers. This dance troupe has continued to the present day, expanding the early vision of their matriarchs and working on the social transformation and cultural revitalization of their communities. They are reclaiming languages and promoting traditional values through singing, drumming, dancing, and extensive research into ancient cultural protocols and practices, and through the creation of visually stunning traditional regalia. The dancers from past and present have also travelled nationally and internationally, educating and delighting people with the richness and beauty of their culture.

Clara devoted twenty-six years of her life to developing First Nations school curriculum, and was honoured with the Governor General's Award for preserving the language and culture of her people. She also played a valuable role in land claim and self-governance negotiations for Yukon First Nations. [71]

In summary, while I have concentrated on a very important aspect of religiousness—social action—this chapter only touches the surface of the varied ways in which Bahá'ís express their religiosity, individually and collectively. Included here are a few examples of how three women acquired their individual understandings of Bahá'í spiritual principle, transformed their habits of thought and behaviour, and endeavoured to translate their faith into service. The life stories Clara, Ruth, and Ethel shared illustrate their conscious awareness of the exigencies of the times, and their particular response to those needs. Now, in the twenty-first century, Bahá'ís are involved in different modalities of fellowship, learning, and dialogue with the societies in which they live, and have new personal and collective narratives to share.[72] ●

Notes

1. The three women included here are Dr. Ethel Martens (who was seventy-nine years old at that time of the interview in Ottawa, ON, 1995), Ruth Eyford (sixty-eight years when interviewed in St. Albert, AB, 1995), and Clara Schinkel (age not given but approximately seventy years old, interviewed in Whitehorse, YT, 2004).

2. William Shaffir, Mary Lorenz Dietz, and Robert Prus, "Field Research as Social Experience: Learning to Do Ethnography," in *Doing Everyday Life: Ethnography as Human Lived Experience*, ed. Mary Lorenz Dietz, Robert Prus, and William Shaffir (Toronto: Copp Clark Longman, 1994), 30–54.

3. Lynn Echevarria, "Working through the Vision: Religion and Identity in the Life Histories of Bahá'í Women in Canada" (PhD dissertation, Essex University, United

Kingdom, 2000). See the methodology section for an examination of the challenges and rewards of the "insider position."

4. Selena Crosson, "Searching for May Maxwell: Women's Role in Shaping Early Bahá'í Culture 1898–1940" (PhD dissertation, University of Saskatchewan, 2012). This is the only Canadian academic study to date that provides a feminist context and in-depth inquiry into the history of a Bahá'í woman. My works are the only studies that include in-depth analyses of extensive life narratives of women and a full feminist inquiry into the many Bahá'í teachings on women. We look forward to the development of more scholarship in these areas.

5. See Echevarria, "Working through the Vision," and Lynn Echevarria, *Life Histories of Bahá'í Women in Canada: Constructing Religious Identity in the Twentieth Century*, American University Study Series 7, Theology and Religion (New York: Peter Lang Publishing, 2011), for those interested in comparisons about women's experience in Christianity and in the Bahá'í Faith, as well as a theoretical feminist inquiry into those subjects.

6. Hasan M. Balyuzi, *'Abdu'l-Bahá: The Centre of the Covenant of Bahá'u'lláh* (Oxford: George Ronald, 1971), 64. The Bahá'í Faith was introduced at this Parliament through a paper read by Rev. George A. Ford on behalf of the Presbyterian missionary to Syria, Rev. Henry H. Jessup.

7. Edith was the first person in Canada to declare her belief in Bahá'u'lláh. See Will C. van den Hoonaard, *The Origins of the Bahá'í Community of Canada, 1898–1948* (Waterloo, ON: Wilfrid Laurier University Press, 1996).

8. Andrew Pemberton-Piggott, "The Bahá'í Faith in Alberta, 1942–1992: The Ethic of Dispersion" (master's thesis, University of Alberta, 1992), 3.

9. Van den Hoonaard, *The Origins of the Bahá'í Community*, 233–35, 240. Each Spiritual Assembly consists of nine members elected from the adult membership of the believers (twenty-one years of age and over). This process involves no electioneering, and is conducted by secret ballot. The Assembly's duties are oriented toward the service, care, and organization of the community in its jurisdiction and service to the larger society.

10. The Feast is the formal community gathering held every nineteen days. It comprises three components: the devotional, the consultative, and the social.

11. Van den Hoonaard *The Origins of the Bahá'í Community*, 252–54.

12. Shoghi Effendi, *Messages to Canada* (N.p.: National Spiritual Assembly of the Bahá'ís of Canada, 1965), 7.

13. Michael McMullen, *The Bahá'í: The Religious Construction of a Global Identity* (New Brunswick, NJ, and London: Rutgers University Press, 2000), 177. See Margit Warburg, *Bahá'í and Globalisation* (Copenhagen: Aarhus University Press, 2005) for an examination of the central doctrine of oneness in Bahá'u'lláh's teachings and how that has featured in Bahá'í communities globally, as well as in Canada.

14. See current demographics and statistics about the Bahá'í Community of Canada: http://ca.bahai.org/bah%C3%A1%C3%AD-community-canada.

15. Bahá'u'lláh left specific guidance concerning the succession of leadership outlined as a covenant between himself and his followers. This is further explained in the next section "Historical Background."

16. This order encompasses two categories of institutions: elected governing councils and appointed counsellors. Counsellors and their deputies play a critical role in the moral development and collective progress of the community. Their duties involve counselling, advising, and encouraging individuals, communities, and Bahá'í institutions. They have no legislative, executive, or judicial authority; cannot authoritatively interpret the sacred writings; and have no sacerdotal functions.

17. See Bahá'í Community of Canada/Act of Canadian Parliament/An Act to Incorporate the National Spiritual Assembly of the Bahá'ís of Canada: http://ca.bahai.org/canadian–bahai.../act–canadian. The section, "fulfill all and whatsoever the several purposes and objects set forth in the written utterances of Bahá'u'lláh, 'Abdu'l-Bahá and Shoghi Effendi," encompasses Bahá'u'lláh's laws regarding equality.

18. Women serve in various positions within the administrative order. For example, at the Bahá'í World Centre in Haifa, Israel, Bahá'í offices at the United Nations in New York, Geneva, and Vienna, as well as on the national and local Spiritual Assemblies worldwide, on committees and councils, and as officers—treasurer, chairperson, secretary—of all the foregoing.

19. See Janet A. Khan, "Promoting the Equality of Women and Men: The Role of the Covenant," *Journal of Bahá'í Studies* 10, no. 1/2 (2000); Echevarria, *Life Histories*; Deborah Kestin van den Hoonaard and Will C. van den Hoonaard, *The Equality of Women and Men: The Experience of the Bahá'í Community of Canada* (Douglas, NB: Self-published, 2006).

20. See Bahá'í World News Service/Human Rights in Iran and Egypt—"Persecution of the Baha'is of Iran," http://news.bahai.org/human–rights/ for updates on the current situation of the Bahá'ís of Iran and information regarding the Bahá'í Institute of Higher Education (BIHE), which has been banned and its educators imprisoned.

In October 2011, some forty-three distinguished philosophers and theologians in sixteen countries signed an open letter protesting the attack on BIHE. See Bahá'í World News Service/Philosophers and theologians worldwide condemn Iran's attack on Baha'i educators, http://news.bahai.org/story/857. See also Romeo Dallaire's speech to the Canadian Senate, November 29, 2011: "We can proudly say that sixty-three of these educators received their degrees here in Canada. We have supported this effort that you would consider subversive if you were an Iranian government official." In Canadian Bahá'í News Service, "Senator Romeo Dallaire Speaks Out about the Bahá'ís," http://bahainews.ca/en/node/691.

21. Hasan M. Balyuzi, *Bahá'u'lláh* (London: Whitefriars Press, 1968), 11.

22. Bahá'u'lláh (the Glory of God), was born Mírzá Husayn-'Alí Núrí in Tehran, Persia, in 1817, to Shí'ah Muslim parents. He became known and distinguished for his knowledge, wisdom, and saintly life, as well as for his services as a counsellor, comforter, and provider. He married 'Asiyíh Khánum, a woman of noble birth, and they had seven children. Only three of these children survived: the eldest son, 'Abbás Effendi ('Abdu'l-Bahá), daughter Bahíyyih Khánum, and Mírzá Mihdí, the youngest son. The writings and prayers of Bahá'u'lláh, the Báb, and of 'Abdu'l-Bahá are considered the Word of God by the Bahá'ís, and they comprise the sacred writings of the Bahá'í religion. The history, major teachings, current global statistics, and other topics of interest regarding the Bahá'í Faith can be found on the website of The Canadian Bahá'í Community of Canada, http://ca.bahai.org.

23. van den Hoonaard, *The Origins of the Bahá'í Community.*

24. Bahíyyih Khánum was known for her saintly life. She became an international administrator and de facto head of the Bahá'í religion for several years. Though she was never able to travel outside the Middle East, she would become pivotal in fostering a culture of change in the Bahá'í community globally. See Khan, *Promoting the Equality.*

25. The texts of the Covenant clearly state that 'Abdu'l-Bahá is not to be regarded as a Divine Messenger, but rather as the perfect human example of Bahá'u'lláh's teachings. 'Abdu'l-Bahá promoted, protected, and administered the religion throughout his lifetime and designated, in his will and testament, the twin institutions of the Guardianship and the Universal House of Justice as his successors. 'Abdu'l-Bahá was known for his wisdom and intellectual brilliance, as well as his compassion and care of the poor. In 1920 a knighthood of the British Empire was conferred upon him in recognition of his humanitarian work. See Hasan M. Balyuzi, *'Abdu'l-Bahá: The Centre of the Covenant of Bahá'u'lláh* (Oxford: George Ronald, 1971).

26. 'Abdu'l-Bahá, *Memorials of the Faithful* (Wilmette, IL: Bahá'í Publishing Trust, 1971), 190.

27. Susan Maneck, "Táhirih: A Religious Paradigm of Womanhood," *Journal of Bahá'í Studies* 2, no. 2 (1989): 41.

28. Asadu'llah Fadil (Jinab-i-Fadil) Mazandarani, *The Wonderful Life of Kurratul-Ayn [Táhirih]*, 1913, http:/bahai-library.com/life of Tahireh-jinab-i-fadil; Shoghi Effendi, *God Passes By* (Wilmette, IL: Bahá'í Publishing Trust, 1957), 72–76.

29. Shoghi Effendi, *God Passes By*, 7, 74.

30. Nabíl-i-A'zam, *The Dawnbreakers: Nabíl's Narrative of the Early Days of the Bahá'í Revelation*, trans. and ed. from the original Persian by Shoghi Effendi (Wilmette, IL: Bahá'í Publishing Trust, 1962), 272.

31. Shoghi Effendi, *God Passes By*, 73.

32. The Promised One of Islám.

33. Shoghi Effendi, *God Passes By*, 32.

34. Ibid., 74.

35. Ibid., 32. See also Amin Banani, "Táhirih: A Portrait in Poetry," *Journal of Bahá'í Studies* 10, no. 1/2 (2000) for more information pertaining to the genesis of her title.

36. Ibid., 3.

37. 'Abdu'l-Bahá, *Memorials of the Faithful*, 202.

38. Maneck, "Táhirih," 47.

39. Shoghi Effendi, *God Passes By*, 75. Táhirih was immortalized in poetry, literature, and plays by such people as Sarah Bernhardt, the actor, Compte de Gobineau, the historian, and E. G. Browne, the Orientalist. See Banani, "Táhirih: A Portrait in Poetry." She has been described as a Persian Joan of Arc, and an originator of the women's movement in Iran. See Shoghi Effendi, *God Passes By*, 76; Banani, "Táhirih: A Portrait in Poetry," 6. Her name was inscribed on the list of pioneers for the emancipation of women at the Seneca Falls Women's Rights Convention. See Banani, "Táhirih: A Portrait in Poetry," 6.

40. Shoghi Effendi, *God Passes By*, 76.

41. 'Abdu'l-Bahá, *Memorials of the Faithful*, 190–203.

42. Shoghi Effendi, *God Passes By*, 7.

43. Eileen L. Anderson, "Qurratu'l-Ayn Táhirih: A Study in Transformational Leadership" (PhD dissertation, United States International University, 1992).

44. Ibid.; Echevarria, "Working through the Vision."

45. The Bahá'í teachings state that there is only one God, though humanity calls that Supreme Being by different names. The Creator sent a progression of prophets or "Manifestations," such as Christ, Zoroaster, Moses, and Muhammad, as part of an eternal covenant to spiritually educate humankind and facilitate the advancement of civilization. This process of divine revelation, "Progressive Revelation," is continuous and suited to the requirements of humanity throughout the ages. In their station as Holy Messengers they are all as one and equal, but differ in the teachings they present according to the spiritual receptivity and needs of humanity.

46. Bahá'u'lláh, *Gleanings from the Writings of Bahá'u'lláh*, trans. Shoghi Effendi (Birmingham: Templar Printing Works, 1949), 249. The words "man" and "mankind" used here mean men and women collectively. This usage could be problematic, suggesting the exclusion of women. Baharieh Rouhani Ma'ani addresses this in "The Effect of Philosophical and Linguistic Gender Biases," *Journal of Bahá'í Studies* 8, no. 1 (1997): 45–66. She states that the writing style Bahá'u'lláh used in a "sizeable portion of His writings" appears sexist when translated into English. In Persian, the original language of revelation, however, it was genderless. She also explains that particular linguistic practices have affected the use of symbolism that was present in the original Bahá'í texts. When the text was translated in the 1950s, the then current mode of scriptural translations (a seventeenth-century model) was followed. This model used the male pronoun and could not account for feminine pronouns in relation to a prophet or manifestation of God. For example, occurrences in which Bahá'u'lláh used feminine terms describing himself as a manifestation of God, and employed the feminine pronoun, are changed to neuter in the English translation. Ma'ani states that according to 'Abdu'l-Bahá, the future universal language Bahá'u'lláh called for will be one that does not have grammatical gender (Ma'ani 1997), 61–62.

47. Bahá'í International Community Statement Library, "World Citizenship: A Global Ethic for Sustainable Development," 1993, http://statements.bahai.org/93–0614 .htm.

48. Ibid.

49. Shoghi Effendi, "The Principle of Oneness," 43.

50. Ibid.

51. See more excerpts from Ruth's and Ethel's stories in Echevarria, "Working through the Vision." For further background to Clara's life, see Lynn Echevarria, "A New Skin for an Old Drum: Changing Contexts of Yukon Aboriginal Storytelling," *Northern*

Review Fall 29 (2008): 39–62. Clara's transcript and oral archive are deposited in the Yukon Government Archives, Whitehorse, YT. Ethel's and Ruth's recordings are in the Bahá'í National Centre archives, Toronto, ON.

52. It is important to mention here that women's identity, according to Bahá'í writings, is not bound up exclusively in either the public or private spheres. Motherhood is viewed as sacred, while women's participation in the affairs of the world is seen as crucial to the advancement of civilization.

53. Echevarria, "Working through the Vision."

54. Ibid.

55. See Rainn Wilson, "The Titanic's Forgotten Survivor," http://www.huffingtonpost .com/rainn–wilson/abdul–baha_b_1419099.html.

56. Robert Prus, "Generic Social Processes: Intersubjectivity and Transcontextuality in the Social Sciences," in *Doing Everyday Life: Ethnography as Human Lived Experience*, ed, Mary Lorenz Dietz, Robert Prus, and William Shaffir (Toronto: Copp Clark Longman, 1994), 396.

57. 'Abdu'l-Bahá, *Foundations of World Unity* (Wilmette, IL: Bahá'í Publishing Trust, 1945), 26.

58. Ibid., 100–104.

59. Universal House of Justice, *"To the Bahá'ís of the World, Ridván 2010"* (Bahá'í World Centre, 2010), 9.

60. 'Abdu'l-Bahá, *The Promulgation of Universal Peace: Talks Delivered by 'Abdu'l-Bahá during His Visit to the United States and Canada in 1912*, 2nd ed. (Wilmette, IL: Bahá'í Publishing Trust, 1982), 72–73. The quotation is addressed to both men and women. Any quotations from Bahá'í texts are English translations from Persian or Arabic. The words "man" and "mankind" mean man and woman collectively. See note 46.

61. Interview with Bob Donnelly, Charlottetown, PEI, 1994.

62. Interview with Bill Carr, Sylvan Lake, AB, 1995.

63. Most of the women in my study, including Ruth and Clara, did not express any personal dissatisfaction with the lack of gender equality in the Bahá'í community. When we turn to scholarly work in this area, however, we find that in the realm of family and community life, progress toward understanding that women are equal with men has been slow, as has been establishing the importance of men and women jointly working for equality. Addressing traditional societal notions of masculinity and femininity, and the corresponding negative behaviours and attitudes, have been areas of struggle for many Bahá'í families. While continued

progress has been made on some fronts such as "a heightened sensibility towards equality" and "the use of consultation in family life," the aforementioned struggle remained the case into the late 1990s, as evidenced in the work of sociologists van den Hoonaard and van den Hoonaard, *The Equality of Women and Men*, 28.

64. Van den Hoonaard 1996; van den Hoonaard and van den Hoonaard 2006; Echevarria, "Working through the Vision."

65. Echevarria, "Working through the Vision."

66. Ibid.

67. For example, two other Yukon people, Chief Mark Wedge and Louise Profeit Le Blanc, served for many years on the National Spiritual Assembly of the Bahá'ís of Canada.

68. 'Abdu'l-Bahá, *Paris Talks: Addresses Given by 'Abdu'l-Bahá in Paris in 1911–1912*, 11th ed. (London: Bahá'í Publishing Trust, 1969), 176–77.

69. Awarded on October 21, 1998, invested on February 3, 1999. See Jeannine Ouellette, "Women in Ottawa: Mentors and Milestones," http://womeninottawa.blogspot .com/2011_07_01_archive.html. Ethel was a pioneer in the field of primary health care and one of the first health educators for Aboriginal communities in Canada. She was lauded for developing "culturally sensitive training programs to enable local people to take responsibility for their own health services." See "Order of Canada," http://www.gg.ca/honour.aspx?id=3991&t=12&ln=Martens.

70. See "Cultural Diversity in the Age of Maturity," http://bahai-library.com/compila tion_cultural_diversity_maturity.

71. I could not find the exact year Clara received the Governor General's award, but see http://www.yesnet.yk.ca/firstnations/pdf/10–11/handbook_10_11.pdf for a description of her services. Clara received many honours and distinctions. She also worked with a number of social scientists over the years on research concerning First Nations.

72. According to the Bahá'í World Centre, this global community has diversified, developing organically through the progressive unfolding and application of the founder's teachings and plans. A worldwide system of extensive learning has evolved wherein Bahá'ís are engaged in four core activities: (1) classes for children, which focus on moral development; (2) moral empowerment groups for junior youth; (3) devotional meetings; and (4) study circles devoted to studying Bahá'u'lláh's teachings through a global curriculum. See The Bahá'í Community of Canada/Building Community, http://ca.bahai.org/building-community.

Bibliography

'Abdu'l-Bahá. *Foundations of World Unity*. Wilmette, IL: Bahá'í Publishing Trust, 1945.

———. *Memorials of the Faithful*. Wilmette, IL: Bahá'í Publishing Trust, 1971.

———. *Paris Talks: Addresses Given by 'Abdu'l-Bahá in Paris in 1911–1912*. 11th ed. London: Bahá'í Publishing Trust, 1969.

———. *The Promulgation of Universal Peace: Talks Delivered by 'Abdu'l-Bahá during His Visit to the United States and Canada in 1912*. 2nd ed. Wilmette, IL: Bahá'í Publishing Trust, 1982.

———. *Women: Extracts from the Writings of Bahá'u'lláh, 'Abdu'l-Bahá, Shoghi Effendi and the Universal House of Justice*. Compiled by the Research Department of the Universal House of Justice. Thornhill, ON: Bahá'í Canada Publications, 1986.

Anderson, Eileen L. "Qurratu'l-Ayn Táhirih: A Study in Transformational Leadership." PhD dissertation, United States International University, 1992.

The Bahá'í Community of Canada. "The Bahá'í Community of Canada." http://ca.bahai .org/bah%C3%A1%C3%AD-community-canada.

———. "The Bahá'í Community of Canada/Act of Canadian Parliament/An Act to Incorporate the National Spiritual Assembly of the Bahá'ís of Canada." http://ca.bahai .org/canadian–bahai.../act–canadian.

———. "Building Community." http://ca.bahai.org/building-community.

Bahá'í International Community Statement Library. "World Citizenship: A Global Ethic for Sustainable Development." 1993. http://statements.bahai.org/93-0614.htm.

Bahá'í World News Service. Human Rights in Iran and Egypt—"Persecution of the Baha'is of Iran." http://news.bahai.org/human–rights.

———. Philosophers and Theologians Worldwide Condemn Iran's Attack on Baha'i educators. http://news.bahai.org/story/857.

Bahá'u'lláh. *Gleanings from the Writings of Bahá'u'lláh*. Translated by Shoghi Effendi. Birmingham: Templar Printing Works, 1949.

———. *The Hidden Words and Selected Writings*. Kuala Lumpur: Bahá'í Publishing Trust Committee, 1985.

Balyuzi, Hasan M. *'Abdu'l-Bahá: The Centre of the Covenant of Bahá'u'lláh*. Oxford: George Ronald, 1971.

———. *Bahá'u'lláh*. London: Whitefriars Press, 1968.

Banani, Amin. "Táhirih: A Portrait in Poetry." *Journal of Bahá'í Studies* 10, no. 1/2 (2000): 1–10.

Canadian Bahá'í News Service. Senator Romeo Dallaire Speaks out about the Bahá'ís. http://bahainews.ca/en/node/691.

Crosson, Selena. "Searching for May Maxwell: Women's Role in Shaping Early Bahá'í Culture 1898–1940." PhD dissertation, University of Saskatchewan, 2012.

Drewek, Paula. "Cross Cultural Testing of Fowler's Model of Faith Development among Bahá'ís: India and Canada." PhD dissertation, University of Ottawa, 1996.

Echevarria, Lynn. *Life Histories of Bahá'í Women in Canada: Constructing Religious Identity in the Twentieth Century.* American University Study Series 7, Theology and Religion. New York: Peter Lang Publishing, 2011.

——. "A New Skin for an Old Drum: Changing Contexts of Yukon Aboriginal Storytelling." *Northern Review Fall* 29 (2008): 39–62.

——. "Working through the Vision: Religion and Identity in the Life Histories of Bahá'í Women in Canada." PhD dissertation, Essex University, United Kingdom, 2000.

Hatcher, William S., and Douglas Martin. *The Bahá'í Faith: The Emerging Global Religion.* New York: Harper and Row, 1985.

Khan, Janet A. "Promoting the Equality of Women and Men: The Role of the Covenant." *Journal of Bahá'í Studies* 10, no. 1/2 (2000): 71–90.

——. *Prophet's Daughter: The Life and Legacy of Bahíyyih Khánum, Outstanding Heroine of the Bahá'í Faith.* Wilmette, IL: Bahá'í Publishing Trust, 2005.

Ma'ani, Baharieh Rouhani, "The Effect of Philosophical and Linguistic Gender Biases on the Degradation of Women's Status in Religion." *Journal of Bahá'í Studies* 8, no. 1 (1997): 45–66.

Maneck, Susan. "Táhirih: A Religious Paradigm of Womanhood." *Journal of Bahá'í Studies* 2, no. 2 (1989): 39–54.

Mazandarani, Asadu'llah Fadil (Jinab-i-Fadil). *The Wonderful Life of Kurratul-Ayn [Táhirih]* 1913. http:/bahai-library.com/life of Tahireh-jinab-i-fadil.

McMullen, Michael. *The Bahá'í: The Religious Construction of a Global Identity.* New Brunswick, NJ, and London: Rutgers University Press, 2000.

Nabíl-i-A'zam. *The Dawnbreakers: Nabíl's Narrative of the Early Days of the Bahá'í Revelation.* Translated and edited from the original Persian by Shoghi Effendi. Wilmette, IL: Bahá'í Publishing Trust, 1962.

Ouellette, Jeannine. "Women in Ottawa: Mentors and Milestones." http://womenin-ottawa.blogspot.com/2011_07_01_archive.html.

Pemberton-Piggott, Andrew. "The Bahá'í Faith in Alberta, 1942–1992: The Ethic of Dispersion." Master's thesis, University of Alberta, 1992.

Prus, Robert. "Generic Social Processes: Intersubjectivity and Transcontextuality in the Social Sciences." In *Doing Everyday Life: Ethnography as Human Lived Experience*, edited by Mary Lorenz Dietz, Robert Prus, and William Shaffir, 393–412. Toronto: Copp Clark Longman, 1994.

Shaffir, William, Mary Lorenz Dietz, and Robert Prus. "Field Research as Social Experience: Learning to Do Ethnography." In *Doing Everyday Life: Ethnography as Human Lived Experience*, edited by Mary Lorenz Dietz, Robert Prus, and William Shaffir, 30–54. Toronto: Copp Clark Longman, 1994.

Shoghi Effendi. *God Passes By*. Wilmette, IL: Bahá'í Publishing Trust, 1957.

——. *Messages to Canada*. N.p.: National Spiritual Assembly of the Bahá'ís of Canada, 1965.

——. "The Principle of Oneness." In *The World Order of Bahá'u'lláh*. Wilmette, IL: Bahá'í Publishing Trust, 1965.

Universal House of Justice. *"To the Bahá'ís of the World, Ridván 2010."* Haifa: Bahá'í World Centre, 2010.

van den Hoonaard, Deborah Kestin, and Will C. van den Hoonaard. *The Equality of Women and Men: The Experience of the Bahá'í Community of Canada*. Douglas, NB: Self-published, 2006.

van den Hoonaard, Will C. *The Origins of the Bahá'í Community of Canada, 1898–1948*. Waterloo, ON: Wilfrid Laurier University Press, 1996.

Warburg, Margit. *Bahá'í and Globalisation*. Copenhagen, Denmark: Aarhus University Press, 2005.

Wilson, Rainn. "The Titanic's Forgotten Survivor." http://www.huffingtonpost.com/rainn-wilson/abdul-baha_b_1419099.html.

Part C

South Asian Religions in Southwest Ontario

8 Being Hindu in Canada

Experiences of Women

ANNE M. PEARSON WITH PREETI NAYAK

Introduction

A young woman in Hamilton is mocked by her friends—"Don't step on that ant! It may be your aunt!"—after they have learned she believes in reincarnation; she smiles awkwardly in response, not knowing what to say. An observant Hindu in Waterloo, used to performing regular ritual fasts with other women in India, loses track of when these special days arrive and is at a loss as to where to find the required ritual paraphernalia in the new Canadian setting. Her daughters, born in Canada, have no interest in following these "arcane" rituals, yet one likes to meditate and is a strict vegetarian, and the other enjoys her Bharatnatyam dance classes. All these women identify as Hindu, yet they, like most Hindu immigrants who are first generation or beyond, find it difficult to articulate exactly what being Hindu in a Canadian setting entails—not just to non-Hindus, but to themselves.

Studies that examine ethnic cultural retention cite religion as a focal point in immigrants' efforts to sustain and transmit culture as religion is often an integral component in keeping one's children linked to their ancestry and cultural backgrounds. Higher levels of religiosity often result in a greater ability to retain culture overall, especially for immigrants from locations where religion and culture are so intimately intertwined, as in South Asia. Further, some studies have indicated that Hindu women have been the primary "carriers of culture" and transmitters of religion to the next generation.[1] We set out to investigate whether Hindu women in Canada view themselves as being responsible for this transmission and, if so, how. We also sought to learn more about the content of that reproduction and transmission, including what gendered norms and practices of Hinduism remain prevalent in Canada and how they have been challenged, if at all. It is clear that such norms and practices (for example, modesty, menstrual taboos, food production, domestic responsibilities, and rituals like fasting for the well-being of family members) are not merely replicated in the new cultural environment; they are adapted, questioned, embraced, rejected, or reinterpreted—a process that begins with the first generation. While there are a plethora of Hindu texts that prescribe or offer models for female behaviour and responsibilities, there is no definitive single source of authority. Thus the interpretation and application of such prescriptions are largely left up to the individual whose perspective is affected by culture, family, education, and personal experiences. The range of possible interpretations is expanded in the Canadian diasporic context where individualism and gender equity are highly regarded. Many young Hindu women growing up in Canada become resistant to particular practices of Hinduism transmitted by their parents that conflict with their developing hybrid values. The resulting "individualized Hinduism" is not perceived as any less legitimate a form of Hinduism. Most of the younger women interviewed felt at ease either rejecting certain practices or transforming their usual meanings to suit their own views. They were able to track the evolution of their religious understanding as they grew older and many cited a trend of creating an individualized Hinduism in Canada that contrasted, they believed, with their mothers' unquestioning assimilative understandings of Hinduism.

The interviews on which a significant portion of this chapter is based were conducted by the authors in 2012 in the cities of Hamilton and Mississauga, Ontario. The twelve Hindu women interviewed at length, and others interviewed more briefly, represent a range of ages (eighteen to seventy), marital status, time of arrival in Canada (1966–2011), and some variety in originating homeland (India, Sri Lanka, and Kenya).[2] Among the married women with children, five were first generation and one was second generation. The six younger unmarried Hindu women interviewed were in their early twenties. Two were born in Canada, and the others emigrated as young children with their families from India, Nepal, Sri Lanka, and the Gulf States. All were either in university or had just completed degrees.

To give the body of this chapter a wider context, we begin with a brief review of the history of Hinduism in Canada and then sketch out features of Hindu diasporic religion. The remainder of the chapter is divided into two sections, the first of which focuses primarily on the views and experiences of first-generation Hindu immigrant women, followed by those of the second generation.

History of Hinduism in Canada

WHILE THE MAJORITY of the world's approximately 950 million Hindus continue to reside in India, there are significant numbers of Hindus in Nepal, Sri Lanka, Fiji, South Africa, eastern Africa, Guyana, and Trinidad.[3] The more recent Hindu immigrants to North America now number approximately 1.2 million in the United States and some 400,000 in Canada with the largest ethnic populations being of Gujarati, Punjabi, and Tamil Sri Lankan ethnic origin.

Hindus began arriving in Canada in the early 1900s. Most of the arrivals were single men who came to the province of British Columbia from India by ship from Hong Kong looking for work in the lumber and other developing industries. The majority of these Indian workers were Sikh, who because of their numbers were able to established gurdwaras. The few hundred Hindus who came were content to attend the newly built gurdwaras as cultural commonalities with the Sikh immigrants outweighed religious differences. Certainly all South Asians in general were viewed by the predominately white British Columbians as the same, all being referred to as "Hindoos." While there was opportunity for employment in Canada and interest in emigrating, growing anti-foreigner sentiment among the dominant Euro Canadian citizenry led to the passing of laws that effectively stifled immigration from South Asia to Canada. Thus, between 1909 and 1943 only 878 South Asians were allowed to enter the Dominion, many of whom were wives and children of men already living in the country. Further, it was only in 1947 with the passage of the Canadian Citizenship Act that Indo Canadians, among others, were granted full citizenship rights, including the right to vote.[4]

The 1950s saw a slow trickle of mostly urban, educated male graduate students and professionals come to Canada from India. A 1962 reform to the 1952 Immigration Act officially eliminated racial discrimination in Canada's immigration policy. Any unsponsored person who had the necessary qualifications could be considered for immigration, regardless of skin colour, race, ethnic origin, or religion. In 1967 the point system was created so that potential immigrants could be assessed, not on race, but on criteria such as education, age, fluency in French or English, and available job opportunities in Canada. The point system was the first major amendment to Canadian immigration legislation that favoured educated and professional South Asian entrance to Canada. A second important policy change that facilitated Asian immigration, including women, was the 1976 Immigration Act, which separated potential immigrants into three classes: family (immediate family members of immigrants in Canada); humanitarian (including refugees); and the independent class (those who applied for landed immigrant status from their home countries and were subject to the point system). By 1986 40 percent of all immigrants to Canada came from Asia, and by 2005, India was among the top three sources for Canadian immigrants. Thus the entry to Canada of a trickle of male Hindus, mostly from northern India, in the first three-quarters of the twentieth century changed into a stream in the last quarter that has lasted into the twenty-first century. This stream included a substantial number of refugees and those fleeing political instability or persecution, such as Tamil Hindus from Sri Lanka arriving in the wake of the civil war starting in 1983 or Hindus escaping violence and political upheaval in Guyana. Hindu immigrants from a wide variety of backgrounds and originating homelands are now found in all provinces of Canada, but the majority have settled in British Columbia and Ontario.

Features of Diasporic Hinduism in Canada

WHILE SHARING COMMONALITIES IN THEIR RELIGION, Hindus do come from a large number of distinct ethnic groups, speak diverse languages, and have distinctive religious and cultural practices. Major differences in ways of being Hindu can appear even within the same ethno-linguistic group, depending, for example, on *jati* (birth-caste) or *sampradaya* (sectarian) traditions. Hindus arriving in Canada from different regions of India and from other nations where Hinduism has long been established thus encounter an almost bewildering diversity of beliefs, practices, and customs among their own co-religionists. Often immigrants only became aware of the extent of the diversity when they meet and try to recreate a communal religious life with their fellow Hindus in a diasporic context.

Since 1988 this recreation of a religious life and a pan-Hindu cultural identity has been enabled by the Canadian government. When Parliament passed the Canadian Multiculturalism Act in July 1988, Canada became the first country in the world to have a national multiculturalism law, one that not only reaffirmed that multiculturalism was an essential component of Canadian society, but provided a cultural space and funding, albeit limited, for its expression, particularly in the heritage language classes. At the same time, government officials expected religious groups to define their own identities, especially when it came to the incorporation of temples or societies that could receive non-taxable status. Such government expectations required Hindus in Canada to identify appropriate spokespeople and to self-consciously determine the "basics" of their common Hindu identity—not an easy task. Some self-identified Hindus may rarely—even never—visit temples, celebrate festivals, or perform puja (worship at home). For others, Hinduism has become a much more defined and salient feature of their lives than it was before emigrating. Some have embraced practices that they never observed in the homeland through interaction with other Canadian Hindus or with visiting Hindu gurus. But for all who identify as Hindu and came from India, there are some common experiences. In India, observing caste distinctions (especially in matters of dining and marriage), avoiding the consumption of beef, and enjoying the traditions associated with annual festivals were a normal part of everyday life. But in Canada, eating meat (and beef) is an everyday occurrence, thus raising questions for Hindus about whether vegetarianism or avoiding beef is a lifelong religious obligation, a practice that need be observed only for holy days, or should even be practised at all.

Another common experience among Hindu Canadians is facing the ignorance among North Americans about South Asian religions. The attempt to address misconceptions forces Hindus in Canada (as it did educated Hindus in nineteenth-century India confronting negative portrayals of Hinduism by European bureaucrats and missionaries) to identify and articulate what it means to be Hindu as distinct from other religions and from Indian cultural practices (including diet, dress, social customs). Hindu identity must thus be negotiated on several overlapping fronts. First, in the early phases of community building and temple construction, it had to be negotiated by co-religionists who brought to Canada a plethora of ways of practising Hinduism.

Second, especially when attempting to gain resources (such as funding) or political power, it must be negotiated in the face of North American secular culture, including government agencies, which tend to know little about Hinduism.[5]

Third, it has to be negotiated with the discourses of neo-Hinduism, which initially emerged in colonial India and have since been reframed and propagated in North America. This discourse has sought to create a pan-Hinduism, to identify and defend what constitutes the boundaries and essentials of a "purified" Hinduism.

Fourth, it must be negotiated in the face of Canadian-born Hindus who are deciding for themselves what differentiates Hindu religion from Indian (or Indo-Guyanese, Indo-Kenyan, Sri Lankan, and so forth) cultural practices and, furthermore, which Hindu teachings and practices they find meaningful and worthy of retaining for themselves, and what thereby they may reinterpret or reject from their immigrant parents.

Part of this process of retention and rejection includes the confrontation with Western stereotypes of Hinduism projected through pop culture (among other sources), which may lead Canadian-born Hindus to feel uncomfortable admitting adherence to particular beliefs or practices. For example, the belief in reincarnation or the anthropomorphic depictions of deities contrast sharply with Judeo-Christian-Islamic frameworks of religion. Moreover, Hindu narratives about gods and goddesses are commonly belittled as mythological rather than legitimate religious sources, making many Hindus feel foolish in admitting they hold such religious ideas. Thus, it becomes easier for Hindus to dismiss their "exotic" beliefs. On the other hand, the commercialization of yoga and the ethical and environmental concerns driving interest in vegetarianism, for instance, galvanize some Canadian Hindus to take ownership of such typical Hindu practices. Thus, Western attitudes toward Hinduism also influence how Hindus choose to characterize their religious identities in the diaspora. Emerging perhaps more strongly in Canada than the United States is also a tendency to identify with fellow South Asians, often referred to as "brown" among youth, in which religious differences are subsumed under new forms of distinctive diasporic cultural hybrids: bhangra music with Western rock riffs; hakka foods that incorporate Chinese, Indian, and Canadian cuisines; and wearing Indian jewellery with Western clothes (though seldom vice versa).

Despite some attempts to create a pan-Canadian Hindu voice and identity through regional and national organizations (these attempts being particularly evident on the Internet), Hinduism in Canada has remained institutionally decentralized, as it is in India. Local organizations have continued to form in order to build Hindu temples, or propagate the message of particular gurus (Sathya Sai Baba, Swami Chinmayananda, and Swami Narayan have been especially popular among Hindus in Canada). Generally speaking, however, Hindus in the diaspora tend to reconcile their personal values with those of whatever is understood to be Hinduism to form a religious identity that works for them. While some diasporic Hindus may try to match their practice of Hinduism with how Hinduism is practised in their homeland community, others feel quite comfortable adapting Hinduism to match how they live life here. Religiosity, therefore, is understood in a variety of ways depending on one's definition of Hinduism and however its "authenticity" in doctrine and practice is measured. Since diversity is typical of Hinduism and, as Steven Vertovec puts it, "ever-malleable,"[6] evaluating religiosity is difficult because there is no set standard of religious adherence. While there are often certain expectations of particular behavioural norms, world views, and practices within Hindu subgroups and families, these expectations themselves may be challenged in the diaspora.

What then does Hindu women's religiosity in Canada look like? Clearly, since making sweeping generalizations about Hindu women's religiosity in Canada (or anywhere else) is highly problematic, we simply offer glimpses of some Hindu women's religious lives in southern Ontario—first through a detailed profile of a sixty-seven-year-old first-generation Hindu immigrant named Parvati in the context of her life history, and then through a discussion of thematic issues derived from interviews with young second-generation Hindu women. The views of other women interviewed, including Parvati's thirty-eight-year-old daughter, Anju, herself now a mother of three, are interspersed with Parvati's profile to indicate where commonalities or differences of opinions and experiences shed more light on Hindu women's religious lives in the Canadian diaspora.

First-Generation Experiences

PARVATI AND HER HUSBAND, NEWLYWEDS, arrived in Canada in 1966. They immigrated to the city of Hamilton, where there was only a handful of Hindus. They emigrated because of the job opportunities in the health care sector. Their fluency in English, their youthfulness and educational credentials, enabled them to settle in a new country far from their homeland relatively easily. While busy raising a family—their three daughters were born in Canada—they went on to set up a successful health practice and are well-known members of the local Hindu community. Both are active religiously—that is, they regularly attend and support the local temple, they sponsor special pujas, they engage in daily rituals at home, and they have sought to transmit their traditions to their children.

Parvati was born the youngest of four daughters in a middle-class Brahmin family in a village in Maharashtra around the time of Indian independence. Her own mother, Rekha, was sixteen at the time of her arranged marriage, but, sadly, Rekha's husband died when Parvati was a baby, leaving her mother to struggle to raise four daughters. Despite only a primary school education, Rekha developed a textile mill and eventually became mayor of her town, an unusual position for an Indian woman. As a widow, Rekha would not do any puja as it was understood to be inappropriate in her inauspicious state. Parvati noted that neither parent had been particularly religious as expressed in ritual activity—they had a "more intellectual approach"—nevertheless Parvati was keen to participate in religious festivals at home, and so she took ownership of the annual Lakshmi puja during the fall festival of Diwali (the festival of light). She organized and observed a fairly simple worship ceremony of the goddess of prosperity, and she lit lamps (*diyas*) all over the house to brighten it up and banish the forces of darkness and bad luck for the year. This practice she later brought to her marital home and it has continued in her daughters' homes in Canada. Her daughter Anju recalled: "My mum would dress up as Lakshmi and she would be honoured with *namaskars* [touching her feet] by everyone, and I do the same. . . . We don't become the goddess, but represent the goddess for that day in the home." Despite her father's early death, Parvati's familial home had been fairly happy. "We children used to have to say the times table out loud each evening, but also Ram Raksha! [a prayer for Lord Rama's protective blessings]—so you don't really think it's 'religion'; it's just what you do."

Parvati's mother viewed education as an important asset for her daughters and so following high school, Parvati went to college in Mumbai. It was there she met her husband, a Hindu, but of another caste. While her mother was initially quite resistant because of the caste difference, this "love marriage" went ahead. Her three sisters similarly found their own partners, yet most of her sisters' children subsequently had arranged marriages in India. Asked why this was, Parvati responded that if a child has not found anybody by a certain age in India (and often in Canada as well), then parents will intervene and ask their child if she or he wants help "because you don't want to be so old" before marrying. With only one female parent, however, it may be more difficult to intervene or arrange a suitable marriage unless the woman's brother or in-laws step forward. Normally, for arranged marriages, parents make sure that the bride and groom's horoscopes match well and they come from the same *jati* (sub-caste), but not the same *gotra* (kin group).[7] In Maharashtra, this meant that the bride and groom did not share the same *kul-devi* (clan goddess), as that would be considered too close.

When you are surrounded by fellow Hindus, you don't question much about why things are done the way they are; but when you come here [Canada], then you begin to ask "What is the meaning of this?" because you want to give explanations to your children. So now we have many more religious books.

These books, mostly compilations of Sanskrit mantras to accompany various pujas, were obtained during return trips to Pune, a city that has a long tradition of training ritual specialists (*pujaris*) as well as religious scholars (pandits), and which in fact has been at the forefront of a movement to train women ritual specialists.[9] "So," Parvati continued, "we can [now] follow the proper rituals." She also noted that sometimes men are found locally who, while they may have other careers, come from families of trained priests and have basic knowledge that they can augment. They thereby are able to fill the ritual specialist vacuum in some communities and will do pujas for others on special occasions. Many priests or unofficial ritual specialists in the diasporic context offer explanations of the rituals in English, in contrast to traditional priests in India who perform the puja without explanation. "So this is a source of knowledge for us [here in Canada]. And the kids respond too, because they [see that the ritual leaders] have education and professions in other areas, yet they still know and believe in these *slokas* (Sanskrit verses) and rituals."[10]

While the vast majority of "priests" in Canada are men, some women are recognized as being able to provide learned discourses as well as ritual services for others, such as the highly accomplished Hindu woman titled Brahmavadini (scholar in theology) Swami (spiritual preceptor) Krishna Kanta Maharaj, who leads the Ram Dham Hindu Temple in Kitchener, Ontario. She was raised in Ludhiana, north India, immigrated to Canada in 1978, and is now spiritual heir and president of the International Brahmrishi Mission.

The boards of Hindu temples often have women members, though they are usually in the minority. When seventy-year-old Aruna, who has been in Canada since 1969 and grew up in Mombasa, Kenya, was asked about this, she responded: "I think women mostly didn't want to [be on temple boards], and when it became so political, they prefer to do the rituals—not get involved in the political side of it; with men it becomes that way.... People don't always get along; men have strong views and insist on them sometimes." She resigned from the board she was on after two years because she had "had enough." "Some women are pretty strong, but they'd rather be doing other things," she reflected. Asked whether priorities might be different if women were running the board, she said, "maybe the goals wouldn't be so different; maybe the priorities would be different and the approach would definitely be different. . . . I think the spiritual side would be more important." She later added that "to me our children are very important . . . otherwise these big *mandirs* and all that are just going to be empty; so I want to work on the children; tell them what it is all about. They can make their own decisions in the end."

Temple attendance is not a requirement or measure of religiosity, whereas many would say home puja is. Home puja can be done by anyone, and can be quite simple or fairly elaborate. Moreover, home puja often takes on a heightened significance for immigrant Hindu women who came from homelands in which Hindus temples were ubiquitous, compared to Canada, where sometimes temples are far away and difficult to get to. Chandra, a forty-five-year-old Tamil Canadian, performed a two-hour puja each morning before she went to work in a room in her home set aside for this purpose. She had taught herself all the verses she recited from Sanskrit texts, along with the Tamil Shaiva text, the *Tevaram*. While she also regularly attended and was well known at the large Sri Lankan Tamil temple north of Toronto, a distant drive from her home, as a woman she was not permitted to assume any official ritual leadership function. Meanwhile, her adult daughter, Meera, has rejected such elaborate pujas, preferring to engage in meditation as a regular practice. In addition, like some other second-generation Hindu daughters in North America, Meera said she had absorbed a great deal of knowledge about Hinduism from her long years of studying classical Indian dance, which often featured the enactment of stories of the gods and goddesses.[11]

In addition to daily prayers, Parvati and her husband observe a puja at their home shrine on the fourth of each month in honour of elephant-headed Ganesh, a god who, since the nineteenth century, has become particularly popular in the state of Maharashtra. Parvati has adopted Lord

Ganesh as her "favoured deity" (*ishtadevta*). Her husband recites the mantras and she acts as the ritual assistant. For the main Ganesh festival in August/September, Parvati gets her daughters to make the special sweets called *modaka* (made with rice flour, coconut, and raw sugar) that are offered to Ganesh during the puja. Indeed, an important way for women immigrants to transmit religio-cultural traditions to daughters is by teaching them to prepare the special festival food, laden with symbolic meanings.[12] Another example is that of Navratri, a fall festival in honour of the goddess, during which different goddesses are singled out for worship each night over nine nights. Many Hindus, especially women, hold a partial fast during this time, so they prepare and eat certain prescribed fasting foods, as well as offer special dishes to the goddess during the pujas. Once offered, the foods are blessed, and the resulting auspicious food is distributed to family members. For some Hindu women it is also crucial to uphold a vow to perform such pujas annually in order to keep auspicious energies in the home. Extended efforts are exercised to keep this commitment, such as Skyping their children who cannot physically attend so that they can receive *darshan* (auspicious viewing) even if not present.

Parvati and her husband have also occasionally sponsored *Satyanarayan Katha*, a popular Hindu practice imported to Canada, in the local temple. *Katha* means "story" and this ritual includes the recitation of several stories whose protagonists, men and women, exemplify unswerving devotion to God (in this case, Vishnu) even in the midst of great hardship and calamity. In the end they are rewarded for their steadfast devotion. Sponsoring the ritual and inviting friends and family to take part itself is deemed religiously meritorious. Parvati said it was about "asking God to take care of things, for luck, and giving thanks for whatever you have." The family of one of this chapter's authors (Nayak) also observes the *Satyanarayan* puja every year. In Nayak's experience, parents vigorously encourage their children to learn the stories because they are a way to re-engage young people in the ritual, which is long and largely meaningless to the youth. Thus, nudged by their parents, the youth take turns reciting a story.[13] Other women interviewed had also participated in sponsored pujas such as *Ram Kathas* (recitations of the *Ramayan*), and *Tulsi-Vivaha* (celebration of the marriage of the goddess Tulsi with Vishnu). Some of them participated in these pujas only after coming to Canada since they were not part of their childhood practices.

Another frequently observed ritual practice among higher caste Hindus is that of *samskaras* (life-cycle ceremonies). There are sixteen (or more) of them described in Sanskrit texts. Most are clustered around the antenatal, postnatal, and childhood periods, and are intended to secure blessings, good health, and the well-being for the child, especially the boy child. Sixty-year-old Sujata, who grew up in Gujarat, described celebrating *godhbarai*, a seventh-month pregnancy ritual common throughout India: "It is like a baby shower here. Men can come, but mostly women do. It is a big gathering, especially of family." Its purpose is to ensure good qualities for the coming child, she said. Rice, coconut, and money are put in the end of the expectant mother's sari. A priest may be invited. Women sing songs and gifts are given for the mother (not the baby, as that is courting disaster—the evil eye). Then after the birth, the baby is taken to the temple to be blessed. Several women interviewed had participated in this ritual in Canada, as well as another popular *samskara* reproduced in the diaspora, the naming ceremony (*nam-karan*). Some women interviewed did this ceremony officially with a hired priest, others, like Parvati, did it informally, with a parent reciting some prayers and inviting friends over to celebrate. As in India, however, the wedding and funeral *samskaras* remain the most elaborately celebrated life-cycle rituals, and for weddings, mothers play a key role in·organizing the events and rituals surrounding the occasion. Even otherwise unobservant Hindu daughters find themselves swept up in the many elaborate ceremonies focused on the bride-to-be, and demurely accept being wrapped in a Banarasi sari, treated with *mehndi* designs on hands and feet, fed and feted with traditional women's bridal songs— perhaps not so dissimilar to what occurs among otherwise secular Canadian brides of nominally Christian families.

A further religious practice common in Hindu communities, and especially among women, is that of ritual fasts. These day-long ritual vows or fasts—observed weekly, monthly, or annually—are described in the Sanskrit medieval texts called *Puranas*. The more popular ones are found, complete with stories to be recited and prayers to be uttered, in inexpensive how-to manuals printed in local languages and sold in temples and market stalls. These days one can also find the popular *vrats* described on Internet websites, including in YouTube videos. In the Sanskrit Hindu texts, these rituals are not considered obligatory (*nitya*), but rather optional (*kamya*), yet there are strong family traditions of observing ritual fasts, especially those linked with annual festivals like *Shivaratri* or associated with particular deities and days of the month, such as *Ekadashi*, observed in honour of Vishnu.[14]

Kalpana, aged fifty-three, who grew up in Haryana, India, and arrived in Canada in the mid-1990s, said that as a girl her family and friends encouraged her to do a *Somvar Vrat* (Monday fast) in honour of the god Shiva, observed in the month of Ashvin (August/September). The fast involves abstaining from salt (thus very plain food or sometimes just fruit is permitted). This ritual fast is usually undertaken by unmarried girls, and a central purpose is to secure a good husband. The authors encountered second-generation Hindu university students who had kept this *vrat* in Canada, though, as in India, the reasons offered also included such explanations as the health benefits of fasting.[15] Married women often take on the practices of their in-laws, and will fast for the well-being of their husbands and sons. Some ritual fasts, like the North Indian Punjabi *vrat* called *Karva Cauth* observed by married women on the fourth day of the fall month of Kartik, have taken on pan-Indian popularity in recent decades and it is a popular *vrat* here in Canada too. Aruna said she used to do this *vrat* because it had been part of her familial tradition in Kenya. In Canada it was "fun" to do it with other women, but because she was busy with her work as a nurse, she stopped it. Instead, for the last fifteen years she has been keeping a Tuesday *vrat* directed to the god Hanuman. She eats only fruit and drinks water and tea, and recites the *Hanuman Chalisa* (hymns of praise in forty quatrains to this god) in front of a small image of him, which she keeps in her bedroom. She started this practice when she was having some difficulties and her sister suggested it. Aruna said she enjoys the discipline and the feeling of peace it brings. A similar sentiment was expressed by Parvati, who, given the familial circumstances of her upbringing, did not keep ritual fasts as she was growing up. However, she did begin a Friday fast directed to her *kul-devi*, Ekvira, after her youngest daughter was born with cerebral palsy. Though her daughter passed away several years ago, Parvati continues with the ritual. "Not as religious-religious [practice] but to give me the discipline, you know, so okay I do this every Friday, so no matter where I am I'll do this." She described the discipline as giving her strength. "What I do for my daughter," she said tearfully, "is my prayer ... so that's the way my religion has been" (sacrificing her time to serve her daughter's needs, and seeking God's help in the process). Despite the demands placed on her by her daughter's condition, Parvati said she never resented it; on the contrary, she said that God had chosen her to take care of this wayward soul—had given her that responsibility.

As she has gotten older, Parvati feels that she has become more religious, both in terms of ritual observances and in terms of the significance of religion in her life. This self-perception of increased religiosity is not the case for all Hindu women immigrants, of course. Some women interviewed averred that they were much less religious in terms of ritual practices than their mothers and grandmothers had been. But certainly a common view we encountered was that the practice of religion here is much more deliberate and informed than it is in India. Parvati thought that compared to her natal family and since coming to Canada, religion has become more self-conscious, "with more understanding." Back in India "they do rituals, follow festivals because everyone else is doing it, so without you even thinking about it, it happens. But here you have to make sure that yes you are doing it because you want to." Others suggested that they have become more spiritual as they have gotten older. Aruna, who worked as an emergency nurse, commented that she has definitely become more spiritual and that this started with the birth of her children:

> But maturity also. Things can change very fast. Like my mother used to say—"it's something you did in your last birth"—sometimes it's the only way to explain things that happen. There's comfort in believing that. Being a nurse also—you see so much suffering. And the outcomes are not always certain.

Asked what she thought was the most important value in Hinduism, Parvati replied "respect for others," a key value similarly identified by other women interviewed. Her daughter Anju concurred, explaining that "the whole idea of respecting knowledge, respecting teachers, respecting your parents—these are the things ingrained by our parents, which we pass on to our own children as core values." Others also mentioned faith, parental devotion, truthfulness, patience, and service to others (*seva*). Parvati later added:

> Also the value of being the mother. People always take gifts for the baby, but for my daughters I always take presents for them; for bringing this child into the world. Their contribution was most important. I think coming from my family of mostly girls, the importance of being a woman is there. There are strong goddesses in India—Lakshmi, Durga. They are all strong.

In their strength they serve as models, Parvati suggested. She went on to describe having recently gone to a Lakshmi puja in a private home, which ended with the ritual worship of invited married women and unmarried girls "who are going to be mothers." Later, Parvati asked the priest for an explanation of what it was all about and he said to all those present that

> the mother's love was feeding and taking care [of the family], while the father's love is more disciplinarian, encouraging children to study, scolding them; mothers protect and give confidence to children. So the priest was saying this puja is about celebrating women.

Parvati seemed satisfied with this explanation as it accorded with her view that women have special roles and responsibilities in Hinduism, women "give birth to children and so have a key nurturing role as mothers." This role has not changed in the Canadian cultural environment. It is the mothers, she affirmed, who "pass on the everyday philosophy; [who give] practical advice and knowledge" to their children in a way that fathers do not.

Asked how she has tried to pass on her Hindu cultural identity to her children, Parvati said that most of the learning took place by modelling behaviour. For example, the idea of respect for elders and for knowledge is demonstrated by showing how one must avoid touching books or another person with one's feet, for that is disrespectful; elders are to be greeted with *namaskar* (palms together), or even by touching the feet of elders, to show respect and humility. Anju confirmed her mother's comments when she noted that her mother was the "driver" of transmitting Hinduism to her children:

> I really felt like spiritually she was able to impart those ideas to us of what being Hindu meant; of what Hinduism was all about . . . and it was more through her action, because she embodied it—never overtly, just "this is how we behave"—it all came down to respect. It was in a quieter way; caring for others. Of course those kinds of ideas transcend all religions. Just be kind. . . . Having compassion. And I think that came especially with the challenges of looking after my younger sister.

While Parvati herself thought that both men and women were responsible as the carriers and transmitters of Hindu culture and religion, others thought that women in fact played the key role. As Kalpana put it, "Women play a very important part in keeping the culture and raising the family and it doesn't matter if they are earning or anything. They are born with this responsibility; what we learn we want to carry on to our kids." She commented further that she had never told her daughter explicitly what she expected:

> They just see and hear and they learn. . . . I'm a modern mom, but there are a few things I wouldn't want my daughter to do and I never had to tell her, she just learned herself. Any [of our youth] they'll see any other South Asian woman and they call her "auntie," but as soon as they see a white person, they'll call her "Mrs. so and so" [suggesting that children key into the appropriate social etiquette in different cultural contexts].

When asked if such roles and responsibilities have changed for Hindu women in the Canadian environment, Aruna affirmed that "there is a big change in men. I've seen it in my own son when he became a father . . . who has been much involved as a parent in nurturing. I think definitely men are developing that side; even in India it's changing." She went on to say, after mentioning that she didn't like how Rama had treated Sita in the epic, *The Ramayan*, that "men and women should be partners in life. There should be a balance. No human being likes to be treated as lesser; as subservient." She bemusedly said that she has these kinds of conversations with her husband "all the time" and with her sons also.

> My father used to say, if he is your *raja* [king], you should be his *rani* [queen]. He instilled that in us. You know how some men feel so bad when they have many daughters? My father used to say he was a very lucky man to have five daughters!

She also indicated that his attitude was rather unusual for men of his era and perhaps even today. In fact, it appears from the experience of other women interviewed as well that if a father or husband was supportive of gender equity, this value was much more likely to have been successfully transmitted to daughters and sons. Even so, as in Western culture, the reality continues to be that women assume more of the caregiving roles in the family.

Asked if her daughters have become more engaged in their religion since they had their own children, Parvati responded, "I wouldn't say necessarily that they're more 'religious,' but they want to make sure that the children understand things the right way." Parvati's husband noted that they were fortunate that both daughters have their in-laws living here, and both sides are observant Hindus (even if from different regions). "They get rituals from both sides," he commented, "but in the end it's all Hindu ritual." Both daughters, he said with pride, "are into maintaining Hinduism and teaching their kids, but they're also into the Canadian community" as active volunteers.

Voices from the Second Generation
Growing up Hindu in Canada

SIX OF THE SEVEN SECOND-GENERATION WOMEN interviewed for this chapter were brought up in traditional Hindu families where rituals such as *vrats*, temple attendance, and Hindu festivals were observed regularly. These practices largely shaped their understanding of Hinduism until their late teens or early twenties when new experiences made them re-evaluate what Hinduism meant for them, especially as women. Canada acted as a site of religious transformation and development for many of these young Hindu women in ways they did not expect. Particular institutions or experiences proved pivotal for them in that because of them, they re-examined their religion and religious roles, which often led to the creation of a personal "customized" Hinduism. This was a form of religious practice that worked for them as individuals, not just as members of their family or ethnic subculture. Such customized Hinduism may mean re-evaluating or dismissing particular practices and views deemed incompatible with gender equality, for example, or simply incompatible with their lifestyle. Indeed, many Hindus we spoke with suggested that the inherent flexibility of the religion was in and of itself characteristic of Hinduism, and when asked what they liked about Hinduism, a common response among the young women interviewed was the "liberal nature" of the religion and its lack of rigid doctrinal or ritual prescriptions.

Not surprisingly, then, attempts to define the parameters of Hinduism produced a variety of responses. Some women believed that not eating beef and doing puja and *arati* were essential to being a practising Hindu, while others disregarded such practices, instead tying their view of what being Hindu meant to a general sense of morality or spiritual connection with God. For example, twenty-one-year-old Daksha commented:

> To me, it's not as much as praying every day and offering certain *prasad* [food for the deities] or doing rituals. . . . To me, it is the spiritual and emotional [aspects of the religion]. I feel that if you are a good person—and I do believe in the gods, I think it [the supernatural world] exists, I don't think the world would be so perfect without them—but it's just like, I believe you can "please" gods in a different way than just offering *prasad* or bathing them.

She paused and continued:

> I think if you're a good person, God will appreciate that. So for me, what it means to be Hindu is to look inside oneself and improve upon that instead of, you know [rituals]. . . . Sure, I'll still do puja and go to temple,

because that is what I have grown up with and it's been ingrained for the past twenty years being a Hindu.

But," she insisted, "it's not what characterizes 'being Hindu.'"

Learning about Hinduism in an academic environment was frequently cited by women we interviewed as a catalyst for further individual research about their religion.[16] It was like opening a door to see a Hinduism beyond what they had learned in their familial context. For most of these women, their learning of religion occurred through years of observation of their parents, particularly their mothers, and participation in various religious activities. But, as Daksha commented, "taking that course [on Hinduism] in university . . . I am kind of starting to open my eyes to what it really means to be Hindu, not just what my mom says to be Hindu. But that's recent . . . for the past eighteen years I am used to just what my mom has said." She went on to explain that the university course introduced her to the theoretical underpinnings of the religion she follows, something her mother never taught her. The course challenged her understanding of what it meant to be Hindu. It made her question deeply if she believed in such concepts as karma and moksha. Questions are often brought home to parents who must grapple with them, which in turn requires self-examination, if not research, as Parvati noted earlier.

The young women interviewed suggested that by their early twenties they had begun to develop an independent understanding of their religion, one that was different from their parents' orthopraxic view of Hinduism. That is not to say that rituals had no significance for these women, as many said that such rituals gave them a sense of self-discipline and order in their lives. Nisha, aged twenty, affirmed that rituals were important:

> Initially, when I moved to Aruba [to study medicine], I let things slip easily. I didn't pray today, because I woke up late; but now I really push myself to pray in the mornings. It's a motivation to get up. It puts me in order; makes me more disciplined. So yes, I have placed more value in it.

Whether ritual keeping was religiously motivated or not, many interviewees accorded great value to the rituals they were taught by their mothers. Fasting gave them a sense of self-discipline, meditation gave them peace of mind, and so forth. However, while such practices may persist in the lives of the young women, their explanation for why they practise them was that they themselves had determined them to be meaningful. For Nisha, fasting was once a part of family tradition, a way, she was told, of ensuring she would get a good husband. Now fasting is a means for her to practise self-control. Moving away from home to attend university led to a new self-consciousness about the familiar and comfortable role that religion had played in her life and about how to deal with its absence. Nisha elaborated:

> Well, initially I did them [rituals] because my mom did them. It became habitual. When I got to Aruba, and I was there all by myself, I had my own apartment . . . it kind of gets lonely and then you start to question yourself. After a certain point of time, I did it [fasted] not because I had to or felt pressured to but because I wanted to and that's when I got really interested in spirituality. [Religion] just gives you a way of life; it tells you that you belong a certain somewhere. It gives you discipline. It basically tells you how to lead your life. A lot of human beings' morality derives from religion.

Although many of the second-generation women interviewed had scrutinized their mothers' way of understanding or practising Hinduism and therefore concluded that what their mothers said and did was a result of growing up in the homeland and blindly adhering to tradition, some asserted that they were more religious here in Canada than they would be if they had grown up in their homeland. When asked why, they responded by saying that Hinduism in their homeland would always be present and inescapable. Its omnipresence would force them to mindlessly engage in practice rather than thoughtfully understand why they were Hindu. As twenty-year-old Radha (born in Nepal, moved to Canada at the age of twelve) noted, "well because I was there, I used to go to more temples. The puja my grandmother used to do was longer. Over there, it's more pronounced, practice is more, you are doing *more* . . . here, everything is toned down." When asked if that made her feel less religious, she responded:

Personally, I don't think so. If I was still living there, I would be forced [to engage in religious practice]. Even when I was living there, I saw everyone fasting but I never saw myself doing that. Here I feel more free [to make up my own mind].

Reconciling Gender Equality with Hinduism

THE YOUNG WOMEN INTERVIEWED also attributed the presence of other religions as a motivation to learn more about Hinduism so that they could explain customs or ideas to those who asked. Being in an environment where Hinduism is not well understood often forces Hindus to re-examine their faith and characterize it favourably. For example, Daksha said that in a society that promotes gender rights and where gender equality is a sensitive issue, one wants to adhere to a religion where patriarchy is not the dominant social norm. This causes many young Hindu women to reject or reinterpret traditional gender norms in Hinduism. They hope to have a more egalitarian relationship with their husbands than their mothers had with theirs. The young women interviewed also believed that their mothers' apparent acceptance of patriarchal norms was a result of their upbringing in their homeland. Here in Canada, by contrast, higher education, among other things, can quickly transform one's perspective. As Radha reflected, "my grandmother studied until grade ten and I don't think even graduating [from] high school is enough to understand this [patriarchy and gender inequality]. I think after going to university and learning about oppression . . . you become much more aware." She went on to observe that the older generation

> tend[s] to generally believe whatever is given to them whereas for me I will listen to what you say and see whether I want to believe it or not. For them, it is not about questioning it. My mom used to say her mom said "don't question me." Thankfully, my mom is not that way. . . . It feels like whenever you hear stories and stuff, for example, the Ramayana . . . it's always about women's suffering and pain. . . . She [Sita] was the one who was kidnapped and had to prove her innocence . . . stuff like that made me so mad.

Radha described how upbringing—namely, education and familial context—had a profound impact on her religious views and interpretation of texts. She said her parents and grandparents likely never questioned Hindu tales that glorified the self-sacrificial suffering of the chaste Sita, the perfect wife, but she has and claimed they perpetuated an unreasonable expectation of women's subservience. In fact, most of the daughters interviewed appeared to believe that their mothers were taught to be passive and uncritical of religion and that this created an outlook on religiously justified gender roles different from their own. Radha, who immigrated to Canada in 2005, lived with her grandmother in Nepal from grade two to grade seven and considers her to be one of the most legitimate sources of Hindu knowledge. Yet, she is clearly also critical of the religious knowledge she received in her childhood from her grandmother.

By contrast, Nisha, who was born in Abu Dhabi and arrived in Canada in 1999 as a child, comes from a family who devoutly follows Durga and identifies itself as Hindu Rajputs. She considers her mother as the most legitimate source of knowledge on Hinduism and affirmed that women are fundamentally different than men. She also believes that women's nature makes them more prone to being carriers of culture or religion:

> We are different in the ways we interact. Even if men do the same things, they don't have the same capacity to explain it to their kids ... they'll do it, but they won't be able to pass it down or teach it properly. So it is more of a communication thing. I don't think men can communicate their thoughts as effectively as women just because we talk a lot more and because we talk to each other a lot more.... Men still have groups of friends, but they are not as emotionally intimate with other men as women are with other women. So yeah ... it is just a communication thing. Women are able to pass it down better.

Nisha feels that women enjoy the cultural roles that are placed on them; this is a natural difference in roles, not an imbalance of responsibilities between women and men. Moreover, she sees herself reproducing these roles when she gets married and has her own children. That is, she sees herself as having the primary responsibility to teach the children about Hinduism. (Interestingly, every interviewee who had a brother stated that she was more religious than him.)

The women whose mothers were more actively religious than their fathers understood that such patterns were passed down to the children who naturally emulated their parents' religious lives. Thus, if changes in roles were to be introduced, it would have to be done deliberately and consciously by both sons and daughters. The young women interviewed had varying views about the desirableness and likelihood of such changes. The stories that accompany ritual practices like *vrats* inculcate the lesson that women have important protective familial roles, which increases their significance in a household. A certain measure of respect is shown for the mother who fasts from morning till night for the well-being of everyone but herself. Nevertheless, many young Hindu women have given up or refused to reproduce such religious rites. Radha, for instance, commented: "I understand the fasting, but what I'm not ecstatic about is that women are doing all the fasting all the time. I mean, there are 800 of those. . . . I like the religion, but I see a lot of patriarchal things."

Other "patriarchal things" mentioned by women included being excluded from worship when they were menstruating. "That is not something men have to deal with," Daksha noted. Asked if she saw this restriction as an impediment to her religiosity, she said yes. Asked if she believed in it, she laughed and said "no," explaining: "I practise it because it's ingrained in my head but I don't think it's valid," adding "I don't think our genders should dictate what we do, as a Hindu. I think my belief in God, for those five days of the month, shouldn't change from all the other days in my life." Such comments exemplify the unease with particular customs or rites that contradict young Canadian Hindu women's belief in gender equality. Daksha, who equated Hinduism with living morally, largely dismissed customs that she felt had nothing to do with living righteously. On the other hand, there were other young Hindu women who respected the intention behind such customs and saw them as compatible with gender equality. As twenty-two-year-old Shreya observed:

> In Sri Lankan culture, women are not supposed to enter the temple during their period. Some say it's just an old cultural thing that during their period

women are "dirty." But others say that the power of the vedic chants can have a negative effect on women who are weakened during their period—so, avoiding the temple is to protect females from the "evil eye."

Shreya thus respected the rationale she had heard for the restriction on women entering a temple during their menstrual period, and was persuaded that the custom was a protective measure for the benefit of women.

Conclusion

RELIGIOUS IDENTITY IS AN INTRICATE CONFIGURATION that is often made more complex by the experience of immigration and the transplantation of religious practice in the diaspora. The Canadian environment has undeniably had an impact on the understanding of Hinduism among both first- and second-generation Hindu Canadian women. Having to explain Hinduism to non-Hindus, taking university courses on Hinduism, as well as meeting fellow Hindus from a wide variety of languages and originating homelands and seeing the multiple ways Hinduism is practised have all fostered a consciousness of, if not an appreciation for, Hinduism's internal diversity, and often a new embrace of what are perceived to be key features of Hinduism: adaptability, tolerance, and respectfulness. All women interviewed for this chapter suggested that there was no single right way of practising Hinduism, and that being Hindu was mostly a matter of identifying with the general world views and traditions of one's extended family. How one chooses to express one's religiosity is largely up to the individual, a matter that, while supported in Hindu texts, is further enabled in the Canadian context, where individualism is positively viewed and where families are separated from their relatives and originating communities. Nevertheless, religiosity is perceived by the women interviewed as connected primarily to the observance of religious rituals (rather than any doctrinal affirmations), and while rituals are malleable, following certain conventions is expected so that the ritual remains recognizable. At the same time, religiosity is also clearly, if implicitly, connected with the maintenance of the Hindu "hearth and home," a role that continues to be associated principally with women, even by the second generation. Marriage and motherhood are still positively valued, and women as mothers remain the principal cooks, caregivers, and trackers of the ritual-festival calendar and often those who maintain the home shrines. As such, women continue to be perceived as the primary transmitters of Hinduism to the next generation. Even so, a commitment to gender egalitarianism inspires younger Hindu women, who see themselves with partners who are equal carriers of religion and culture.

Hindu mothers in Canada also often work outside the home, and those with careers both model the possibility of "doing it all" and convey to their children a modern view of the powerful Hindu mother figure—less passively self-sacrificing and more assertively capable in multiple roles (the interpretation of Shakti or divine feminine power increasingly defined by women themselves, rather than male Brahmin pandits). Because so much of Hindu religiosity is expressed in the home and orthodoxy and its arbitration has relatively less significance in Hinduism than in other religions, it is not surprising that the women we interviewed expressed little desire for positions of religious leadership in the temples—as priests or on temple boards. On the other hand, Hindu women have been active as participants, creators, and leaders in establishing classes for Hindu children at temples and in organizations such as Indo Canadian societies, South Asian cultural associations, and associations for South Asian seniors.[17] Here they can and do have an impact beyond their immediate families. The Canadian socio-political environment, which welcomes such community initiatives, the importance diaspora South Asian families place on professional education for children of either sex, and the acceptance, if not need, for women to contribute to family income have been further facilitating factors, allowing women to quietly assume more economic and social power and influence than has traditionally been the case in their originating homelands. In these ways, Canada has been a catalyst of change for Hindu women to re-inscribe positive valuations of their traditional roles while assuming new ones that effectively begin to erode patriarchal norms. ●

Notes

1. See Vanaja Dhruvarajan, "Ethnic Cultural Retention and Transmission among First Generation Hindu Asian Indians in a Canadian Prairie City," *Journal of Comparative Family Studies* 24, no. 1 (1993): 63–79; Anne Mackenzie Pearson, "Being Hindu in Canada: Personal Narratives from First and Second Generation Immigrant Hindu Women," *Religious Studies and Theology* 23, no. 1 (2004): 55–88; Anne Mackenzie Pearson, "Mothers and Daughters: The Transmission of Religious Practice and the Formation of Hindu Identity among Hindu Immigrant Women in Ontario," in *Hindu Diaspora: Global Perspectives*, ed. T. S. Rukmani (Montreal: Concordia University, 1999): 427–42; Steven Vertovec, The Hindu Diaspora: Comparative Patterns (London: Routledge, 2000); Prema A. Kurien, *A Place at the Multicultural Table: The Development of an American Hinduism* (New Brunswick, NJ: Rutgers University Press, 2007); Nancy Nason-Clark and Cathy Holtmann, "Perpetuating Religion and Culture: Hindu Women," in *Growing Up Canadian Muslims, Hindus, Buddhists*, ed. Peter Beyer and Rubina Ramji (Montreal and Kingston: McGill-Queen's University Press, 2013), 145–66.

2. While I (Pearson) had never interviewed the women whose views form the substance of this chapter before, many were already known to me because of my long association with the Hamilton Hindu community. The interviews were usually conducted in their homes using an interview schedule, adapted for the second-generation interviews in Burlington and Mississauga. The names and certain other identifying features of the women whose comments are included in this chapter have been altered to protect their privacy.

3. Portions of this section on Hinduism in Canada are adapted from Anne Mackenzie Pearson, "Hinduism," in *World Religions: Canadian Perspectives—Eastern Traditions*, ed. Doris Jakobsh (Toronto: Nelson Education, 2013), 30–85. On the history and formation of Hinduism in Canada, see also Paul Younger, "Hindus," in *The Religions of Canadians*, ed. Jamie Scott (Toronto: University of Toronto Press, 2012), 219–60; Harold Coward and S. Banerjee, "Hindus in Canada: Negotiating Identity in a Different Homeland," in *Religion and Ethnicity in Canada*, ed. Paul Bramadat and David Seljak (Toronto: Pearson Education, 2005), 30–51; Harold Coward, "The South Asian Religious Diaspora in Britain, Canada, and the United States," *Nova Religio: The Journal of Alternative and Emerging Religions* 8, no. 2 (2004): 127–29.

4. After 1908 Indo Canadians could not serve on juries, act as school trustees, enter public service jobs, nor could they vote in provincial elections; in 1920 the Dominion Franchise Bill prevented them from voting federally.

5. Hindus formed organizations such as the Hindu Federation of Canada in order describe themselves to governmental institutions, the media, and the larger culture. On its website, the Federation describes Hindus in the following way: "We the Hindus of Canada came from different geographical references, speaking many different languages and being exposed to many different cultural and traditional customs. We have accepted that our religion is Hinduism and our country is Canada and have made great strides in preserving our great heritage in this wonderful country." The website goes on to note that Hindus have been very successful in creating places of worship where they have been able to practise their religion and provide an opportunity for the next generations to develop an appreciation of the Hindu way of life. The site also urges all Hindus to become involved in their communities' welfare "with the conviction that in the eyes of the rest of Canada we [Hindus] are all one," and thus should address issues "as a community working together." There is also a concern expressed that Hindus in Canada need to be seen as "progressive and a major contributor to the Canadian society." See *Hindu Federation*, www.federationofhindutemples.ca.

6. Vertovec, *The Hindu Diaspora*.

7. Gita, a forty-five-year-old from Maharashtra living in Hamilton, also had a "love marriage," but with a non-Hindu non-Indian. She was the first in her large extended family to have such a marriage. She met her husband while studying abroad, but sought approval from her father. Concerned about his daughter's plans, he had her fiancé's birth chart (horoscope) cast. Traditionally, she said, one wants at least eighteen points to be compatible and in her case all points were, so the astrologer said to her father "even God can't stop this marriage so don't even try!" With that, her father's misgivings were set aside.

8. Sixty-year-old Sujata, for instance, who came to Canada from Gujarat in 1972, said that she and her husband became followers of the Chinmaya Mission after a Chinmaya *brahmacharya* (acolyte) came to Hamilton and started a study group focused on the Bhagavad Gita. They started to attend Chinmaya week-long "camps" held in hotels in Toronto, where they practised yoga, meditation, watched videos of the guru Chinmaya and heard discourses, along with hundreds of others. Her practice of meditation and study of the Bhagavad Gita (both taken up after her move to

Canada) has enabled her, she said, to be detached, to "let go" of problems. Sujata said the Chinmaya Mission teaches "change yourself, don't try to change anyone else," and for her this is now the central message of Hinduism.

9. The first schools opening their doors to the training of women priests were in Pune, Maharashatra. The Sankar Seva Samiti began in the mid-1970s and was followed by the school Gyan Prabhodini, which opened year-long training programs for women. Women are trained to conduct rituals using Sanskrit mantras for such events as life-cycle rituals, new business and house openings, and festivals.

10. As noted by several scholars, this act of offering explanations in English of the ritual is just one of a number of adjustments made to ritual and temple Hinduism in the diaspora. See T. S. Rukmani, ed., *Hindu Diaspora: Global Perspectives* (Montreal: Concordia University, 1999); Kurien, *A Place*; and Younger, "Hindus." Making Sunday the special day for community gathering at temples, creating Sunday "services" with sermon-like talks by priests, and passing out transliterated copies of the mantras, *stotras*, and *bhajans* are other practices in North America that remain uncommon in India, but serve to educate and reinforce religious identity among Hindus in the diaspora.

11. Meera and Chandra are described in Pearson, "Being Hindu."

12. The importance of festival foods as repositories of cultural knowledge for Hindus cannot be overestimated. Foods are linked to the agricultural seasons, to astrology, to the preferences of particular deities, to colours, to diet, and to health. Food represents both physical and spiritual or cultural nourishment. In addition, the Hindu kitchen, as in other religious traditions, is an important space for female bonding. See also Nason-Clark and Holtmann, "Perpetuating Religion."

13. Nayak recalled that she has heard the Satyanarayan stories since she was a young child. She and her cousins sometimes found it hilarious because aspects of it seemed nonsensical. For example, when Sadhu (one of the protagonists) tries to deceive Lord Vishnu, his boat is filled with "creeper plants." Such punishments were very amusing for us and we used to re-enact this story with exaggerated accounts of what happened. While we recall the amusing performative aspects of the ritual, the adults' intentions are fulfilled too—youth learned the moral of the story (don't lie, be grateful for your blessings, always eat *prasad*) because of this puja—and we will likely carry on the tradition even if we poke fun at it because dramatic narratives are an effective mode of teaching religion to children.

14. See Anne Mackenzie Pearson, *"Because It Gives Me Peace of Mind": Ritual Fasts in the Religious Lives of Women in North India* (Albany: State University of New York Press, 1996).

15. See ibid. and Pearson, "Being Hindu."

16. The influence of university courses about Hinduism on Hindu Canadian students is also affirmed by the findings of Nason-Clark and Holtmann, "Perpetuating Religion."

17. Further research on such topics as how Canadian Hindu priests view women's changing roles and religious aspirations, how Hindu Canadian cultural associations provide avenues for women's leadership and self-understanding, how immigrants (especially women) of traditional low-caste status create Hindu identity in Canada, the religious status of widows, and what ideas or institutions in Canada affect a Hindu's commitment to cultural and religious retention would help shed further light on the continuing emergence of Canadian Hinduisms.

Bibliography

Coward, Harold. "The South Asian Religious Diaspora in Britain, Canada, and the United States." *Nova Religio: The Journal of Alternative and Emergent Religions* 8, no. 2 (2004): 127–29.

Coward, Harold, and S. Banerjee. "Hindus in Canada: Negotiating Identity in a Different Homeland." In *Religion and Ethnicity in Canada*, edited by Paul Bramadat and David Seljak, 30–51. Toronto: Pearson Education, 2005.

Dhruvarajan, Vanaja. "Ethnic Cultural Retention and Transmission among First Generation Hindu Asian Indians in a Canadian Prairie City." *Journal of Comparative Family Studies* 24, no. 1 (1993): 63–79.

Hindu Federation. www.federationofhindutemples.ca.

Kurien, Prema A. *A Place at the Multicultural Table—The Development of an American Hinduism*. New Brunswick, NJ: Rutgers University Press, 2007.

Min, P. G. *Preserving Ethnicity through Religion in America: Korean and Indian Hindus across Generations*. New York: New York University Press, 2010.

Nason-Clark, Nancy, and Cathy Holtmann. "Perpetuating Religion and Culture: Hindu Women." In *Growing Up Canadian Muslims, Hindus, Buddhists*, edited by Peter Beyer and Rubina Ramji, 145–66. Montreal and Kingston: McGill-Queen's University Press, 2013.

Pearson, Anne Mackenzie. *"Because It Gives Me Peace of Mind": Ritual Fasts in the Religious Lives of Women in North India*. Albany: State University of New York Press, 1996.

——. "Being Hindu in Canada: Personal Narratives from First and Second Generation Immigrant Hindu Women." *Religious Studies and Theology* 23, no. 1 (2004): 55–88.

——. "Hinduism." In *World Religions Canadian Perspectives—Eastern Traditions*, edited by Doris Jakobsh, 30–85. Toronto: Nelson Education, 2013.

——. "Mothers and Daughters: The Transmission of Religious Practice and the Formation of Hindu Identity among Hindu Immigrant Women in Ontario." In *Hindu Diaspora: Global Perspectives*, edited by T. S. Rukmani, 427–42. Montreal: Concordia University, 1999.

Rukmani, T. S., ed. *Hindu Diaspora: Global Perspectives*. Montreal: Concordia University, 1999.

Shukla, Sandhya. "Locations for South Asian Diasporas." *Annual Review of Anthropology* 30, no. 1 (2001): 551–72.

Vertovec, Steven. *The Hindu Diaspora: Comparative Patterns*. London: Routledge, 2000.

Younger, Paul. "Hindus." In *The Religions of Canadians*, edited by Jamie Scott, 219–60. Toronto: University of Toronto Press, 2012.

9 Women in Hinduism

Ritual Leadership in the Adhi Parasakthi Temple Society of Canada

NANETTE R. SPINA

Introduction

In the broadest sense, this chapter is set within the context of North American Hinduism and the migrations of Hindu people. As the local Adhi Parasakthi Temple Society of Canada (ATSC) in Toronto is part of the larger global Adhi Parasakthi (Ātiparācakti) organization, it maintains a connection to the "mother" temple in Melmaruvathur, India.[1] In this regard the study of this local, predominantly Sri Lankan Tamil community is an example of a Hindu tradition in both its diasporic and transnational dimensions.

This chapter will address issues of religiosity, gender, and identity within the Adhi Parasakthi Temple Society of Canada based on ethnographic fieldwork from 2007 to 2009. The first part of the chapter introduces the Adhi Parasakthi tradition and the Toronto temple society, including a brief history and the specific aspects of worship style within this tradition. The remainder of the chapter discusses the rich ritual and cultural life of this community.[2]

One of the most prominent aspects of this tradition is that women are privileged as ritual leaders; this is a marked shift from Brahmanical ritual authority and Hindu social convention. My research foregrounds the influence of women's ritual authority and leadership in cultivating this Tamil religious tradition in Toronto. The study illustrates the ways in which women's ritual authority and a collective style of worship have offered a revised definition of worship patterns from priest-mediated ritual performance to a collective style of ritual participation. This worship pattern affords members of the community more opportunity to become active in formal puja or rituals of devotional worship, and a number of attendant daily rites. This movement in worship style has, in turn, been instrumental in fostering a community identity in the Canadian setting by emphasizing inclusivity regarding caste and gender in communal worship patterns. This inclusivity is now a clear ethical preference within the community. Prioritizing these ritual initiatives has extended ritual authority and hence ritual participation to a wider demographic and removed a historically embedded form of social discrimination. This aspect of the tradition is often mentioned by both the men and women of the community, partly because it is seen or interpreted as a step in the direction of greater social equality or at least a move toward "equal opportunity." In speaking with members of the community, a number of people have expressed the view that such principles have an ethical appeal and value, one that they find compatible with the lifestyles and values they are choosing to cultivate in their Canadian diasporic setting.

The approach that seemed best suited to this project combined both qualitative and quantitative research methodologies. In addition to participant observation, I conducted personal interviews, informal group discussions, and designed a survey questionnaire. I have used pseudonyms for all informants with the exception of Vasanthi, who, as the president of the Adhi Parasakthi Temple Society, permitted me to use her name. Taking their cue from Vasanthi, the members of the community have been uniformly co-operative and often helpfully suggested new avenues of information. In this way, I want to highlight their voices when conveying their perspectives. I acknowledge that my presence as a researcher has also played a role in the way that our collective experiences at the temple or *mandram* have unfolded.[3] I recognize that I, as a researcher, have brought my own perceptions to bear on my interpretations of the research material. For these reasons, I have tried to leave room for alternate interpretations, and include descriptions of my role in the *mandram* community as best as I can.

The Local Temple Community

THE ADHI PARASAKTHI TEMPLE SOCIETY OF CANADA is located in Scarborough, the easternmost district of Toronto. The Canadian Sri Lankan Tamil community has grown larger especially during the mid-1990s. Most of the members of this community immigrated to Canada during the 1990s largely due to the civil war in Sri Lanka. In the earlier years this community took the form of a chanting group in one woman's home. Over the course of several years, the group of devotees meeting together, mostly women, increased in number. As the size of the group increased, there was a greater need to find a larger space. Eventually, encouraged by her guru in Melmaruvathur, Vasanthi and a few devotees selected a location in Scarborough.

Many residents of Scarborough are immigrants or descendants of immigrants; the two largest groups represented are those of South Asian and Chinese descent. In proximity to this area are numerous privately owned ethnic stores, restaurants, service-oriented businesses, and places of religious worship. From retailers selling clothing, jewellery, dry goods, or groceries to real estate dealers and lawyers, one can find an abundance of services aimed to attract Tamil-speaking clientele from Sri Lanka. In the whole of Toronto, this is one of the most intense centres of South Asian activity and commerce.

The *mandram* itself serves as a worship centre with complete ritual hall equipped with facilities for the performance of all weekly and festival rituals, including occasional fire rites or *yajñams*. The *mandram* is open seven days a week for puja or worship services. Pujas are offered on weekday evenings and on Saturday and Sunday mornings.[4] All worship services are followed by a traditional Sri Lankan Tamil community meal (vegetarian). Newcomers and the general public are welcome to attend all worship services and festival occasions. In this location, the community opened the doors to the Adhi Parasakthi Siddar Vaara Vazhipattu Mandram of Canada in September 2002.

The People of the Temple Society
Community Survey

A bilingual (English and Tamil) community survey was conducted on four separate occasions during 2008 in order to reach a wide range of participants. The survey sheet was distributed among members of the community who were asked to fill out the questionnaire only once in as much detail as possible. Participants were informed that they could decline to answer any of the questions by simply leaving the space blank. Participation in the survey was voluntary and all participants registering information on the questionnaire remained anonymous. Ninety-two survey sheets were collected.

Demographic Profile

As with any voluntary survey, the data collected represent only a portion of the total community population. In my estimate, based on average attendance counts for Sundays,[5] a little more than half of the weekly membership completed the survey. As the survey was known to have Vasanthi's support, I assume the half who participated included most of the leaders in the community. Of the ninety-two people surveyed, forty-seven were female, twenty-five were male, and twenty people did not respond to the question on gender. Of those who responded to the questionnaire, 83 percent indicated that they were born in Sri Lanka. According to the survey data, the largest age group was the one between the ages of thirty-six and fifty-five. Forty-three percent of the people surveyed were in this age range. The next largest age group was made up of children and young adults under the age of twenty-one. According to the survey data, much of the *mandram* membership comprises first-generation Sri Lankan immigrants, many of whom have children under the age of twenty-one.

From the broader body of survey material that I collected, some important points should be noted about the Adhi Parasakthi community in Toronto. There is a strong sense of Sri Lankan Tamil solidarity in Toronto, which is reflected within the Adhi Parasakthi community. When asked to identify their ethnicity, many survey participants self-identified by adding the term "Sri Lankan" in some way. This identification was more common than the term "Tamil." The Adhi Parasakthi community clearly takes pride in the solidarity of the broader Sri Lankan community of Toronto, and members happily participated in the nationalist initiative that took place in Toronto and Ottawa in 2009 to raise awareness in protest of civil war in Sri Lanka. These protests received wide media coverage and drew public attention to Sri Lanka and the ethnic identity of Sri Lankan Tamils in Canada. In this way, we see the importance of ethnic identity for members of this community and their desire to participate as a distinctive community.

One of the reasons the Adhi Parasakthi community enjoys worshipping together at the *mandram* is because they can share the Sri Lankan Tamil heritage with others in the community. As the *mandram* is an ethnic-based worship centre, Sri Lankan Tamil culture and language are given preference. The survey results regarding language indicated a strong commitment to language preservation within the community. Several children take Tamil language classes after school and most of the parents speak Tamil at home. One of the most significant elements of ritual performance at the *mandram* is language; every aspect of the worship is conducted in Tamil, and the Jaffna dialect is often evident. In this regard, ritual performance reflects a preference within the community that members both appreciate and enjoy.

The sense of family is very strong within the *mandram* community and Vasanthi and the other women take special care to see that the children are not left out in any way. There were always children present at the *mandram* whenever I was there. The majority of second-generation children are high school age or younger. A special youth group has been established at the *mandram* and is directed by a woman with leadership responsibilities in this community. The children and young adults have formed important friendships with one another, friends with whom they share both culture and religion. In this way, they feel they have a place of their own within the community, and the parents also feel that they will benefit from the Sri Lankan Tamil environment that has been cultivated through the women's leadership at the *mandram*.

The *mandram* community experienced significant growth between 2002 and 2008. The increase in numbers in 2007 was nearly double that of the previous year and the last three years show the most growth overall. The survey results also show that twice as many people went on pilgrimage to Melmaruvathur, India, in 2007 than in 2006. In this way we can see the importance of Melmaruvathur for the local community. (Melmaruvathur is the seat of religious authority in this tradition, the site of sacred pilgrimage and the home of Guru Bangaru Adigalar, the founder of this tradition.)

The Melmaruvathur Adhi Parasakthi Tradition— Tamil Nadu, India

Historical Perspective

The ATSC in Toronto is part of the larger transnational Adhi Parasakthi organization (Om Sakthi) dedicated to the worship of the goddess Sakthi (Śakti). This religious organization, founded in the 1970s under the leadership of Adhi Parasakthi Guru Bangaru Adigalar, is based in Melmaruvathur, Tamil Nadu, and is now a global network comprising religious centres; medical, educational, and vocational training institutions; and charitable foundations.[6] The organization has further established service programs, including free medical camps, ecology awareness organizations, blood donation camps, and AIDS-awareness outreach. Located southwest of Madras, the temple to Adhi Parasakthi is one of the most popular pilgrimage places in south India, especially during the *Taipūcam* and *Āṭipūram* festivals when pilgrims number in the tens of thousands.[7]

According to literature published under the auspices of the Melmaruvathur Adhi Parasakthi organization, this tradition began with the discovery of a *svayambhu liṅgam* (an aniconic symbol of generative energy within Hinduism) in Melmaruvathur, India, in 1966. In the aftermath of a fierce cyclone, an uprooted neem (*nīm*) tree revealed the presence of a *svayambhu liṅgam* resting in the ground.[8] According to the organization's literature and oral tradition, the goddess Sri Adhi Parasakthi had been residing in the form of that *liṅgam*, waiting for an opportune time to make her appearance in the world.[9] At that time, the *liṅgam* was carefully drawn from the soil and a temporary shelter was constructed around the *liṅgam* by Gopala

Naicker, the landowner and father of Adhi Parasakthi Guru Bangaru Adigalar.

A temple was built on Naicker's land in 1977 and a stone image of Adhi Parasakthi was installed there. The *liṅgam* is now installed in the *garbha griha* or sanctum sanctorum of this temple in Melmaruvathur, or Marvathur as it is more commonly known, below the pedestal of the Sri Adhi Parasakthi image. After a decade and a half, the surrounding land was gradually developed into the current temple complex.

The Guru

Adhi Parasakthi Guru Bangaru Adigalar or Amma, as he is affectionately known by devotees, is an avatar of the goddess Adhi Parasakthi according to the organization's literature. Most members of the temple society have described him to me as a *Cittar* (*siddha*) or enlightened master of meditation and teacher, and some add that he has become merged with the divine Śakti principle or formless goddess.

Many devotees describe Adigalar in terms of his gift of "divine speech," or *aruḷvākku*. Within the tradition, the goddess is understood to inspire Adigalar's words speaking through him. Most often the English term used in the organization's literature for *aruḷvākku* is "oracle." The historical literature from the Adhi Parasakthi organization cites the first occurrence of *aruḷvākku* in 1970, when Adigalar was a young man living in Melmaruvathur. This practice is continued by Adigalar today. Adigalar currently resides at the *Siddhar Peetam* in Melmaruvathur, India.[10]

The utterance of *aruḷvākku* is generally understood by devotees as a source of guidance and healing. There are varying interpretations, both literary and oral, as to the meaning and significance of *aruḷvākku*.[11] Specific interpretations of the phenomenon within the Toronto Adhi Parasakthi community differ from individual to individual. Among the more common interpretations, two are most salient. One conveys the notion that Adigalar has "merged" with the goddess Adhi Parasakthi as her devotee, and the second conveys the view that Adigalar has "merged" with the Śakti Principle, the goddess. In this tradition the goddess is worshiped reverently as supreme Śakti and mother. Both the goddess and the guru are referred to by devotees as Amma, which means "mother" in Tamil. Any differentiating factors must be derived from the context of the conversation. That gender difference may be less marked in the context of extraordinary people such as gurus, saints, and renunciants is a notion found among some followers of Hindu-based guru traditions.[12]

An Innovative Tradition

Under the leadership of Guru Bangaru Adigalar, this South Indian religious tradition has implemented an innovative structure of ritual authority that allows for and supports women's leadership roles in ritual instruction and performance. One of the more notable aspects of this tradition is the directive that privileges women as ritual leaders and does not impose purity restrictions that would prohibit women from ritual performance at any time. Lifting purity restrictions for women entering ritual space is in itself a marked shift from traditional Hindu Brahmanical ritual authority and gendered purity restrictions, which are by now well-established social conventions throughout South Asia and the diaspora. Such restrictions have prohibited women from entering and worshipping in temples during their menstrual cycles, and generally forbid them from roles in ritual leadership.

According to both oral and literary sources within this tradition, the primary imperatives of the Adhi Parasakthi organization have been set forth by Amma in her *aruḷvākku* or "voice divine." The mission objectives are divided into four parts and focus on cultivating spiritual and psychological wellness, a practical dedication to improving conditions within human society, and a commitment to the educational and spiritual uplifting of women. In alignment with these objectives, widows (traditionally discriminated against) are given access to educational/vocational training institutions and encouraged to participate in ritual as well.

The objectives as articulated within the Om Sakthi publication, *Glory of the Mother Divine: Amma Melmaruvathur*, are as follows:

1) to inculcate faith in the divine and foster spirituality,
2) to raise the status of women both socially and spiritually,

3) to promote the cause of education and health, and meet the cultural needs of the society, and

4) to cater to the needs of the weaker sections of the society and the help-less suffering masses through self-help measures and philanthropic undertakings, and to interest and enthuse them in spiritual activities as well.[13]

In Hindu traditions, the goal of human life is to attain liberation from the cycle of rebirth (saṃsāra). This may be achieved by practising one of the three main paths (marga) or, as some Hindus prefer to describe it, three aspects of one path: karma yoga, the path of selfless action or service; jñāna yoga, the path of knowledge, more specifically the realization of one's true nature with the nature of the universe; and bhakti yoga, the path of devotion, that is, the path to union with the divine through loving devotion. Within the Adhi Parasakthi tradition, cultivating a relationship with the divine by adhering to this path, which combines three aspects, one comes to under-stand the goal of yoga: awakening, liberation, mokṣa or in other terms, union with the divine. The Adhi Parasakthi tradition incorporates elements of the three disciplines above, including meditation, chanting, fasting, yajña, scrip-tural study, and puja (ritual forms of worship) as do a number of other Hindu guru-based traditions. In addition to the specific directives from the Adhi Parasakthi tradition, devotees are encouraged to cultivate and integrate knowledge of society, science, and spirituality in a proper balance in order to lead a productive and fulfilling life. The temple welcomes people from all faiths, an inclusivity expressed by the devotee's slogan "One Mother, One family," indicating that all of humanity is one.[14] Devotees at both the temple and the mandrams often wear red, a colour associated with the goddess and a reminder that Śakti dwells within all people.

The directives encouraging women to hold positions of leadership have been instrumental in shaping this tradition. To support and empower this objective, educational opportunities have been made available for women under the auspices of the Adhi Parasakthi Charitable, Medical, Educational, and Cultural Trust (established in 1978) and Adhi Parasak-thi Siddhar Peetam Women's Trust (established in 1989). The priority for applying the directives continues to inform and shape the structure and mission of this movement both in India and abroad. The Adhi Parasakthi organization currently has chapters in several countries, including Canada, the United States, France, Britain, Australia, Sri Lanka, and Singapore.

The Start of the *Mandram*

THE CURRENT *mandram* in Toronto was officially registered in Canada as part of the Melmaruvathur Adhi Parasakthi organization in 2002 under the name Adhi Parasakthi Temple Society of Canada.[15] The community consists of approximately 250–300 members and is growing steadily. The president of the Adhi Parasakthi Temple Society is a woman whom the community calls "Vasanthi." Vasanthi first immigrated to Canada with her husband and sons in 1996. Following the beginning of the civil war in Sri Lanka, Vasanthi spent time with family in India where she studied Ayurvedic medicine. While studying in India, she attended the main temple of the Adhi Parasakthi organization in Melmaruvathur. Before immigrating to Canada, she shared news of the impending move with Amma (Adigalar) and after some time in Toronto was asked to form a community group. Soon after her arrival in Canada she met the women of a *bhajan* (devotional singing) group and others, and with permission from the Melmaruvathur temple organization, Vasanthi began establishing a more formal *mandram*. As president of the Temple Society, Vasanthi oversees all operational aspects of the *mandram*. There are committees for the management of tasks required for ritual services and others for operational management, including weekly puja services, special holiday occasions, festivals, supply acquisition, accounting, rent/utilities, and communications. All members of this organization contribute to the organization on a volunteer basis.

Women
Ritual Performance

AS BRAHMIN PRIESTS do not serve as ritual specialists in this tradition, one quickly notices their absence. Upon entering the ritual space of the *mandram*, it is likely that one will first notice women performing puja. Both men and women serve in leadership positions; however, women have been encouraged to take more active roles, and in Toronto at least they assume the dominant roles.

This aspect of the temple society was brought to my attention time and again, notably by welcoming practitioners, who, upon meeting me for the first time, delighted in pointing out this particular aspect of their tradition. It is a point of honour in the community to be able to serve in this way and I was often reminded that women perform puja for the goddess directly in Melmaruvathur and in worship centres around the world.

The *Śakti Pīṭham* or Primary Shrine

THE FOCAL POINT of the main hall is the *śakti pīṭham*. The *pīṭham* holds three framed pictures placed side by side, usually adorned with flowers, neem leaves, and flower/lemon garlands. All three pictures are set behind framed glass and ritually anointed before each puja with turmeric paste and *kumkum* (vermilion) in the form of the circular *poṭṭu*. The centre picture portrays Adigalar sitting at the feet of the Adhi Parasakthi *mūrti* or image and *svayambhu liṅgam* [*linkam*] under worship in Melmaruvathur. Directly below this picture is a brass statue of the same composition set on the shelf below the frames. Next to this statue is a small flame lamp. As one faces the images, at the right is the picture of Guru Adigalar's feet. Positioned below the picture is an *āratī* tray upon which is set a metallic representation of the guru's sandals or *padam*.

The picture at the left is Adigalar seated in a chair wearing a red robe and smiling benevolently. At both ends of this *pīṭham* are statues of Vināyaka (Ganesha), anointed and adorned with garlands. Vināyaka is the only other deity represented in the *mandram*.[16] At the base of each picture is a brightly coloured silk fabric on top of the long altar. After the puja service members of the congregation form a queue to receive *darśan* (divine glance or grace of the divine) in front of the *pīṭham*. Many devotees move closer to the photographs, icons, or the guru's sandals and bow in reverence (*pranām*). Often they leave offerings, such as flowers, loose petals, neem leaves, coins, bills, or small fruit, at the base of each image. The centre image of the goddess usually has multiple fresh flower garlands of varying lengths, the longest of which reaches nearly to the floor. The *pīṭham* is carefully adorned with rich, colourful designs.

About Ritual Performance

IN ONE CONVERSATION WITH VASANTHI, I asked which aspects of the Melmaruvathur Adhi Parasakthi tradition first attracted her attention. She said that three aspects came to mind: (1) women were performing rituals in the temple; (2) she could worship in her own language (Tamil); and (3) women were not prohibited from worshipping in the temple even during their cycles.

For Vasanthi and several other women with whom I spoke, these aspects of tradition seemed innovative and appealing. In one regard, these aspects seemed to bring the act of worship closer to the worshipper. By inviting women to perform rites in the temple and *mandrams*, access to ritual was extended to those who were usually excluded from this domain of authority. While women are given priority as ritual performers, men are not excluded from these positions. When I spoke with men regarding ritual performance in the Adhi Parasakthi tradition, often one of the first points noted was that anyone could perform rites in the temple and *mandram* without regard for caste.

By extending such performance opportunities beyond customary parameters, relatively new modalities in worship have been implemented and this appeals not only to the women of this community, but to the men as well, even though some men focus on caste inclusiveness more than on gender. Of the people I spoke to, no one expressed feeling marginalized or excluded at the *mandram*. Second, for some members of the community, the idea of worshipping in one's own language made the language of liturgy more "down to earth," making ritual participation more accessible and meaningful. In the *mandram* community, use of the Tamil vernacular reaches more first-generation Tamils and makes the worship experience more personal. One of the community members, Mr. Thevaram, expressed his perspective in this way: "I am an educated man, but I do not understand Sanskrit. Here, we chant and worship in my own language. I can speak to Amma in my *own* language;

this, I prefer." For Mr. Thevaram, and other worshippers, the language used in ritual performance is as important as the rite itself. They are not separate but equally significant aspects of a holistic experience, two parts of the worship experience that draw the worshipper closer to the Divine. By choosing to attend the puja services at the *mandram*, worshippers are exercising their agency in making selections from the local options available. They are making choices that affirm a sense of identity and the life-style practices that they find suitable in this diaspora location.

Lastly, as noted above, a unique feature of the ritual structure in the Adhi Parasakthi organization promotes opportunities for women to assume leadership roles as ritual specialists. Women may perform rituals unrestricted by orthodox purity precepts regulating much of contemporary and historical Hindu religious practice. Because gendered purity restrictions that affect menstruating women have been lifted, many women feel less constrained by the socio-religious customs and more at ease in performing puja within the community.[17] This entitlement has been positively received by women in the community. It is viewed as supportive of women and has helped expand the purview of religious expression and agency. Some women have expressed feelings of freedom, acceptance, support, encouragement, and exoneration. In one young woman's words, "a woman's cycle is natural, it does not make her polluted. Why should we stay outside?" Many women share an attitude of participatory inclusivity; they do not feel excluded from collective rites or puja services based on more traditional attitudes about women and purity, and they have set aside the religious gender restrictions many were taught as children. This is a marked shift in attitude and differentiates them from many of their Hindu contemporaries in North America and abroad.[18]

As Corinne Dempsey has aptly noted, "the fact that a menstruating woman will rarely enter a temple during her period is well known in India." She further observes in her study of Indian Catholic women in Kerala that even while the church hierarchy discourages such purity taboos among Kerala Catholics, Hindu notions of purity/pollution carry over into Christian worship and some women will not enter certain churches or shrines of Catholic saints during their menstrual cycles.[19] One can concede, that the religious ordinance removing purity restrictions within the Adhi Parasakthi organization constitutes a significant paradigmatic shift in values with regard to what it means to be female in this Hindu religious context. While the concept is supported by the Adhi Parasakthi organization itself, there is clearly additional enthusiasm for this shift in Toronto. Furthermore, it seems that North American attitudes and the social mores of the diaspora setting add additional support in facilitating a transition to this course of Hindu religious customs.

In examining this issue it becomes clear that the diaspora setting can serve as a liminal place where the social mores from the homeland are in a state of flux in the host country. It is likely that over time some observances may give way to permanent change. It is also true that attitudinal changes may more easily take root in a new setting. To a certain degree, new attitudes and personal priorities are forged as the result of a transitional phase during which negotiations between one's former location or social role within the homeland culture shifts to a new social context with different cultural norms and expectations in the host country. It is not surprising that in the process of resettlement, one might re-evaluate former notions of self, identity, social class, and gender, but it is a bit surprising to find that this discussion is taking place within the context of an intensely traditional worshipping community.

Several women have expressed relief in finding that the pressures to accommodate or yield to social and familial expectations from back home have been upset, or are at least temporarily unsettled, in the diaspora. Several women expressed the view that socio-cultural expectations and pressures were bound to be less pronounced in North America. In adapting or revitalizing their personal identities, women seemed less constrained by the social obligations and considerations they felt bound to prioritize in their homeland. For some women, life in the diaspora has provided greater opportunities to choose, and in exercising their own choices they came to experience their own sense of authority in new and different ways.

Patrick Olivelle comments, in discussing the rise of cities in India and some of the challenges to Vedic religious ideals that the urban environment fosters, that "all culturally created worlds, however, are intrinsically unstable. . . . They are constantly challenged by new experiences, by changes in geography, climate, and economics, by social upheavals, and by individuals and groups seeking better answers and new meanings."[20] The diasporic context for new immigrant communities also represents a certain destabilization, a move from a familiar homeland environment and generations of kinship ties within a community. For the Adhi Parasakthi community, the expansive geography implied by the term "homeland" may be further specified to the predominantly Tamil Jaffa peninsula of northern Sri Lanka. Further destabilization occurs through the process of migration from towns and villages with a relatively contained and closely knit web of interdependent relationships that create reciprocal rights and obligations to a more loosely knit or open (perhaps somewhat impersonal) urban multicultural environment and an increase in the individual's power to choose from a variety of options. In that process and processing, a space opens, allowing room for renegotiations of boundaries and reformulations of tradition in the new diasporic context.[21]

Through the increased opportunities to share in ritual performance and to assume ritual authority, members are afforded greater agency in self-expression. Such opportunities offer community members the opportunity to take a more active role in self-determination; in identity expression; in one's own personal, spiritual, and emotional support; and in the support of others. By increasing the opportunities and roles in which one can serve one's community and oneself, one's capacity to grow and accomplish one's goals is increased as well. Such measures empower both men and women.

Devotional Worship
Ritual Performance in the Adhi Parasakthi Tradition

THE HEART OF ACTIVITY in the *mandram* centres on worship in the form of ritual performance and there is a strong element of communal participation in the rituals performed at the *mandram*. A variety of individuals play leadership roles as the ritual process proceeds. In addition, on certain occasions individualized rituals are performed within the group setting as well. This worship style has been very well received within the *mandram* community. One example of this type of individual-based collective style is the *villakku* puja, which will be described below. This ritual style demonstrates direct participation, or what one might think of as a "hands-on" approach to ritual within the community. The *mandram* hall teems with ritual activity, and the ritual performers are the members of the community. This ritual style has become a characteristic marker for this community among the broader Hindu community in the Toronto area. When I asked Adhi Parasakthi participants/devotees how this tradition was different from other temple traditions in the area, quite often community members responded by saying, "Here, we can do the rituals ourselves. There are no [Brahman] priests here."

This perspective seems to be one of the foundational convictions of the community of worshippers. Such statements are commonly used to characterize worship within the Adhi Parasakthi tradition when members are speaking to newcomers and outsiders alike. In this way, it seems that much of the community has identified personal ritual performance as a salient value within the community. Being directly involved in ritual performance as a practitioner and, by extension, experiencing a sense of ritual authority as well, are elements of this tradition in which many community members take pride.

Based on participant observation and my conversations with devotees and newcomers alike, I would say that the attitude toward ritual performance in the *mandram* reflects a deep sense of devotion expressed in attending the goddess, and the rituals are a means for cultivating one's relationship with her.[22] Ritual performance in the *mandram* is viewed as a privilege that participants accept with honour and humility. As within any religious community, there are members who take more active roles in participation than do others; however, the opportunities for participation and access to ritual performance remain open to the entire community. Certain rituals, such as *abhiṣekam* or the ritual bathing of the residing deities, are performed daily before each puja service commences, and any person from the community or guest who wishes to attend and participate in these rites may do so.

The Operation of the *Mandram*

MAINTAINING THE HALL, THE OFFICE, AND THE KITCHEN requires a number of different tasks, some of which are long-term responsibilities performed by members of the community. Such responsibilities are considered *seva* or selfless service, understood by members of the community as offerings to the goddess Adhi Parasakthi or Amma. For example, each month a family, a small group, or a committee of four or five people takes responsibility for puja services one day a week. During this month they ensure that all the puja preparations and the subsequent communal meal are prepared.

With regard to ritual performance, responsibilities are assigned and rotated so that each section of the puja service is coordinated under the supervision of an experienced ritual leader or assistant. Most ritual proceedings, but not all, are orchestrated under the ever vigilant direction of Vasanthi.

While not everyone in the community has been specifically instructed in the various rituals in the *mandram*, there are usually plenty of knowledgeable volunteers on hand to assist in guiding ritual participants. There is also a regular group of core volunteers who guide and manage each proceeding. Sunday puja services and special holiday and festival occasions draw the largest number of devotees to the *mandram*. Such large-scale occasions require somewhere between twenty-five to thirty-five volunteers. In order to manage all that needs to be done in preparation for the ritual performance, volunteers work together in groups at the various tasks: cleaning the hall, cooking for the communal meal, hanging decorations in the hall, serving as hall monitors, preparing puja offerings, constructing a ritual fire pit for certain occasions, *yantras*, stringing garlands, making the rice *kolam* designs, adorning the *kālasam* pots, monitoring oil lamps, arranging seating, distributing puja materials for collective puja occasions, leading chants, assisting with ritual performance, and other responsibilities.

Preferences and Priorities

The Adhi Parasakthi ritual tradition has a collective style in which members of the community are drawn into ritual leadership and participation. This dimension is even more prominent in the diasporic context as newer immigrant ethnic communities try to find their own identities in the face of numerous others. Women in particular realize that the traditional restrictions they knew in the Hindu temples back home no longer apply. In this sense the ritual rules have a very direct social impact on how men and especially women engage them. To gain greater access to the sacred is to cultivate a relationship with the divine and share in the implementation of ritual authority within the community. What this means in practical terms is that by creating opportunities for ritual performance within the community, opportunities to access ritual authority are created as well and personal agency is enhanced. These ritual opportunities bestow new access to sacred power. Sometimes this power is configured in personal terms as new strength, grace, or divine guidance, and sometimes it is a more passive power in the sense of "having the ear of the divine." Within this tradition, the sacred source of power, the divine Mother Śakti, is accessible through the performance of ritual practices and devotion. A large number of the women I interviewed said they felt a particular privilege in performing puja in the *mandram*, and that this has become a special aspect of relationship with Amma. For many women, and men as well, this relationship itself is a source of power and strength. While puja may also be performed at home, the *mandram* houses the *śakti piṭham*, and as ritual responsibilities may be shared by a number of community members, this allows for increased participation on a larger, more elaborate scale.

A Place of Support and Compassion

A number of the women at the *mandram* maintain jobs as well as managing the household and caring for their children. One woman named Nitya explained to me that after coming to the pujas at the *mandram* and speaking with other women there, she found compassion and support for considering her own needs as well as those of her family. She explained to me:

> Sometimes, I am exhausted and I want to come here to be at peace.
> Here, when I am doing puja, I feel free; my mind feels free. I can think
> about what I need so that I can go home and help my children. I used to
> pray only for my daughter's health and recovery; she has a respiratory

condition. One woman I know here knew about my situation and my daughter and invited me to come and do puja here. I was not going to a temple for ten years or so.

She went on to share with me that she had been feeling worried about and disappointed with the way her life was going. After coming to the *villakku* pujas and praying to Amma for a couple of months, she decided that she would make a trip to Melmaruvathur to see Amma. She was able to speak to Adigalar and receive Amma's blessings. Her experience there was profound, and Amma's words (*aruḷvākku*) are with her every day. She shared with me that during her visit to India she realized that her daughters would not benefit from the care of an exhausted, fearful, and intensely worried mother. That was more a disservice, rather than benefit, to her children. Adigalar had asked her to turn her worries about her daughter's health over to Amma and to take better care of herself from now on. Nitya also explained that over time her daughter's health had begun to improve. "Not a cure," she said, "but we are grateful that her condition is not as severe as it was." Nitya also shared the sense that she now felt less anxiety about her current circumstances. When I asked if she had been going to other temples again, she said, "No, I am only coming here. I feel no need to go anywhere else."

For Nitya, one of the gifts or benefits she received from her experiences at the *mandram* was renewed faith and the availability of choices. Her renewed awareness of these was revitalized by the initiatives she had taken and through her fellowship with others. From the experience of doing puja, from the compassion and support of other women in the *mandram*, and from her pilgrimage to Melmaruvathur to receive Amma's *darśan*, Nitya accessed previously unavailable *means* to address and cope with her concerns. Whether to allow one's state of mind to dictate one's experience of the world or whether to alter that state and be healed is a choice she felt everyone had, even though people may not recognize it. According to Nitya, the sum of these experiences helped her to help herself. "The understandings came in a natural way," she said. For Nitya, understanding her circumstances and the change in perspective she attained came partly through the environment she chose to enter (she had the support of the people she associated with at the *mandram*) and partly through the experience of religious practice she had (ritual performance and pilgrimage).

The *Villakku* Puja

A significant aspect of ritual performance within the Adhi Parasakthi tradition is the elaborate large-scale *villakku* puja occasions. These rites are conducted regularly during full moon *purnima* days and special holidays as well. *Villakku* puja is performed by making offerings of flowers, *kumkum*, rice, and incense while the sacred names Vināyaka and Adhi Parasakthi are recited before a flame-lit lamp.

The *villakku* puja is considered an auspicious and powerful means of attracting the grace of the goddess. On such occasions each person who takes part in the ritual may initiate his or her own individual puja offerings from his or her own place in the communal ritual configuration. While the layout of the configuration may change, what is significant is that the collective is worshipping together as one community. Each person is given the same ritual offerings to perform worship while sitting before a lamp. In this way the space in front of each person serves as that person's altar and for some, individual prayers may be considered more efficacious.

By employing the familiar concept "the one in the many; the many in the one," ubiquitous in Hindu artistic styles and religious iconography, these ritual occasions incorporate the numerous devotees into a single collective ritual space and in so doing, map a familiar religious concept onto the sacred space of the ritual. From one perspective, the participants can be considered collectively as the ritual embodiment of this sacred principle. On a smaller scale, such puja occasions are performed at the Adhi Parasakthi Temple Society in Toronto as well. This means of worship in the greater Toronto area offers a shift from priest-mediated puja to an individually based collective style of ritual performance. In this configuration, we see a visible decentralization of power whereby the central focus gives way to a multiplicity of peripheries. These pujas are extremely well attended, and are especially popular among women. While this style of puja is not singularly unique or new, it is significant because it has been identified by the local community as a defining feature of this tradition in Canada. The practice of *villakku* puja offers not only a personal experiential shift, but also has a democratizing effect as well. This ritual style provides for Canadian Hindus another pattern of worship wherein the focus is no longer on the priest but on the many participants or congregation.[23]

Attendance for the collective *villakku* puja, which draws newcomers and the friends and relatives of devotees, has clearly increased between 2007 and 2009. More than once I listened to the personal narratives of newcomers who said they had been hesitant to visit the *mandram* or perform *archana* before now because they "didn't really *go* to temples that much" or "just weren't that religious" or "hadn't been going to temples much since childhood." Their reasons for attending the Adhi Parasakthi *mandram* varied and were personal in nature, but at the same time, several people acknowledged that something had recently changed in their life or really needed to change.

The topic of the conversations I initiated stemmed from my interest in the reasons these women continued to worship at the *mandram* after their initial introduction to the tradition. As one might imagine, there were various responses, but one common conversation stood out and helped me clarify what I was hearing from a number of devotees. Several people told me that they came to the *mandram* because they could perform the rituals there, and for many, performing the rituals for Amma brought peace, relief, and a deep sense of gratitude that was given expression through ritual for their relationship with the Divine Mother. In this ritual setting, individual prayers seemed more efficacious.

Women and Leadership Roles

Influential examples of empowerment and leadership for the women of the Adhi Parasakthi *mandram* in Toronto can be found in a number of sources. Some come from traditional Hindu lore to which the women would have been exposed in their childhood. Some examples of more aggressive female power are goddesses described in popular lower-caste Tamil stories, and other examples are Tamil women, who, in the context of the recent civil war, acted heroically. And then, of course, there were the comments from some of their daughters based on their North American feminist experience. While the women at the *mandram* were familiar with models of feminism in North America, these women would rather be selective when it comes to values, even though they eagerly sought out their own means of empowerment from within a Tamil social and religious framework.[24] While North American role models might be an ideal for which some of their daughters may strive, gender ideals can perhaps be *actualized* in the context of community wherein one defines one's interactions with others. For a number of devotees, the *mandram* provides a supportive community context in which their gender ideals can be shared, encouraged, and manifested.

Many of the women with whom I spoke were familiar with pan-Indian narratives and the various role models of women portrayed in Hindu textual sources such as the *Mahābhārata* and the *Rāmāyaṇa*. Though there are a number of differences between north and south Indian/Sri Lankan cultures, everyone I asked was familiar with the figures of Rāma and Sītā, the revered couple from the epic *Rāmāyaṇa*. While examples of Rāma and Sītā have been cited by numerous scholars and recalled by many Hindus as traditional role models for the ideal husband and wife, in the *mandram* women smiled politely when I asked if they thought of Sītā as a role model. While women took some pride in showing their respect for traditional Hindu cultural sources, it was clear that they did not particularly admire the passive, obedient Sītā, but were drawn to stories of women, saints, and goddesses with a sense of agency and strength. But they never paused to discuss the fact that one particular experience of the goddess comes largely through the mediation of a male guru figure. Within this tradition, Adhi Parasakthi is understood to manifest herself in a myriad of forms. In this regard, the composite image is one that transcends gender.[25]

Examples of feminine agency frequently mentioned included the fiery Tamil heroine/goddess Kaṇṇaki from the epic *Cilappaṭikarām*, and the mystic *bhakti* poet-saint Kāraikkāl Ammaiyār (sixth to seventh century), author of devotional hymns to the god Śiva in her native Tamil language. She is one of only three women to be recognized as a saint in the Tamil Śiva-*bhakti* tradition, and is often pictured in sculptures as an emaciated but unwavering female ascetic. But most common of all were references to real women in their own lives whom they respected, such as Vasanthi and others, and women they knew well through times of adversity and joy.

A number of the women at the *mandram* were not only inclined to acknowledge gender influences in their immediate environment, but described their own interest in these matters as current and something they were currently working out. As a matter of practicality, some of the models recalled from their past were no longer relevant in their new circumstances. Women currently in leadership positions exerted the most influence on their constructions of gender because their example worked within the present context. The models of leadership that women such as Vasanthi presented were catalyzed from the circumstances of their own life histories, which were very similar to those of other women in the community. These women had authority and were leaders in the community in no small part because they had demonstrated an ability to meet and address the circumstances in the local diasporic setting. The fact that Vasanthi has been able to achieve and maintain the level of leadership and respect within the temple community that she has is testimony to her dedication, hard work, and perseverance. It is also due, no doubt, to her integrity and her sense of service as devotion to Amma. It is worth noting, in appreciation of diversity, that though distinct from the orthodox Brahmin priests in the neighbouring temples, her authority rests on her ritual knowledge and her demonstrated ability to lead from within the experience she shares with the other women and members of the community.

In dealing with the challenges of emigrating from Sri Lanka, those coping with the complexities of war and adapting to a new homeland, reuniting family, securing financial resources, and planning for the future of one's children, the models of leadership that the women looked to most were those who radiated strength and perseverance. These virtues are needed to face the challenges addressing many in the community. In this way such role models point to the possibility of re-envisioning notions of identity and gender as community women take on their own roles in the new Canadian environment.

The Goddess in Tamil Culture

AMONG THE PEOPLE OF SOUTH INDIA, local traditions of feminine deity worship have a long history. Adhi Parasakthi is both Tamil and pan-Indian and in this aspect she is different from most local and regional Tamil deities.[26] Goddess temples and shrines frequented by devotees are a visible part of Tamil life, rural and urban, and the presence of goddess worship is part of the Tamil ethos. Goddess worship constitutes part of a cultural and psychological awareness that has permeated various aspects of material culture as well. Amalgamated with Devī worship, in India and Sri Lanka villagers and non-villagers alike take their daily offering and prayers the Divine Mother who is known by many names and forms.

The attributes of the goddess Adhi Parasakthi that seem most admired within the *mandram* community coincide, to some degree, with the human role models of female figures in history and literature, and of real-life women. A number of women at the *mandram*, as well as men, respect the sense of ultimate authority, wisdom, and compassion found in the metaphor of the divine Śakti principle as a Mother/matrix. In this sense, the image of the goddess as mother is not particularly as a fertility goddess, meant to reflect women in their reproductive capacity alone. Rather, the attributes that draw devotees to the goddess focus attention on the goddess's divine authority, sovereignty, and power to make things happen and to act on behalf of her devotees.[27] The image of the Divine Mother in this setting focuses on her power to act, protect, and fortify her devotees. Focusing on these aspects or dimensions of the goddess is not unique to this community or to Śāktas in general, yet they express the qualities of the goddess that are emphasized by a particular community and also shaped by local custom.[28] Devotees express confidence that the goddess Adhi Parasakthi can "command even the gods." In contexts such as these the power of the goddess is considered supreme—that is, not derived from a male deity. For devotees she is the universal goddess, also referred to as Devī, a goddess with many forms richly portrayed in regional and pan-Indian narratives and devotional traditions across India and Sri Lanka.[29]

The popularity of the independent goddess in myriad forms (protective of her devotees, identified in certain forms as fierce or bitter about injustice) garnered devotional and narrative significance in India and Sri Lanka (Pandian 1982; Kinsley 1986; Hawley and Wulff 1996; Craddock 2001; Pintchman 2001; Foulston and Abbot 2009).[30] This is but one example of the way in which cultural and religious paradigms survive and persist within a cultural ethos.

Interpretations of the Goddess

As various interpretations of gender and a variety of female role models are possible within one community, it is perhaps not so surprising that the attributes that inspire and empower women to assume roles in ritual and leadership are emphasized. Paving the way as leaders in their community, some women do cultivate such qualities on their own terms and to some degree through interaction at the *mandram* feminist values and social mores begin to take shape locally. The sense of religiosity conveyed to me as I spent time talking with the women as they volunteered, collecting individual histories and participating in temple activities was consistently one of relationship with the goddess characterized by intense devotion and service, and also reciprocity.[31] The goddess, the source of sacred power, is understood as Śakti, immanent and transcendent, and the women of the *mandram* continue to look to real women for leadership and friendship to create practical new currents in thought and action. From one viewpoint, the women at the Toronto *mandram* have taken a proactive stance on ritual authority and leadership.

When considering the ways in which religious authority and leadership roles impact *mandram* women's notions of gender and identity, there is no formula to follow and not everyone reacts in exactly the same way. From one perspective, the women are interpreting and envisioning models of female authority and strength that at once affirm a belief in the power of the divine as Adhi Parasakthi and her ability to act in the world for the benefit of her devotees. At the same time, they are also affirming the ability of "real women" with *śakti* to act as well, both in the temple and beyond for the benefit of self and others (i.e., family, friends, community, etc.). As Rita D. Sherma aptly notes, "Hindu perceptions of the divine feminine inform and shape Hindu expressions of female agency and authority that are beginning to be articulated in a different key from the Western feminist ideals."[32] As I mentioned earlier, while the women at the *mandram* are somewhat familiar with North American feminism (some more so than others), these women would rather not emulate and assimilate all feminist ideals, even though they eagerly seek out their own means of empowerment within a Tamil social and religious framework. I would suggest that women's interpretations of the divine feminine and the relationship that is cultivated with the goddess enable them to address the immediate concerns in their own lives with a sense of foundational support in the new local context. In this community, the central means by which this relationship is cultivated and maintained is through devotion and ritual.[33] Women's direct ritual participation and leadership at the temple affirms female authority and agency. This is one way in which the women feel supported as Sri Lankan Tamil Hindu women in North America on their own terms, and they do not believe that this makes them more North American or less Tamil. The fact that the women have willingly assumed leadership responsibilities within the community attests to their sense of vision and also enables them to support one another as they continue to make valuable contributions and move through the future stages of shaping this tradition in Canada.[34]

Conclusion

WHILE ENCOURAGED AND SUPPORTED by Guru Bangaru Adigalar in India and the Melmaruvathur Adhi Parasakthi temple organization, the local Toronto community is deeply rooted in Sri Lankan Tamil culture and in the practical options accorded to it at the local level of Toronto.[35]

The community of women of the Adhi Parasakthi *mandram* has created a local space that welcomes and invites all. The women who come to the *mandram* have found a place where they can expand the parameters of ritual participation and, in some ways, their religious identity. For most of them the *mandram* is a place where they can engage in volunteer positions and communicate with other like-minded women. Most important of all, it is a place where they are entrusted with ritual authority outside the home, perhaps for the first time.

One of the reasons women have not been entrusted with ritual authority is based on Hindu notions of ritual purity/impurity that regard the female body as subjected to pollution during the menstrual cycle, after childbirth, and whenever she has had to deal with a death in the family and other occasions. During such times women are generally prohibited from entering Hindu temples, and in some regions women are not allowed to attend outdoor festivals either.[36] Most women at the *mandram* with whom I spoke expressed appreciation that the Adhi Parasakthi tradition does not recognize these particular taboos. The Adhi Parasakthi temple is the only one in Toronto that explicitly rejects prohibitions of women entering or performing rituals in temples or *mandrams*.

By participating in a community where women are empowered to empower others, there is also an opportunity for these women to promote positive change in their domestic lives. The *mandram* is, first, a place of worship for a community of devotees, and, secondly, a centre where people can come together in service, and the women are intensely engaged in both activities. In both roles, the *mandram* provides women with an engaging and supportive environment outside their home in which they as individuals can interact in meaningful ways.

Postmodernism rejects neatly packaged definitions of gender, recognizing that the experience of womanhood differs among women. Mimi Arnstein notes that "women develop identities based on multiple positions (e.g., economic, racial, cultural) and therefore challenge totalizing definitions of women."[37] Conceptual notions of selfhood within the Hindu social structure have often been understood in relational terms rather than in terms of the individual, and at times traditional constructions of female gender have been closely related to socially determined roles associated with marriage (i.e., wife, mother, and daughter-in-law). These roles are still highly valued by the women at the *mandram* and yet at the same time interpreted somewhat differently. In some ways women's leadership roles and authority are affirmed through modes of performance that carry important responsibilities both ritually and administratively, publicly and domestically. Women's leadership in the temple casts women as individuals, working together in mutual support of one another, family, and community. As I consider some of the salient examples that continue to influence *mandram* women's notions of authority and gender, I see the important ways in which the divine feminine is envisioned within the community, the inclusive discourse in terms of gender and caste, the collective patterns of worship, women's responsibilities for daily pujas, and the administrative maintenance of the *mandram*. These factors together constitute both means and support for enacting this particular interpretation of Hindu socio-cultural and religious life.

If to a certain degree identities are constructed not only through interaction with others but also through the skills and knowledge we attain, the accomplishments we achieve, and the contributions we make to a larger collective, then the time the women spend at the *mandram* is a means to reshape, redevelop, reconstruct, and reinvent potential aspects of personality and identity. The influence of women's ritual authority and leadership at the *mandram*, and the support they give one another have provided women with a common venue where they can express their own sense of identity in an affirming environment. The responsibilities and ritual practices with which they are entrusted have engaged women as individuals, both personally and publicly. In some cases, these opportunities may inspire a fresh perspective or influence current notions of identity in new ways. ●

Notes

1. Alternatively transliterated *Ātiparācakti* in Tamil and *Ādiparāśakti* in Sanskrit. For this chapter I have chosen to use the spelling found in the literature from the organization used by the local community in its written material. Names of deities, other than purely Tamil deities, and most technical ritual terms are transliterated from more readily recognizable Sanskrit forms. Other names and terms, including the names of festivals at the Adhi Parasakthi temple, are given in their Tamil forms. Following a helpful style solution used by C. J. Fuller, "The Divine Couple's Relationship in a South Indian Temple: Mīnākṣī and Sundareśvara at Madurai" (Chicago: University of Chicago Press, 1980), 321–48.

2. The ethnographic fieldwork on which this essay draws was carried out between 2007 and 2009 while living in the Toronto area and additional follow-up visits in 2014.

3. When community members are speaking English, the word "temple" is often used interchangeably with the word *mandram*, which implies a smaller worship centre, satellite to Melmaruvathur.

4. The puja schedule varies from time to time. On my most recent visit (2014), the evening programs were held on Tuesday and Friday primarily and on a number of special observance dates.

5. Sunday pujas consistently have the highest attendance.

6. Separate registration for the temple and the Adhiparasakthi Charitable, Medical, Educational, and Cultural Trust was done in 1978. Donations to the Trust are tax-deductible.

7. See Knut A. Jacobsen, Helene Basu, Angelika Malinar, and Vasudha Narayanan, eds., *Brill's Encyclopedia of Hinduism* (Leiden; Boston: Brill, 2013), s.v. "Melmaruvathur Movement."

8. E. C. Sakthi Chandrasekharan and Sakthi Dr. C. Thirugnanasambandham, *Glory of Mother Divine: Amma Melmaruvathur* (Melmaruvathur, India: Adhiparasakthi Charitable, Medical, Educational, and Cultural Trust, 2004), 88–89.

9. Although the linga is usually connected with Śiva, it is spoken of as the abode of Śakti. See Sundara G. Moorthy, *Mother of Melmaruvathur and Her Miracles* (Madras, India: Oxford Printers, 1986), 10.

10. Though spoken of as guru/avatar/*siddha* during his early life, he married and had four children and now has several grandchildren. His family is also involved in this tradition.

11. Moorthy, *Mother of Melmaruvathur*, 13. Moorthy notes that "the voice is that of an ancient female *siddha* who chose that place as her abode."

12. Lisa L. Hallstrom, "Anandamayī Ma, the Bliss-Filled Divine Mother," in *The Graceful Guru: Hindu Female Gurus in India and the United States*, ed. Karen Pechilis (New York: Oxford University Press, 2004), 106; K. Pechilis, "Introduction," in *The Graceful Guru: Hindu Female Gurus in India and the United States*, ed. Karen Pechilis (New York: Oxford University Press, 2004), 222–23.

13. Chandrasekharan and Thirugnanasambandham, *Glory of Mother Divine*, 88–89.

14. Moorthy, *Mother of Melmaruvathur*, 19.

15. At the time of my earlier field research (2007–09) there were two smaller groups affiliated with the Adhiparasakthi organization located in the greater Toronto area. However, as of 2014 only one remains.

16. During Navarātrī there are representations of the goddess set on a special side shrine assembled each year for this occasion.

17. Ritual ablutions are part of the protocol on these days and call for adding a particular herbal mixture with turmeric to one's bathing regimen.

18. For interesting research and points of ethnographic reflexivity from her own experience of these restrictions in the field, see Orianne Aymard, *When a Goddess Dies: Worshipping Mā Ānandamayī after Her Death* (New York: Oxford University Press, 2014), 37.

19. Corinne Dempsey, *Kerala Christian Sainthood* (New York: Oxford University Press, 2001), 71–72.

20. Patrick Olivelle, *Saṃnyāsa Upaniṣads: Hindu Scriptures on Asceticism and Renunciation* (New York: Oxford University Press, 1992), 29. He further notes that the freedom to choose encouraged by the new urban environment was at the heart of challenges to the Vedic religious ideal from outside (i.e., renunciants), but also engendered challenge and change from within.

21. Olivelle, *Saṃnyāsa Upaniṣads*, 43. See also Richard Gombrich and Gananath Obeyesekere, *Buddhism Transformed: Religious Change in Sri Lanka*, vol. 8 (Delhi: Motilal Banarsidass Publishers, Pvt., 1988), 57–58, for a summary of the conclusions that A. Ghosh, *The City in Early Historical India* (Simla: Indian Institute of Advanced Study, 1973), 38, draws as to how rapid social change may engender a spiritual malaise and how urbanization changes social organization and may contribute to radical changes in outlook and lifestyle.

22. My field research within the community regarding ritual performance has been based on participant observation, interviews, ritual instruction that I received there and my conversations with ritual specialists, devotees, and newcomers.

23. Another example in ritual of a decentralization of power is noted by Loriliai Biernacki, "The Kālī Practice: Revisiting Women's Roles in Tantra," in *Woman and Goddess in Hinduism: Reinterpretations and Re-envisionings*, ed. Tracy Pintchman and Rita D. Sherma (New York: Palgrave Macmillan, 2011), 192, writing on ritual in the context of Shree Maa's temple/ashram. While the example is not identical, as it involves a sequence of participants performing *āratī* one at a time, Biernacki speaks to the intuitive strategy employed by Shree Ma (though not stressed or remarked upon in self-presentation), which effects a decentralization of power by "democratizing and hence dissolving the very space of center." She further notes that the centre becomes multiple and localized, and in a sense ceases to exist. See Loriliai

Biernacki, "Shree Maa of Kamakkhya," in *The Graceful Guru: Hindu Female Gurus in India and the United States*, ed. Karen Pechilis (New York: Oxford University Press, 2004), 179–202.

24. A number of women at the temple hold feminist values, however defined on their terms: See Chandra T. Mohanty, Ann Russo, and Lourdes Torres, *Third World Women and the Politics of Feminism* (Bloomington: Indiana University Press, 1991); C. T. Mohanty, *Feminism without Borders: Decolonizing Theory, Practicing Solidarity* (Durham, NC: Duke University Press, 2003); Saba Mahmood, *Politics of Piety: The Islamic Revival and the Feminist Subject* (Princeton, NJ: Princeton University Press, 2005).

25. Jacobsen et al., eds., *Brill Encyclopedia of Hinduism*, s.v. "Melmaruvathur Movement." The identification of Adhi Parasakthi with Bangaru Adigalar seems to have grown over the years. In the early years of his youth, the goddess is said to have spoken through him intermittently, gradually increasing the frequency of *aruḷvākku* over time culminating in the experience of constant presence, the experience of becoming one with the goddess.

26. Ibid.

27. For engaging research, including this facet of goddess worship and community, see Elaine Craddock, "Reconstructing the Split Goddess as Śakti in a Tamil Village," in *Seeking Mahādevi: Constructing the Identities of the Hindu Great Goddess*, ed. Tracy Pintchman (Albany: State University of New York Press, 2001), 145–69.

28. Tracy Pintchman, ed., *Seeking Mahādevi: Constructing the Identities of the Hindu Great Goddess* (Albany: State University of New York Press, 2001), 6–8; Thomas Colburn, "Devī the Great Goddess," in *Devī: Goddesses of India*, ed. John S. Hawley and Donna M. Wulff (Berkeley: University of California Press, 1996), 43–44.

29. With regard to the history of goddess worship in India, the Devi-Mahatmya or "Glorification of the Goddess" is an early text of approximately the sixth century CE. Thomas Colburn notes that "the Devi-Mahatmya is not the earliest literary fragment attesting to the existence of devotion to a goddess figure, but it is surely the earliest in which the object of worship is conceptualized as Goddess, with a capital G." Colburn, "Devī the Great Goddess," 31–48.

30. There is much interesting scholarship on Hindu goddesses, including: Jacob Pandian. "The Goddess Kannagi: A Dominant Symbol of South Indian Tamil Society," in *Mother Worship: Theme and Variations* (Chapel Hill: University of North Carolina Press, 1982), 177–91; David R. Kinsley, *Hindu Goddesses: Visions of the Divine Femi-*

nine in the Hindu Religious Tradition (Berkeley: University of California Press, 1986); John S. Hawley and Donna M. Wulff, eds., *Devī: Goddesses of India* (Berkeley: University of California Press, 1996); Tracy Pintchman, ed. *Seeking Mahādevi: Constructing the Identities of the Hindu Great Goddess* (Albany: State University of New York Press, 2001); Lynn Foulston and Stuart Abbott, *Hindu Goddesses: Beliefs and Practices* (Portland, OR: Sussex, 2009). In south India one of the most common narratives of an independent goddess was that associated with Māriyamman, who healed the scourge of smallpox during the hot season and brought the monsoon rains to give life to the land. In Sri Lanka the traditional story of Kaṇṇaki was more prominent. At times Buddhist villagers conflated stories of her with their traditional goddess Pattini, who, like Kaṇṇaki, was distinguished by her anklet.

31. On the relationship between the goddess and human women in this context, Flueckiger suggests that "the relationship is not one of imitation or modeling, but an empowering relationship in which their shared nature as possessors of *Shakti* (female power) is asserted and performed." See Joyce Flueckiger's work and rich ethnographic accounts of ritual, narratives, and festival in the context of Gangamma worshippers in south India. Joyce B. Flueckiger, *When the World Becomes Female* (Bloomington: Indiana University Press, 2013), ix.

32. Rita D. Sherma, "Introduction," in *Women and Goddess in Hinduism: Reinterpretations and Re-envisionings*, ed. Tracy Pintchman and Rita D. Sherma (New York: Palgrave Macmillan, 2011), 11.

33. On my most recent visit to the temple, I had the opportunity to spend full days there with the president and some of the ritual specialists opening the temple in the morning, completing ritual preparations for the formal puja, participating in puja, observing daily operations, cleaning, and closing the temple for the night. Whether weekday or weekend, it was not uncommon to see devotees stopping in for short periods of time during the course of their daily work or errands or for some, while on the way to or from work. During these brief visits, devotees (mostly women) might stop to pray and/or make a small offering at the *śakti pīṭham* in the main hall, or drop off an item that was needed at the temple and continue on with their day. After a while I began to think of this as a common occurrence that had seamlessly become part of the devotees' average day in their relationship with Amma.

34. There are a broad range of women's concerns in the Toronto context, a number connected to the complexities of migration such as loss of support networks, life

cycle transitions and attendant ritual concerns, family separation, children, education, and economic concerns. There are a number of ways in which the women have been able to compensate and support one another collectively through the temple from providing avenues of support for individuals or families in crisis to establishing the youth group for cultural education and activities. In this way, it is possible to see how female paradigms of authority have begun to manifest in a manner of grassroots feminism (for lack of a better term). Women's initiative and leadership have succeeded in providing solutions, in some ways imagining a new range of actions and possibilities. My thanks to the anonymous reviewers for their comments, which helped me to think through some of these aspects more closely.

35. When it is possible for community members to travel to the Melmaruvathur temple on pilgrimage, families and individuals do go as this is considered an important and valuable experience within the community.

36. Else Skjonsberg, *A Special Caste? Tamil Women of Śrī Lanka* (London: Zed Press, 1982).

37. Mimi Arnstein, "Consciousness Razing," in *Feminist (Re)Visions of the Subject: Landscapes, Ethnoscapes, and Theoryscapes*, ed. Gail Currie and Celia Rothenberg (Landham, MD: Lexington Books, 2001), 161.

Bibliography

Arnstein, Mimi. "Consciousness Razing." In *Feminist (Re)Visions of the Subject: Landscapes, Ethnoscapes, and Theoryscapes*, edited by G. Currie and C. Rothenberg, 159–78. Landham, MD: Lexington Books, 2001.

Aymard, Orianne. *When a Goddess Dies: Worshipping Mā Ānandamayī after Her Death*. New York: Oxford University Press, 2014.

Berger, Peter L., and Thomas Luckmann. *The Social Construction of Reality: A Treatise in the Sociology of Knowledge*. Garden City, NY: Anchor, 1966.

Biernacki, Loriliai. "The Kālī Practice: Revisiting Women's Roles in Tantra." In *Woman and Goddess in Hinduism: Reinterpretations and Re-envisionings*, edited by Tracy Pintchman and Rita Sherma, 121–45. New York: Palgrave Macmillan, 2011.

——. "Shree Maa of Kamakkhya." In *The Graceful Guru: Hindu Female Gurus in India and the United States*, edited by Karen Pechilis, 179–202. New York: Oxford University Press, 2004.

Colborn, Thomas. "Devī the Great Goddess." In *Devī: Goddesses of India*, edited by John S. Hawley and Donna M. Wulff, 31–48. Berkeley: University of California Press, 1996.

Craddock, Elaine. "Reconstructing the Split Goddess as Śakti in a Tamil Village." In *Seeking Mahādevi: Constructing the Identities of the Hindu Great Goddess*, edited by Tracy Pintchman, 145–69. Albany: State University of New York Press, 2001.

Dempsey, Corinne. *Kerala Christian Sainthood*. New York: Oxford University Press, 2001.

Flueckiger, Joyce B. *When the World Becomes Female*. Bloomington: Indiana University Press, 2013.

Foulston, Lynn, and Stuart Abbott. *Hindu Goddesses: Beliefs and Practices*. Portland, OR: Sussex, 2009.

Gombrich, Richard, and Gananath Obeyesekere. *Buddhism Transformed: Religious Change in Sri Lanka*. Vol. 8. Delhi, India: Motilal Banarsidass Publishers, 1988.

Hallstrom, Lisa L. "Anandamayī Ma, the Bliss-Filled Divine Mother." In *The Graceful Guru, Hindu Female Gurus in India and the United States*, edited by Karen Pechilis, 85–118. New York: Oxford University Press, 2004.

Hawley, John S., and Donna M. Wulff, eds. *Devī: Goddesses of India*. Berkeley: University of California Press, 1996.

Jacobsen, Knut A., Helene Basu, Angelika Malinar, and Vasudha Narayanan, eds. *Brill's Encyclopedia of Hinduism*. 6 vols. s.v. "Melmaruvathur Movement." Leiden and Boston: Brill, 2013.

Kinsley, David R. *Hindu Goddesses: Visions of the Divine Feminine in the Hindu Religious Tradition*. Berkeley: University of California Press, 1986.

Mahmood, Saba. *Politics of Piety: The Islamic Revival and the Feminist Subject*. Princeton, NJ: Princeton University Press, 2005.

Mohanty, Chandra T. *Feminism without Borders: Decolonizing Theory, Practicing Solidarity*. Durham, NC: Duke University Press, 2003.

Mohanty, Chandra T., Ann Russo, and Lourdes Torres. *Third World Women and the Politics of Feminism*. Bloomington: Indiana University Press, 1991.

Moorthy, Sundara G. *Mother of Melmaruvathur and Her Miracles*. Madras, India: Oxford Printers, 1986.

Narayanan, Vasudha. "Brimming with Bhakti, Embodiments of Shakti: Devotees, Deities, Performers, Reformers, and Other Women of Power in the Hindu Tradition." In *Feminism and World Religions*, edited by Arvind Sharma and Katherine Young, 25–77. Albany: State University of New York Press, 1999.

Olivelle, Patrick. *Saṃnyāsa Upaniṣads: Hindu Scriptures on Asceticism and Renunciation.* New York: Oxford University Press, 1992.

Pandian, Jacob. "The Goddess Kannagi: A Dominant Symbol of South Indian Tamil Society." In *Mother Worship: Theme and Variations,* edited by James J. Preston, 177–91. Chapel Hill: University of North Carolina Press, 1982.

Pechilis, Karen. "Introduction." In *The Graceful Guru: Hindu Female Gurus in India and the United States,* edited by Karen Pechilis, 1–49. New York: Oxford University Press, 2004.

Pintchman, Tracy, ed. *Seeking Mahādevi: Constructing the Identities of the Hindu Great Goddess.* Albany: State University of New York Press, 2001.

Sherma, Rita D. "Introduction." In *Woman and Goddess in Hinduism: Reinterpretations and Re-envisioning,* edited by Tracy Pintchman and Rita D. Sherma, 1–16. New York: Palgrave Macmillan, 2011.

Skjonsberg, Else. *A Special Caste? Tamil Women of Śrī Lanka.* London: Zed Press, 1982.

Conclusion

The chapters in this volume by Bowman, Echevarria, Gold-berg, Lee, McCann, Morgan, Pearson, Power, and Spina represent an early and modest effort at capturing the religious experiences of women in Canada, both historic and contemporary. We hope that the works of these authors will inspire and encourage further research about the religiosities of women in Canada.

The gaps in this volume are obvious. Most prominently missing from a volume on Canadian diasporic religiosities is First Nations spirituality. Some might argue that the peoples of the First Nations are not in diaspora but displaced internally to treaty reserves. However, in the past decade increasing attention has been paid to "indigenous diasporas." As James Clifford explains, "diasporic ruptures and connections—lost homelands, partial returns, relational identities, and world-spanning networks—are fundamental components of indigenous experience today."[1] Although a chapter on indigenous women's religiosities would enhance this volume, we believe that the topic deserves to be treated apart from settler communities in a dedicated volume.

Also absent are Islam, Asian traditions, and indigenous South Asian traditions except for Hinduism, to say nothing of the religiosities of the African diasporas and new religious movements beyond nineteenth-century Theosophy and Bahá'í. In short, there is much work to be done, and only tentative conclusions can be drawn from such a small body of work. Nevertheless, several features of women's religiosities are already evident:

individual agency invested in both conservation and transformation of tradition, and conversion to a new religion; strong communal affinities; and an early openness to global influences that resulted in a contemporary Canada that is diverse and richly plural.

The nineteenth-century Theosophists and Bahá'í faithful that McCann and Echevarria respectively examine brought multiple versions of the "East" to the "West," making inroads for new immigrant populations like the twentieth- and twenty-first-century Hindu communities in the heartland of southwest Ontario that Pearson and Spina write about. But variance is captured not only in change; it is expressed in the continuity of traditional beliefs and practices too. Bowman's and Morgan's studies of women of the historical Roman Catholic and Anglican churches in the outposts of Newfoundland offer a sharp contrast to the new religions and new immigrant communities covered in some of the other chapters. Lee's account of the interplay between Roman Catholic women and the church's institutions reminds us that differences are present not only between traditions but also within them.

As the Roman Catholic and Anglican women's communities considered in this volume challenge the stereotype of mainstream liberal Christianity, so Goldberg's analysis of Jewish non-affiliated groups in Toronto and Power's of the Church of Latter-Day Saints in small-town Alberta belie any stereotypes about immigrant religiosities.

When all nine chapters are taken together, provocative themes and questions suggest themselves. What differences, if any, would we find if we were to compare rural, suburban, and urban religiosities? How might the women from the Albertan LDS Church and the Ontarian Hindu communities (or any of the groups studied here) encounter each other in the context of multiculturalism? In what ways do race and ethnicity shape Canadian religiosities? And how do economic forces, especially expressed in globalizing pressures on the hinterland, influence women's beliefs and practices?

There are, of course, many more questions to be asked and researched. It is our sincere hope that this volume will function as a catalyst in encouraging and focusing more scholarship on women and their religiosities in Canada. ●

Note

1. James Clifford, "Varieties of Indigenous Experience: Diasporas, Homelands, Sovereignties," in Indigenous *Experience Today*, ed. Marisol de la Cadena and Orin Starn (Oxford and New York: Berg, 2007), 217.

Bibliography

Clifford, James. "Varieties of Indigenous Experience: Diasporas, Homelands, Sovereignties." In *Indigenous Experience Today*, ed. Marisol de la Cadena and Orin Starn, 197–224. Oxford and New York: Berg, 2007.

Bibliography for Women and Religion from 1951 to 2013

'Abdu'l-Bahá. *Women: Extracts from the Writings of Bahá'u'lláh, 'Abdu'l–Bahá, Shoghi Effendi, and the Universal House of Justice.* Compiled by the Research Department of the Universal House of Justice. Thornhill, ON: Bahá'í Canada Publications, 1986.

Alcoff, Linda, and Elizabeth Potter, eds. *Feminist Epistemologies.* New York: Routledge, 1993.

Atkinson, C. W. "Precious Balsam in a Fragile Glass: The Ideology of Virginity in the Later Middle Ages." *Journal of Family History* 8, no. 2 (Summer 1983): 131–43.

Aune Kristin, Sonya Sharma, and Giselle Vincett, eds. *Women and Religion in the West Challenging Secularization.* Aldershot, England: Ashgate, 2008.

Bakht, Natasha, ed. *Arbitration, Religion, and Family Law: Private Justice on the Backs of Women.* National Association of Women and the Law. Ottawa: National Association of Women and the Law, 2005.

Bannerji, H. "The Paradox of Diversity: The Construction of a Multicultural Canada and 'Women of Colour.'" *Women's Studies International Forum* 23, no. 5 (2000): 537–60.

Beaman, L. "Church, State, and the Legal Interpretation of Polygamy in Canada." *Nova Religio: The Journal of Alternative and Emergent Religions* 8, no. 1 (2004): 20–38.

———. "Molly Mormons, Mormon Feminists, and Moderates: Religious Diversity and the Latter-Day Saints Church." *Sociology of Religion* 62, no. 1 (2001): 65–86.

Beaman, Lori, Nancy Nason-Clark, and Rubina Ramji. "The Difference That Gender Makes." In *Growing up Canadian Muslims, Hindus, Buddhists*, edited by Peter Beyer and Rubina Ramji, 235–61. Montreal and Kingston: McGill-Queen's University Press, 2013.

Beavis, M. A., with E. Guillemin and B. Pell, eds. *Feminist Theology with a Canadian Accent: Canadian Perspectives on Contextual Feminist Theology*. Ottawa: Novalis, 2008.

Bednarowski, Mary Farrell. "Outside the Mainstream: Women's Religions and Women Religion Leaders in Nineteenth Century America." *Journal of the American Academy of Religion* 48 (1980): 207–31.

———. *The Religious Imagination of American Women*. Bloomington and Indianapolis: Indiana University Press, 1999.

Beecher, M. U. "Mormon Women in Southern Alberta: The Pioneer Years". In *The Mormon Presence in Canada*, edited by B. Y. Card, H. C. Northcott, J. E. Foster, H. Palmer, and G. K. Jarvis, 211–30. Edmonton: University of Alberta Press, 1990.

Bendroth, Margaret Lamberts. "Millennial Themes and Private Visions: The Problem of 'Woman's Place' in Religious History." *Fides Et Historia* 20, no. 2 (1988): 24–30.

Benowitz, June Melby. *Encyclopedia of American Women and Religion*. Santa Barbara, CA: ABC-CLIO, 1998.

Berktay, Fatmagul. *Women and Religion*. Translated by Belma Otus-Baskett. Montreal: Black Rose Books, 1998.

Besant, Annie. *Annie Besant: An Autobiography*. Adyar: Theosophical Publishing House, 1995. First published in 1893 by T. F. Unwin.

Bowman, Marion. "Devotion to St. Gerard Majella in Newfoundland: The Saint System in Operation and Transition." Unpublished MA thesis, Memorial University of Newfoundland, 1985.

Braude, Ann. *Sisters and Saints: Women and American Religion*. New York: Oxford University Press, 2008.

Brekus, Catherine A. *The Religious History of American Women: Reimagining the Past*. Chapel Hill: University of North Carolina Press, 2007.

Bronner, Leila Leah. *From Eve to Esther: Rabbinic Reconstructions of Biblical Women*. Louisville, KY: Westminster John Knox Press, 1994.

Campbell, Peter. *Rose Henderson: A Woman for the People*. Montreal: McGill-Queen's University Press, 2010.

Castelli, Elizabeth A., and Rosamond C. Rodman, eds. *Women, Gender, Religion: A Reader*. New York: Palgrave, 2001.

Cima, Gay Gibson. *Early American Women Critics: Performance, Religion, Race*. Cambridge: Cambridge University Press, 2006.

Clark, Elizabeth A., and Herbert Warren Richardson, eds. *Women and Religion: A Feminist Sourcebook of Christian Thought*. New York: Harper & Row, 1977.

Collier-Thomas, Bettye. *Jesus, Jobs, and Justice: African-American Women and Religion*. New York: Knopf, 2010.

Conway, Sheelagh. *A Woman and Catholicism: My Break with the Roman Catholic Church*. New York: PaperJacks, 1987.

Cook, Sharon Anne. *Through Sunshine and Shadow: The Women's Christian Temperance Union: Evangelicalism and Reform in Ontario, 1874–1930*. Montreal: McGill-Queen's University Press, 1995.

Cornwall, M. "The Institutional Role of Mormon Women." In *Contemporary Mormonism: Social Science Perspectives*, edited by M. Cornwall, T. B. Heaton, and L. A. Young, 239–64. Chicago: University of Illinois Press, 1994.

Cort, John E. "Models of and for the Study of the Jains." *Method & Theory in the Study of Religion* 2, no. 1 (1990): 42–71.

Coulter, J. "Remarks on the Conceptualisation of Social Structure." In *Philosophy of the Social Sciences* 12, no. 1 (1982): 33–46.

Coward, Harold. "The South Asian Religious Diaspora in Britain, Canada, and the United States." *Nova Religio: The Journal of Alternative and Emergent Religions* 8, no. 2 (2004): 127–29.

Cranston, Sylvia. *H. P. B: The Extraordinary Life and Influence of Helena Blavatsky, Founder of the Modern Theosophical Movement*. New York: Jeremy P. Tarcher/Putnam, 1993.

Crellin, John K. *Home Medicine: The Newfoundland Experience*. Montreal and Kingston: McGill-Queen's University Press, 1994.

Cressy, David. "Purification, Thanksgiving, and the Churching of Women in Post-Reformation England." *Past & Present* 141 (November 1993): 106–47.

Crosson, S. "Searching for May Maxwell: Women's Role in Shaping Early Bahá'í Culture 1898–1940." PhD dissertation, University of Saskatchewan, 2012.

Curly Tó Aheedlíinii , Berard Haile, Irvy W. Goossen, and Karl W. Luckert, eds. *Women versus Men: A Conflict of Navajo Emergence*. Lincoln: University of Nebraska Press, 1981.

Danylewycz, M. *Taking the Veil: An Alternative to Marriage, Motherhood, and Spinsterhood in Quebec, 1840–1920*. Toronto: McClelland and Stewart, 1987.

Dempsey, Corinne G., ed. *Kerala Christian Sainthood Collisions of Culture and Worldview in South India*. Oxford: Oxford University Press, 2001.

Dixon, Joy. *Divine Feminine*. Baltimore: Johns Hopkins University Press, 2001.

Dossa, Parin. *Racialized Bodies, Disabling Worlds: Storied Lives of Immigrant Muslim Women*. Toronto: University of Toronto Press, 2009.

Drinnon, Richard. *Rebel in Paradise: A Biography of Emma Goldman*. Chicago: University of Chicago Press, 1982. First published in 1961 by University of Chicago Press.

Ebaugh, Helen R. F. "The Muslim Veil in North America: Issues and Debates." *Sociology of Religion* 66, no. 2 (2005): 201–2.

Echevarria, L. "Life Histories of Baháʼí Women in Canada: Constructing Religious Identity in the Twentieth Century." In *Theology and Religion*. American University Study Series 7. New York: Peter Lang Publishing, 2011.

Eglin, P. "Members' Gendering Work: 'Women,' 'Feminists,' and Membership Categorization Analysis." *Discourse & Society* 13, no. 6 (2002): 819–25.

Ehman, Daniel, CSsR. "The Mothers' Saint." Toronto: The League of St. Gerard, 1951.

Eisler, Riane. *The Chalice & the Blade*. New York: HarperCollins Publishers, 1987.

Elder, J., C. O'Connell, and Canadian Corporation for Studies in Religion. *Voices and Echoes: Canadian Women's Spirituality*. Waterloo, ON: Published for the Canadian Corporation for Studies in Religion/Corporation Canadienne des Sciences Religieuses by Wilfrid Laurier University Press, 1997.

Ellwood, Robert S. "The American Theosophical Synthesis." In *The Occult in America: New Historical Perspectives*, edited by Howard Kerr and Charles K. Crow, 111–34. Urbana: University of Illinois Press, 1983.

Enzner-Probst, Brigitte. "Waiting for Delivery: Counseling Pregnant Women as an Issue for the Church." *International Journal of Practical Theology* 8, no. 2 (2004): 185–201.

Eskenazi, Tamara Cohn, and Andrea L. Wiess, eds. *The Torah: A Women's Commentary*. New York: URJ Press, 2008.

Fall, V. J. *"Except the Lord Build the House . . .": A History of the Catholic Women's League of Canada 1920–1990*. Winnipeg: Catholic Women's League of Canada, 1990.

Farley, Ronnie. *Women of the Native Struggle: Portraits and Testimony of Native America Women*. (The Library of the American Indian.) New York: Orion Books, 1993.

Fay, T. J. *A History of Canadian Catholics: Gallicanism, Romanism, and Canadianism*. Montreal: McGill-Queen's University Press, 2002.

Foster, L. *Women, Family, and Utopia: Communal Experiments of the Shakers, the Oneida Community, and the Mormons*. New York: Syracuse University Press, 1991.

Gerhart, Mary, Morny Joy, and E. K. Neumaier-Dargyay, eds. *Gender, Genre, and Religion Feminist Reflections*. Waterloo, ON: Wilfrid Laurier University Press for the Calgary Institute for the Humanities, 1995.

Grant, John Webster. *A Profusion of Spires: Religion in Nineteenth-Century Ontario*. Toronto: University of Toronto Press, 1988.

Greenspan, Frederick, ed. *Women and Judaism: New Insights and Scholarship*. New York: New York University Press, 2009.

Greer, Mary K. *Women of the Golden Dawn: Rebels and Priestesses*. Rochester, VT: Park Street Press, 1995.

Griffith, R. Marie. *Born Again Bodies: Flesh and Spirit in American Christianity*. Berkeley: University of California Press, 2004.

Holden, Pat. *Women's Religious Experience*. London: Croom Helm & Totowa, NJ: Barnes & Noble, 1983.

hooks, b. "Choosing the Margin as a Space of Radical Openness." In *Yearning: Race, Gender, and Cultural Politics*, 145–53. Toronto: Between the Lines, 1990.

——. *Feminist Theory: From Margin to Center*. 2nd ed. Cambridge, MA: South End, 2000.

Houlbrooke, Margaret. *Rite Out of Time: A Study of the Churching of Women and Its Survival in the Twentieth Century*. Donington: Shaun Tyas, 2012.

Jakobsh, Doris, ed. *World Religions Canadian Perspectives—Eastern Traditions*. Toronto: Nelson Education, 2013.

James, Gene. "Religion and Women's Roles." *Dialogue & Alliance* 2, no. 3 (1988): 3–94.

Johnson, E. Pauline, ed. *The Iroquois Women of Canada*. Marlborough, England: Adam Matthew Digital, 2007.

Kassam, Zayn, ed. *Women and Islam*. Santa Barbara, CA: Praeger, 2010.

Keller, Rosemary Skinner, and Rosemary Radford Ruether. *In Our Own Voices: Four Centuries of American Women's Religious Writing*. San Francisco, CA: Harper San Francisco, 1995.

Keller, Rosemary Skinner, Rosemary Radford Ruether, and Marie Cantlon, eds. *Encyclopedia of Women and Religion in North America*. Bloomington: Indiana University Press, 2006.

Keough, Willeen. *The Slender Thread: Irish Women on the Southern Avalon, 1750–1860*. New York: Columbia University Press, 2006.

Khan, J. A. "Promoting the Equality of Women and Men: The Role of the Covenant." *Journal of Bahá'í Studies* 10, no. 1/2 (2000): 71–90.

——. *Prophet's Daughter: The Life and Legacy of Bahíyyih Khánum, Outstanding Heroine of the Bahá'í Faith*. Wilmette, IL: Bahá'í Publishing Trust, 2005.

King, Ursula. "Gender and the Study of Religion." In *Religion and Gender*, edited by Ursula King, 1–41. Oxford: Blackwell Publishers, 1995.

Knödel, Natalie. "Reconsidering an Obsolete Rite: The Churching of Women and Feminist Liturgical Theology." *Feminist Theology* 5, no. 14 (1997): 106–25.

Kraft, Francis. "Orthodox *Minyan* Has Torah Honours for Women." *Canadian Jewish News*, November 6, 2008.

Lacelle, Elisabeth J., ed. *La Femme et la Religion au Canada Français: Un Fait Socio-culturel, Perspectives et Prospectives*. Montreal: Éditions Bellarmin, 1979.

Leonard, E. "The Process of Transformation: Women Religious and the Study of Theology, 1955–1980." In *Changing Habits: Women's Religious Orders in Canada*, edited by E. M. Smyth, 230–46. Ottawa: Novalis, 2007.

L'Estrange, Elizabeth. *Holy Motherhood: Gender, Dynasty, and Visual Culture in the Later Middle Ages*. New York: Manchester University Press, 2008.

LeVine, Sarah. *The Saint of Kathmandu: And Other Tales of the Sacred in Distant Lands*. Boston: Beacon Press, 2008.

MacDonald, H., and E. Smyth. "Imaging *Perfectae Caritatis*: Viewing the Consecrated Life through the Mother House Museums of Canadian Women Religious." In *Vatican II: Experiences canadiennes — Canadian Experiences*, edited by M. Attridge, C. E. Clifford, and G. Routhier, 476–94. Ottawa: University of Ottawa Press, 2011.

Macey, Marie. *Multiculturalism, Religion, and Women: Doing Harm by Doing Good?* Basingstoke: Palgrave Macmillan, 2009.

MacIntosh, Heather, and Dan Shapiro. *Gender, Culture, and Religion: Tackling Some Difficult Questions*. Calgary: Sheldon Chumir Foundation for Ethics in Leadership, 2012.

Malone, M. T. *Women and Christianity*. Vol. 1. Ottawa: Novalis, 2000.

McClory, R. *Turning Point: The Inside Story of the Papal Birth Control Commission, and How Humanae Vitae Changed the Life of Patty Crowley and the Future of the Church*. New York: Crossroad, 1995.

McNamara, J. A. *Sisters in Arms: Catholic Nuns through Two Millennia*. Cambridge, MA: Harvard University Press, 1996.

Min, P. G. *Preserving Ethnicity through Religion in America: Korean and Indian Hindus across Generations*. New York: New York University Press, 2010.

Moorthy, K. K. *Mother of Melmaruvathur and Her Miracles*. Madras, India: Oxford Printers, 1986.

Morgan, Cecilia Louise. *Public Men and Virtuous Women: The Gendered Languages of Religion and Politics in Upper Canada, 1791–1850*. Toronto: University of Toronto Press, 1996.

Morgan, Sue, and Jacqueline deVries, eds. *Women, Gender, and Religious Cultures in Britain, 1800–1940*. New York: Routledge, 2010.

Morrill, Susanna Morrill. *White Roses on the Floor of Heaven: Mormon Women's Popular Theology, 1880–1920*. New York: Routledge, 2007.

Murray, Hilda Chaulk. *More Than Fifty Percent: Woman's Life in a Newfoundland Outport, 1900–1950*. St. John's: Breakwater, 1979.

National Film Board of Canada. *Behind the Veil: Nuns*. Montreal: National Film Board of Canada, 1984.

Neis, Barbara. "From 'Shipped Girls' to 'Brides of the State': The Transition from Familial to Social Patriarchy in the Newfoundland Fishing Industry." *Canadian Journal of Regional Science* 16, no. 2 (1993): 185–202.

Northup, Lesley A. *Ritualizing Women: Patterns of Spirituality*. Cleveland: Pilgrim Press, 1997.

O'Connor, Karen, ed. *Gender and Women's Leadership: A Reference Handbook*. Thousand Oaks, CA: Sage Reference, 2010.

Opp, James. *The Lord for the Body: Religion, Medicine, and Protestant Faith Healing in Canada, 1880–1930*. Montreal: McGill-Queen's University Press, 2005.

Orsi, Robert A. *Between Heaven and Earth: The Religious Worlds People Make and the Scholars Who Study Them*. Princeton: Princeton University Press, 2005.

———. *The Madonna of 115th Street: Faith and Community in Italian Harlem, 1880–1950*. New Haven: Yale University Press, 1985.

———. *Thank You, St. Jude: Women's Devotion the Patron Saint of Hopeless Causes*. New Haven and London: Yale University Press, 1996.

Palmer, Susan J. *Moon Sisters, Krishna Mothers, Fajneesh Lovers: Women's Roles in New Religions*. Syracuse, NY: Syracuse University Press, 1994.

Pearson, Anne M. *"Because It Gives Me Peace of Mind": Ritual Fasts in the Religious Lives of Women in North India*. Albany: State University of New York Press, 1996.

———. "Being Hindu in Canada: Personal Narratives from First and Second Generation Immigrant Hindu Women." *Religious Studies and Theology* 23, no. 1 (2004): 55–88.

———. "Mothers and Daughters: The Transmission of Religious Practice and the Formation of Hindu Identity among Hindu Immigrant Women in Ontario." In *Hindu Diaspora: Global Perspectives*, edited by T. S. Rukmani, 427–42. Montreal: Concordia University, 1999.

Pechilis, Karen, ed. *The Graceful Guru: Hindu Female Gurus in India and the United States*. New York: Oxford University Press, 2004.

Pike, Sarah M. *New Age and Neopagan Religions in America*. New York: Columbia University Press, 2004.

Pollock, Griselda, and Victoria Turvey Sauron, eds. *The Sacred and the Feminine: Imagination and Sexual Difference.* London: I. B. Tauris, 2007.

Ray, Donna E. "A View from the Churchwife's Pew: The Development of Rites around Childbirth in the Anglican Communion." *Anglican & Episeopal History* 69, no. 4 (2000): 443–73.

Read, Donna, Martha Henry, Merlin Stone, Jean Shinoda Bolen, Charlene Spretnak, and Starhawk. "Goddess Remembered." In *Women and Spirituality.* National Film Board of Canada. Montreal: Studio D, National Film Board of Canada, 1989. Reproduction 2007.

Redekop, Gloria Neufeld. *The Work of Their Hands: Mennonite Women's Societies in Canada.* Waterloo, ON: Canadian Corporation for Studies in Religion/Corporation Canadienne des Sciences Religieuses and Wilfrid Laurier University Press, 1996.

Rieder, Paula M. "Insecure Borders: Symbols of Clerical Privilege and Gender Ambiguity in the Liturgy of Churching." In *The Material Culture of Sex, Procreation, and Marriage in Premodern Europe,* edited by Anne L. McClanan and Karen Rosoff Encarnación, 93–114. New York: Palgrave, 2002.

——. *On the Purification of Women: Churching in Northern France, 1100–1500.* New York: Palgrave. 2006.

Rieti, Barbara. *Making Witches: Newfoundland Traditions of Spells and Counterspells.* Montreal and Kingston: McGill-Queen's University Press, 2008.

Ross, S. *Companions on the Journey: The Catholic Women's League of Canada 1990–2005.* Winnipeg: Catholic Women's League of Canada, 2007.

——. "For God and Canada": The Early Years of the Catholic Women's League in Alberta. *CCHA Historical Studies* 62 (1996): 89–108.

Ross, Tamar. *Expanding the Palace of Torah: Orthodoxy and Feminism.* Lebanon, NH: Brandeis University Press, 2004.

Ruether, Rosemary Radford, ed. *Religion and Sexism: Images of Woman in the Jewish and Christian Traditions,* 150–83. New York: Simon and Schuster, 1974.

——. *Women-Church: Theology and Practice of Feminist Liturgical Communities.* San Francisco: Harper & Row, 1985.

Ruether, Rosemary Radford, and Rosemary Skinner Keller. *Women and Religion in America.* San Francisco: Harper & Row, 1981.

Savage, Candace. *Our Nell: A Scrapbook Biography of Nellie L. McClung.* Saskatoon: Western Producer Prairie Books, 1979.

Schmeigelow, Phillipa. "Canadian Feminists in the International Arena: A Retrospective." *Canadian Woman Studies* 17, no. 2 (1997): 85–87.

Skjonsberg, Else. *A Special Caste? Tamil Women of Sri Lanka.* London: Zed Press, 1982.

Spiegel, Fredelle Zaiman. *Women's Wages, Women's Worth: Politics, Religion, and Equity.* New York: Continuum, 1994.

Swidler, Arlene, and Leonard, eds. *Women Priests: A Catholic Commentary on the Vatican Declaration.* New York: Paulist Press, 1977.

Trothen, Tracy J. *Linking Sexuality & Gender: Naming Violence against Women in the United Church of Canada.* Waterloo, ON: Canadian Corporation for Studies in Religion/ Corporation Canadienne des Sciences Religieuses and Wilfrid Laurier University Press, 2003.

van den Hoonaard, D. K., and W. C. van den Hoonaard. *The Equality of Women and Men: The Experience of the Bahá'í Community of Canada.* Douglas, NB: Self-published, 2006.

Warne, R. R. *Literature as Pulpit: The Christian Social Activism of Nellie L. McClung.* Waterloo, ON: Wilfrid Laurier University Press, 1993.

Wehr, Kathryn. "Understanding Ritual Purity and Sin in the Churching of Women: From Ontological to Pedagogical to Eschatological." *St. Vladimir's Theological Quarterly* 55, no. 1 (2001): 85–105.

Wessinger, Catherine, ed. *Women's Leadership in Marginal Religions: Explorations outside the Mainstream.* Chicago: University of Illinois Press, 1993.

Wheeler, Rachel M. "Women and Christian Practice in a Mahican Village." *Religion and American Culture* 13, no. 1 (2003): 27–67.

White, O. K., Jr. "A Feminist Challenge: 'Mormons for ERA' as an Internal Social Movement." *Journal of Ethnic Studies* 13, no. 1 (1985): 29–37.

Whiteley, Marilyn Fardig. *Canadian Methodist Women, 1766–1925: Marys, Marthas, Mothers in Israel.* Waterloo, ON: Canadian Corporation for Studies in Religion/Corporation Canadienne des Sciences Religieuses and Wilfrid Laurier University Press, 2005.

About the Contributors

MARION BOWMAN lectures in Religious Studies at The Open University, UK. A former president of both the British Association for the Study of Religions and The Folklore Society, she works at the interstices of religious studies and folklore. Her research focuses on vernacular religion, religion as it is lived in specific locations, including Newfoundland and Glastonbury (a microcosm of contemporary spirituality in the UK). In 2012 she co-edited *Vernacular Religion in Everyday Life: Expressions of Belief* (Routledge) with Ulo Valk.

LYNN ECHEVARRIA received her BA and master's degrees from York and Carleton Universities in Sociology and Women's Studies, and a PhD from the University of Essex, UK. She was instructor and coordinator for Yukon College Women's and Gender Studies Program 2002–2012. Lynn is the author of *Life Histories of Bahá'í Women in Canada: Constructing Religious Identity in the Twentieth Century* (Peter Lang, 2011), and several reviews, book chapters, and journal articles. Currently she enjoys living a country life and as a Professor Emerita continues her research and writing.

AVIVA GOLDBERG teaches in the Humanities department of the Faculty of Liberal Arts and Professional Studies at York University, specializing in the area of Religious Studies. Her research interests include contemporary Jewish theologies, women's rituals, and spirituality. She is the rabbi of Congregation Shir Libeynu, an unaffiliated liberal and inclusive congregation in downtown Toronto. Dr. Goldberg is a lecturer, teacher, moderator, and adult education workshop leader in the areas of Jewish liturgy and ritual.

BECKY R. LEE is an Associate Professor of Religious Studies in the Humanities department at York University. Her teaching and research interests include the intersection of gender and religion, the methods and theories of gender histories, and medieval and modern religiosities. Her recent publications include "Unwed Mothers in Medieval England" (2014) and "The Historian as Translator of Past Cultures: Translation(s) of Margery Kempe and her *Book*" (2012). She has published several articles on the churching of women in medieval England.

GILLIAN MCCANN is an Associate Professor in the Religions and Cultures department at Nipissing University, North Bay. Gillian graduated from the Centre for the Study of Religion, University of Toronto, in 2002. Her research interests include Theosophical utopianism, the connection between occult movements and Eastern philosophy, and problematizing the idea of secularism. She is the author of "A Pilgrim Forever: The Life and Thought of Albert Smythe" (2010) and *Vanguard of the New Age: The Toronto Theosophical Society, 1891–1945* (McGill-Queen's UP, 2012).

BONNIE MORGAN holds an MA (History) from Memorial University and a joint MLIS/LLB from Dalhousie University. She was awarded a PhD (History) from the University of New Brunswick in 2014. Her dissertation, "Conceiving Christianity: Anglican Women and Lived Religion in Mid-Twentieth-Century Conception Bay, Newfoundland," explored connections between women's work in the family economy, the construction of gender relations, and the expression of religious belief and practice in rural communities.

ANNE MACKENZIE PEARSON teaches in the Department of Religious Studies at McMaster University. She specializes in Hinduism and South Asian studies and is the author of *Because It Gives Me Peace of Mind: Ritual Fasts in the Lives of Hindu Women* (SUNY, 1996) and a number of articles and book chapters on Hinduism and Hindu women in Canada, among other topics. Preeti Nayak, her co-author, is a young Konkani-Canadian living in the Greater Toronto Area. She holds a M.Phil. in Education (University of Cambridge) and a BA in Anthropology and Religious Studies (McMaster University).

KATE POWER is a critical discourse analyst, who earned her PhD in Applied Linguistics at Lancaster University, UK. Her doctoral thesis looked at how people give off a sense of their religious identity when talking about contemporary social issues, such as Canadian multiculturalism. While teaching academic research and writing at the University of British Columbia, Kate continues to research and write across academic disciplines—with interests in religiosity, gender/sexuality, international development, economics, and popular culture. Kate is currently Secretary for the International Gender and Language Association, and Managing Editor for the journal *Secularism and Nonreligion.*

NANETTE R. SPINA is an Assistant Professor of Religion at the University of Georgia. Her research interests include Hindu traditions in India, Sri Lanka, and North America; religion and migration; and religion and gender. She has conducted field studies among religious communities in South Asia and North America. Currently she is focused on transnationalism and diaspora communities, and foregrounds the common boundaries that associate religion with notions of identity, gender, and ethnicity in North America.

TAK-LING TERRY WOO teaches in the Humanities department at York University. Her research interests include theories about women in Chinese religions and their lived experiences, and Chinese religiosities in diaspora. She is the author of "An Integrated Approach to a Philosophical Study of Women from Tang to Song" (Bloomsbury, 2016), "Chinese and Korean Religions," in *A Concise Introduction to World Religions,* 3rd edition (Oxford UP, 2015), and "Chinese Popular Religion in Diaspora: A Case Study of Shrines in Toronto's Chinatowns" (2010).

Index

Bahíyyih Khánum, 237, 258n24

Baird, Elsie, 49

Baker, Carolyn, 153

Barr, Dudley, 217

BCP (Book of Common Prayer), 39, 40

Beaman, Lori, 161

Bednarowski, Mary Farrell, xi, 199

belief story, 8

Bennett, Gillian, 8

Besant, Annie, 199, 201, 205, 211

Biernacki, Loriliai, 330n23

Birt, Anita, 87

birth control, 80–82

Blackwood, Algernon, 207

Blavatsky, Helena, 199, 204, 220

body: and religious belief, 36–37, 56n5, 56n7; women's, 37–38

Book of Common Prayer (BCP), 39, 40

Bostonians (James), 206

Bouclin, Marie, 89

Bourgeoys, Marguerite, 68

Bramadat, Paul, x

brides of Christ. *See* women's religious communities (nuns)

Bridle, August, 211

British North American Act (1867), 69

Bronner, Leah Leila, 116

Brown, Penelope, 165, 166

Brubaker, Rogers, 145

Bruns, Gerald L., 116

Bucholtz, Mary, 145, 146

Buddhism, 205

Bury, Fred, 206

Bussey, Minnie, 47

Butler, Gladys, 44–45, 49

Campbell, Peter, 198

Canada: and birth control, 80; Christian history in, 65, 68, 203; harmonial religions in, 207; immigration policy, 272; multiculturalism in, 170, 273; women in mid-twentieth century, 240–41. *See also* Upper Canada

Canadian Catholics for Women's Ordination/Catholic Network for Women's Equality (CCWO/ CNWE): approach to, xiii–xiv, 65, 66–67; beginnings of, 83, 84; and Canadian Conference of Catholic Bishops, 85, 87; mandate of, 84–85, 86–87; marginality of, 87, 88, 91–92; membership decline of, 90; name change of, 86–87; opposition to, 86; ordination of members of, 88–89; recent activity by, 90, 91; relationship with media, 87–88

Canadian Citizenship Act (1947), 272

Canadian Conference of Catholic Bishops (CCCB): and Canadian Catholics for Women's Ordination, 85, 87; and Catholic Women's League, 76–77, 78; on *Humanae vitae*, 80–81; on sanctity of life and women's issues, 83, 84, 85

Canadian Council of Conservative Synagogues, 111

Canadian Multiculturalism Act (1988), 170, 273

Canadian Theosophist (journal), 211, 212, 220

Canadian Yeshiva and Rabbinical School, 111

Carr, Bill, 249–50

Carroll, Francis, 76

caste, 273, 277, 299n.17. *See also jati*

Catholic Church. *See* Canadian Catholics for Women's Ordination/Catholic Network for Women's Equality; Canadian Conference of Catholic Bishops; Catholic Women's League of Canada; devotional magazines; devotional objects; Majella, Gerard, St., in Newfoundland; Roman Catholic Church; Roman Catholic feminist movements; women's religious communities (nuns)

Catholic Church Extension Society of Canada, 73

Catholic feminism, 74–75. *See also* Roman Catholic feminist movements

Catholic Network for Women's Equality. *See* Canadian Catholics for Women's Ordination/Catholic Network for Women's Equality

Catholic Women's League of Canada (CWL): approach to, xiii–xiv, 65, 66–67; agenda of, 75–77, 78–79; beginnings of, 73–74, 95n60; and birth control debate, 81–82; and Canadian Conference of Catholic Bishops, 75–77, 78; Catholic feminism of, 74–75; and mainstream feminism, 79; marginality of, 75–76, 78–79, 91–92; membership decline of, 90; political action by, 77–78; recent activity by,

90, 91; and sanctity of life issues, 82–83; success of, 78

CCCB. *See* Canadian Conference of Catholic Bishops

CCWO/CNWE. *See* Canadian Catholics for Women's Ordination/Catholic Network for Women's Equality

Centre for Life (Newfoundland and Labrador Right to Life Association), 25–26

CEWA (Church of England Women's Association), 44, 49

Chabad-Lubavitch, 131n10

Charity Chicks, 157. *See also* Claresholm LDS Relief Society members

Charles, Maggie, 166–67

chazzanut (cantorial duties), 119, 125–26

childbirth, 36, 41, 44. *See also* churching; lying-in; Majella, Gerard, St., in Newfoundland; midwives

Chinmaya Mission (Hindu), 297n8

Chown, Alice, 200

Christian, William A., Jr., 3–4

Christian Guardian (newspaper), 205–6

Christianity: in Canada, 65, 68, 203; patriarchy in, 200–201. *See also* churching; Church of England; Roman Catholic Church

Christian Science, 201, 204, 221

chuppah, 115, 133n38

churching: approach to, xiii, 35–36, 338; beliefs about, 38–39, 39–42, 43, 52, 54–55; in Eastern Orthodox Church, 56n15; and gender and sexuality, 53–54; history of, 39–42;

and midwives, 47–48; perceived
unpopularity of, 57n22; practices
related to, 42–43, 47, 50–52, 52–53
Church of England, 38, 39–42, 68. *See also*
churching; Conception Bay (NL)
Church of England Women's
Association (CEWA), 44, 49
Church of Jesus Christ of Latter-Day
Saints: and African Americans,
182n112; in Claresholm (AB),
144–45, 168; on common terms for,
180n82; Correlation Program, 144;
history of, 142–43; in southwestern
Alberta, 143–44; women in, 144.
See also Claresholm LDS Relief
Society members
Church of Jesus Christ of Latter-Day
Saints Relief Society: approach
to, xiv–xv, 338; history of, 142;
membership in, 148–50; work of,
144. *See also* Claresholm LDS Relief
Society members
Claresholm (AB), 144–45, 168
Claresholm LDS Relief Society members:
approach to, xiv–xv, 141–42, 146,
170, 338; on belonging, 147–52;
on non-belonging, 152–56; other-
categorization of, 156–60; self-
identification by, 170; stance-taking
on non-religious matters, 160–69;
transcription symbols used for,
178n63
Claresholm Ministerial Association,
145, 168
Clarke, Brian P., 72

class, social: and churching, 38, 39, 52,
53–54
Classical Judaism, 111
clerical sexual abuse scandal, 24, 29
Cleverdon, Catherine, 208
Clifford, James, 337
Codd, Clara, 217–18
Committee for Social Reconstruction
(TTS), 209
companionate marriage, 201, 223n19
Conception Bay (NL): approach to
churching in, xiii, 35–36; childbirth
in, 36, 44; churching in, 41, 47,
50–52, 52–53, 54–55; lying-in in,
45–46; midwives in, 44–45, 47–50.
See also churching; lying-in
Congregation of the Most Holy
Redeemer. *See* Redemptorist Order
Congregation Shaar Hashomayim
(Montreal), 131n23
Congregation Shir Libeynu (Toronto):
approach to, xiv, 338; analysis of,
123–24; author's participation in,
117–18, 122–23; and Leah, 116–17;
mission statement of, 119; overview
of, 118–19; services and prayers at,
119–22, 134n48; as unaffiliated, 119,
124; venues for, 119, 134n46. *See also*
Jewish women; Judaism, in Toronto
Conservative Judaism, 110–11
consultation (Bahá'í), 246–48
Cooper, Frederick, 145
Corriveau, Fr. Ray, 26
Cort, John E., 198
Covenant (Bahá'í), 18

Crellin, John, 50

Cressy, David, 38–39, 47

Curran, Charles, 86

CWL. *See* Catholic Women's League
    of Canada

Dakhká Khwáan Dancers, 254–55

Danylewycz, Marta, 69, 70

Davis, Lelia, 209

Davis, Natalie Zemon, 44

Dawe, Eliza Jane, 45, 48, 49

Dawe, Judy (Rideout), 51

Dawe, Marge (Saunders), 47, 50, 51

Dawe, Rachel, 49

Day, Richard, 168

Dempsey, Corinne, 313

Denison, Flora MacDonald, 209–10, 213,
    223n11

Despard, Charlotte, 199, 202, 223n11

Devi, Rukmini, 199

devotional magazines (Roman Catholic):
    and children named after
    St. Gerard Majella, 13; *Madonna*
    (magazine), 10, 12, 13; on medals,
    12–13; participatory aspect of,
    13–14; popularity of, 12; and
    St. Gerard Majella, 9–10, 12, 14

devotional objects (Roman Catholic):
    importance of, 19; medals, 9, 12–13,
    16; statues, 23; of St. Gerard Majella,
    9, 16–17, 19–20

diaspora: indigenous, 337; and social
    mores, 314–15; use of term, x

divine feminine, 325–26. *See also* goddess
    (Hindu)

diya (Hindu), 277. *See also arati;* Hindu
    immigrant women

Dixon, Joy, 198, 202, 203, 211

Douglas, Mary, 169

Driver, Tom F., 118, 124, 128

Droogers, André, 142

Dunne, Veronica, 83

d'Youville, Marguerite, 68

Eastern Orthodox Church, 56n15

Ehman, Daniel, 11

Eikon (magazine), 10

Eisler, Riane, 221

Eller, Cynthia, 221

Ellis-Bolles, May, 234

Ellwood, Robert, 199, 205

embodied religious practice, 36–37, 50.
    See also churching

emic perspective, 198

enclavist (Judaism), 112–13, 129

Engelke, Matthew, 29

enlightenment: and religion, 141, 198–99

ethno-hermeneutics, 117

Eyford, Ruth: introduction to, 241,
    242–43, 255n1; roles of in Bahá'í
    Faith, 247–48, 250–51; on spiritual
    growth in Bahá'í Faith, 244–45

Fagan, Rachel, 47

faith healing, 37

fasts, ritual (Hindu), 282–84, 290, 293

feminism: Catholic, 74–75; on
    marginality, 66, 197; Marxist,
    on religion, 198–99; Mormon, 144;
    movements within, 93n27; and

Roman Catholic Church, 65–66.
See also feminist theology

feminist spirituality. See feminist
theology

feminist theology: explanation of, 38;
Stuckey on, 118, 123, 127; and
Theosophy, 202, 220, 221

Finegold, Rachel Kohl, 131n23

Finke, Roger, 207

First Nations peoples: and Bahá'í, 236,
251–52, 253–55; spirituality of, 337;
and Theosophy, 205, 220

Fitzgerald, Richard, 161

Flueckiger, Joyce, 332n31

Foucault, Michel, 53

Fuller, Robert C., 221

Ganesh (Hindu deity), 280–81

Geertz, Armin W., 117

gender: and churching, 53–54; and
faith healing, 37; and religion
and spirituality, 29; Theosophical
debates on, 202–3; and women's
theology, 38. See also gender
equality; gender roles

gender equality: in Adhi Parasakthi
organization, 301–2, 308, 309, 312;
in Bahá'í Faith, 236, 249–50, 257n18,
260n46, 261n63; and Hinduism,
291–94

gender roles: changing among
immigrant Hindus, 286–87;
and women religious, 67

Glazer, Henry, 119

goddess (Hindu): Adhi Parasakthi/Śakti,
306, 307–8, 324, 325–26; Durga, 285;
history of, 331nn29–30; Kul-Devi,
277, 283; Lakshmi, 277, 285; Navratri
festival, 281; and women, 332n31

Godwin, Joscelyn, 204

Goffman, Erving, 165–66

Goldman, Emma, 210

Gore-Booth, Eva, 202

Grant, John Webster, 203

Greenberg, Blu, 108

Griffith, R. Marie, 36–37

Guerin, Bullele, 74

Guide for the Halachic Minyan (Bar-Asher
and Bar-Asher Siegal), 127

Gutteridge, Helen, xv, 197–98

gynocritical approach, 117

Haines, Enid (Porter), 47

halacha/halachic (rabbinic law), 108–9,
116, 127

Hall, Kira, 145

Harding, Sandra, 117

Harding, Suzanne, 167

harmonial religions, 207

Hay, Agnes, 77–78, 79

healing: alternative, 215; faith, 37;
traditional, 46–47, 50; women's
rituals for, 123

Heavenly Mother (Mormon), 144

Heilman, Samuel, 112

Henderson, Rose, xv, 197–98, 200

Hinckley, Gordon B., 164, 166–67

Hindsley, Madeleine, 217

Hindu immigrant women: approach to, xvi, 269–70, 276, 294–95, 338; and changing gender expectations, 286–87; and festival foods, 281; and gender equality, 291–94; and home puja, 280; increased religiosity of, 284, 290–91; individualized Hinduism for, xvi, 270, 288; key Hindu values for, 284–85, 297n8; and menstrual taboo, 293–94; and Navratri (goddess festival), 281; participants in study of, 270–71, 296n2; and ritual fasts, 283–84, 290; and *samskaras* (life-cycle ceremonies), 282; second generation, 280, 287–91, 291–93; and sponsored pujas, 281–82; studying Hinduism by, 289; as transmitters of Hinduism, 286, 292–93. *See also* Adhi Parasakthi Temple Society of Canada; Hinduism; Parvati (case study); puja

Hinduism: festival foods, 298n12; goal of human life in, 309; history of in Canada, 271–72, 297nn4–5; issues facing in Canada, 273–76; and marriage, 277, 297n7; practices particular to North America, 279, 298n10; ritual fasts in, 282–84, 290, 293; ritual purity/impurity taboos, 293–94, 313–14, 327; *Satyanarayan Katha*, 281, 298n13; selfhood in, 327; and Theosophists, 205, 218; university courses about, 289, 299n16; women in, 279–80, 285, 295,

298n9. *See also* Adhi Parasakthi organization; Adhi Parasakthi Temple Society of Canada; Hindu immigrant women; puja

hippies, 219–20

Hirsch, Samson Raphael, 112

Holden, Pat, 200

holy pictures. *See* devotional objects

homosexuality (Theosophy), 215

hooks, bell, xiv, 66, 91

Houlbrooke, Margaret, 39, 40

Housley, William, 161

Hughes, Katherine, 73

Humanae vitae (Paul VI), 80–81

human dignity (*kevod haberiyot*), 108, 124–25, 129

identity, 145–46, 165–66, 173n11

ideological dilemma, 166

immigrant communities and social mores (Hindu), 314–15, 317–18

immigrants, Catholic, 69, 71, 73

Immigration Act, 272

indigenous diasporas, 337

individualism, 294

International Perpetual Rosary for Life campaign, 25

Islam, 337

Ivanič, Roz, 173n11

James, Henry: *The Bostonians*, 206

jati (Hindu), 273, 277. *See also* caste; Hindu immigrant women

Jayyusi, Lena, 147

Jensen, Marilyn, 254

Jewish Orthodox Feminist Alliance
(JOFA), 108, 129. *See also* Jewish
women
Jewish Theological Seminary, 111, 130n2
Jewish women: approach to, xiv; and
badeken (veiling), 115; biblical
exegesis by, 116; and Congregation
Shir Libeynu, 123–24; and
egalitarianism, 110–11; future for,
129–30; involvement in Judaism,
107–8; Jewish Orthodox Feminist
Alliance (JOFA), 108, 129; and
kevod haberiyot (human dignity),
108, 124–25, 129; and *Koren-Sacks*
prayer book, 129; and Leah, 113,
116; methodologies for studying,
117–18; and *Siddur Eit Ratzon*
(prayer book), 119–20; and Toronto
Partnership Minyan, 127–28, 129;
and unaffiliated synagogues, 109,
116–17, 124
Jews: in Canada, 110; Sephardic, 131n10;
and Theosophy, 220. *See also* Jewish
women; Judaism
Jinarajadasa, C., 220
JOFA (Jewish Orthodox Feminist
Alliance), 108, 129. *See also* Jewish
women
Journal of New Thought, 206
Journal of Psychosophy, 206
Judaism: biblical exegesis in, 116;
Classical, 111; Conservative, 110–11;
enclavist, 112–13, 129; Modern
Orthodox, 112–13, 116, 126, 129,
131n23; non-affiliated, xiv; Orthodox,

107–8, 109, 112–13, 129; seminary
graduates (2013), 130n2; women's
involvement in, 107–8. *See also*
Congregation Shir Libeynu; Jewish
women; Jews; Judaism, in Toronto;
Toronto Partnership Minyan
Judaism, in Toronto: approach to, xiv;
Conservative Judaism in, 110–11;
conservative milieu of, 112, 113;
as enclavist, 113, 129; funerals in,
113, 132n24; future for, 129–30;
synagogues in, 110. *See also*
Congregation Shir Libeynu;
Toronto Partnership Minyan
Judge, William Quan, 204

Kapustin, Shlomo, 110–11
Kāraikkāl Ammaiyār, 322
Karant-Nunn, Susan, 38
karma, 208, 212, 215
Kealey, Linda, 203
kevod haberiyot (human dignity), 108,
124–25, 129
King, Francis, 204
King, Ursula, 117
Klein, Isaac, 115
Kneil, Loretta, 73–74
Knights of St. Columba, 25
Knödel, Natalie, 38
Koren-Sacks prayer book (Jewish), 126, 129
Krishna Kanta Maharaj, 279

Labor Advocate (newspaper), 208
Lacey, Tom, 213
Lakin, Sarah, 212–13, 213–16, 218–19

mechitza (partition), 125

medals, devotional, 9, 12–13, 16

Melmaruvathur (India), 306. *See also*
Adhi Parasakthi organization

membership categorization analysis
(MCA), 142, 146, 179n76

menstrual taboo (Hinduism), 293–94,
312, 313–14, 327

Mercredi, Ovide, 163

midwives, 44–45, 47–50

minhagim (rabbinic customs), 115

"Miriam's Song," 120–21

modernization: and religion, 141

Modern Orthodox Judaism, 112–13,
116, 126, 129, 131n23

Mol, Hans, 169

Morgan, Beulah (Porter), 45

Morgan, David, 16

Morgan, Eve, 49

Morgan, Joyce (Andrews), 47

Morgan, Sue, 53–54

Mormon feminism, 144

Mormon women, 144. *See also* Church
of Jesus Christ of Latter-Day Saints
Relief Society; Claresholm LDS
Relief Society members

Morrill, Susanna, 48

Morrisson, Mark, 206

Moss, Aron, 133n38

motherhood: in Anglicanism, 37–38;
in Bahá'í Faith, 261n52; among
Hindu immigrant women, 294–95;
in Roman Catholicism, 85; and
St. Gerard Majella, 4, 10, 11–12, 14, 18

Mother of Perpetual Help (magazine), 10

Mothers' Saint. *See* Majella, Gerard, St.,
in Newfoundland

multiculturalism, 161, 162, 164–65, 166,
167–68, 170, 273. *See also* Canadian
Multiculturalism Act (1988)

Murray, Hilda Chaulk, 7

Myers, Greg, 165

Nadell, Pamela, 107

National Synagogue Directory, 110

Navratri (Hindu goddess festival), 281

Nelson, Lynn Hankinson, 202

neo-Romantic movement, 204

New Age movement, 215, 220–21

Newfoundland: Catholicism in, 6–7, 7–8,
24–25, 29; Catholic women in, 24–25,
29; life in outports, 6, 8; pro-life
activity in, 11–12, 25–26; women in,
7. *See also* churching; Conception
Bay (NL); Majella, Gerard, St.,
in Newfoundland

Newfoundland and Labrador Right to
Life Association (Centre for Life),
25–26

new religions, xiv, 221, 337. *See also*
alternative religions; Bahá'í Faith;
Church of Jesus Christ of Latter-
Day Saints; Theosophy

New Roman Missal, 87, 98n97

New Women, 200–201, 202, 203, 208.
See also Theosophical women

non-affiliated Judaism, xiv

Northup, Leslie, 118, 123, 124, 128

nuns. *See* women's religious
communities

occult underground, 199, 203, 204–5, 206.
See also Spiritualism

Ochs, Elinor, 161

Olcott, Henry Steel, 204

Olivelle, Patrick, 314, 330n20

oneness, principle of (Bahá'í), 239–40

Ontario: religion in, 203

open-ended interviewing, 233

Opp, James, 37

oral history, 198

Order of the Golden Dawn, 206

organizations. *See* women's
organizations

Orsi, Robert A., 3–4, 10, 17, 37, 56n7

Orthodox Judaism, 107–8, 109, 112–13, 129

Outside the Mainstream (Bednarowski), 199

Owen, Alex, 199, 205

participant observation, 117–18, 233

Parvati (Hindu immigrant women case
study): increased religiosity of,
284; key Hindu values for, 284–85;
life of, 276–77; and marriage, 277;
and religious education, 278–79;
religious practice of, 277, 278,
280–81; and ritual fasts, 283–84; and
samskaras (life-cycle ceremonies),
282; and *Satyanarayan Katha*, 281;
on second generation, 287; as
transmitter of Hinduism, 285–86.
See also Hindu immigrant women

patriarchy: in Christianity, 200–201;
and Church of Jesus Christ of
Latter-Day Saints, 144; and female
sexuality and maternity, 37–38; and

Hindu immigrant women, 291, 293,
295; in Roman Catholicism, 87, 88;
and women religious, 67

Paul VI (pope): *Humanae vitae*, 80–81

Perrin, Eunice, 49

Playle, Ruth, 212–13, 216–19

Point Loma community, 199

Pontifical Biblical Commission, 84

popular beliefs. *See* embodied religious
practice; lived religion; vernacular
religion

Porter, Mary (Petten), 47

Porter, Mildred (Butler), 42–43, 44, 47

Primiano, Leonard, 28

Procter-Smith, Marjorie, 219

pro-life activism, 11–12, 25–26, 81

Protestantism: in English-speaking
Canada, 65, 68

Protestant women's organizations,
72–73, 207

puja: at Adhi Parasakthi Temple, 303,
311–12, 317, 320–21, 329nn4–5; for
celebrating women, 285; Parvati's
practices of, 277, 278, 280–81;
training in, 279; *villakku*, 320–21

Pune (India), 279, 298n9

purification ritual. *See* churching

Quakers, 200

Quebec (Lower Canada), 68

Rabbinic Council of America, 109

rabbinic customs (*minhagim*), 115

rabbinic law (*halacha/halachic*), 108–9,
116, 127

Ram Dham Hindu Temple (Kitchener, ON), 279

Ramayan (Hindu epic), 278, 281, 287. *See also* Sita

Ray, Donna, 39, 40, 41

Realm, The (journal), 206

Redemptorist Order (Congregation of the Most Holy Redeemer): contemporary activity of, 26–28; devotional magazines by, 10; missions of, 9, 14, 27; in Newfoundland, 8, 23–24; promotion of St. Gerard Majella, xii–xiii, 3–4, 6, 10, 14, 29; purpose of, 5–6; St. Teresa's Church, St. John's, 27; and women, 27. *See also* League of St. Gerard; Majella, Gerard, St., in Newfoundland

Redfield, Robert, 7

reincarnation, 202, 208, 212, 213, 218

Relief Society. *See* Church of Jesus Christ of Latter-Day Saints Relief Society; Claresholm LDS Relief Society members

religion: and body, 36–37, 56n5, 56n7; characteristics of empowering for women, 199; and cultural retention, 269; embodied religious practice, 36–37, 50; Enlightenment view of, 141, 198–99; lack of interest in institutional, 221; lived, xvi, 29; Marxist feminists on, 198–99; and modernization, 141; within multicultural society, 166, 168–69; self-identification in, 169–70; and

sexuality, 37–38, 53–54; and social change, 330n21; vernacular, 4, 28. *See also* academic religion inquiries; alternative religions; new religions

religiosity, x–xi, xi–xii

religious membership categories (RMCs), 147, 179n75

"Rerum novarum: On Capital and Labour" (Leo XIII), 73

responsa (authoritative rabbinic replies), 108

Rideout, Myra (Porter), 43, 45, 58n51

Rideout, Prudence (Morgan), 51

Rieder, Paula M., 38

Rieti, Barbara, 50

ritual performance (Jewish), 118, 128, 330n23. *See also* women's ritualizing

RMCs (religious membership categories), 147, 179n75

Roe, Jill, 198, 201, 211

Roll, Susan K., 38

Roman Catholic Church: on birth control, 80–81; deacons in, 97n89; and feminism, 65; history of in Canada, 68–69; New Roman Missal, 87, 98n97; Pontifical Biblical Commission, 84; and sanctity of life issues, 82–83; sexual abuse scandal, 24, 29; social teaching of, 73; ultramontanism in, 69, 70, 71, 78; Vatican I, 70–71; Vatican II, 25, 79–80, 80–81, 84, 89; and women's ordination, 83–84, 85, 88–89, 99n106; women's organizations, 71–72, 73. *See also* Canadian Catholics for Women's Ordination/Catholic

Toronto Theosophical Society (TTS): approach to, xv, 198; Committee for Social Reconstruction, 209; decline of, 219; gender balance in, 211–12; hostility towards, 214; membership of, 207–8, 227n83; Ruth Playle's experience, 217–19; Sarah Lakin's experience, 213–16, 218–19; topics addressed by, 206–7, 212; women in, 212, 221–22. *See also* Theosophical women; Theosophy

Trudeau, Pierre Elliott, ix

TTS. *See* Toronto Theosophical Society

turban affair, 161–62

Ulrich, Laurel Thatcher, 60n70

ultramontanism, 69, 70, 71, 78

United Synagogues of Conservative Judaism, 111

Upper Canada, 68, 69, 143

van Leeuwen, Theo, 168

Vasanthi, 310, 312, 323

Vatican I, 70–71

Vatican II, 25, 79–80, 80–81, 84, 89

vernacular religion, 4, 28

Vertovec, Steven, 275

vrats (ritual fasts), 282–84, 290, 293

Walton, Jim, 243, 252

Warford, Emma (Petten), 50–51

Waterstone, Penny, 199

WCTU (Women's Christian Temperance Union), 207

Webb, James, 199

Weber, Max, 205

Wessinger, Catherine, 199

White, William (Bishop of Newfoundland), 41

Williams, Sarah, 39, 52

Winnipeg Statement, 80–81, 84

women: characteristics of empowering religion for, 199; in mid-twentieth-century Canada, 240–41. *See also* churching; feminism; motherhood; women's ordination; women's organizations; women's religious experiences

women-church, 88

Women's Christian Temperance Union (WCTU), 207

women's healing rituals, 123

women's ordination: Orthodox Jewish, 109; Roman Catholic, 83–84, 85, 88–89, 99n106. *See also* Canadian Catholics for Women's Ordination/Catholic Network for Women's Equality

women's organizations: Catholic, 71–72, 73; Protestant, 72–73, 207. *See also* Canadian Catholics for Women's Ordination/Catholic Network for Women's Equality; Catholic Women's League of Canada

women's religious communities (nuns): approach to, xiii–xiv, 65; associate programs, 90–91; history of in Canada, 68–69; marginality of, 68, 69, 91–92; as subversion of gender roles, 67, 70, 93n19; and Vatican I, 70–71; and Vatican II, 89

Women's Religious Experience (Holden), 200
women's religious experiences, ix–xii,
    337–38. *See also* Bahá'í Faith;
    churching; Claresholm LDS
    Relief Society members; feminist
    theology; Hindu immigrant
    women; Jewish women; LDS
    women; Majella, Gerard, St., in
    Newfoundland; Roman Catholic
    feminist movements; Theosophical
    women

women's ritualizing (Jewish), 118, 123,
    128. *See also* ritual performance
women's suffrage, 207, 210
women's theology. *See* feminist theology
Woolgar, Pat (Morgan), 46
world citizenship (Bahá'í), 239–40

Yang, Mayfair, x
Yeshivat Maharat, 109
Yoder, Don, 28
yoga, 275, 309

Studies in Women and Religion
Études sur les femmes et la religion